DIRECTORS CLOSE UP 2

Interviews with Directors Nominated for Best Film by the Directors Guild of America

2006–2012

Moderated and Edited by Jeremy Kagan

THE SCARECROW PRESS, INC.

Lanham • Toronto • Plymouth, UK

2013

Published by Scarecrow Press, Inc.
A wholly owned subsidiary of The Rowman & Littlefield Publishing Group, Inc.
4501 Forbes Boulevard, Suite 200, Lanham, Maryland 20706
www.rowman.com

10 Thornbury Road, Plymouth PL6 7PP, United Kingdom

British Library Cataloguing in Publication Information Available

Library of Congress Cataloging-in-Publication Data

Directors Close Up, Second Edition was cataloged by the Library of Congress as follows:
  Directors close up : interviews with directors nominated for best film by the Directors Guild of America / edited by Jeremy Kagan.—2nd ed.
    p. cm.
    Includes index.
    ISBN 0-8108-5712-X (pbk. : alk. paper)
    1. Motion pictures–Production and direction. 2. Motion picture producers and directors–United States–Interviews. I. Kagan, Jeremy Paul.
  PN1995.9.P7D5643 2006
  791.43'0233092273—dc22   2005025790

Directors Close Up 2: Interviews with Directors Nominated for Best Film by the Directors Guild of America 2006–2012
  ISBN 978-0-8108-8391-8 (paper : alk. paper)

∞™ The paper used in this publication meets the minimum requirements of American National Standard for Information Sciences—Permanence of Paper for Printed Library Materials, ANSI/NISO Z39.48-1992.

Printed in the United States of America.

CONTENTS

PART III: POST-PRODUCTION

Benjamin Button Storyboard Sequence

PART IV: THE WORST AND THE BEST

LIST OF ILLUSTRATIONS

PHOTOSPREADS

PROLOGUE

What you are about to read is a compilation of seven years of in-depth interviews with the Directors Guild of America's nominees for Best Director of a Feature Film from 2006 through 2012. It is a sequel to the edition of *Directors Close Up* published in 2006, which covered the DGA's Meet the Nominees symposia from 1992 through 2005. I have had the privilege of being the moderator of these events since they began. For those who make movies and those who love them, this is a unique opportunity to find out how master directors work.

Now, this book is not necessarily meant to be read from cover to cover. Of course, you can do that, and it will be an informative experience and entertaining. But you can also dip in anywhere and that is the way this book is designed. If you are interested in a certain aspect of directing like casting or shooting or editing, just look up that topic and you will find a variety of gifted feature film directors speaking about how they deal with this subject. You can also check in on directors you like and find their various entries throughout the book. Or you can start at the end and work your way back.

These interviews explore the director's role. Actually the word 'roles' is more appropriate. Famed American director Elia Kazan once gave a discourse on what makes a director. He talked of all the fields with which a director needs to have familiarity: literature, theater, dramaturgy, comedy, music, painting, history, movement, design, costume, lighting, camera, sound, editing, architecture, topography, nature, acting, psychology, eroticism, economics, politics, food, and self-knowledge. His entire speech is included in the first volume of this book series and is online at the Directors Guild website as a downloadable pdf document (http://www.dga.org/The-Guild/Committees/Special/Special-Projects.aspx).

Please note that the words written here are those of the directors themselves, spoken during these interviews; and as we wanted you to get a feel for how they actually sound, forgive some of the phraseology and more colorful language.

The bottom line for all these conversations, of course, are the films themselves. They are the expression of the brilliance of the directors included in this collection. This book, then, is a companion piece to watching their stimulating movies.

If you want to encounter more interviews with other master directors of our time, go to the Directors Guild of America website (www.dga.org) and look at the Visual History Collection where we have amassed hundreds of hours of videotaped conversations. If you look at the search functionality on this site, you will see it is organized by topics like this book, and you will be able to access a wide range of subjects to hear and see how many directors meet their challenges (http://www.dga.org/Craft/VisualHistory.aspx).

Words themselves are often limiting, but they can set a context for the complex process that is directing, and that is the goal of these collections. What you will also be experiencing here is the continuity of this profession and art form, for these directors are part of a heritage from which they have learned, and to which they are now contributing. They have adapted the past and individualized their creations and they now are passing on their visions and knowledge to us.

We hope you learn, expand and enjoy.

—Jeremy Kagan

Acknowledgments

Like making movies, putting this book together has been a collaborative undertaking. I want to start by thanking director Arthur Hiller, for it was under his administration as President of the DGA that these interviews began. And I owe my appreciation and admiration for the work of the staff of Special Projects of the DGA, led by Gina Blumenfeld and so ably assisted by Alison Russ, Matt Gamarra, Ruby Sindher and Kristina Huff. They spent many hours amassing all the materials you are about to see. I also want to acknowledge Stephen Ryan at Scarecrow Press who transformed my manuscript into this book.

We also are grateful for the help of the assistants to the directors and to the production companies, distributors and studios who aided us in obtaining the images in this volume. And, most importantly, I want to thank all the directors who took part in these symposia for their forthrightness and exceptional talent. It has been an honor for me to take part in conversations with such masters of the art of directing. And I want to personally thank all my filmmaking teachers, and my parents who supported me on this journey to be able to call myself a student and colleague of the directors in this book.

—Jeremy Kagan

Nominees in Attendance, 2006–2012

2006
George Clooney, *Good Night, and Good Luck.*
Paul Haggis, *Crash*
Ang Lee, *Brokeback Mountain*
Bennett Miller, *Capote*
Steven Spielberg, *Munich*

2007
William Condon, *Dreamgirls*
Jonathan Dayton, *Little Miss Sunshine*
Valerie Faris, *Little Miss Sunshine*
Stephen Frears, *The Queen*
Alejandro González Iñárritu, *Babel*
Martin Scorsese, *The Departed*

2008
Paul Thomas Anderson, *There Will Be Blood*
Ethan Coen, *No Country for Old Men*
Joel Coen, *No Country for Old Men*
Tony Gilroy, *Michael Clayton*
Julian Schnabel, *The Diving Bell and the Butterfly*

2009
Daniel Boyle, *Slumdog Millionaire*
David Fincher, *The Curious Case of Benjamin Button*
Ron Howard, *Frost/Nixon*
Christopher Nolan, *The Dark Knight*
Gus Van Sant, *Milk*

2010

Kathryn Bigelow, *The Hurt Locker*
James Cameron, *Avatar*
Lee Daniels, *Precious*
Jason Reitman, *Up in the Air*
Quentin Tarantino, *Inglourious Basterds*

2011

Darren Aronofsky, *Black Swan*
David Fincher, *The Social Network*
Tom Hooper, *The King's Speech*
Christopher Nolan, *Inception*
David O. Russell, *The Fighter*

2012

David Fincher, *The Girl with the Dragon Tattoo*
Michel Hazanavicius, *The Artist*
Alexander Payne, *The Descendants*
Martin Scorsese, *Hugo*

Part I

PRE-PRODUCTION

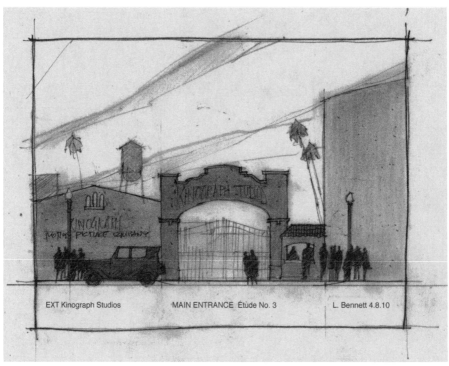

EXT Kinograph Studios MAIN ENTRANCE Étude No. 3 L. Bennett 4.8.10

Sketch of exterior "Kinograph Studios," main entrance for *The Artist*. Courtesy of La Petite Reine, The Weinstein Company LLC, Gregory Hooper, and Laurence Bennett.

Why Make the Film?

STEVEN SPIELBERG, *MUNICH*

I think my film is asking a very difficult and perhaps an impossible question to the audience, and that is: Everything you've ever heard or known or thought you knew about the Middle East and about the conflict between the Palestinians, the Israelis for so many years, many generations—is it possible, the film asks, that you can come into this experience and leave everything you're certain about at home. Can you leave your certainty behind when you watch what the film is attempting to question? We don't have the temerity to try to be solving this problem. I can't do it. The world has been struggling to do this for years, but we simply ask a lot of questions about both sides. And the film really risks offending people by saying: "Please leave everything that you thought you knew about this behind you." I just want the audience to see it through a lens, and that's what films can do so well. Films give you a tremendous perspective. Something you thought you knew all about, you're seeing it anew, because you're seeing it filtered through the point of view of the author and the director and the collaboration of performance art. You're seeing it through a lot of different filters. And a subject like this, which dares not to solve any of the problems but instead dares to bring up very difficult, painful questions, asks a lot from the audience, and one of the things it asks the audience is: "Will you be patient with us?" Just listen, because the problem that we've been having in the Middle East for all these years is people don't listen to each other. We tend to become very entrenched in our own positions and we stay there, and there's no movement to the center. And peace can only be achieved from the center.

MARTIN SCORSESE, *THE DEPARTED*

The script written by William Monahan was based in Boston. That's what got me hooked on the project. I loved the script. I read the first page. And then, I turned to the second

182   CONTINUED: 115.
                                                                   182

                         COSTELLO
            So Dignam's the only one with the
            keys to the kingdom.

                         COLIN
            He's *fucking* resigning. He put his   *PARANOIA*
            papers in. He's not talking.

                         COSTELLO
            Give me his location. Tonight.   *
     PARANOIA   ①TRACK BACK w/COLIN - F.G. ACTION *He STOPS*
     COLIN wanders through the room. People working. On a table he
     sees a plastic EVIDENCE BAG which contains Queenan's   ②P.O.V.
  Looking   bloodstained cellphone ③He glances around, and ⑥picks it up.
  it in   Blood gets on his fingers. He moves into the office, and seen   *Evidence*
  ①②   through the glass, he seizes the phone and with trembling   *BAG*
            fingers punches up the last incoming number ⑤   ④ *Reverse - He*
                                                                Comes to Camera

183   INT. BILLY'S MOTHER'S APARTMENT KITCHEN. NIGHT   183
     ①*CU-CUP*   *PARANOIA*   *Thr. glass office*
  Table ①BILLY is looking at a chipped SANTA MUG from his childhood *
  level and is eating something--sheer maintenance, and drinking wine
  phone in from the bottle. His phone rings ③He looks at the ID and is ④now
  F.G. stunned⑤Queenan's number ⑥He picks up the call but remains *over Billy*
            silent. The caller is also doing the same. *on phone up to*
                                                        HEADON CU-Billy
                                                  SAME AS →⑥ →COVER → ③*Colin*
184   INT. COLIN'S OFFICE #2. CONTINUOUS   184   *looks*
      ①*on His Ear + p/home "click" He TURNS TO Xter*   *at E.*
     COLIN hears that the other side has hung up the phone. He   *C.T. Phone*
     sees ②ELLERBY looking at him through the glass. But Ellerby
     hasn't seen the phone. *Blocked FRAGMENT PARANOID (M3)*

185   INTERCUT BILLY'S MOTHER'S APARTMENT/COLIN'S OFFICE #2.   185   *
           CONTINUOUS ①*wipe* ③*Tight B... (PAN long/lens)* ②*Tight Billy*
                      PACES ②SLOW TRACK; Jump Action
     BILLY is agitated. Exhausted. Frightened. He paces, and looks
     at the phone ④He begins to pack, taking things ⑤money, ~~from~~
     ~~his safe~~⑥Finally, like a man committing suicide--it's that   *
     intense-- he dials the number. INTERCUT.

  ⑥*on*   BILLY   *PARANOIA CURVES into CU*
  Billy med   You called this number on a dead
  Headon   guy's phone. Who are you.   *
  Tilt Down
  To phone   COLIN   ⑦*Move in on C.*
  He Takes in   So you're the one.   *To match CU*
  up To B.   BILLY
  Track in   Who are you?
  To CU as He
  Dials - in
  CU Pov 1st line "who are you?"
  (Continue to move fr. 22 "who are you?"   (CONTINUED)
  Tighter and do ALTERNATE Hold... 1 of "who are you?")

page. And then I went to the third, and then it was a long process. I started looking at this thing—Irish-Catholic, Irish-American. I was reticent in terms of certain issues, because it's similar territory I'd done before. What else could I add that would be new to it? But it was like the sirens calling you in a way. I was still drawn to the project.

It's a gangster picture. I mean I don't know what they are anymore, in a sense, because it's a different world. I mean it's the first film I've done in the modern world. I don't really know what people wear or how. I don't know how to use cell phones. I mean I do kind of, no, I don't.

Ultimately, this picture became the same picture I've been making over the years, the father and the sons, and I guess I owe everything to still trying to talk about family. I just pretty much owe it all to my father and my brother, basically. I'm still working that out, and maybe it'll never work out because this film is rife with it. And, particularly, there is no good, and there is no bad. The morality of our moral ground is zero. The only place to go from there is up, if you can. Everybody winds up paying for it. Sometimes it's a pleasant thing, and sometimes it's extremely unpleasant.

GEORGE CLOONEY, *GOOD NIGHT, AND GOOD LUCK.*

My father was an anchorman and I'd grown up around the news, and I started reading [Edward R.] Murrow [an American broadcast journalist]. I was very familiar with the story of Murrow and [Joseph] McCarthy [an extremist right-wing Republican Senator

George Clooney with Dianne Reeves on the set of *Good Night, and Good Luck.* GOOD NIGHT, AND GOOD LUCK.—Licensed by Warner Bros. Entertainment Inc. and 2929 Productions LLC. All Rights Reserved.

during the 1950s who falsely accused people of being Communists]. I started reading some of Murrow's speeches again and listening to him say we should succeed not only in the area of bombs, but in the area of ideas. And you started listening to these words that someone wrote in 1954 better than anything anybody could say today. It was like Paddy Chayefsky [a famed American playwright and screenwriter] and I thought, this is a great place to sort of house dissent without it being on the nose and saying, "Come on over to the left. It's beautiful." Saying, "Listen, I welcome all arguments to this issue, but I won't be told I'm a traitor for asking questions. I won't allow that." That was the motivator. I think people are allowing a certain amount of dissent in again.

BENNETT MILLER, *CAPOTE*

The film aspires to do what is often the domain of a novel, which is to find a way to express something, which is never made explicit in a life. You see who this person is, his public self, and the film peels back the layers and gets to that private part, that part of a person that will be concealed perhaps for a lifetime. And so you have this charismatic public figure, and this is the very private and internal tragedy of a public figure. He talks about there are two Americas. He is both of those Americas. But to me, the film was never just about America or even Truman Capote, but it always felt like a very classic, timeless, universal tragedy that people have been writing about this for 2,500 years. It's about somebody who wants something so badly that he becomes insensitive to what he's trampling upon to get it. I wanted to make a sobering film. I think so many of us have got our passions that intoxicate us, and we lose sight of, in the pursuit of that, that the day's going to come when there's going to be some kind of reckoning. I do believe that your character is your destiny and that you're going to face yourself and the consequences of what you've done. And I think that's true for every person. I also think corporations work that way, and I think nations work that way.

ANG LEE, *BROKEBACK MOUNTAIN*

I think theme is very important for *Brokeback*. There are obvious themes like don't beat up gay guys. That's the obvious one. Leave him alone. Let him fall in love. It's a love story. Because our main target is women, we don't want to say it's a western. That's a turnoff for women. I'm doing a realistic love story of true people. It's a real West, real people, ranch hand, people doing hard work. So what really struck me is what do you want the audience to get? I think a movie should have a taste. A taste you gather or aftertaste. When I read the short story, I got choked up. I want to do justice to that, and I want to share that with the audience. But why I get choked up is a mystery, and that was why I make this movie. You know, gay ranch hands in Wyoming is like as far from me as possible. Why did I cry? What is the connection? It takes a movie to find out. And I didn't realize what I was doing. That taste or aftertaste I was after is actually after I finish shooting when I see the assembly [when the film is first edited]. It is in that process I realize the movie is about missing. I was dealing with both sides of the mountain of the western, both sides of America, one is Jake [Gyllenhaal], one is Heath [Ledger]; one conservative, the other is "go for it." *Brokeback Mountain* is the illusion of love. It's almost like paradise. Enigmatic love is the more elusive, more existential, the grander it looks, like a western; and you just have to be humbled by the emotion. We don't give statements. We're not pretending, especially like politicians who say, "We have answers. We're simplified. We categorize people." For us let's ask the questions. Let's respect the unknown. That's what it is. That's what life is.

I was very ambitious the two movies prior to this. I think I went through my midlife crisis, a lot of cinematic ambitions I had since student days, I just want to exercise it. And I was exhausted and I sit back to make this movie. I thought I just wanted to make something like my first movie, shoot actors and do it quickly, and somehow it's quite magic.

TOM HOOPER, *THE KING'S SPEECH*

I think because I started making films at twelve, I always assumed that I had nothing interesting in my life to talk about, but film. I thought all I could talk about was becoming obsessed about directing films at the age of twelve and making films which seemed to be a pretty self-referential topic. But because I'm half Australian and half English myself, there were aspects of this story that related very specifically to aspects of my upbringing. The way my Australian mother unpacked the effects of my father's childhood and I found that not only was the connection very definite, but I could even draw on, talk with my parents about that time to help enhance the script and it's funny to me because people assume that I have some interest in the monarchy. I don't. I saw in this film the opportunity to talk about aspects of that childhood experience. I suppose I learned the power of being personal even if you siphon it through other characters.

STEPHEN FREARS, *THE QUEEN*

It's what Jean Renoir [French director of masterpieces like *Rules of the Game* and *Grand Illusion*] said, that in the end, you make films that are very, very different, and then they all turn out to be the same film. So you learn all films somehow become bits of your character, and somehow your character gets into them in a way that I never quite understand. Making this film, I learned about women of a certain generation, of which my mother was a member. You certainly learn about the role that the Royal Family has in your life. I mean the queen has been in my life for sixty years.

PAUL HAGGIS, *CRASH*

When I came up with the story, I didn't know why I was writing it, didn't know why the stuff was coming out of me. And then when we were actually shooting it, I didn't think anyone would ever see it, but what did bother me a lot is the fact that my questions were all about things that troubled me personally, things that I thought about myself, not the good things, the darker side of who we are, the darker side of good people. And so that's what I wanted to explore. I wanted to explore how good people can do terrible things; because it doesn't really interest me how terrible people can do terrible things. That we know because they're terrible. So I really wanted to do a film about the contradictions that we all embody because I think as human beings that's who we are. I mean at least that's what I've come to discover in my 10 years in television, that we can be the hero and the villain in our own lives, and we are, moment to moment. I think movies often put white hats on this group of people and the black hats on this group of people, and I want to fuck with that a little bit.

JULIAN SCHNABEL, *THE DIVING BELL AND THE BUTTERFLY*

Jean-Dominique Bauby wanted to prove to everybody that he wrote that book by blinking his eye and people thought that he couldn't do it, so there was this documentary and it really served a purpose but when I showed that film to my wife she looked at me and said, "You are out of your mind. Everybody's saying this guy Schnabel is so heavy. Everybody dies. This is the most depressing thing in the world. What are you, nuts? Two years I have to live with this?" and I said, "No, it's really funny, it could be really funny. You don't really see it the way I see it."

JASON REITMAN, *UP IN THE AIR*

My best advice did come from my father [Ivan Reitman who directed *Ghostbusters*] and I've spent more time around him than any other director I know. You know growing up there wasn't a room that I wasn't allowed to be in. I was in the editing room; I was on my father's sets. I was even in writing rooms sometimes. The access I got to the process—it's kind of unbelievable looking back on it and he gave me a lot of advice. I suppose the best advice I ever got from my father about directing was your job is to capture authenticity, and it's very easy while you're writing or while you're on set or while you're in the editing room to lose sight of what you're doing, because your barometer for comedy and your barometer for drama is actually nowhere as good as your barometer for honesty. While you're on set you shouldn't be worrying about what's funny or not. You actually don't know. You won't know until you're sitting in an audience and you're feeling it through them, but what you do know is whether it feels true, and so he said this to me, actually right before I went to make my first film. He said, "Just ask yourself that all the time. Does this feel real? Would someone do that? Would someone say that? Would they say it in that way? Would they walk in the room that way? Would they sit down or would they stand up while they were talking. Would someone respond that way?" And I've used that advice all the time and I find it's so simple that it's easy to forget or not to think of, but actually it speaks very truthfully to what directing is.

JAMES CAMERON, *AVATAR*

Right before I was making *Terminator*, I worked for Roger Corman and he was remarkable at creating an environment where like people would find each other and they

James Cameron on the set of *Avatar*. AVATAR ©2009 Twentieth Century Fox. All Rights Reserved.

were all crazy, passionate, ready to work all night long for no money. He didn't actually sort of hold class. You didn't sit at Roger's knee, although he did tell me once when I was directing, I should sit down a lot, which was good advice I guess. He also said, "Make your day [finish the work scheduled for the day]," which I have been seldom able to apply in practice. I respected and wanted to be like Walter Hill [director of *48 Hours*] and I actually was writing *Aliens* before I directed *Terminator* and I was trying to emulate his very cursory kind of haiku-style. Walter's big advice to me when I started *Aliens* was, "Don't fuck this up." I thought that was actually pretty good advice. It was implicit that if you fuck it up, you're never going to get to do it again and, you know, I think that's a pretty sound thing to remember all the time. In the five years of the making of *Avatar,* it's in my mind every day, you know. The other thing he said, actually, that was helpful had to do with casting, but I think it sort of applies to everything, is don't go to the center, push away from it. Now, at the time I was like "What does that mean?" because my tastes were very kind of mainstream and my film schools were the drive-ins of Orange County, you know, but I think it's great advice.

KATHRYN BIGELOW, *THE HURT LOCKER*

I would say probably the best advice was inspiration in watching film after film after film that I loved like *The Wild Bunch,* everything from [Sam] Peckinpah [director of *The Wild Bunch*], everything from [Sam] Fuller [director of *Steel Helmet*], everything from Sergio Leone, Robert Aldrich, and Anthony Mann. Absorbing their films in a way that you then can internalize and hopefully one day make your own. Walter [Hill's] advice was, "Spend time with people who are doing what you want to do."

MICKY (cont'd)
It's for me. I can't keep goin'
like this, ya know, Kasie, I gotta
do somethin' -

KASIE
(nods, lays back down)
I love you, Daddy.

Micky pauses before he leaves, looking back at his daughter
on the couch, and heads out the door...

STAIRS - MICKY'S APARTMENT ABOVE GARAGE - EARLY MORNING

Micky stands at the top of the stairs, old blue gym bag slung
over his shoulder, breath white in the cold early morning.
He looks out at the day, the sun just starting to rise...

CUT TO:

B.H.C. - INSIDE YARD, 1ST FLOOR - DAY

Days later, winter morning. Dickie's running, shadowboxing
around a track, gray hooded sweatshirt soaked with sweat,
noisy crowded square 75-by-75 yds, solid brick up 20-feet,
open sky except for a three-foot overhang that wraps around,
razor-spiraled barbed wire rising another 10-feet into the
sky, cement floor covered with white painted lines separating
several basketball and handball courts...over the loudspeaker,
"Visit for Dickie Ecklund."

VISITOR'S ROOM - 1ST FLOOR, B.H.C. - DAY

...Dickie sitting in a wooden chair, sweatshirt still wet,
matted hair, his two boys on his legs, Little Dickie and TOMMY
ECKLUND, 6, half-Cambodian, half-Dickie...Alice sitting across
from them smoking up a storm.

DICKIE
(talking fast to his
boys, mouth dry,
nervous)
- and I get down on my hands an'
knees every mornin' and thank
Gahd. Every day's a test for me.
All the drinkin' and druggin',--
I hurt a lotta people, but I gave
up cryin' about that, ya know.
Yous guys're the most important
things to me now. And I ain't
afraid a tellin' you this,-- I was
a piece a shit, but no more, okay?

Dickie pulls both boys close to him, hugging them tight.

❷

The Script

RON HOWARD, *FROST/NIXON*

Every movie winds up kind of defining itself differently and winds up looking, sounding, feeling different and it really starts with a script. Using Peter Morgan's [the playwright and script writer] own analogy, this was sort of a thinking person's boxing film.

What attracted me to the material I think is that everything is operating at two or three levels thematically, in terms of what's entertaining about it. It can be funny one second and intense the next, but I always wanted to work against a look, a feel that was theatrical, that was presentational. When I was watching the play, as much as I was loving it, I was having this little fantasy of grabbing a camera and jumping up on stage and starting to bore in on these guys and pan in from this person to that, make you an observer in the room while these things were going on.

The big challenge was our opening, because, of course, it was a play and in the play there's a narrator and basically Nixon walks out and resigns and then gives a second farewell speech, and Frank Langella [who played Nixon in the play and the movie] is extraordinary. At first he doesn't look anything like Nixon and eventually he begins to win you over. We shot all of that, and the question for us was how do we make the audience accept this man as Nixon and what is the story that we are actually telling, and we found that it was important to shift it. First we use documentary and newscast stuff and so forth to orient people who may not know anything about it. You know you sort of define Watergate and everything leading up to Nixon resigning. Then we decided to tease in Nixon and you're seeing hands, you're seeing an ear, that kind of thing, hearing a voice. Catching a glimpse of him, but on a TV monitor and it isn't til much later that we actually see him, but even when we see him in a shot in helicopter, he doesn't speak yet and it's much more about the predicament that the world is facing, that the country is facing. This man is resigning and it's about David Frost getting an idea and that's quite a bit different than the play. Then we went back further because now we're removing all of that exposure to Nixon. His next couple of scenes are sort of all awkward charm and talking about money in its own way, kind of ingratiating stuff. So I went back under titles, blended in real Nixon from real tapes to again on some level, even if it was subliminal, just to remind people. That was just a big shift from the play, which used narration very well, but in a very theatrical way. By the way, Michael Grandage's production, which I happened to see at the DonMar Warehouse and I saw again on Broadway, was spectacular. I mean daunting and very visual, but in a very theatrical way, so I was really challenged by that, but they used a lot of theatrical devices, basically stopping and narrating the story from time to time. Some of it was very helpful from a narrative standpoint. It was funny. It keyed certain jokes, counterpoints and so forth, and Peter Norton [the script writer] was ready to get rid of it altogether and I said well why don't we imagine a sort of documentary. This whole thing is about television. In the play there was this fantastic thing, which is this whole bank of television monitors over the actors' heads and whether there was an image on there or not, you were always reminded this is about making a big ol' television show.

As much as some quest for the truth, David Frost was this entrepreneur who saw this incredible opportunity and so you know that was one of the ironies I liked about it, and I thought Grandage [the theater director] had sort of captured it that way. So every opportunity I had to use TV, I did and I thought let's also divide up the characters, the narration amongst the characters because the other thing I wanted to do in the adaptation was broaden the perspective and I felt like that in the play, the characters were used almost as symbols: The liberal guy, the neo-con guy. And I felt like it was going to be much easier to relate to the drama that was going on if you didn't try to solely connect to Nixon or to Frost. But if you began to believe in [James] Reston's passion, Sam Rockwell's [who played Reston the journalist] passion or what was at stake for Oliver Platt [who played Bob Zelnick, the professor of journalism who did research for Frost with Reston] or what it meant to Kevin Bacon [who played the former US marine officer and political aide to Nixon], then the drama would be intensified.

STEVEN SPIELBERG, *MUNICH*

I had a close-to-perfect screenplay by Tony Kushner. It was literature: the quality of the writing, the dialogue, the instruction inside the lines of who these characters were to each other. It was so complete for me that I felt for the first time in my career that I was directing a stage production more than I was directing a motion picture because like directors on Broadway, I had Tony Kushner right here sitting with me every day. He was on the set every moment. And he was on the set just listening very carefully to how his dialogue was being spoken by the actors. It was nice having the author with me, and I would recommend that. I certainly had that experience with Steve Zaillian on the set of *Amistad*, where he was with me every single day of that production, and that's a good thing when that happens.

We were telling a story which is, in principle, the truth. We also made up scenes for dramatic reasons and to enlighten and illuminate what the story was about and who the characters were and who they were representing and how they were representing themselves.

The actors brought the lines to life, but the actors didn't suggest improvements on the dialogue. I've had other movies where actors have come over to me with reams of notes that they had done, rewriting the screenplay the night before, rewriting all of their scenes, and by the way, rewriting everybody else's scenes that day. And I've had to basically mediate these tremendous potential explosions of emotion by making sure that the other actors didn't see the lines that this actor rewrote for them.

ANG LEE, *BROKEBACK MOUNTAIN*

I spent three years working the script and the actor rewrote it, and then they probably spent weeks on that, on those rewrites, and you just want to kill each other.

KATHRYN BIGELOW, *THE HURT LOCKER*

The script opens with that quote by Chris Hedges, "War is a drug" and so you know there's a sense that James is only complete in that venue, in that world and not that he's some kind of psychological apparition. I don't mean that. As Chris Hedges speaks about in this amazing book, "War is a Force That Gives Us Meaning," he talks about it's a volunteer military. You have to take that into consideration. These are men and women that are there by choice and there is a kind of allure that the battlefield can hold for certain individuals and that's what the film finally unpacks. What is that allure for this particular individual. It's obviously not for the other men, not for Sam, not for Eldridge, but for this man it's to the exclusion of all else and so somehow you find the visual equivalent to that.

JULIAN SCHNABEL, *THE DIVING BELL AND THE BUTTERFLY*

I basically knew what I was going to put in there, in the script. Even the things that were not scripted I knew where they were going. The truth of the matter is Inés, whose real name is Florence, is really the one who took care of Jean-Dominique Bauby [Bauby wrote the book after his stroke]. And the mother of his children showed up at the hospital only a few times. But he left the book to the wife and the mother of his children so it was like an annuity for them so I didn't feel the same way about leaving her out. I talked to her so I wanted to show that though he was living with another woman when he went to pick up his kid [when he had his stroke] when he said that, "I could be with the women I love," I wanted to show that he was really in love with her.

I had written a script to the book *Perfume* and I had a really impossible lack of dialogue, anyway, I wrote a great script that never was used but there were things I thought of, going up on top of the mountain and all the way to Egypt or seeing

toucher le gagnant. Etais-je aveugle et sourd ou bien fallait il nécessairement la lumière d'un malheur pour m'éclairer sur ma vrai nature ?

winner. Had I been blind and deaf or did it take the harsh light of disaster for me to find my true nature?

CLOSE ON HIS EYE AS IT CLOSES

BLACKNESS. The sound of footsteps.

His POV opens to the clock on the wall, which reads 5:01 am. A NURSE turns on the TV. An early morning program is beginning. Dawn light on the window.

CLOSE ON JEAN-DO'S EYE AS IT CLOSES

Script page from *The Diving Bell and the Butterfly*. THE DIVING BELL AND THE BUTTERFLY—Licensed by Miramax, LLC, and Pathé Pictures International.

ecosystems falling apart, so I thought Jean-Dominique Bauby could do it too with his imagination and his memory, and really all this stuff happened. At the same time I wasn't going to do this film. But my father was dying, and the script came. The man who gave me the book in the first place was in the room with my dad and I thought it was in the first person, both of these things were in the first person, so I liked the idea that we know what's going on, but other people in the movie don't. It's like when you see William Holden lying in the pool [in Billy Wilder's film *Sunset Boulevard*] he says, "There I am, dead in the pool."

STEPHEN FREARS, *THE QUEEN*

Well, the writer, I think, believed a connection between the Queen and Blair more than I did. I kept saying, "Well, you can't really advance it as a sort of psychological theory that he thinks that she is like his mother, but I could see you could make a joke of it and maybe it'll sneak in around the back."

I found the idea of attributing psychology or a psychological explanation for the characters' actions very difficult. I didn't think that was my job, but with the writer, that was sort of his eureka moment. "Oh, I see. He thinks she's his mother." I was less convinced and ended up agreeing with him.

PAUL THOMAS ANDERSON, *THERE WILL BE BLOOD*

We [Paul and Daniel Day-Lewis] talked about the film for a few years. We tried to get it off the ground and didn't for a number of reasons and it just gave us the benefit of talking over the telephone for about a year, just bullshitting really, not talking that much about the movie, but getting used to each other, I suppose.

There is no dialogue in the first fifteen minutes of the movie. That would be the decision as a writer, and it just didn't seem like there was anything for them to say. I guess I imagined what it would be like to prospect for silver or oil which was very lonely, quiet work that you do by yourself, that the labor was so hard at no point would you say, "Golly! Look at all this oil we've got here!" You know? Or something like that. I just couldn't think of anything for them to say. It just presented itself as a good idea. Hopefully not feeling like a novelty or anything like that, but they literally had nothing to say to each other and that the first time we would hear him [Daniel Day-Lewis] speak he would say, "Ladies and gentlemen." Seemed like a good idea.

ETHAN AND JOEL COEN, *NO COUNTRY FOR OLD MEN*

ETHAN: In the course of adapting this book you just dump 70 percent of what's in the novel because you're making a feature length movie and there's no way you're going to shoot an entire novel. Half of the novel is just a lot of interior monologue of Tommy Lee Jones's character. It's kind of just a threshold writing question. We thought, we're adapting the novel, what do we do with that? The obvious thing to do would've been to render it all as voice-over, which we didn't really want to do except in dramatic scenes, and then in the one instance to introduce the movie, we decided to make that voice-over. It's funny, it seems perverse to have voice-over of a character you weren't going to meet for a while, but we just didn't worry about it.

JOEL: And we'd actually did it before in the movie, *Fargo*. We'd also done a movie before where really the principal character didn't come in until thirty of forty minutes into the movie.

TONY GILROY, *MICHAEL CLAYTON*

The script opening in the very first version had a sweeping helicopter that came through Sixth Avenue and this oceanic vision, and that gradually got stripped away not by economics, but good taste over time. A lot of the things that start, then practically, with the limitations, they end up, if you're in the right hunt, they end up having some larger effect that you were hopefully, instinctively, going for. As we got to the end of doing the opening there was a lot of resistance against, "Oh, it's confusing," but I began to realize when we did the opening that the real meta by-product of it was that it was okay to give people permission to pay attention, but not pay attention. So much information is coming and I want you to take it in, if you want to, but there is a permission you have to give to the audience. You don't have to know everything that's going on here, just feel this. I also want to say you got to lean forward. I'm not going to fuck around, I'm not going to stop here. I'm not going to explain anything. You have to hang in with me here, but the journey, when it arrives, they begin to realize that it is sort of like a mini version of the movie, which is, if you stay with me, and you don't fall off the cart, I will get you some place at the end of it. And it started to work that way, at least that was my argument, you know, when people wanted to cut it out later on.

CHRISTOPHER NOLAN, *THE DARK KNIGHT*

There's a strange thing that happens in the writing, which is you start to construct narrative scenarios to demonstrate your character points. Who's the hero? Who's the villain? How you're going to resolve all the different character issues going on and the one thing that's completely flexible in the writing is the physical environment, so you say, okay, we need Batman to be able to save the boy, as Harvey flips his coin, so they've got to be at the edge of a huge drop, so that means in an earlier scene they've got to go up ten flights of stairs and then we want them at the bottom. So they can go down to the bottom, Batman has to run off and wind up over here. You ignore any type of reality when it comes to what this building is going to look like. You write this whole scene and then you're stuck with all the departments who are trying to figure out how on earth this physical geography can exist in the real world.

And in this case, you're presenting a very iconic character that your audience is very familiar with in a different inclination, so the whole thinking behind what the opening of the film needed to be was all based on definitively, aggressively, presenting Heath's [Ledger] portrayal in a sequence that would excite the audience and show them the way in which we were reinterpreting the character and re-contextualizing in a more, I call it, a more realistic context, more like a conventional action character, as opposed to a superhero comic book movie. The way the Joker was portrayed in the past (obviously, most famously by Jack Nicholson) rules, but also there's Cesar Romero, these guys are very much in the popular imagination and Nicholson's portrayal particularly was absolutely authoritative and definitive inasmuch as one can remember, so we were up against these huge odds with that, so we tried to construct a sequence that would be overpowering for the audience, that would not allow the audience to reject the portrayal in any way. I wanted Heath to have a really iron-clad opening. We wanted to conceal who he was and let his body language start the show, that there's something different about this character, he's wearing this mask and in the moment where he reveals the mask, my original pitch to Heath and this is actually what we did, is we shot the whole sequence using IMAX cameras and we took the first six minutes of the film when it was finished long before anything else was finished and we, about six months before the film was released, we put it in IMAX theaters, just IMAX theaters not regular 35mm theaters, in this incredible format, which is sort of eight stories high and has an incredible resolution to the image and so forth because we really wanted to aggressively make the statement that what Heath was going to be doing with this character was going to be fresh and different, yet true to the iconography, and these movies are very much about iconography and iconic presences and when you do a franchise film, a film that has so much baggage that it carries with it, with your opening you're really making two films in a strange way. You're making a film that says this is a fresh and different exciting story. You're also making a film that answers the audience's questions about how the iconography is going to be dealt with within this kind of a story. They want to relax with it slightly and recognize it, but you also want it to be fresh, so you kind of have these two parallel tracks working.

GUS VAN SANT, *MILK*

We had problems with just the beginning of the movie, the back story. We did, sort of, resort to telling the ending of the movie in the beginning: The announcement that Harvey's [Milk] been shot and the mayor of San Francisco has been shot. We needed to establish, I think, the sexuality of the characters and like the reason they were living in the Castro [District] in the first place and the reason they were forming together, protesting. So to show their sexuality and that it was illegal. That was 1959 footage in Miami that we had found in a stock footage search and we were going to use a lot of stock footage in the film as well so we sort of set that up. In the script Lance Black [the writer] had indicated there was to be stock footage of Anita Bryant, so that's sort of where we began with Anita and as we were looking for Anita footage, we found all this other footage and we decided to keep the Dianne Feinstein documentary with the announcement by her of Mayor Mascone and Harvey Milk being shot and then we really started to go crazy with a lot of documentary footage.

I think that a lot of people that have been in the situation of creating in their film, that you're sort of always rehashing the beginning and you're sort of pulling the audience in. You're kind of revisiting the complexities of the beginning and we had so much story to tell. After the beginning there's a tape recording of Harvey recording his will actually to be played after his death, so that he can assign the person in office to follow him in City Hall. So after that we sort of go to the real time of the movie and he meets Scott and they have a quote unquote sex scene to sort of clear the air and show two guys making love and then proceeding with their travel to San Francisco, and I think that was the scene that was originally taken out of the script as we sent it out to actors just not to scare them off as they were reading, so they could get past page 20. Sean [Penn] was the recipient of the script and we had a meeting and he said you know you really need a sex scene upfront, so we understood and we put it back in.

Before we started shooting we decided to use the will as an encasement of the whole story and it sort of cheats because his will is being recorded in 1977, but in fact in our story it goes throughout 1978, so it's kind of a fudge. It was a way to, like, not just have a voice-over but to have a source of the voice-over. I guess we were just playing that Greek tragedy card.

ALEXANDER PAYNE, *THE DESCENDANTS*

The book had wanted the literary ending and I was just thinking a movie always needs a kind of landing strip. We brought the plane the whole way and what kind of landing strip is it going to have, and this is not a movie where they live happily ever after or the killer is caught or something like that. It's just one of those films where you have to suggest somehow life goes on, so that was just what I somehow came up with to suggest that life goes on. So the ending scene on the couch, I didn't know what the hell they were going to be watching on TV or that it was going to be Morgan Freeman narrating *March of the Penguins*, which turns out to work so well. The entire family is represented because that yellow quilt had been the mother's childhood quilt, which we had seen cover her in the hospital. So it's in a way the four of them now together on that and it was in the screenplay that they would all be covered by that quilt, slightly corny, but we got away with it.

I try to think about transitions as much as possible in the screenplay, even suggesting wipes and dissolves. Sometimes they work out. I'd say three-quarters of the time, they work out and the other part of the time, no, no, no, a cut is better.

JAMES CAMERON, *AVATAR*

I wrote a treatment in '95 and a lot of it changed over time from the script that was written in '06 to the final version of the movie. A lot changed and the whole beginning of the movie shot was taken out and everything changed, but the one thing that never changed was the last shot, and right from the initial treatment, which was the slow kind of hovering perspective that came solely on his eyes. His eyes open and you cut to black and there's the title, because to me I just never thought of anything better, frankly, but I thought it worked and the way it worked to me thematically was the whole movie was about opening your eyes, changing your perspective. The whole conceit of the film is this guy arrives in this place and everybody tells him it's the worst place in the world. He arrives at a place called Hell's Gate on a planet called Pandora and they tell him that everything out there is going to try to kill him and pretty much it does right away, but then his perceptions change. His perceptions about these people that he meets changes and the entire audience goes on that journey with him and at the end, the entire audience or most of it, except for some conservative pundits, seem to pretty much go with the idea that we're going to root against ourselves. We're going to root against humanity, which of course they're really not because the Navi represent our higher version of ourselves. They are the repositories of that and the humans in the story are our more venal selves and how we're trying to evolve one to the other, so really it's all about human experience. But if you can take an audience on a journey where at the end of that journey they are literally cheering against themselves, then you've succeeded cinematically and that's the beauty of cinema. You can do things like that, so at the end, the character completes his journey in the last frame of the movie. I always wanted to do something like that, a little bit of a stylistic conceit.

At the premiere, it was so satisfying to see the audience explode to their feet at that cut to black, you know what I mean? I mean, literally they got it, you know, and it's tricky, you know, you're making a commercial picture and it had to be a commercial picture, it had to work around the world in order to justify its expense. You know you don't want to get too artsy, but you also want to have some style to it and be making some cinematic statements. You don't want everybody going, "Hmmm, what the fuck was that?," you know, at the end of the movie. You don't want to leave it on a flat note. It's a unity between the character and the audience at that point. We've become him.

JASON REITMAN, *UP IN THE AIR*

The endings of my movies are tricky because my films all deal with politically polarizing idea. My first film was about the head lobbyist for tobacco. The second one was about teenage pregnancy and this one was about a guy who fires people for a living and it also has that kind of political decision to live alone with nobody and nothing in his life. And I find that at the end of each of these films the audience is always kind of looking to me to give them an answer, particularly on how I feel about the subject and what I wish them to think and I don't believe in that. I think that's a cop-out. I don't want to tell my audience what to think. I want to leave them on a note that lets them think for themselves and I certainly like the films that do that for me and that's tricky because once you get to the end people are looking for anything and they're looking for a sign, any piece of action or production design or the way you shoot it as to what I think politically on the subject matter. And so most people when they watch *Up in the Air*, half the audience thinks that he's getting on a plane to go find a woman to settle down to share his life with. The other half thinks that he's going to live cyclically for the rest of his life doing the same thing and that makes me very happy, that lets me know that I did the right job. So the movie ends with a guy looking up at a large board of destinations. When I read the book *Up in the Air*, that was one of the first ideas that hit me to end the movie this way, how I feel when I walk through airports. I look at these boards of destinations and I see alternate lives that when you're in an airport, you could literally get on any of these flights, go to a city where you know nobody and have nothing and begin a different life. I think there's something exhilarating about that.

DANNY BOYLE, *SLUMDOG MILLIONAIRE*

When I read the script, there was no sense of flashback, so we tried to make sure that it didn't feel like you were going backwards and forwards. We made this decision that we would have three different ages of actors playing it and that's it and that's really the only indication you'll get of what time you're in. We wanted it to feel like it was all present day even though it's clearly five years ago and ten years ago according to the ages of the characters. So that was one of our guiding principles. So there's about five different timelines in it and we tried to mix all those up, so that you would establish that principle for the audience that we were going to go everywhere. And the other thing was we wanted was to try and tumble everybody into the film because there's a big dilemma particularly as a Brit, because we ruled in India until sixty years ago and you go back there to make a film, which is not about a British character or a white character. It's about a guy who grows up in the slums and I thought the only way we'll ever make a half decent job of it is if it feels as subjective as possible, so we tried to tumble people into the film.

I'm hopeless at improvising, absolutely hopeless. I work hard on the script beforehand, but then we lock it and that's it. I'm really script dependent, absolutely script dependent. Sometimes you get all this wonderful applause and things, and you do have to say that it was in the script, you know, it's just true.

MICHEL HAZANAVICIUS, *THE ARTIST*

There was a big difference during the writing process because you have to write with images and no words, so the technique is different. The goals are the same and you want to make a story with characters you care for. You want entertaining sequences or two touching seconds of funny sequences, but you don't have the same tools. So technically, it's different. During the writing, I started to watch silent movies and kind of had the obsession to have as few as possible cuts. I think I would love to make an entire film with no cuts. And at a certain point, I said, "Actually, it's not my obsession. I don't care about cuts."

DAVID FINCHER, *THE CURIOUS CASE OF BENJAMIN BUTTON*

Get a good script. It'll never stop you from being a genius.

We had this framing device for better or worse, which (actually) allowed us to make the movie a lot shorter because we could leap forward story-wise with these other people who were telling the overarching story. The Clock was an odd flight of fancy and it is a dangling participle . . . it is this thing that doesn't make any real sense until the last shot of the movie. I mean you keep coming back to it, but you're not meant to really understand . . . it's sort of like, well, this could've happened in a past New Orleans if a "Magic" Frenchman had made this clock that had run backwards. Eric Roth [the screenwriter] had this idea that we could see people moving, or running in reverse, we see footage played in reverse and this was something very simple and great. It visually allowed for an abstract explanation of Benjamin, in cinematic terms . . .

I feel like you shouldn't see anything you don't *need to see* and to me the thing about the baby [in the opening of the movie] was it was only going to bridge the gap between what you were imagining and what you could possibly make out of radio-controlled airplane parts, so it seemed to me that the notion was let's tease it as much as possible. I'm more interested in the IDEA of a baby left on a doorstep and people squirming, "Oh my God." That to me was more powerful than anything we could cast out of silicone.

Heath Ledger and Ang Lee on the set of *Brokeback Mountain*. Courtesy of Universal Studios Licensing LLC.

❸

CASTING

JAMES CAMERON, *AVATAR*

In casting, don't do the obvious.

I am in the casting room with people for hours. It's me and a casting person in a room.

Avatar was a much bigger film than I had done before and it was going to be a longer time commitment and that wound up being four and a half years. At the time we started, we figured it was going to be over three and we didn't really know what we were getting into, but we knew it was going to be this huge, huge roll of the dice. The casting decisions become more and more critical in a sense, even more so since we were not doing stars, which I wasn't particularly interested in. I didn't even think of Sigourney [Weaver] as a star. She was a friend of mine, someone I'd worked with before. I didn't really cast her particularly for star power, but you know, obviously, Jake Sully was a character that the whole movie would ride on whoever I cast as that. And I looked at all these young guys because I wanted him to be sort of twenty-five-ish, young enough that you felt the kind of the heartbreak of a guy all of whose options and potential were taken away by his injury and you don't feel that if it's a forty-five-year-old embittered by something that happened in his distant past. I wanted it to have been fresh for him and also the fact that you see that he's an unbowed kind of warrior that just happens to have a disability, so I looked at a lot of these young guys, names, no names. Margery Simkin was my casting director and she's very opinionated and very good. You've got to have a good dynamic with your casting director. They've got to challenge you and push you and push buttons and have ideas and all that. Sometimes she would read and sometimes I'd have my actor-friend come in and work with the person, so it would be actor to actor so I could operate the camera. Sometimes I'd read with them myself. Sometimes I'd throw the camera down and say, "No, let's do it like this," and I would read the other character to kind of push them a little bit. I looked at a lot of these young guys and, of course, they were all easy on the eyes from a female perspective, but I was trying to find somebody who would speak to men as well and it was getting thin. You know, when I found Sam he had a super thick accent like Crocodile Dundee [Australian character from the movie of the same name] and I thought, oh shit, how are we going to do this, but you know you put your faith in actors. You put your faith in their ability to prepare for a part. I didn't need to hear him do the character in an American accent. I just needed to hear him do the character and Sam and I hit it off right away because he was a brick layer before he was an actor and I was a truck driver and a machinist and all this stuff, so from the blue collar connection, we both knew that we had a work ethic and that inspired something in him. He inspired something in me to kind of step up as a director 'cause he was very, I don't want to say combative, but he was confrontational until he was comfortable and I actually like that, you know. I liked, in a way, to have to prove myself to him. About getting the studio talked into it, I had to eventually put him on a 3D audition, shoot him with the actual cameras that we were going to make the film with. Sam appeared on camera and as a CG [Computer Graphic] character.

But Zoë [Saldana] appears only as a CG character and she's absolutely beautiful. When I met her I said that the only tragedy if you do this part is that the world won't see you. They'll see a CG version of you. She was the first one we cast. She basically won us pretty quickly. You know this one fairly long audition, I went through a number of scenes with her and she was just very, very fluid in her process and was able to reach an emotional state very quickly. She was able to catch anything I lobbed at her and we did movement exercises to get to some kind of feral, animal behavior, and then she incorporated that, and when she read the scene completely differently after we had done that, she became much more kind of catlike and snarled in the middle of the dialogue. Things like that that really led me to believe that she could create an interesting character. I saw lots of actresses, but then when I met her, that was pretty much it.

I don't think you can spend too much time, but I don't want to be someone's friend. I don't want to hear about the drive over to the meeting or what you did last night and all that shit. I want to get down to business. I want to work on the scenes. I want to work on the scenes a lot, like for as long as it takes for me to know that they're going to be comfortable with me and break through all the bullshit that actors walk through the door with in terms of how they prep the night before with their acting coach, and all the things that got them screwed up sitting in the waiting room looking at the other actors. Whatever it is, we got to get past all that stuff. You're not going to do that in fifteen minutes or ten minutes watching them do the scene. It's about finding out if I can work with them and they can work with me and if they have a comfort factor. Yeah, we're going to have some laughs around the process of creating a character together and for me that's magic, and I want to see that magic in that moment and it takes time for them to relax. I say right up front, "Okay, we're not going anywhere until we have some fun with this and we discover something together," and I'll give them a couple tries at the way they've prepped it their mind and then for me, that's the point where we get busy. The other thing is I shoot my own films now, I operate the camera myself except for steadicam [a stabilizing mount for the camera], but I do all the handheld, I do all the wheels, all the dolly stuff and all the virtual camera stuff, so I like to work with the camera with the actor. I like to see how their face takes the light and I don't want to intimidate them with lights when they walk in the room, so I set it up very carefully where there's a window, and it's sort of designed ahead of time so it's self-lit in a way that's not obvious. But I'm going to look at how their face takes the light, how the light hits their eyes, how photogenic they are while they're acting. I will find out how quickly, if I start lobbing stuff at them, how quickly they can take that and shake off the preconception that they've walked in the door with. I think I can find out in an hour or however long it takes, maybe less, maybe more, what our working relationship is going to be because if I cast that person, I'm going to be working with them for six, seven months and I've got to have a sense of what that process is going to be. How can they express what they're feeling to me? How can I express what the character is feeling to them, and take that and run with that? Can they change up quickly? It becomes like a dance, or maybe it's like two jazz musicians riffing off each other, and I want to feel that. I can't look into somebody's soul like a CRT scanner in one second. I mean people are deceptive, and by the way, they're actors, you know. They can be your best friend and zero to sixty in four seconds. I'm not going to be seduced by that. They might be a complete narcotic mess, you know, halfway through your shoot. And also you've got to see if there's enough magic within their soul that they can bring out, that they can focus to the task of creating an emotional being.

I say, take the time. It's the most important decision you're going to make. When the process breaks down, we rely on instinct and when we're starting out and we don't have the luxuries, we have to be a lot more instinctive. I think the instinct comes first. You apply analysis, you apply process to it later when you know. You start thinking about what you were already doing. And also you can't reduce the casting process to one sort of plan that works for everybody, I mean it was very different for me finding a kid to be the main character in my $100 million movie *Terminator 2* when all I saw was just a long string of kids who had been in commercials. I mean I looked at a lot of kids and I just wasn't finding any kid that felt real to me, didn't feel street to me, didn't feel like he had a "fuck you" attitude about adults. And Mali Finn, who cast three of my films, was an absolute genius at finding completely raw talent that had no acting experience. She was at the Boys and Girls Club out in South Pasadena and saw this guy standing against a fence and walked over to him and asked, "Hey, have you ever acted?" and he thought she was like some kind of a molester or something. And he said, "My dad films my videos at birthday parties. That's the only time I've ever been on camera," and it was true. He was completely raw and I think that was the toughest decision on the whole picture. It was budgeted at $87 million and it almost went to $100 million. At the time you know that was some serious money in 1991! That's pretty serious money now.

Memorization is not that important unless they want to. Because I'm not going to do two or three scenes. I'm going to do five or six scenes. It's more talking about the character and what that person sees in it and what they would bring to the character, and frankly I want to see that person say these lines. It's that simple. Do they strike me as the character. I mean it's not a hard fast rule, but I like to have actors read. I didn't have Kathy Bates read for *Titanic*. I kind of figured she may know what she's doing! My point is it was a lot of fucking money by anybody's standards and it was hanging on a kid who'd never acted before. I didn't make my decision looking into his eyes. I had him read.

The way I like to do it is have the casting director see a lot of people and even reach out to other casting directors that they know. She didn't travel to England, but she had an associate of hers in England send us a lot of people, and an associate from Australia sent us a lot of people and I look at hundreds on tape, maybe thousands over the course of making a film for all the different characters, and then I narrow it down to a short list that I want to meet. I don't want to meet everybody. I don't want to spend that kind of time with everybody. You got to have a pretty good indication before the fact, but I think you know the camera doesn't lie. People either work on camera or they don't, and you can have an amazing moment with someone socially and then you see them on film or on tape and there's nothing there.

BENNETT MILLER, *CAPOTE*

In casting Clifton [Collins Jr. as Perry Smith, one of the killers] we looked at a lot of great actors. A lot of great actors didn't want to do it. Anyway, it got to the point where a decision had to be made. We needed an actor, and I'd flown out here to meet one of them. Somebody was willing to read who you might not have imagined would have read, and I came out, and he was amazing but not right. And somebody came into the room and said, "I've got one more thing to show you." This guy's sister put him on tape like in his apartment or something like that, and it was Cliff. And I looked at it and said, "Could he come in?" And a couple of hours later, he was there. Everybody else was gone, and so I'm like putting the tripod down and shooting him doing the confession scene, at which point he finishes and then he just breaks down, and I leave the camera rolling for two minutes. I watch this person, who I don't know, four feet away from me just trying to recover from that experience. And I said, "If you could learn to control yourself, we could probably make it work!"

We got to know a lot of prison guards. All of the prison guards in the movie are prison guards because they were not working. They were on strike. Every performance in that movie, save eight people who we were permitted to bring in, came from within ten miles of downtown Winnipeg. That's a big challenge, and it's not desirable.

GEORGE CLOONEY, *GOOD NIGHT, AND GOOD LUCK.*

You've got to understand that David Strathairn [who plays Edward R. Murrow] showed up the day before the first day of shooting. I'd never met him. We called him up and said, "You want to play Murrow?" and he goes, "Okay," and then I saw him like six months later and he had a white beard like this and long white hair and he sat there, and we'd never auditioned him or anything. I was like, "He's the right guy." Because to me it's about a feeling, and I knew what he looked like without the white beard and the white hair. He looked like the right guy, and there's the weight of the world on David's shoulders always in every scene, in every movie he ever does, and Murrow always felt like he had the weight of the world on his shoulders. So although David's voice was a little higher and there were some issues and things, he was the right actor. But when he showed up with his white beard and his white hair and he sat down, I'm like, "Holy shit!" And then he shaved and put some boot polish in his hair and put a cigarette in his hand with, "Good evening," and we were actually high-fiving. It was fantastic.

PAUL THOMAS ANDERSON, *THERE WILL BE BLOOD*

We found this wonderful ten-year-old boy in Fort Davis, Texas, which is just a town right next to Marfa where we were shooting. To be really blunt, we looked at child actors from Los Angeles and New York. That was not the right thing to do. They seemed very professional in the wrong way. There is an idea that you cast the parent as much as you cast the child and it can be a tricky situation. The casting person went to some schools in the area and more or less said we're looking for a man in a ten-year-old body and just described the character a little bit, "Do you have any boys like that?" And they'd say sure, and one of them said, "I know just who you want to talk to. It's this boy named Dillon Freasier," and so she met him, talked with him, and it was just instantly clear that he would be able to do this. I just met with him, and talked with him about the film and got to know him as a person and didn't really read any scenes at all. It didn't feel necessary, honestly. The first time we read the scenes we auditioned some girls to play the young girl that he would have scenes with, and he would read it with them. That's more or less how it went. Finding the boy was going to be the hardest part, going into it.

For character roles I'll read the scene with them. My casting person will be there sometimes. She'll do it or I'll do it. Mostly I don't know how much that can really tell you. It's a little bit more like getting to know somebody and knowing that they are someone you want to be around more than anything else.

There is a terrific actor, he steps off the train, he's a competitor. But he's not an actor, he runs an independent oil refinery down in Long Beach and we went down there to scout because we were going to shoot down there and he's just such an amazing character. He's got a claw for a hand, he's got this amazing face, this amazing voice, when he's talking. He could have just come from a lunch meeting, which was at a strip club nearby with one of his competitors from another oil refinery across the street, and he was talking about it and it was just too good to be true. I asked him if he would like to be in the film and he said, "Well, yeah, I'll consider it." So then I gave him the scene and I said read it over and if you want to do it please come down to Texas and do it and he said okay. So then he called me and finally said, "Yeah I'll come down and do it," and by the time he had gotten down to Texas he had these sides [the pages of a script] and he thought that he was playing the lead, you know, so he had all of the lines of Daniel [played by Daniel Day-Lewis] memorized. I said, "No, no you're not Daniel. That's Daniel." He was very quick to have his own lines memorized and what was great was that I showed people the film and they see him and they say, "It's so great you brought that old actor back. I missed him he was terrific." He just has that kind of presence about him.

We had the most wonderful extras in Texas. You could give them a line. You could have them do anything. They were so dedicated, they were so into it. We got back to California and the extras here are just so jaded, and angry, and they wanted a line, and if they didn't get a line they were pissed off that they didn't get a line. But out there, there were so many wonderful people that you just wanted them to talk and you wanted them to be a part of the scene, and they were an active part of scenes.

RON HOWARD, *FROST/NIXON*

I've done movies where I'm neurotic with casting. I'm bringing people back three and four times and trying combinations and trying to determine chemistry on, you know, all kinds of levels. This one was different. Once we decided to go with Michael Sheen and Frank Langella, which was a long, thoughtful process [both actors were in the original play]; ultimately I just felt like that these guys so understood the characters and had learned so much about them that I felt like everyone else was going to be playing a hopeless game of catch up and I would be too.

At every level, I really wanted to cast people who were incredibly competent be-cause we were going to be moving quickly and I knew these guys [Sheen and Langella] owned their characters. I didn't want to waste takes, but I also wanted people who were incredibly comfortable in front of the camera and were loose. Kevin Bacon isn't very comfortable improvising. Sam Rockwell, Oliver Platt are, but I wanted that feel-ing of comfort, spontaneity, and a sort of green light to all those secondary characters that we were going to flesh them out and risk a take, try something, do whatever comes to mind, and pump lots of spontaneity in and around the brilliant writing. Certainly we were going to calibrate and we were going to explore and look for nuances, but basi-cally I knew what those performances more or less were going to be, so I didn't audi-tion any of the other leads except maybe Rebecca Hall who I just didn't know. I had met Sam, and I kind of knew I wanted to work with Sam. I'd always wanted to work with Oliver. I had been dying to work with Kevin Bacon again. Matthew MacFadyen, I had liked a lot on another thing, but he hadn't got the part, and Peter Morgan [the writer] said the real John Birt is not so much like the guys in the play. And we talked about it and he said Matthew MacFadyen is more like the real John Birt, so it came together very quickly because the material was rich and interesting and I just promised everyone that the parts were going to get bigger because you were going to be able to breathe life into it. Some of it's going to happen in the writing and some of it's going to happen on the day and I think that'll be the excitement of it, and it was. That went on to the characters with one, two and three lines. You know my brother's talking through the movie and he has no scripted lines except "5, 4, 3, 2 . . . 1." And as this was a thinking person's boxing film, you know how important the corner men are in terms of helping us define the ups and downs on a nuance level of the conflict that we are watching, and I knew that it was going to be a chance to create suspense and also broaden their sense of character. I did audition a number of people, but I wound up using a lot of people from *Apollo 13*. It just started happening. Jane Jenkins, who cast *Apollo 13*, cast this and it was sort of like, Andy Milder [who plays Frank Gannon], I wonder if he'd want to be in it. Oh, okay great, let's get him and it went on down the line that way, so a lot of those characters were filled out with people who I've worked with more than once.

I used to read with the actors when I was still acting. In fact, I did it and they seemed to respond to it and I felt good about being able to give them 100 percent. And then I sort of drifted away from it because it was easier for me, better for me to watch. I was judging a little too much by our chemistry was which was totally irrelevant, of course. And then at one point about five years ago I decided it would be good if I tried reading the scenes. I didn't know it was because it was with children or an actor who I was a little sensitive about casting, but I did read and I was so bad, I realized I was way worse than the casting person and I gave it back to Jane Jenkins and said you better do it.

I've come to audition less and less, but again, every movie is different, and with Rebecca Hall [who plays Caroline Cushing, Frost's girlfriend], it was really important for me to get her and Michael in the room together along with a couple other women who auditioned and actually see what that was going to look like, and that was the closest thing to a formal audition process.

STEVEN SPIELBERG, *MUNICH*

I don't like actors to read for me. I just like to meet them. I mean, if I like the person, I know he is or she is going to acquit the role. And if I've seen other samples of their work, I know they can act and they're going to be good. I don't like readings, and when I do read, I never read with the actor in the room. I find that when actors come in to meet with me, there's a whole other thing that happens that makes them all nervous. So I let the casting folks read all the actors for the secondary roles and they'll read ten, twelve, fifteen actors for each part and I'll make a selection. And I don't usually meet the actors until they show up on the set for the first day of shooting.

There were many challenges in casting for this film, but I had time on my side. When I was supposed to make *Munich*, the script wasn't ready, but I had already cast half the film and I'd spent a year, almost a year, casting. And when you can take your time casting, you get the best results. When you rush casting, you don't get the best results at all. We had 165 speaking parts, and I think we had 80 cast on the day that I decided to make *War of the Worlds* first, and then we just had to go and hope that all the actors would wait, and they all did other jobs, and then almost to a person, they came back and did *Munich*. The biggest challenge, I guess, was because for 80 percent of the actors in *Munich*, English was not their first language. They came from Damascus, Syria; they came from Saudi Arabia, they came from Egypt. There were Arabs that came from Israel. There were Arabs that came from New York whose parents came from the Middle East. Everybody could speak Farsi or Arabic, and some of them were Arab British, some of them were Arab Americans, but most of them were actually from Syria or Libya. We had an actor from Egypt. And it was fascinating because I didn't quite know what to expect. So it was getting them to show up and speak English where you could hear what they were saying. And if I had to do anything over and over and over again, it wasn't so much about performance, it was so the English would be clearer. We had many dialect coaches assigned to different actors, and that was the biggest challenge, just getting the words out.

I produced a movie called *Road to Perdition* that Sam Mendes directed, my company produced it, and at the very beginning, there's this wonderful performance by Ciarán Hinds playing a man who is intoxicated at a funeral and he's talking out of turn in front of Paul Newman, who's kind of the Don, you know? And they have to go up onstage and get him out of that building before he says too much that could basically sign his own death sentence. And it was just one of those wonderful moments. Sometimes you see a movie and there's a secondary role that is extraordinary so you just somehow retain it. You leave the theater and you remember some guy that had seven lines. And I tend to write things down because my memory never had been good long-term, so I write everything down. And I remember writing his name down once I found out who that was and kept him in mind, and then I flew him out to LA to meet me, then offered him the part of Carl.

ALEJANDRO GONZÁLEZ IÑÁRRITU—*BABEL*

Well, for me, this experience in *Babel* was the first time that I have worked with non-actors. In the case of Morocco, beside Cate Blanchett and Brad Pitt, all the people that you see in the Moroccan stories are real people from these humble communities, no plumbing, no electricity. They have never seen a camera before in their lives, and it was a very scary moment. Seventeen days before we start shooting, I didn't have one single actor, and I was very close to canceling the film because I didn't know what to do because all the actors that I was hoping to work with were not working. They have bad habits from the bad TV soap operas in Morocco. The skills were not good for the kind of story that I was looking to do, and it was very scary, very, very scary. So then I decided to turn the casting people to the towns in Morocco, and the mosques, and we start to announce that there was a film that was looking for people. The men came out from there and they were not praying. They were just forming lines, hundreds of them. So we taped them, and basically I started looking at the faces of these guys and kids. And I was like, okay, this kind of makes sense. And then when I was interviewing them, like I was looking for a tough guy, and I said something to stir him and, obviously, I have a translator, a fantastic actress, and she always helped me not only to translate, but she was my emotional bridge to the people. So we were doing some improvisations, and these guys have very tough faces, Biblical faces almost, hundreds of deserts marking their faces. But when they laughed they were like kids. They were the most nice guys. If you put those faces in the *New York Times*, they become portrayed like terrorists, whatever, but they are the kindest, most beautiful and innocent people. It's very difficult to attach that thing that you are looking for to the faces, and it's complicated. It was complicated. I was lucky to find these people and for the strangest reasons. For example, the guy that takes care of Brad Pitt and Cate Blanchett, he was a computer guy, a systems guy. So I said, "I have better plans for you. You will be with Brad Pitt in a film." Or there were kids playing football in the plaza. And Alfonso, a great guy that was my second unit director said you have to come to see this kid playing football.

Look at that face. So I saw him, and I said, "I just want to you to say a couple of lines. I don't want you to answer, I just want you to react." So I said to him, for example, "Your mother has just died." And he just looked at me and he starts crying, but not overacting, and my skin gets bumps. And then I said, "Your football team has just won the World Cup," and he has a range, immediately natural. The father of the boys in the movie is a carpenter, and the veterinarian was the realtor of this little town.

All my casting in Mexico was completely redone, and that's why I took almost a year because all the things that I have done before, nothing was used. I was glad that that happened, that crisis in Morocco, because that made me decide to use non-actors, and I think the film benefited from that.

In the Japanese section, the funny thing was that I wanted desperately to get a deaf Japanese girl because I thought that politically it was the good thing to do. All the other girls who were around her are deaf, except the main character. I went one year before shooting, and I started casting, but none of them was really good enough and spiritually, emotionally, they were not there. But Rinko Kikuchi, I did a reading with her. She was fantastic, but she wasn't deaf, and I said, "Oh, my god, she's not deaf." Then I was struggling, but then she took nine months of sign language classes, and when I returned, she was better than anybody. And I said, well, acting is the art of transformation. A blind man or man with some physical disease can be played better by actors because the actors can see 360 degrees and then transform themselves, and the blind man cannot see himself. So it was interesting, and very frustrating. I remember the casting with the Japanese, the deaf Japanese, I have to translate from my Spanish to my English, my bad English, to the Japanese translator, then the Japanese translator to the sign language Japanese translator.

ALEXANDER PAYNE, *THE DESCENDANTS*

I've never directed children before and even harder than directing children is casting, and I would say I finally learned how to do it late in the process. The problem is not the kid; the problem is the parents. I'd see the kids on tape. "Wow, she's terrific. Bring her in." So she'd fly in from Memphis or something and by the time the actress would reach me, the parents would have drilled the hell out of her to do it a certain way. And I would say, "Okay. That's great. Now, try it a little bit more this way or a little bit more that way." They can't do it. So the advice is simple, which is make sure your child knows the dialogue, but do not rehearse your child, and I learned that too late, yes.

DANNY BOYLE, *SLUMDOG MILLIONAIRE*

Anil Kapoor [who plays Prem, the MC on the show] is a superstar in Bollywood. He's incredibly risky with what he does and that was one of the things that's really interesting about him as an actor. A lot of Bollywood stars are worried about how they're perceived, that whole chestnut of, "Does this make me look like a hero or . . ." The biggest star in Bollywood is this guy Amitabh Bachchan, who is the guy that the kid tries to get the autograph from. His heir apparent in the '90s was Anil Kapoor. Now Anil's star has faded a little bit since then and Anil as part of that reduction of his superstardom has begun to explore lots of different roles and he's a very bold actor. We tried to cast everything in Bollywood. There's a huge and extraordinary range of actors there all of whom are weirdly busy at all different levels, not just the big stars, the medium players, the day players, they're all kind of juggling all the movies and adverts. It's kind of weird and it's a big difference from Hollywood and the UK, the two places I'd worked before. In the UK, actors tend to be unemployed most of the time, you know, and therefore a bit paranoid when they turn up. In Bollywood it's like the opposite. There's this confidence about doing it but they have to adjust their style a bit, and you find that there's a lot of fantastic talent there. But we had been looking for this eighteen-year old lad, and most of the lads there when they're going into the system are body builders basically. You've got to have a really buff body. You've got to look like you can take your shirt off because they often do for the dances and stuff like that. So these guys had come in and sat down in the auditions and they were lovely. They were eighteen, so their heads were still quite small, petite, but there were these kind of Michelin man bodies underneath them and they just looked like heroes, you know. They looked like they were heroes in hiding. I've lived with a casting director for many years and we have three children together and our youngest daughter said see this guy Dev Patel who's in this show "Skins" on TV in the UK. He had played a small part. He was a very funny comic character and then when we brought him in and met him in the room he was like comedians often are: He was really unfunny. Almost sour. And they're weird like that and I really liked that about him although he was like only sixteen when we cast him. I had a different casting director in India, an extraordinary woman Loveleen Tandan who casts everybody in India, but auditioning Dev, we mostly auditioned Dev in London to begin with. And I act with them. I virtually always act with them and that's just one of the things I've enjoyed. I come from a theater background, so I always used to do that in the theater as well. And we auditioned him a number of times and put him on tape and showed him around different people to feel that he had won the part.

In the casting sessions with the kids, apart from talking to them, I'd play a lot of games. I'd play that game where you put your hands together and slap each other's hand. They love that game. I was worn out by the end because they just want to play it all the time once you introduce those games. There's a ruler game. You get a kind of ruler. If you hold it and you drop it, you got to catch it before it falls where you aimed it and they would play that and it would last forever, and you get so bored playing it. It's just kind of creating the right emotion for them, the right sympathy and the right space. And on set it's making sure that the crew don't behave like monsters to them. In the casting you get them to perform the script and then you give them notes where you want a bit more this way or a bit more that way. I guess you're checking out whether they can deal with the fact that there's a camera, not to look in the camera and things like that. You're checking that there's no inhibitions about the circumstances they're going to be working in on a slightly larger scale than is in the casting room.

None of the Latikas had acted before. The middle Latika had danced, which is an important thing because there was something in the script that clearly implied that she was assaulted sexually, that she was used sexually and that is quite a big thing for a young girl at that age, and the initial girl that we cast turned it down in the end. Her mother wanted her to do it, but she said in the end she didn't want to do it and you have to respect that. I'd explained very carefully that nothing would be seen, but you know I can understand they can look at a script and think who knows what would happen so the fact that we got a dancer for the middle girl helped because she had a physical confidence that she was able to kind of see her way through that.

I saw the older Latika on a tape and I had one of those moments. I remember having it with a girl in *Trainspotting*. It was a girl who again hadn't acted before and you have an instinctive response and you just bet that's her. And you go through the whole process of seeing all these beautiful girls, which is hard work. Six hundred beautiful girls and you're performing the part with them. It's really tough! But I kept coming back to her and she hadn't much experience in terms of acting, but you know they learn and you trust them. It's trusting your instinct. They kind of learn how to do it. I've been amazed by the two of them, Dev and Freida [Pinto] and the way they've learned to handle press duties and all that kind of stuff. You see them grow in front of you.

The fat cop is played by Saurabh Shukla and he is a writer-director-actor. Wonderful kind of character actor and he wrote a wonderful film called *Satya*, quite a serious film there. Loveleen brought him in and he came in and you know what it's like, you sit with these great character actors that you just think straight away it's going to be him. It's got to be him and you fight for him then because he's doing adverts for whisky and nappies, and then he's got all these writing commitments and it's just such a hurly burly and everything is done personally. There's no agents. It's all telephone numbers, everybody's calling each other. They deal with you directly about their fee. You're on the phone with them about their fee. It's just incredible you know and it's all like, no contracts. It's all, "Okay I'll do that, I'll be there."

Danny Boyle on the set of *Slumdog Millionaire*. SLUMDOG MILLIONAIRE ©2008 Twentieth Century Fox. All Rights Reserved.

KATHRYN BIGELOW, *THE HURT LOCKER*

Jim [Cameron] said very early on, "Be very careful in your casting choices because those are irrevocable decisions no matter how great your script is, no matter how great you shoot the film, no matter how wonderfully, it's mixed, etc. If you have made a mistake in your casting choice, that's it."

What was so interesting that none of us anticipated in going to Jordan where there were refugees from the occupation, Iraqi refugees. At the time we were there, there were close to a million refugees in Jordan. Also, what I never realized was that in Baghdad there was a really thriving theatrical community, so many of those refugees were actors. I mean this was just like the most serendipitous of events, so we had this huge pool to choose from. Virtually every single background player and bit player that needed to be Arabic were actually Iraqis, many of which, like even the butcher man at the beginning, have blue eyes, so they are very specific looking and to somebody who's really knowledgeable about that area, the fact that those are Iraqi, I mean, it was important to me, obviously, but it instills the kind of truth in the movie that was important also to the Arabic culture. To be respectful of the fact those individuals were cast as who they were meant to be. That gentleman [Black Suit Man who was tied to a bomb], his name is Suhail [Aldabbach] and he was a very famous Baghdad stage actor living in Amman at the time we were shooting. He thought he would probably never act again. Homeless, you know, he's a refugee, and thankfully we had a Jordanian casting director who knew of him and brought him in, and I worked with an interpreter, but you just see that face and there's so much emotion and he's so magnificent looking that he was absolutely the man that was scripted, and he was so grateful too.

But the young boy who plays Beckham, that was the most challenging part. There were a lot of young Arabic or Jordanian and Iraqi kids that came in and that was very, very difficult. You know I wasn't sure how we were going to figure that one out because they're very uncomfortable, had never acted and I always believe that obviously your main characters are critical but you will let them down if the bit players that they're playing with are not up to their caliber. They can't carry the entire scene. It's a dialogue. So Tony [Anthony Mackie, actor and producer] happened to have been at the Dead Sea and there was a kid playing the piano at one of the hotels, just a tourist. He was playing this piano. His eye went right to him obviously because he's playing this piano, beautiful, beautiful young boy. He also had a Jordanian father who happened to be an arms dealer and a mother who's from Texas, so he was bilingual and he just was a natural, but I did spend a lot of time with him just to make sure. I threw a lot of things at him just because he had never been on a film set. We spent quite a little bit of time with him over a few days just making sure that he was alright if we were to throw something new into the sequence, if we wanted to re-sculpt the scene a little bit, was he okay with that, and he was just absolutely a natural. It was one of those great gifts.

I went to Kuwait and I spent time at a military base, which was the last staging area before, if you were a member of the military and meant to do your turf duty in Iraq, you would go into Iraq. One day when we had lunch at this mess hall, there were maybe twenty-five hundred men and women in uniform with their M4s and I was just really feeling that it was very, very, very important that those particular three men in our movie, James, Eldridge and Sanborn, be very familiar, but unfamiliar. That they kind of be every mother's son in a way, and just kind of have a beautiful anonymity that would also underscore this kind of fragility because I looked across this room and there were all these idling buses. The sergeant major noticed me watching them and he turned to me, or I turned to him, and I asked, "What's going on?" and he said, "Well those buses leave here full, but they never come back that way." So it was very important for me when I gazed across those faces, you want to underscore the fragility. On the other hand, all these three actors have a tremendous body of work behind them. They're just not household names, so I set about looking at hundreds if not maybe a thousand independent movies. I mean I was looking. I was interested in somebody who had a certain amount of work behind them, so I could get a sense of their range and dexterity and flexibility, but at the same time the first person I needed to cast was James because he's kind of your anchor. I found *Dahmer*, where Jeremy Renner plays a serial killer and it's a magnificent movie and obviously that's a character for whom you would never imagine having any compassion. You watch this movie, you have compassion and it was the real strength and genius of this particular performance. Renner was shooting in London at the time. We sent him a script. He loved the script. He called. We spoke on the phone and probably spoke for, I don't know, two, two-and-a-half hours. It was just so interesting the questions that he asked and I often think that great acting, you must have an incredible imagination obviously, but a really acute imagination and kind of a flexible intelligence, which is what he had on the phone. I mean he just came at it from all these different areas and having that incredible performance behind him, in my mind at that moment, he was the guy. Now I hadn't met him yet. He had a break in his shoot, so he was going to come. I was going to meet him, but I began casting, in my mind, the other characters as if he was the guy. I had never, you know, shaken hands yet, but a large part of casting is instinct and that kind of starts the process, but then of course, the actors like Ralph [Fiennes] and David Morse, Guy Pearce, I specifically had them in mind when we were kind of crafting those characters.

I spend time with the actors and sort of get a sense that we could communicate really well with one another. And because I sort of tend to be shy by nature, I wanted to make sure that I could break through that, and we just became very familiar and I felt that there was a real ease, plus when there's a body of work, it's not like I have to start from scratch. I mean look at *Half Nelson* that's a phenomenal performance and every time Anthony Mackie has ever been on screen. Now Brian [Geraghty] had done the incredible small piece in *Jarhead* and I thought all right, he's got the right fragility, the right vulnerability, the right sort of twitchiness to a character to give it a lot of interest. At the same time you don't feel his strength, his ability to rise to any challenge, but he had been shooting all night long. He showed up and this time we actually were reading and Jeremy was there, so I was reading him for the character of Eldridge. I had many Eldridges there reading with Jeremy. He hadn't read the script, he hadn't slept, he couldn't find where we were going, so he was lost. It was like ten in the morning, his eyes were bloodshot and he was just a wreck. I have to say in the audition process, I just feel their pain. I feel more their pain than their prowess, so it's like somehow I have to dig through that, put that aside, just look at what they can do. He came in and he was ready to cry and I'm like, "You're perfect." But he was almost shaking and he was like, "I don't even know if my character lives or dies." But his honesty, that was it. He didn't try to just come in and bullshit me. He was just, "Look I don't know, I haven't slept, I've been working, I couldn't find this place."

JULIAN SCHNABEL, *THE DIVING BELL AND THE BUTTERFLY*

I watched a bunch of French movies. I had seen Mathieu Amalric in a movie called *Late August, Early September*, a film by a guy named Olivier Assayas. About ten years ago I was on a jury in San Sebastian and his wife Jeanne Balibar had won best actress that year. I had seen a remake of Jim Toback's film, *Fingers*, called *The Beat That My Heart Skipped* and I saw Niels Arestrup, who played his father and looks like a cross between Brando and Chris Walken after they have been left in a glacier for about thirteen hours. He's got this crazy look in his eyes, brilliant actor. I saw a film called *I'm Not Here to Be Loved* with Patrick Chesnais and Anne Consigny. Patrick Chesnais ended up playing the doctor. I had an ensemble cast but nobody knew who they were. I never asked anybody to read anything. I met all the people myself, talked to them directly, met them, shook their hand, said, "Do you want to do it?" They said, "Yes" and that was it and they're all great, I mean they were great, every single one of them and I couldn't believe they said yes.

They had two children in real life, but I thought they should have three in the movie. Because two children is a little sad. The boy is ten, the daughter is eight. Then I met this girl Talina Boyaci, she was six or something like that, but she was so smart and so funny and it's like giving the kids a dog or a toy. I'm serious about this if you want any directing tips stick an extra kid in there because the daughter gets to pick up the other child so that she can speak to her father and this little kid was invaluable and they were all good. The little boy was always ready to cry. Somebody made a tape of the kids and so I had seen them. Many of the actors that were quite good in Paris were too polished already, they were acting already and this kid had nice qualities, but he wasn't perfect so I thought that was good and in fact the way I cast them, I acted like I was paralyzed, and I had Mathieu tell them that I was their father so they had to tell me a game and also answer my part of the game. Hangman was one game. It's amazing what these kids will say and you can see where they could go.

TONY GILROY, *MICHAEL CLAYTON*

You start bringing in all these kids in and you see everybody. There's two things: you have kids who are really, really polished and then you have kids who are total civilians. I had never done this before. I was taking a flyer on a huge bunch of other things and, you know, a kid comes in and kind of reads like a machine and you're going, "Well, that's acceptable, I am going to put him in a car with George Clooney, I have one day to shoot this and a half a day to shoot this and I have a bunch of other kids who are sort of spooky," and you're terrified. I don't think that changes. You can sort of protect yourself by hiring brilliant actors that at least you know, they're going to be reliable, but the kid, what do you do? I actually called Steven Soderbergh because I had these two kids and I had one who was kind of a machine who was reliable who would have been acceptable and kind of looked like George and I can triangulate the mother, cast the mother so it would look alright, and I had another who had no idea what he was doing but he was so sweet and eager. And I called Steven and he said, "Pick the one with the most soul and let the camera do it and trust it. It will work out." He's got that face you know and it's the reason that you sort of take the gamble because he's a really soulful kid and he was scared you know, in a good way, he was scared in the right way. So I started to work with him and I was nervous about it so I thought, "I'll work with him a bit" and I literally went up to the house and I got fifteen minutes into a conversation with him, sort of easing into that he had to learn all the things. There's a game and a book and a whole life that the kid in the movie has that I really wanted and ten minutes in I was like, "All I am doing is making this worse." If I take this apart I will never know how to put it back together again, but I wanted him.

You're looking for somebody fresh. There's the brother playing a cop. It's the kind of part that is just so easy it slips into a cliché, it's right there on the brink. I saw a lot of people, almost settled and then Sean Cullen came in and we were just like, "Who is this guy?" Never seen him before, just fantastic. And there was Sydney Pollack's part, but Sydney [who was a well-known feature director] kept dropping out on me, then there was nobody else on that list. You'd think that there's all these people who can do this part and you sort of start crossing off and define somebody who has the age and the authority and is fresh enough and someone who can take every scene from George. I mean he has to dominate George in every scene and you know actors of a certain age, they are either very well-known or they're not automatically dominant, let's just say. There's been something over time that you know they have been beaten by things along the way, and I really needed someone who was really going to kick George. And so Sydney was in, he was out, he was in, was out and he was in and when he was out it was a nightmare because it was a very shitty list.

I have a lot of directors in the film. They were really greedy to be actors. I have all kinds of small parts: Doug McGrath and Tom McCarthy and Brian Koppleman.

I made sure that when people came in and auditioned for the parts of the killers, I was casting people that are handy. One guy came in, Terry Serpico, who had a lot of stunt stuff on his resume. The other actor, Robert Prescott, who came in, and this has happened to me several times, was someone I knew as a friend and I had happened to play golf with him. He's one of the best golfers I've ever played with in my life. He's an extraordinary athlete and he came in and I thought well he's a great athlete. Good for it.

LEE DANIELS, *PRECIOUS*

I got two minutes to hit it and quit it, so I got my gut and that's all I got. So can you do this job lady, let me look in your eyes real quick, you know what I mean. It's really that.

I read over 400 people for Precious because you know I was looking for the truth. I'm always looking for the truth, so I'm going to the McDonalds, I called somebody at

ICM [a big talent agency] and said, "Do you have a four-hundred pound . . . ," and they just said what are you talking about, then I went to McDonalds. I went on the train. I went all around the city looking for her and I learned so much about Precious, the creation of Precious, by the time I cast her because a lot of those girls I read had been abused. All of them were invisible because nobody wants to see them. I learned about my own prejudices. I learned that a lot of them were illiterate. HIV girls came in that were living with AIDS, that were all over three-hundred-fifty pounds. They were from almost white to the color of tar and it was not the color that was really the issue, but rather the girth and the feeling of just being invisible and so it was the incredible jour-ney. I learned so much about Precious by the time Gabby [Sidibe] came into my office, I had a vast experience of Preciouses that were real. When Gabby came in and after the audition, she was as good as the ten girls I had narrowed down to. But homegirl [Gabourey Sidibe] started talking like a white girl from the valley. She was like, "I love *Monster's Ball*." I was like, well who are you? Who are you? But I knew if I cast any of the girls who were the truth, I would have been exploiting them because they would not have been able to talk articulately and eloquently as Gabby does because she's acting. She'd done a play. The other girls had not done anything. I think she had an understanding. She came from a really privileged background, but because of her girth and because of her physicality, she was invisible. She knew that she was invisible, but Gabby is a different type of girl. She's in a state of denial about who she physically is, or she's so elevated, she's a gift from God because she holds herself up with absolute dignity. You think you're talking to somebody's who's ninety pounds, with blonde hair. That's how she holds herself and I think she was my gift.

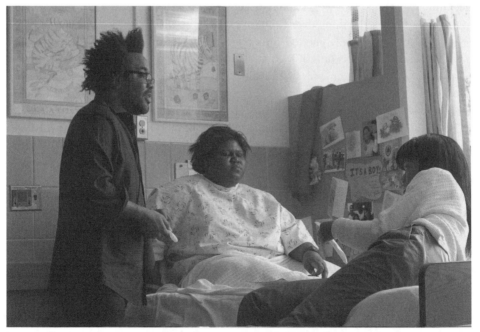

Lee Daniels, Gabourey Sidibe, and Xosha Roquemore on the set of *Precious*. Courtesy of Lionsgate and Elephant Eye Films.

The rest of the cast, it was really two minutes with all the girls in the room. The girls that were in Each One Teach One [the school in the movie] were girls that I knew personally. I knew that if she came in and she moved a certain way or if she cocked her head a certain way or closed her eyes a certain way, I forced myself back into high school and just replicated every one of those people I went to school with, and I knew that they were the truth, or my understanding of what an environment of school was.

With Mariah [Carey], we're very good friends. Helen Mirren [the actress who won the Academy Award for *The Queen*] was supposed to play the role and Helen is so sweet you know, she said: "Lee darling I can't do this, I just can't do this." Why Helen? She had a bigger pay regular job. We don't pay no money, so three hours later Mariah called and said, "Darling, come over for some champagne," and I said, "Mariah I cannot, I'm working, I'm doing a film called *Push*." She knew the book and a light bulb went off and I called Helen and I asked Helen, "What do you think of Mariah replacing you," and she said, "Lee, I can do this with my eyes closed. If you can pull something out of Mariah, then you're on to something." I mean it's not that deep, but it's just the way it works. Literally, I went from one thespian to the next thespian.

The casting of Ms. Rain [the teacher] was really important to me, you know, because I had a crush on the only woman I've ever had a crush on, which is my grade school teacher and she was in eighth grade and she was the most beautiful thing that I'd ever seen before, and she inspired me to learn French, and I only stayed in that room because she was so intoxicating. And so I cast Paula Patton who just reminded me of my junior high school teacher. I never asked her to read. We sat down, we talked, you know, we vibed. I used to direct theater and then I managed actors, so I think that the auditioning process is quite humiliating for an actor. I think the best auditions are far from good actors. It's just a game. It's a scam. It's a game and so you know a person by digging into their soul and looking into their eyes and feeling them. So for me, it was about feeling her and I felt her.

I think you have to play around with the words, especially with Precious. I don't believe in the auditioning process. I think that you sit down with me and talk to me and we talk about everything under the sun from sex to gossip to Lenny Kravitz to sunglasses to bling bling and we connect the spirits because before I yell, "Action," we are not rehearsed, we're one. We're moving along as a spirit.

My sister who's a casting director found Mongo [played by Quisha Powell]. It was a very difficult casting. She has Down syndrome, but don't let it trick you. She smart. She's very smart. She was just brilliant. She set the tone for the scene when the social worker comes, because we had to work around her. Her mother is as dark as Precious, so you know people of color come in all different colors, so it's really interesting to see her. She's really the highlight of the movie for me. She's really quite spectacular.

The little girl Precious gives the scarf to at the end, she was an extra. I had cast Ruby because I had read kids for Ruby. This is what happens when you read people. This girl read for me and she got to the set and she didn't do it and everybody got mad because I fired her. The little girl went home crying, but I gave her a dollar or two or something and then I said to this little extra, you can do it, come on in here, sit in here.

I had theater experience too and I think theater comes into the whole casting process because there's the trust. You know when they're bullshitting you. You know that when an actor sits down there, you know that they're actors, which is a great thing, but you know that you have an instinct that knows even with this, it's an act. That behind all that shit is still going to be something that you're going to have to deal with, so that's an intuitiveness that comes out.

QUENTIN TARANTINO, *INGLOURIOUS BASTERDS*

Christoph Waltz is literally an example of the casting process working at its best. One of the best decisions I think I made on this film was that I was told the way normal international productions do it is, especially if you're casting out of Europe a lot, is you hire a British casting director and then they deal with a French casting director. They deal with a German casting director and I go, "No, I'm not going to do that. That's not the way to go on this. What I'm going to do is I'm going to have a French casting director. I'm going to have a German casting director cast the Germans and an American casting director to cast the Americans, and that's what it's going to be." I set that in place and I also set up that when I was in Los Angeles and I was casting the Americans, I don't care if the greatest German actor on the planet Earth lived on Sunset and Cahuenga, I would not see him in America. I had to see him in Berlin. I had to see him where I was casting the Germans. I had to really compartmentalize the process, so this was just about the Basterds, and this is just about the Americans. When that was done, then I went to Germany and it was just about the Germans and then when that was done, I went to Paris and then it was just about the French. But during that time, Christoph came in and I was aware enough to know that Landa's probably the greatest role I've ever written and one of the greatest roles I'll ever write, so I was obviously precious about the thing. So when he walked in, I didn't know who he was. He was a TV actor. My casting director brought him in. They do a lot of miniseries in Europe, so he was like the third lead on miniseries stuff, and the trick was this, especially in the case of Landa, is Landa had to speak German, French and English. A lot of the actors coming in could more or less do that, actually. They were fluent in English and most German actors can stumble through French to one degree or another, but can he say *my* dialogue in English and that's the trick. I write very specific, very rhythmic. I write stylized dialogue so the casting process is a whole gigantic process for me. It's gigantic insofar as not every actor can pull my stuff off. I put my heart and soul into writing it and I usually go right into production as soon as I finish the script, so one of the first things down the line is going to be casting and to me it's when you see if this material genuinely works. It's my first time when I really get to play with the material and I get to hear people say it. I'm always reading the scenes and playing all the characters. I'm hearing the dialogue. I'm hearing the bad notes. I'm hearing the good notes.

And with Christoph, he came in and it's just one of those things you hope happens. He just comes in and the way I've always heard it in my head was how he did it. On a character like that you don't just say "my dog," you have to sing it and he had to sing it, in a bunch of different languages and he could sing it. And when I read other German actors who were amazing actors and they couldn't do my dialogue in English, it wasn't because they weren't fluent. I could talk to them for the next three weeks in English, but you know, it wasn't their language for poetry and there is a poetic quality to my dialogue. It's part poetry, it's part stand-up comedy, it's a little bit of rap, it's a little bit of wordplay. It's all that together and it ain't for sissies. You got to be able to do it.

When I read scenes to somebody else, I do all the characters. I'm only hearing it through my voice, so now I'm letting go. It's a small process of me letting go, but even then I'm always acting with the actors. If I'm reading the French farmer, then I'm doing Landa for the entire twenty pages and then you leave and somebody else comes in and I do it all over again and it's tiring and stuff, but it's also to me like pre-rehearsal. It's almost like a director's school for me.

During the casting my thing is I owe them their best performance. I want to get their best performance out of this room and even if I know that they're not the one I'm probably going to go with, look, they're here right now and I want to get their best work from them and that's also reminding me how to get the best work from an actor and how to go about it different ways, and even if you know I'm not going to cast this dude, let me explore if I did cast him. Let me explore the character from this direction, and I find shit that's wonderful there. See, I always do a tiny, tiny dialogue polish after I get through the casting process because I've tested dialogues now.

When I did *Reservoir Dogs*, the piece of advice that I got that I always have to remind myself to use was from Harvey Keitel, from an actor. Actually, old salty dog actors gave me good advice, and one of the things Harvey did when he was auditioning for *Reservoir Dogs* was he said, "I know you're going to have a temptation to do this. Don't tell the actor anything when they do their first reading. An adjustment is the easiest thing in the world to give, but you'll never know what they came in with on their own. Always let them do that first one themselves. Then you give them an adjustment, so you're not cutting off something you don't even know about." Now that's harder when it's like hour eight and you're exhausted and you kind of just want to get the goods, but you always have to let them do their thing.

Casting Fredrick Zoller, Daniel Bruhl, he's as perfectly cast as Landa is in the film. Now that was a situation where unless he fucked up in the room, or unless I thought he was an asshole, I was all prepared to give him the role because I saw him in *Goodbye Lennon* and I thought he was so fantastic, and I fell in love with him. When I saw him in that I was like, "Oh my God, this is the perfect guy. This is the German Audie Murphy. This is the poster boy." This could be the guy Goebbels would cast as the lead of his own movie, and then I knew some people who had worked with him, who knew him, so he was somebody I really wanted, and so I didn't actually read other people for that part. When he came in and he did a good job, I was, like, boom, "You're cast," but after I cast him, I went to Paris to cast Shosanna and after I did my first big round with a bunch of Shosannas, I narrowed it down to about eight to come and do callbacks, and then I brought Daniel back with me so I could see the Shosannas and Daniel together, and literally it was a situation when Melanie [Laurent] walked in and they did the scene together. It was like, "Oh my God, this would be the MGM 1943 version of the movie," because it was like the German movie star and the French movie star and they were gorgeous, but they were terrific and they were captivating. It was wonderful.

Casting Hitler, is interesting enough, because your Hitler is *your* Hitler. That was a case, actually, where frankly I had to beg that actor to play that role. His name was Martin Wuttke. He's very, very famous in Germany. I mean he's considered one of their finest actors, like their Gene Hackman or something, and he's actually done probably Germany's favorite performance of Hitler ever and he did the Bertolt Brecht play where Hitler transforms into a dog, all right. He did that play on the Berlin stage and it's considered the performance of Hitler of all time in Germany. It's just renowned like Brando and Kowalski so when I go to talk to him, he's a star of a *Law and Order* kind of show right now, so it was very hard to work out his schedule, so I go to talk to him about it and he said, "I'd rather play a schnitzel than play Hitler." So he was not entranced by the idea of playing Hitler one iota. He said: "Look I'll play two lines, but I won't play Hitler." He turned me down, but then he called back. He called back three days later because he told his friends and his friends were like: "What are you kidding, you've never done it on film. If you're going to do it on film, you could do it for Quentin, I mean Jesus Christ, I mean get over yourself, all right!" So he called back and talked to me and said, "Yes." Half the thing about the performance that was so great that he's done on stage was that just almost everybody in Germany, they've heard Hitler so often, they can impersonate Hitler. He's got a certain way of talking. Germans always can do it, it's really funny when they do it. We can all do Reagan and they can all do Hitler, all right. I just felt lucky to get him. But the thing is, though, you know it was a combination of his vocals, his vocal patterns were so amazingly perfect when he would do the speeches, but then part of it was based on the metamorphosis of the dog thing, so it wasn't just this bio thing, it was really, really terrific, and in this I'm going for Hitler at full rant. The entire performance is Hitler at full, childish-losing-his-sensibilities, rant. Similar to what Luther Adler did in *The Desert Fox*. I was very inspired by that sequence.

DAVID FINCHER, *THE CURIOUS CASE OF BENJAMIN BUTTON*

As it relates to the many Benjamins—we knew we were going to do a lot of "head replacement." We knew we were going to lop their heads off and put Brad Pitt's onto them and we knew we needed this progression of sizes, progression of different body types. We knew that coming out of the wheelchair and muscling onto the crutches, we needed actors. Obviously height had a lot to do with it, but also whether or not they could take direction and be "present" and "responsive" because they needed to inspire everyone in the room. You needed people to want to touch them and do the things that the story required of them, in any given scene. I didn't want it to just be like "here's the person to be replaced later" so we brought in Robert Towers, who played Benjamin as a ten- to thirteen-year-old—he was the first actor we ever worked with on the film. We did a shoot with him in 2002 or 2003 to test specific "head replacement" techniques we would later develop—then we found Peter Badalamenti who's the first Benjamin, the four- to eight-year-old. Originally, I think we thought we were going to have five stages and then we refined the plan and ended up going with three. Tom

Everett is the last, the teenager. You know, it was kind of: "What walks on two wheels in the morning two legs in the afternoon and three legs at night?" It was just a process of refinement, as always. You think you're going to need all these different options and then you get down to it and say: "Well, he's just going to need to act a little bit more and then he's our bridge to the next character iteration." We asked them each to walk on crutches. We asked them to do the scene where he tries to walk for the first time. We did a lot of improvisational stuff. It was just play, just screwing around. Try this and try that. Laray Mayfield did the casting and also cast a lot of the extras. She went down to Louisiana and did all the REAL "legwork." Laray reads the auditionees mostly. I read actors sometimes if I feel like I want to get an idea of what the give and take is like with a specific person. If I want to give them that attention, I apologize in advance and tell them that I'm going to suck at this, because I'm going to be reading and then I'm going to be scrutinizing what they do, but for the most part I like to watch. If they've done a great job reading, then they've got the role. We freak people out every once in a while, we'll go, "Okay, great, let's move on" and they're like, "I should do what?" "No, you've got the part." They're like, "You sure you don't want to . . . ?" and we're trying to be convincing: "No, you've got the part." I've definitely had situations where people who auditioned really amazingly just evaporate under extreme pressure, but there's no getting around pressure—we're here to make diamonds.

DAVID FINCHER, *THE GIRL WITH THE DRAGON TATTOO*

I work to find somebody who I can unleash, as opposed to find somebody that I have to coddle. The journey of finding Rooney [Mara] was finding somebody who I could say: "Whew, that's handled." I'm looking to get work—or "decisions" off of my plate. It is her creation. We talked a little bit about stupid stuff. I did say to anybody who came in to audition "She's not a wound; she's a scar. She doesn't feel anymore. She doesn't bleed; she doesn't cry. She doesn't have access to that." I said: "She's got to be androgynous . . . Now, how do we work on that?" I mean, Rooney's very feminine and lovely and mature, and so I said "This girl is emotionally retarded from the age of 13 because of this traumatic experience. I need an androgynous teenager." So we talked about that and one of the things that we did was, I convinced her—"I want you to learn how to skateboard" because skateboarders don't stand like anybody else. Their center of gravity is like two feet to the left of wherever they are, and they look very boyish. She went out and she did that. So, man, you find the right person, you get the fuck out of their way.

ETHAN AND JOEL COEN, *NO COUNTRY FOR OLD MEN*

JOEL: When we made our first movie, the casting person said to us, "What do you do? How do you cast?" and I think neither of us had ever met any actors before so we just said, "I don't know, we don't know, what do people do?" and he said, "Usually what they do is they have people come in and you meet people and then if you like them you ask them back and read a scene," so we spent like five days meeting scores and scores of people and then he said, "Who do you want to have come back?" and I said, "Everybody, I like everybody." So we subsequently decided to skip the first part of the process and go straight to the reading and that's kind of pretty much what we do. We also find that we can't find anything by seeing people on tape. We have to be in the room with them.

We saw a lot of people for Josh [Brolin's] part. Josh has told this story and people may have heard it, but it's true. He had actually been making a movie with Quentin Tarantino and Robert Rodriguez. He sent us a tape that Robert directed and Quentin shot. We both looked at it and afterwards Ethan said, "Who lit that?" We weren't really interested in Josh. It wasn't until much later we got in a room with him and did some scenes with him and then it was just the opposite. It was sort of immediately apparent.

ETHAN: That was just totally like the right kind of a vibey thing. That was weird because we went into the movie, and I think we went in blithely thinking that there were dozens of people in Hollywood or somewhere that could play that and we were slowly disabused. We met like a lot of people. It was definitely a nail biter.

JOEL: We weren't even sure what we were looking for when we first started out. We thought, as Ethan said, it was a much easier proposition from a casting point of view. Then we realized he has to be able to sort of believably inhabit the region. So much of the movie is about the physical process in watching him do things.

ETHAN: At that point we'd already cast three more or less equal parts: Tommy Lee [Jones], Javier [Bardem], and this open part and having cast those two guys, Tommy Lee and Javier, we were acutely aware that we didn't want to be cutting between these three separate stories. In a way, Tommy Lee's compelling and Javier we thought would be compelling and then the dull guy, we set the bar kind of high.

JOEL: In casting his wife, a Scottish actress, we didn't want to see her actually. We had our arm twisted to see her because we both thought why would we cast a woman from Glasgow with a heavy Glasgow-Norwegian accent and as this woman is in a trailer in West Texas? Kelly [Macdonald] was in New York to go to a wedding and we went, "Okay, come on in," and she got on the phone with a friend of hers. She just has an amazing facility with accents. I mean she got on the phone with her friend from Texas for an hour before she came in and did pretty much what you hear in the movie, which is quite remarkable.

There's an interesting amazingly deep talent pool of actors in Texas I have no idea why, if you go one state over to New Mexico, nothing.

CHRISTOPHER NOLAN, *THE DARK KNIGHT*

Because it was a sequel we were very fortunate. We already had a great ensemble in place and that helps. You know you've got a certain number of the roles already cast.

That takes a load off, but also helps attract a lot of other actors to it because they see all these whether it's Michael Cain or Morgan Freeman, Christian [Bale who plays the Batman], all these guys give you a huge advantage. We faced two enormous challenges. One was casting the Joker. Heath [Ledger] was the first person who I talked to about it before we even had a script and as far as I was concerned, I was done, you know it was great because I could just look into his eyes and see that he had something to express within and we were on the same page about how you would reinterpret this icon in a fresh way, so that for me was fairly effortless. It took a while to commit to everybody else, but because he'd never done anything like it, it was exciting. I think and that's the funny thing with casting, you can't just be looking to things people have done in the past. You really need to be trying to make these characters fresh in some way for the audience. It gets very difficult with some of the small roles as well. We had ninety-seven speaking parts to cast, which took an enormous amount of time. We had to cast in three different places as well. We cast some in LA, some in Chicago, some in London. Our casting director John Papsidera, I've worked with since *Memento*, so we have a good shorthand, a good relationship and he is just very great at finding really interesting actors to do these odd little roles that I think can let down a film enormously if they're not done right. I started watching Hollywood movies with a fresh eye after I'd been through that casting process and you see these great actors, these great performances from the leads and very often what you're seeing in the supporting characters is not as impressive. You don't notice while you're watching the movie because you're carried by the lead and what I was finding out as I was getting into the big-scale filmmaking is there's a very specific reason for it, which is you shoot the leads all day and then in the last ten minutes before the light goes, you throw the poor day player [an actor who works for one day only] and go, "Okay go and he's got all the exposition." It's very unfair to them. It's really tough. There's nothing you can do about it. It's just the way movies are made. That's the reality, so you have to have a casting director who can find you people who are hungry for it and come prepared and know how to just grab that little moment they get.

We just bring in a lot of people and we go very fast and it's a horrible process for them. I cannot imagine being an actor. I feel very guilty during the whole process because you're sitting there kind of judging people and you have to go through it very fast, and it's very impersonal in a way. John reads with the actors. I've done it before in the past with casting directors who've brought an actor in to read with the other actor, but I don't like that. It makes me uncomfortable because I find that the other actor can't help, but perform and so the gravity of it shifts in an uncomfortable way. I like just seeing a very flat reading from the casting director and just letting the person who is coming to audition have their say. If I'm interested in them I will try a couple of different things with them as quickly as possible just to see whether they can be flexible or whether they can do it in different ways. I've been very burned before. There are definitely actors who can audition incredibly well and give you something very subtle in the audition and it's on the tape and it's translated and then you get on set and they aren't actually capable of reproducing that or making it fresh. That complexity of what they were doing in that very pressured environment, you like to try and see it a few different ways and see if they can be flexible, because it's very different sitting in that you know funny little office with a video camera. Then when you get on set there are hundreds of people and it's just a much bigger deal.

One of the things I like about John is he's very polite, he's very good to the actors and that helps ease the whole thing. In the room is me and John and my producer. We keep it small because we don't want a whole committee of people. We try and keep it intimate. Some of it you wind up having to do on tape near the end because you're shooting as you're casting. I try and minimize that, but that's where having a relationship with your casting director really helps because at certain points with John I've actually had to call him up and say, "Look, you just have to send me somebody to play this cop on this day and they've got to have a sense of humor and they've got to be able to . . ." I know he'll send me someone who can really work. Obviously that's not ideal, but on a film that big it gets down to that sometimes.

I think the villains in this kind of movie are very tough to cast because it's back to this question of baggage and audience expectation. Everybody has this sort of old TV show in their mind with henchmen with, you know, matching silver jackets or whatever, and you sort of try to look at the real world and villainous people in the real world. You also try to look at other movies and come up with a sort of balance of reality or apparent reality or hyper-reality with these characters. One of the things we did in *The Dark Knight* with our mob boss was we made him a Chechen. We've now had so many movies and TV shows and everything with that type of Italian mob presence, you're actually looking for ways to present faces to the audience and voices to the audience that will threaten them a bit in a fresh way. At the same time you're trying not to distract from your main villains and you're trying to keep a clarity with who the significant bad guy is.

Down to a lot of the extras it's very difficult to find the big thug who would stand behind him or whatever. It's really tough to get great faces of people who can really find their place in the scene and either not do too much or too little and distract. And we even got to the point where there's a couple of ADs [Assistant Directors] who are actually playing Chechen thugs in the background. It's one of the things you run into on a film that shoots in other countries, and I now watch these sort of blockbusters from the '70s very differently, because you turn a corner from New York and you're in Pinewood [Studios, which are in London]. I was watching Dick Donner's *Superman* recently and I showed it to my kids and there's a moment when you realize he had the same problem I had, which is they wouldn't pay for that actor to go from New York to England, so he does this brilliant thing in *Superman* where you see the gun stick out the alley and he kind of beckons him and then when they cut around [shoot in another direction], and there's the actor there he wanted and I thought I know exactly how that's come about.

PAUL HAGGIS, *CRASH*

I mean the casting process was very, very difficult. It took a year and a half to cast it, and we kept losing terrific actors because we'd have to push because we didn't have a green light [when the movie is financed and able to be shot] until we got all eleven actors together.

STEPHEN FREARS, *THE QUEEN*

I did a TV film with Michael [Sheen] playing Tony Blair, so I was very keen to bring him on. I wanted Helen [Mirren who plays the Queen] immediately, but the truth is when you're making films about real people, of course, in the end, what you really want are talented people. Whether they resemble them, whether they don't resemble them, what license you take, it's pretty arbitrary. You know what these people look like, so I suppose you're looking toward actors who more or less resemble the person, but in the end, of course, you need good actors.

I mean it wasn't particularly hard to cast, but it was really just working out where you draw certain lines, which, of course, you're absolutely willing to abandon at any moment because you want to do something else.

Nobody reads for me [which is when an actor plays the part from the script for the director in a casting session]. When they walked into the room I knew they were good actors, so there's confidence that they're going to be very, very good and that their intelligence informs their performance and all those sort of things. The truth is, before an actor comes into the room, either you know or you're told who is good. It's not very difficult to find out that someone is good, particularly in this country, where their reputations precede them. What really matters is sort of instinctive: Do I actually believe in this person, does this person have the qualities that make sense to me? And that's a much more invisible process and largely depends on your instincts. Are they witty, are they interesting, are they bright, things like that. It doesn't seem that reading particularly reveals this. So

Laurence Burg, Michel Gay, and Stephen Frears on the set of *The Queen*. THE QUEEN—Licensed by Miramax, LLC.

I tend to go on my instinct much more than on auditions. So I'll do just idle gossip about where they were the night before. I mean when people are very young, you ask them to audition maybe, but with experienced actors, I know too much about them before they come in the room.

In a way, the most striking piece of casting was James Cromwell, the Duke of Edinburgh. In British social life, he's a sort of comic fascist, and British actors I thought of, which included someone like Bill Nighy, would've come across as sort of figure out of pantomime. When Jim Cromwell's name was suggested, and it wasn't my suggestion, I grabbed hold of it because it immediately dealt with that problem of casting someone who was very, very familiar certainly to a British audience but would actually be capable of playing the character as more considerable than just a pantomime character. I'd worked with him before and curious enough, he had met the Duke of Edinburgh, so he was naturally on the Duke of Edinburgh's side.

The actor who plays Prince Charles was actually suggested by Michael Sheen, but he'd been very, very good playing George Bush in David Herz's play, and he'd always wanted to play Prince Charles, so again, it wasn't particularly difficult. It just involved whether your minds on the same track.

The problem is that the people in the film, they are sort of ridiculed all day. They're very, very familiar to all of us, and at the same time, you're trying to make a film which is not particularly a satire, which presumes that the people you're making a film about are intelligent and smart and modern and all those things. So you're trying to get behind the caricature. Can I actually break the caricature convincingly? Again, in the end, you're choosing from actors who share that point of view and who would instinctively not just wish to make fun of the characters or anything like that.

Some of the parts in Scotland were more difficult, and in fact, the man who takes the queen to see the dead stag, he's an Irish actor. He's not even a Scottish actor. And that was hard because they're really the products of a feudal system. I mean you know they come from this part of Scotland, which is quite feudal. And I suppose most modern actors, that wouldn't come naturally to them. You find an Irish guy, and he does what you want.

The children were a separate problem. It seemed to me that it would be intrusive to start filming the children, after all, the real children lost their mother, and it just seemed clear that you shouldn't go near them. At the same time, they were there, and their position in the family was central. So I wanted them there, and I didn't want to linger on them. I know a woman who's very, very good at casting children. I probably saw a number. I mean there, you were more casting for physical resemblance. One of the boys has red hair, doesn't he, which Harry has. So because there's no other quality to go for, you're not actually asking them to give performances in the normal sense of the word.

GUS VAN SANT, *MILK*

I tried to be open to who might be able to play the characters. I think originally we were just trying to get gay people that could play in the movie and we really were coming up with kind of crazy ideas like David Geffen [a very successful producer and executive] playing a part because we couldn't find gay actors. It was hard for us to do that. Howard [Rosenman, a producer] is gay and Howard plays The Advocate owner, David Goodstein, he looked exactly the same, so it was partly a visual thing of this imposing large man with a beard. He was the heavy in his part. We brought him in and he did a good reading. I mean, he passed.

Francine Maisler was our casting agent. We cast mostly at Paramount at Jinks/Cohen Office, our producers, in a very small room. The camera was packed into the corner and it was uncomfortable which is good because if the actors can do it under pressure like that with bad furniture, you know, bad sound and bad traffic outside, then they're doing well. A lot of people were very nervous in our casting sessions for some reason I'm not sure why. A lot of facial tics that I think were just nerves. I'd never seen that before and I'm not sure if it was the roles or if they were really pushing themselves into the roles. I'm usually sitting there watching and the casting directors are reading or somebody else is reading with the actor and I guess I take photographs sometimes. Sometimes I look at the photographs afterwards and sort the footage as well and review it, get into it. If we're calling back an actor, there's something specific. Maybe it didn't go so well the first time and you know you want to give them a second try or they weren't quite ready.

One of the main parts we had was Sean [Penn]. We were building around Sean. Emile [Hirsch] pretty quickly said he was going to play Cleve Jones. I think we did a number of Cleve Jones tryouts, but then I think one of the main ones was Scott Smith who was Harvey's lover and that was sort of trying to find the right Scott. James Franco eventually plays the part, but before we found James, a lot of people came in and I must have gone through fifteen or sixteen readings. Francine was curious as to how Sean thought of that part and I think he had said, "Just imagine you're my mother and I'm being sent to prison for twenty years and you're choosing my cell mate," which is a kind of Seanism and eventually I think without really reading James, he offered to play the part and just in my mind's eye I thought they would be good together. We didn't have any of that thing where you see them together or acting together. I had known James, for about ten years, so I had known him pretty well, but usually you try and get them in the same place because they were the two lovers and the leads. In this case we didn't because we were happy that he was willing to do it.

In the other parts like Anne Kronenberg, Dick Pabich, Jim Rivaldo we had visual references. Sometimes it was a visual thing. Joe Cross came in to read for Cleve and he was willing to play Dick and he's an amazing sort of lead character, then a side character. It was different each time. We were always in that same like small room, but each person gave a different performance. I was also looking for people in San Francisco who are not actors. It was hard to find anyone that was good enough. While I had had a lot of success in other movies casting high school students that were just novices, in this case it was hard to find anyone that was right. I guess because maybe when you get to a certain age, in your twenties or thirties or forties, you've left behind "let's pretend." When you're nine to twelve you still have a little bit of that and when you're sixteen you can call that up, but by the time you're twenty-six it's sort of going away or you don't really have it. Or perhaps they're not even interested in being in a film. If you want to cast a real politician in one of the roles, it's hard to find enthusiasm.

All the roles were pretty difficult. Matt Damon was going to play Dan White and then he had a conflict because we pushed our schedule, and we went through the Hollywood directory of like possibilities and eventually Josh [Brolin] was able to play the role. I had met Josh at a festival so I knew him personally and I had seen *No Country for Old Men*, and he was Sean's suggestion actually. But it was one of those things that we could only offer it to a person for like three days and we would have to move on. We were desperately trying to fill that role so it was difficult.

MARTIN SCORSESE, *THE DEPARTED*

I was just talking to my guys about doing the film, I guess, a B film in a sense, a genre film, and at the same time, Leo DiCaprio read it, and Leo and I have been working together for a few years. He wanted to play that part. Kenny Lonergan, who's a wonderful writer/director, who did a film called *You Can Count on Me*, he's good friends with Matt Damon. He said, "You know, Matt Damon should play the other part." The studio agreed. They talked to me about it. Matt came from Boston, and I've always liked his work. With those two elements, then I said, "Well, then you need for the character of Zeus, so to speak, or the god, the father, you need someone who can permeate the whole picture because he's in less scenes." I thought Jack [Nicholson]. I said, "Let's get Jack." Jack I know. He has the history of Hollywood. He goes back to the late '50s. He went through Roger Corman [director and producer of B movies who gave many people their first break, like Scorsese and Coppola and Ron Howard, and Jack Nicholson had worked in his movies]. He understands genre. He understands different types of genre coming out of the American cinema and also European cinema and Asian cinema and all that sort of thing. I've always wanted to work with Jack, and so I presented the idea to him. I gave him a call. I said, "I've got this thing. It's a gangster picture, I think." So we started talking, and he became more interested. But he wanted something else. I think he wanted something a little more, and I thought so, too. This is facile to say, but I've done a number of films based on these types of people and these worlds and, therefore, there are figures like Jimmy Conway, played by Robert De Niro in *Goodfellas*, characters in *Mean Streets*, the characters like Danny Day-Lewis in the *Gangs of New York*. So we needed something special here to be on that level. And Bill Monahan [the writer] came up with the idea that we base it upon the actual "Whitey" Bulger, a famous Irish American gangster from Boston. Nobody knows where he is, or they claim not to know where he is. Once we began to read the books on these people and the situation in Boston at that time, nothing that we did in the film was, in a sense, exaggerated in any way. In fact, it was less. Whitey Bulger actually made a deal with the FBI to give up anybody around him, particularly the "organized" Italian mobs from Providence, Rhode Island, and in this way, he was left to be given kind of a carte blanche to do what he wanted in Boston. Jack heard that, and he said, "That's interesting because then nobody knows where anybody stands."

The part of the young woman was difficult because in a movie like this, a story like this, ultimately it's male-driven in a sense, but I wanted the woman to at least be emotionally integral to the story and to the people in the picture. That took over a year and a half of work. Ellen Lewis, my casting director of so many years now brought me a film called *Down to the Bone*. Debra Granik directed, and I thought it was really a good picture, pretty interesting film. I liked the way the actors were all working together with the director and the writer in the film. They told me about the process. I thought Vera Farmiga was great. She came in, she read. I thought she was terrific. She had the intelligence and the grace and the understanding. "Look, you're always going to be the addendum, in a sense, but if she is integrally worked emotionally into the story, I think we might achieve something."

Ellen pulled everybody together from Boston. The rest of the cast of one-liners, we read everybody. We saw a lot of people. The one-liners are very difficult. I'm thinking of the fellow who tells Leo that that Jack's character is an FBI informant. He's screaming. He goes, "Oh, my God. I'm in shock. They told me it wasn't supposed to hurt." He was terrific. We brought him in twice, because I said it can't be [just once]. He's really good. Let's bring him in again. Let's hear it again. He did so well. I said, "Great. Let's go with him." And a number of other people like that just livened the whole thing. Of course, there were many, many real policemen in the film who have done some acting, and also some denizens of the neighborhoods.

When I bring in actors, I have them sit down and talk, have a little fun. I like to hear you say the dialogue, and then if you've got the right tone and the right attitude, I may ask you to change some of it and put in your own words. Like, for example, those two guys who were shaking down the Indian man in the luncheonette, that came out of an improvisation we did with their words. That one is actually an ex-policeman. He understood the shakedown. And the Indian man was really great. He just came in a few times, and he just did one line. I thought he was fine.

David O'Hara [who plays Fitzy], I've seen him in a number of pictures, and he's remarkable. And Ray Winston [who plays Mr. French]; I've always wanted to work with Ray. He's not Irish, but that was one of the issues. He couldn't improvise within the language, the accent, so he decided to play it cool, like a wall, and not trust anyone.

MARTIN SCORSESE, *HUGO*

Asa Butterfield came in the room for the audition and I liked his presence and I liked the fact that he hesitated. That meant he was thinking. You could see him thinking. He had to be a boy that was hiding. He had to be a boy that something was broken inside that had to be fixed in a way. So I liked that very much, that reticence. Very often, like a silent film, we'll cut to his face and you read whatever you want into it in a way. Chloe, on the other hand, was very expressive and irrepressible, jumping around, dancing around and that was good.

Martin Scorsese with Asa
Butterfield on the set of *Hugo*.
HUGO ©2012 Paramount Pictures.
All Rights Reserved. 2012 GK
Films, LLC. All Rights Reserved.

JONATHAN DAYTON AND VALERIE FARIS,
LITTLE MISS SUNSHINE

VALERIE: We didn't have a studio when we were casting the movie. We had been
at a studio for three years trying to cast the movie the way that studios cast a movie,
and it wasn't working. So when it actually came to the point where we had the money
and we had a start date and it was independently financed, casting was very quick. It
just sort of came together quickly because you have a date and you have an offer on
the table, and so for us, we had been thinking about these characters for four years,
and we had thought through many actors for those parts and had some favorites and
we pretty much went to our favorites, and somehow the stars aligned and we got
everybody we wanted.

JONATHAN: I mean, there were always a couple of people that we thought could work
in each of the roles, and it really depended who would fall into place in some of the
other roles in terms of building the family. But Greg Kinnear was the first actor we met

with when we got the job, and we just loved him. We felt like he had all the qualities, that he could handle the comedic needs of the film, but he was also capable of being a real, an honest performer.

VALERIE: In casting we just talk, and we already know their work for the most part, so it's really just, here's how we see the film and how we want to approach it, and see if that scares them or sparks their interest. And I think you know so much from a conversation. I mean, we were fortunate for the role of the little girl, Olive. We had to audition for that, and for us, as soon as we got this job, we said we have to find this girl because we can't assemble a cast and then not have her, and compromise on that role, because the whole film really was dependent on her. You had to love her. So the first part we focused on was finding her, and we actually found her when she was six. We auditioned her, and then it took another three years to get the movie made. So luckily, she grew a little bit but not too much. She was such a great listener, and she was so reserved and really simple. I mean she's a very smart actor and a smart person, but she doesn't think too much about it. She's very instinctual. And really when it came time to make the film and we had this three-year-old audition, you know, she was six, we said, "Is there anything we can see that would tell us more about what she's like now?" And they had a tape of her on the *Jay Leno Show*, and in just looking at that, looking at her ability to sit and just focus . . .

VALERIE: She looked right at him the whole time and was just completely engaged in the conversation with him and talking about poker and playing poker with her brother, and we just thought she had no awareness, really, of the audience. She was just totally engaged.

JONATHAN: And genuine.

VALERIE: Yeah, and was still just a real kid.

JONATHAN: For the part of Dwayne, we read a lot of people. And that was really tricky because he's a character that doesn't speak, and it was very interesting. It was very clear that certain actors would pantomime and try and communicate a whole lot through their gestures, and what was important, of course, is that this is a character who was not interested in communicating. He was trying to shut off. So what Paul Dano did so well was to appear to be trying to keep the world out, and yet in his very subtle gestures was communicating so much. He had that internal life.

VALERIE: But he wasn't communicating what he was writing. That was just to placate the people around him, and Paul's just a really natural, incredible actor. We did like three scenes, and one was when he burst out of the van, runs down the hill, and says his first word, which is "fuck." And how the actors played that scene told us everything, because first it's a very emotional scene, but it's very easy to overplay that and over-dramatize it, and there was also this kind of sweetness that had to come through in that scene when his mom comes down and tries to get him back in the van. So just having the complexity in understanding that situation, Paul's just a very smart actor. He's just an interesting guy to watch, and there's a lot going on.

JONATHAN: The casting people would read with the actors so we could just focus on the performances, but it's so interesting because this was our first time going through this kind of work, and you really find that the people who do the least amount of stuff are the most interesting, who are just more reserved and that have those details that really make you interested in them.

VALERIE: But there are no rules either. That's the funny thing. I feel like you just sort of know when the person and the character line up in the right way, and I think it's always a slight risk, but I felt like we were so lucky and the other challenge was can they feel like a family because Alan [Arkin] and Greg don't exactly look like father and son, but then the challenge is, okay, we have to make them feel like a family. We have to build the family.

BILL CONDON, *DREAMGIRLS*

Effie is 90 percent of casting that movie. There's no question on stage it was a legendary performance by Jennifer Holliday, who I guess still thinks she should be in the movie, but it is twenty-five years later, and we needed to find somebody who could fill those shoes, basically. And it is a movie, so it's realistic. So she's eighteen when she enters the film, so it's got to be someone who's young, so you knew it wasn't going to be someone that we knew. It was going to be a newcomer in some way or another. The whole idea was to have this open-door policy. If anyone who wakes up in the morning, looks in the mirror, and says, "I could play Effie on film," we would give her a shot, you know? So we had open calls around the country. We did some in England. And slowly went through those tapes and really winnowed it down, and then I started to meet people. The only rule was that they couldn't sing "And I'm Telling You" just because, first of all, I didn't want to hear it 800 times, but it was just something that you wanted to be able to have some input on. In fact, one of the problems with Jennifer Hudson initially is that she had sung "And I Am Telling You," and it was on her website, and I already made the mistake of looking at it. She sang it when she was a kid, and it was just sort of blared out. It wasn't acted. It wasn't felt in a way. And it was actually in the beginning hard for me to get over that. But it was interesting with Jennifer, because I went to New York, auditioned her, worked with her, and I felt it.

You spend many, many hours because, again, you're working with someone who's not acted before and also you're then putting on a number. You know, she gets to rehearse for a few hours with a piano accompaniment and then we did it. Eventually we did it over a series of days with costumes, and so it's a real old-fashioned Hollywood screen test, you know, blocking and shooting over two days and things like that. But the first time in the casting office, it was really working through several hours working on the scenes, working on the song until we went to shoot it. And what happened to me is that I felt a real spark. I felt excited by her. And then I went home and looked at the tape, and it didn't seem to be there. And that's what kept me looking, kept me going and looking at a lot of other people. And Larry Mark, actually, the producer, reminded me, "You know, the one time I've heard you be really excited was in the room with her, although it didn't translate." So I said, "You're right," and I brought her back and then did the proper screen test, and that's when it became clear that you could get it onto tape. Unfortunately, in a movie like this, part of it is you decide on somebody and then you're selling that person. So there are an awful lot of people with opinions here, too. So I was iffy on it, but I knew what I'd seen, but then everybody else looked at it and said, "No, it's not there." So then she was not rejected but certainly put on a kind of questionable list. I guess there were about ten or twelve that I tested seriously, but I have to say by the time I did Jennifer's test, I was hell-bent on making it work because I didn't really believe in any of the others. So it was a really scary position to be in because we had everybody else in the cast. It was two weeks before we were going to start rehearsing. And you realize that you could get everything else right in this movie, but if you didn't have an Effie to anchor this, you'd really be in trouble.

Deena was a big question for me about Beyoncé, who came after us for the part. And she did agree to audition. I think mostly you know actors. It's not a question of auditioning. It's really a question of sitting down, chatting with them. But in this case, with both her and Jennifer, these are people who really weren't actors, and you really had to be sure that they could pull off the role dramatically. In her case, too, it just feels as if you've worked with some sort of big divas. When they develop such a strong stage persona, to ask them to really shed that and become something completely different, you look at Beyoncé on a stage, and her powerful sexuality, that has nothing to do with Deena Jones or this period. So I really needed to see that she could do that, and she did it beautifully. That was one of the cases where I didn't even have to look at the tape. It was so clear that she was getting it.

When the script was done, it went to David Geffen's [the producer] house. "Who would you like?" I said Eddie Murphy and Jamie Foxx and then we went about trying to get them. And, again, it's certainly not auditioning them, it's me auditioning for them, certainly in Eddie Murphy's case. You know, go to lunch and what was thrilling there is to, from the first moment, be on the same page, him not wanting to peek out from behind the character, really wanting to turn into something completely different and do something he'd never done before. Jamie Foxx agreed to do it. We met and then he won the Academy Award and wanted a lot of money. And I can tell you that because he talks about it all the time. And then as Eddie Murphy came on board and Beyoncé and people who were cutting their fees drastically, he decided it was something he needed to be a part of, so then he came back.

I think the thing that happens that's interesting is that if you really look at what a part demands, those lists get very short, and I think it becomes very scary when you think you won't get those one or two people who were so right. Here, one of the challenges was simply having a lot of movie stars who had incredibly busy schedules a year out, and would we get the twelve-week period when Eddie Murphy, Jamie Foxx, and Beyoncé Knowles could be in the same place together? And truly until about two months before, it felt as if we were always going to have to sacrifice one of them. And then, finally, *Miami Vice* finished, and we got Jamie.

Then Danny Glover, getting him in this musical was kind of a nail-biter, you know. There are seven main characters, and it's such an epic story that takes place over fifteen years actually, in a way you need somebody like that who comes with so much resonance.

We've been watching him for so many years now, and he represents a kind of royalty of a certain generation of actor, you know? And when he drops out of the movie and then reappears twenty minutes later, there's just something on his face and him being his real age now that tells you so much about what the character's gone through. And I did feel as if there weren't that many other Danny Glovers out there. Initially we went through the agent and then a call to Danny.

This part of the young girl, I wanted her eyes to well with tears at the end, so that's the first thing, and there were three girls who could do it beautifully, and the one that we got did the scene and then you're so moved that you cry, and then suddenly this thing happens. Well, this one girl, I mean I think there may be a disorder there or something because she's so facile. She cried in every take, and then she'd run to the monitor and look at it and watch herself cry and then start to cry watching herself.

JASON REITMAN, *UP IN THE AIR*

I wrote a role for Vera Farmiga. I was always worried, will George [Clooney] say yes? That was it. I mean if George says no, I really don't know who I make this movie with. In fact, my second choice for *Up in the Air* was so different. It was Steve Martin. I was going to completely rewrite the movie for Steve Martin if George had said no. When George said yes, I said great I'll go get Vera. I found Vera was seven months pregnant and we were about to shoot and this blew my mind and this was oddly in that moment that I realized that Vera and Anna [Kendrick] are just as irreplaceable as George. I didn't really know anyone else I could use and I sat with Vera more than once and I remember telling her, you can't do this, I've had a baby and I know what you're about to go through. An idea that you could shoot a month after having a baby, I don't want to tell you what you can't do, but it's impossible and she made me believe. It was kind of the strangest things. She forced me to believe, she came back at me as if I was saying nothing. She was like, "Oh no, no, no, it's going to be fine," and she talked at me so directly and in those moments I realized you are the character. I mean she was so confident that it oddly made me realize even more that I picked the right actress.

On *Up in the Air*, there's eight or nine of the characters I wrote the roles for them and I find it a lot easier to tailor a part for an actor that I know, hopefully that I have already worked with. If I haven't worked with them, I've met them before, know how they speak and I know a bit about who they are. I mean to a certain extent, I like the characters to mirror the people that are playing them. I like my actors to be doing some sort of self-examination in playing the role. Now, when you get down to people who have like one line in the film it's kind of a fairly typical casting process. People come in, they read a line and you tell them, "Thank you very much." I mean that's kind of it and you know I found that there are not great mysteries. I do put them on tape, but you know right away. It's so funny because so much is made of the casting process and the great mystery of it, how you find someone that works and I find it relates to almost everything in directing, which is you just know that it's very hard to write a book about directing, it's very hard to describe how it's done, that it's your gut and either your gut is good or your gut is bad, and when I watch actors, you know in the first take, you know in the first line, and it doesn't take long to get a feel for whether they are real or you believe them or not. You just see something in their eyes. You sense a certain honesty and realism. The harder thing is when for whatever reason they come in and just knock you out on audition and you get to set, and you realize they don't have the goods. That's the scarier thing.

Zach Galifianakis, well I got screwed there because I picked Zach Galifianakis, this kind of underground comedian that me and my friends knew. He had to go do *The Hangover* and become a movie star and it really frustrated me because now my movie opened and it was supposed to be on a guy and perhaps you knew him, perhaps you didn't, but he was getting fired but now you knew him as this guy who jerked the baby off on *Hangover* and you're just waiting for him to make a joke, waiting for him to be funny. It's like, no, he's getting fired. It's not that funny, and people would be laughing at the wrong moments, so that actually worked out strangely.

I find that what's nice about reading with actors is looking in their eyes and seeing that okay, this person's soul is right, but a part of it is actually just seeing what is the functionality of working with this human being, and that's the part that you don't get looking into someone's eyes.

David O. Russell with Christian Bale on the set of *The Fighter*. THE FIGHTER ©2010 Fighter, LLC. All Rights Reserved.

4

REHEARSAL

QUENTIN TARANTINO, *INGLOURIOUS BASTERDS*

Once in a while on something like *Kill Bill* because we had all that fight training, and it got in the way, but I try to do two weeks rehearsal on a movie. The optimum situation and if it can work out is you have a week in a rehearsal room and then the next week on whatever locations that you can get or even whatever standing sets or even in whatever stage there are you can go to. I rehearsed for two weeks on this. As an example the scene in the tavern, I rehearsed that for four days and what happened was the first two days of rehearsal we had the German table over here with the German soldiers and we had our hero guys over here. Everybody was there and then you had the proprietor and the bar maid and once again the other thing that's important about a rehearsal, so important about a rehearsal like this is that the idea of the direction is not going to just be Michael Fassbender and Diane Kruger. The direction is going to also be the proprietor of the bar and the bar maid, all right, so they're not just standing around looking dopey, all right, but they're actually working at the place. They actually become characters. The audience gets to know who they are. You know the real work is actually making those four soldiers play that game and have them be interesting and have them play that game on their own and come up with different things and by the time we got to the third day of rehearsal, we could do the scene from beginning to end, all right. Not the Brad [Pitt] stuff, but like from the point the Germans are playing the game to the point where everybody shoots everybody. By the third day we could do it from beginning to end, so we just did it eight times, all right, from beginning to end, boom boom. I could have put it on the Berlin stage and then the fourth day, Brad showed up and we did his part of the scene.

Everyone was really nervous, all right, when they came in. One, I had actually fired somebody, so they were like, "Shit, I could be gone. I could be gone, all right." So they were very trepidatious and they have this gigantic piece of material, like it's scary for me, well it's even scarier for them. Believe it or not it was pretty scary for me. Anytime you bite that big scene and start chewing, it's trepidation about it, but then you just get down to the work. The best way to start it off was I had the German soldiers show up first, the first two hours and then I just came up with four more versions of the game that weren't in the script, so they could just keep playing the game, keep playing the game and then I would just rewrite stuff and, "Hey, do this and, okay, now you're Anna Karenina. Now you're playing Anna Karenina," until we came up with a couple of things, but by that two hours, I gave them tons of activities to do for the next two weeks when we shot the scene, but again that was the thing. I wasn't dealing with the scene as an entirety. I was just dealing with that moment and that got us all into the groove and that got us into it. We all went out drinking at the end of the night and August Diehl, who is magnificent in the movie, he plays the Gestapo guy who comes in and he has about as difficult stuff as Christoph [Waltz] has to do in the movie. Like I said, I fired somebody before, so it fucked everybody up. I gotta tell ya, I don't know if I want to do this as a trick, but boy it fucking worked, man, all right. Because it was just like, "Oh shit, he can fire him. Fuck we could all go. I mean this is an audition that keeps goin' on. We are out of here and if we ain't pulling, If we ain't doin' his lines right, we're out the door, tout de suite." So the thing about it was they all went out to drink and Eli and August were talking and August was like, "Man, this has been so intense, we are just in the hot seat all the time, because we could just fucking go. It's the hot seat, but you know I understood something, I just love the hot seat, the hot seat is what I need to sit all the time."

RON HOWARD, *FROST/NIXON*

I usually try to get at least two or three weeks of rehearsal and it always varies film to film. But I did not want to rehearse the two of them together at all and in fact we didn't really. Salvatore Totino the cinematographer and I kind of landed on this approach for the film which I had never really done before, which was we did almost no blocking on the day. I always like to touch on every scene at some point just to get the actors talking about, to see if there are any red flags, give them a sense of what I'm looking for. When it's going to be pages and pages I find it is helpful even though you always keep having to remind them and yourself that you're going to have to re-block on the day [when you are actually shooting], but it might be the difference between fifteen minutes of very quickly sort of reorganizing versus having to take an hour and really figure it out, so some of the group scenes we did block in rehearsal.

But in our whole rehearsal period, I never had Michael Sheen and Frank Langella together because they had done it three hundred on the stage and I wanted it to be as fresh as possible when we were filming, but we did sit and just talk. I was explaining the adaptation and why and what we changed from the play, and what we were thinking about. But it was also me just trying to understand what it was these guys had learned and also try and open up a channel, so that they would realize when we were filming this was going to be their final stamp on the characters and I was going to do a lot of angles and I was going to do a lot of takes and just trying to earn their trust, so that when we were filming it was almost back to the beginnings of rehearsal of the play for them, but with this breath of knowledge.

During rehearsal, I'll kind of wander around a little bit and I never try to get anyone to play a scene up to speed. That's the one thing. I want to get a sense of what they're going for, but the one thing that I do always sort of say to them is, "Hey, we're getting a feel for it," and I don't want them to feel like they left it in the rehearsal stage ever. I want them to feel excited about the moment of actually shooting. We did a week of just sort of meeting without any blocking whatsoever in New York because Michael and Frank were still doing the play and then we did another rehearsal a week and a half in LA where we were going to shoot. We again were talking through the adaptation. Peter Morgan [who wrote the play and the screenplay] was there and also trying to understand what was working in the play, what they had learned about the characters, what did they understand, so that they would never feel that at some arbitrary level I was leaving behind what they had already come to understand about it and yet at the same time I was trying to excite them about the possibilities of what we could do and the makeup and hair test, though they weren't all that extensive, they were really important to us especially for Frank Langella because he's not a very self-conscious person. I don't think he's ever really looked at a lot of pictures of himself as Nixon or his interviews like the video version of the play or anything like that and he doesn't think about the camera when you're filming at all. Though he's done a lot of films, he kind of blocks it out. He built Nixon from the inside out, so certainly for the stage character he's enough of a technician to have tried to physicalize him in certain ways. But it meant a lot to him to go to the makeup and hair tests and hear himself speak. I have been talking about how much nuance the camera would get and he would completely embrace that and understood it in the makeup and hair tests and I was almost afraid he would panic and go too far, which he didn't. The really interesting thing about him is there's nothing of Nixon in Frank Langella or vice versa. There's nothing of himself that he could draw upon and yet he had really come to understand this guy in a very soulful level. I was in Washington for the inauguration and these politicos and journalists are saying, "My God, he doesn't really look anything like him, but he got him," and when you talk to Frank about it, it's not watching tapes of Nixon, which he did a little bit of. It's really that he said he went and sat in Nixon's home at the Nixon library, and just sat there in the loft that he had lived in with a couple of his tubercular brothers and he said, "I just started to get a sense of what drove this guy, what made him so afraid."

I was once talking to Mike Nichols maybe seven, eight years ago about rehearsing and I've never directed theater and I always intended to rehearse to get more of the physical problems out of the way and I was delving into some more complicated kind of material and I was talking to him and I said, "What do you use rehearsal for?" He said, "The actors to discover as much of the character in themselves as possible without ever really intellectualizing it or pointing at it. I try to create a conversation flow that allows them to see these little things, for the little light bulbs to go off" and I thought it was a brilliant thing.

PAUL HAGGIS, *CRASH*

We had no time to rehearse and no money to get the actors to do it, so we were all grabbing time whenever we can and we're rehearsing at my home. I would set the thing up and work it out and the actors would improvise the stuff. We'd string stuff around the dialog. I knew I wanted to rehearse the scene that was in the upside-down car, and so I just turned my chairs in the living room upside down. And Thandie [Newton] and Matt [Dillon] are just laughing their asses off at me, "Oh, yeah, this is going to work." I just wanted to get the basic blocking down for them to understand it so when we got there inside this car and set it on fire and had them act, that we could get to the moment where he saw in her eyes that she would rather burn to death than be saved by him. Because that's the moment, what would that do to a man to see that in someone else's eyes? And he has to get to that moment. And because of the way we rehearsed it, when they got there, it made a difficult scene work much better.

BENNETT MILLER, *CAPOTE*

I think Phil [Seymour Hall] had prepared for six months. Together, we'd worked for about two-and-a-half months rehearsing.

Bennett Miller and Philip Seymour Hoffman on the set of *Capote*. Courtesy of MGM Media Licensing. CAPOTE ©2005 United Artists Films Inc. All Rights Reserved.

ALEJANDRO GONZÁLEZ IÑÁRRITU, *BABEL*

Maybe it's because I'm not very experienced and I'm not trusting in myself so I have to explore everything that can be better every time so I complicate things for myself a lot. I try to rehearse. I studied two years theater, so I came from a theater background, so I like to explore. I had a great teacher that said, "The only thing you have to add when you arrive to the set is whether the actor will be standing up, sitting, or laying down, right?" That is the question. Okay, but I find in rehearsal that moment that I can understand even better who these guys are, and I enjoy seeing the process of the actors because I think when the actors arrive to a part that you have been working on two years in your head, I know who these characters are, and when they have problems or questions, I maybe can solve them or I can help them to solve who these guys are or why. And I don't like too much over-rational thinking, like with all those questions that some actors bring to you getting me crazy like what was the cereal that he liked when he was a seven-year-old. See, I don't care, right? I mean what kind of wine do you think the character drinks, all those things, I don't believe it. But I think good things that can trigger good conversation, then they're rehearsing. And I try to be very clear, about what is the objective of the scene, and then what is the objective of the character, what he wants. And then both of us find what is the best way to achieve that. There could be multiple ways to find the same thing.

With the Muslim actors and with the Moroccan actress we really rehearsed a lot, a lot, a lot, in order that when we arrive to the set, we didn't lose time because I didn't have a lot of time. We used classical rehearsal techniques like very basic dramatic objectives, you know? So it was a very basic way to open up because for me, at the end, this film has very few dialogue lines. And although the Japanese story is almost a silent film in a way, what was most important for me is what happened between one line and the other. I don't care about talking people. So for me, it was more about what I can feel about these guys. So the rehearsing for me was a huge advantage.

CHRISTOPHER NOLAN, *INCEPTION*

Some actors like to rehearse a lot. Most of the actors I've worked with are a bit like Leo [DiCaprio] and they don't really like to rehearse too much but they like to go over the script a lot. And really talk about it and talk about it. I mean over months. So by the time we begin to shoot a scene we very exhaustively have gone over what the ideas were which should be there. For me, it wouldn't have been much point in rehearsing because we shoot in a real location, you know, like they're sitting on window ledges twenty feet apart, there's traffic noise, you know, so it wouldn't have made any difference if we rehearsed in a small rehearsal room, like just the way they're having to shout.

ALEXANDER PAYNE, *THE DESCENDANTS*

Film has a wonderful capacity to lie, as we know, and the actors had spent about two weeks together before shooting, so there was some familiarity and really, all they then have to do is just sit there.

TOM HOOPER, *THE KING'S SPEECH*

In *The King's Speech* I did three-week rehearsal before the shoot even started. Which is really a workshop for the script because I don't tend to get actors to constantly put it up on their feet in rehearsal. I find the process of going through the script in incredible detail and working out where it does and doesn't work, tells actors a huge amount about character. You know even the choice of a word can tell an actor a lot about character. And so I use that process. This script helpfully or unhelpfully, after the first line which indicates the stutter, says from here on the stammer will not be indicated for the rest of the script. So the whole thing was an open book. It might sound strange but Colin [Firth] and I didn't spend a lot of time rehearsing the stammer. We made a decision about the type of stammer. We got footage of the real King George VI and there was some archive that literally brought tears to Colin's and my eyes because it was so poignant, the struggle to do the right thing and these drownings in these terrible silences. But I'd studied Colin's work very carefully and I felt he was an incredibly minimalist actor. And when you work with Colin, he's incredibly articulate explaining why he should do very little. I mean he can be very persuasive so I felt armed against that because I thought he was going to be brilliant at this way and that he should do very little. And sure enough on the first day when we started to really work with the stammer his instinct was to really hold it back and I think that the most important thing was me getting him to push it and go much further than I think he was expecting to go. I think he was afraid, possibly quite rightfully, of issues of pace, of issues of the thing getting too slow, but I wanted him I suppose as an actor to switch off the editorial part of his brain that was censoring the level of the stammer. I needed him to be so free that if he actually went into a hole which he didn't come out of for thirty seconds that that was okay. Because the point about stammering is it's about the surrendering control. And when you're facing that abyss, you don't have a part of your brain saying six seconds is enough and now I'm going to stop. So I knew to get him in the moment I had to kind of say it's not your role to decide. You've got to let that go and you just got to be in the moment. And that was quite successful because after about three or four weeks he stopped having the ability to choose to stammer. He started stammering anyway.

LEE DANIELS, *PRECIOUS*

The rehearsal process was really getting to know each other, their rehearsal process was to stay in a room for three hours a day, four times a week until they really got a sense of camaraderie.

Each one of the actors has his own rehearsal. We have our own rehearsal process. With Mariah Carey, she had to change herself physically. You see Mariah wears stiletto heels and she was born, as an embryo, she was in stilettos, seriously, so she had to learn to walk on the palms of her feet and open and so she's walking like a duck and it was really hard for her to un-Mariah herself. People talk about the taking the makeup off and her hands trembling. It really was not that. It was learning how to walk and I believe it all starts with the walk and so for her it was the walk. We never rehearsed. We talked and

I love actors, so the words, if you got great words and you trust your actor then that's it. With Mariah, her rehearsal was the walk. With Mo'Nique, we simply talked. We talked, we talked, we talked and normally Mo'Nique did it in one take for the most part.

Mariah and I had so in depth talked about our lives together, you know we both live the same, all of us. Mariah comes from extreme poverty. She knew this woman. Mo'Nique knows this woman. I think us African Americans, we're only a generation away from "the projects" and so this was all something that was in our DNA that just poured out on screen. There was no rehearsal for them. You know it was what it was.

Precious was a lot of rehearsal with her because Gabby walks with pride, as with Lenny Kravitz too. They walk like a rock star. Well, dude, you just came out of jail and you ain't even a nurse, you a nurse's aide, so you had to hunch your shoulders and he's not used to that, you know. He's the one, so he's not used to coming in like that. With Gabby, Gabby has been trained and conditioned because she's either in denial or on another plane. She holds herself with dignity. You almost forget about her girth, so I had to remind her of her girth, so that means slouching down lowering her voice, you know working from your gut, slowly walking, not looking up at people in the eyes and slowly, slowly be able to look people in the eyes, and slowly learning how to smile, so that was the real rehearsal.

The girls were a party. They had gotten together as a group and had become friends and they'd say the lines and it was really wasn't that deep.

STEPHEN FREARS, *THE QUEEN*

I remember a day's reading [the script]. I don't remember any rehearsal time beyond that. I'm not very good at rehearsing like all the marks on the floor and things. Once you put people in the real situation, it seems to sort itself out. I mean, generally, people sort of coming in or pouring cups of tea or things like that, it's not exactly complicated stuff. I remember seeing Robert Mitchum being interviewed about Charles Lawton, and the guy making the film said, "What did Charles Lawton say to you when he was doing *The Night of the Hunter*?" And Robert Mitchum said, "Well, he didn't say anything." And the guy said, "Well, he must have said something." And Robert Mitchum said, "Well, he said, 'Today we're doing page 34.'" Listen, if my actors are as good as Robert Mitchum, that's fine by me. There are generally a few technical things to work out: when you come in here, and they do it, and then you might say, "Well, actually, it's better if you come over there because the light is better." You're trying to maneuver them around to suit what the cameraman might have to say. But it is quite straightforward stuff, and British actors, they can sort of do it blindfold, and they do know the characters very, very well. I don't have any insight that they don't all have. So it does sort of sort itself out.

KATHRYN BIGELOW, *THE HURT LOCKER*

With each film it's different, but with this one, it was actually very pragmatic. I mean what was interesting for me was to have these guys, I mean obviously they're not going to be actual bomb techs, I mean if they were to face an EOD [Explosive Ordinance Disposal] they would run like all the rest of us, but I wanted them to have the confidence that they could actually do it, so the most important thing for me was to have them spend time with EOD techs both here and in the Middle East and actually detonate live explosions, which is a whole different thing than pyrotechnics that are created for movies. They would go out for instance to Barstow and work with the EOD training sergeants and actually detonate cars, you know live ordinances found in the ground and they would figure out how to do it. It was obviously very, very, very carefully handled, but that I think gave them a tremendous amount of confidence, and spending time with those guys and getting kind of in, as I had done. They needed their own kind of one-on-one with those individuals that don't run from an opportunity to disarm a live ordinance in the fields. So rehearsal was giving them that kind of confidence and language and motor skills. For instance, what Jeremy [Renner] had to do was get comfortable in the suit. He would put the suit on and one of the very first things they'll do to see if you're claustrophobic or not, it's not unlike diving. You put this suit on. First of all you're breathing inside a contained device, it's only 120 degrees outside, so that was not fun. You're given a pile of paper clips. You have to move those paper clips in this hundred pound bomb suit from over here to twenty feet away. Nothing, right? You're in this suit, if you can do it, which Jeremy did beautifully, but that's like the lesson number one and that will like winnow out a lot of people apparently. You know you've already passed the IQ test, your engineering skills, so you can go into either atomic physics or EOD and you have the motor skills of a surgeon. They've already figured out you have that and so now you're at the paper clip test and that winnows out virtually like 90 percent of the people fail that test. It's very, very, very hard. It takes hours to do and you're in this suit. Anyway, so it's the practical kind of getting the scenes, getting the material, getting the character up on its feet.

That's what I call rehearsal. Anything else, I start to hear the performance but at the same time if you're replicating a conflict, the authenticity is absolutely a kind of moral imperative, so you know these guys, even the snipers, even the Anthony Mackie and Eldridge character, you know the ranger and the specialist, they're trained. They're trained so on the set we would walk through before we would do any of those big set pieces.

Pragmatics did sort of throw a monkey wrench into the rehearsal process because Anthony Mackie, he wasn't available until the day we started shooting, but I was determined to have him. I wasn't going to re-rig the schedule and also I had only a finite period of time.

MICHEL HAZANAVICIUS, *THE ARTIST*

The stars Jean Dujardin and Bérénice Bejo didn't dance before. They learned for the movie and they took lessons for four months, maybe five months. Bérénice took lessons of dancing, tap dancing, and the choreographer I think has been very clever. He did something very simple. He taught them the basics and once he saw which steps were the best for them, steps they were comfortable with, then he did the choreography with what they knew how to do. He didn't try to make something too difficult. And actually, I told them very soon, "Don't worry about your feet. Just smile. Look at the camera. If you smile, nobody will look at your feet, and anyway, I'll put the sound in later. So don't worry about your feet." But no, they worked very hard for a long time. She worked so much really, and the dancing lessons were very important for her, but not awful.

Bérénice really worked on being an American actress and it's very different. If you look at French movies and American movies, there's something that reflects something larger than just cinema, I think. The way we live in small cities that came from the Middle Ages, with small streets and small apartments, and you have a lot of room, and you really can see how Americans are more open. I mean, you use the space because you have space and we don't have it. So you can really see that with actors. The way they occupy the space, it's really different, and she really worked on that. And also, there's something about the '20s. There was something really crazy. I mean, all these young ladies, the flappers. She watched a lot of Joan Crawford clips, but the young Joan Crawford who was really different from the old Joan Crawford, and she was really crazy, and, she really worked on that.

DAVID FINCHER, *THE CURIOUS CASE OF BENJAMIN BUTTON*

I don't rehearse the same way I used to rehearse. I used to tape stuff out on the floor and kind of go through it all. I'm more interested in having a dialogue. I'm more interested in tailoring the material, tailoring the suit for whoever has to wear it. So it's usually conversations, reading stuff, and yakking about it. We did have prosthetic rehearsals, and it turned out to be a very valuable thing and I would recommend it for anyone who's doing prosthetic stuff. We ended up doing six weeks of just putting them in a chair and they had already taken life casts and had started sculpting pieces, but we would just take pieces off the shelves that Greg Cannom [Special Makeup Creator] had lying around and slap it on their faces, so that Brad [Pitt] and Cate [Blanchett] could start to get an idea of what this silicone was going to do to them, like how they were going to be able to perform through it, and also the first pieces that were cast for them were just far too thick and we really had to focus on that and when we finally got it down they were membranes, they were ridiculously thin by the end of it, but it started off being just PLAY.

When we rehearsed we discovered, did the scene need to be as long as it was? Or, did it need to be longer? Was there something not being said that needed to be said or was there something being said that we could really do without and in most cases that's what you find when people read over and over is that, especially with great people "I don't need to say that," and you chastise yourself "Duh, of course." Most of it is that—it's just that "let's play dress-up, let's hear it" but not too many times. I don't want them to get bored, let's hear it enough times that we can answer, "What's wrong with this? Cate was amazing. There was a big scene in the movie that troubled both studios. It was the scene where Brad leaves her with the baby and everyone was advocating "He shouldn't know that she's pregnant" and we were mulling it all over

"Yeah, I don't know if it has enough power. I don't know if it seems like a good enough dramatic decision," and she was the one who offered: "No, no, the problem with the scene is that I'm asleep when he leaves. I should be awake." I said, "Well what are you going to say?" and she said, "I'm not going to say anything. I just look at him." I said, "We're done with this. Let's move on. Next page." It's like it just suddenly works.

DAVID FINCHER, *THE GIRL WITH THE DRAGON TATTOO*

Rooney Mara learned to kick-box, she learned to ride a motorcycle. She did all that stuff. We talked about how she was going to smoke. We wanted her to smoke like she was in a foxhole. We wanted to make it so she was a girl who smokes on the subway and so she learns how to smoke in a way that people won't necessarily see her. We all talked about her look. Trish Summerville designed the wardrobe and we had Pat McGrath, who's an amazing makeup artist, come in and play with Rooney's face. She has an amazing face. I mean, that was one of the things that I knew from *The Social Network* was that at times she looks like she's invisible. She looks like a boy. And then the light catches her and you go, "Oh, my God, she's Audrey Hepburn." It's like she has that mercurial thing and you have to be careful of it too. There are times when you reshoot a take where, "Keep your chin down because I don't want you to hit me with both headlights and those cheekbones, I need you to stay away. I need you be sheepish." And Trish Summerville was exactly the right person to dress her and she just went wild, but again, that's the thing you hope to do. You find collaborators that you can wind them up and turn them on and send them into the world. You want to talk to talented people, you want to be able to interface with them, but you also want to be able to inspire and protect them.

JAMES CAMERON, *AVATAR*

I've moved away from rehearsing at all, ahead of time. I used to do that, get everybody together for a couple of weeks and we do that. We'd try to treat it like a stage play and I just realized over time that the day you shoot is the crucible where everything good happens and the take is the moment of the magic and so what I do is a fairly cursory read through so that everybody actually understand what the words mean and they all get to sit in a room together and laugh and joke and talk it through and then there'll be some rehearsal that literally is just stand up, say the words to each other, so everybody's got each other's measure a little bit just so the actors are comfortable with one another and so they're not dreading the scene on the day. Then, to me it's all about the day and I think having a set or having a location is very important. Now meanwhile, I've rehearsed the crap out of it in terms of the physical staging even to the extent of doing pre-visualization or in the case of performance capture having doubles come in and just show me what the basic positions might be to stand within the space and get an idea of what angles, what angles work, but then on the day I just clear the crew back and we rehearse just enough to get it going.

For me, the words are the easy part. Becoming the character is the hard part, so I am much more interested in processes of helping actors find their characters, not playing the scenes. You know we went to Hawaii and tromped around in the jungle in Hawaii for three days and did like bow hunting and stood out in the forest in the rain and talked about the characters and we'd just go up some path and we'd kind of squat down in the rain and talk about their characters, you know, and it was very, very helpful. For Sigourney, I found a botanist for her to go off with, do some botany in the woods and learn how to do science and collect specimens, how to think like a scientist. I took Sam [Worthington] and Zoë [Saldana] down to the river and had them like, it wasn't a fish, but it was like a palm leaf, but they had to bow fish and I said, "Well, now what are you going to do?" and it's kind of drifting by in the current after Sam shot at it and I said, "Well, you're going to jump in and get it" and he said, "What, jump in?" and I said, "Yeah" and I jumped in the water, went over and got the thing and came back out and he said, "Oh, okay." Zoë did three months of movement training with a Cirque du Soleil choreographer to create a motion vocabulary for the Navi. We had a little acting troop who played various background characters: old ladies and young girls, even kids sometimes. So everybody learned to be Navi and move like the Navi all at the same time. They did archery, they did horseback riding. For Sam, I put him with my brother Dave who was a marine for six years and fought in Desert Storm and they went out and did weapons training. They just went out in the canyon and shot machine guns and stuff and crawled around. He had him on the ground and crawling around kind of a mini boot camp. Sam wasn't interested in going through the boot camp psychology part of it. He was more interested in studying the marine, so I put him with four marines for the week and they dragged his ass in the dirt, but he was interested in studying their mindset kind of indomitable spirit. Sam sought out on his own, and I encouraged him, to find disabled guys and be with them and he practiced with the chair a lot, but it was all about creating an environment where they could become their characters. I think the actual scene work itself is relatively straightforward if you know who you are, if you come to the table with that. You know the language for Zoë and the other actors that were playing the Navi and even more difficult than the language was the accent, because it quickly would become either French or Japanese or something recognizable. It's very, very hard to find an accent in English that some existing language group hasn't already got staked out. It's hard to define new turf and it came from Paul Frommer who worked with the dialect coach. Paul Frommer was the guy who created the language. He said there are these ejective consonants, so those should be incorporated into the accent and so Zoë, because she had the most lines in the accent, in the Navi-accented English, she got to establish the accent, and then all the other actors had to go to school on that and match her, match her accent, and because she's bilingual in Spanish and English, she put in some tapped Rs that made it easier for her to pronounce it and then pushed it away from a Hispanic accent using the ejective consonants and stuff like that. It took her a long time to master that, but everybody was pretty much ready to go by day one with three months of build up to it.

MARTIN SCORSESE, *THE DEPARTED*

I had serious actors' availability issues. Certain actors were only available for a specific amount of time. The rehearsal process was really with Bill Monahan [the writer] and the actors and myself. We were rehearsing and also rewriting. Things would come up as we were shooting. We'd call Bill. Bill would come in. We'd work with Bill in a trailer, go back out for a scene the next day.

Two weeks before shooting, maybe we had six days of that sort of thing, and then every day on the shoot, we'd spend time to work on the following scenes, scenes that would come up next.

MARTIN SCORSESE, *HUGO*

Asa Butterfield [who plays Hugo] trained from pre-production on learning magic tricks, a very, very, very good magician in London taught him so many things. We tried to get more in there like the raising of the cards and that sort of thing, but he became pretty adept at it and he was doing it for maybe four months, I'd say.

GUS VAN SANT, *MILK*

We had a normal rehearsal time. We usually go for two weeks with some kind of rehearsal and the rehearsal period is usually only three hours a day around that time when you're choosing costumes and makeup, hair and everyone's sort of getting to know each other. It's sort of a goofing-around period and I usually just start by reading through it and talking. Then you can get into and really do the scenes. A lot of times the things that happen in rehearsal are things that you will never get on the set because it's so loose and it's so safe in the rehearsals space that you only hope you can get it when there's a crew around. It's just kind of like I guess an exercising period. My first time experiencing the rehearsal possibility was *Drugstore Cowboy*. I sort of just opted for this two-week period because I wasn't really used to rehearsing. I was more of a visual filmmaker and not really doing things that involve acting. I kind of just arrived at this and it's an important time for everyone to kind of just hang out. I discovered a lot during the rehearsal. One of the things we wanted to do in *Milk* was we had these great plans to make things up, and improvise or at least I had all these great plans. But it became very obvious that we weren't going to get very far because it was period improvisation within this political discussion. Usually the dialogue was around something that anchored it politically, enough that the actors, unless they did a lot of studying, couldn't really go off the lines too much. I think Emile Hirsch was the best at it. He could just sort of go off and wander around. I think Josh Brolin also really could do weird things with his performances. We pretty much stuck to the script. But I think for me the hardest thing is blocking the scene in the location so you kind of need the real location and I heard that Sidney Lumet

Gus Van Sant with Sean Penn on the set of *Milk*. Courtesy of Universal Studios Licensing LLC.

[director of *Network, 12 Angry Men, the Verdict*] I've heard, he tapes out marks [in the rehearsal hall, where furniture and doors and walls will be on the real sets]. I guess you could do it that way. Once you have the real location, which is only the day you're shooting, the blocking is so varied you could do almost anything. It's kind of like your own rehearsal period and the actors are happening right there on the set that day and you have to sort of make quick decisions, let everyone go their ways no matter if there are five actors in the scene, have them go every which way, then decide whether or not it's possible to do it that way and then you're in conjunction with the DP [cinematographer] and you're trying to figure out how you would shoot that and if you want to limit it or extend it. It's pretty vast, the possibilities, but it's the most important thing I think besides the performances.

I think one of the strong things about the film is Sean [Penn's] portrayal of Harvey Milk. Harvey himself is like a very intense character and funny, almost like Groucho Marx or Abbie Hoffman [political revolutionary of the sixties and seventies]. There was a lot of footage of Harvey that we had available from libraries and that was something that Sean did with sort of my supervision on the side, but really by himself. He locked himself into this area where he could try different things out, absorb the recordings of Harvey, recording his will or speaking or Harvey debating or Harvey campaigning, so it was sort of something that was coming about through his own work. During the rehearsals you could see certain things, but I don't think I really saw it until the first day of the real thing. There was so much footage of the real guy, but Sean forged his own version of a character that was coming as much as it could from Harvey and somewhere between Sean and Harvey there was a synthesis of character.

BILL CONDON, *DREAMGIRLS*

I crave rehearsal because that's when you discover so much, and that's where actors are so smart and they often come in with great ideas and great turns of phrases and things like that. For example, when Effie walks out of a performance on CBS and she has this sort of toe-to-toe argument with Jamie Foxx, I'd taken some of the dialogue from the stage and it didn't work. And just getting to know Jennifer [Hudson who plays Effie] a little, I was able to kind of make it more colloquial and a little more oblique and I think much more powerful. So things like that, I'd listen to it, it doesn't work, go home, write something else, try it the next day, and it would be better.

We rehearsed solidly for two months, and then there are people like Eddie [Murphy] who didn't like to rehearse. But he'd come to the recording studio and pre-record the songs, so that became a way for Anika [Noni Rose], for example, who acts all of her scenes opposite him and who craves rehearsal, to kind of sneak in rehearsals because she'd just hang out and she'd sort of push through and get to know him, and they wouldn't literally do scenes, but they'd get to know each other and start to talk about the movie.

I mean the trick about a musical, obviously, is that these performances are committed vocally before you shoot a foot of film. Of the two-hour running time, it's probably ninety minutes of it that's musicalized, and I would always be relieved when I'd finally get a scene that I would treat in a more kind of traditional way, more open. I think one of the things a director has to be sensitive to the needs of the actor, and in this case with Jennifer Hudson, it really was that kind of specific, making it real, until she really got comfortable with it. It was like, "Lift the glass there, turn the thing," that sort of thing at the beginning, and then she would find it on her own.

So to go from that extreme to the Eddie Murphy extreme, which is sort of just you give him one idea like that this number's a nervous breakdown on stage, and he says, "Okay, I got it," and he goes and does it, and then there are little adjustments you make. You need to be open to whatever an actor needs.

CHRISTOPHER NOLAN, *THE DARK KNIGHT*

You sort of fit rehearsal around prep [the period of preparation before shooting], but what I sort of really gravitated towards is more getting actors together, particular ones who haven't performed together before and just reading a scene, not really rehearsing as such, more talking about it. Reading a scene together is a great way to then pick out things to talk about and in that way you just start to get a dialogue going between those actors and with those actors. One of the other things I've found is that the hair and makeup tests actually and wardrobe tests when we film them on film, everything is a great way for everyone to dip their toe in the water a little bit either on the crew's side, but also particular for the actors. I mean certainly in Heath [Ledger's] case, we had a whole look to develop for the Joker and we did that through hair and makeup tests and on camera. What I saw him use that for was to start showing us what he figured out in terms of how the character would move and how the character would talk. He'd throw in a line and just gradually you get a little what the characterization was going to be.

You need to see it in a context with wardrobe and everything. You need to get used to it yourself, so it's a very useful process to have a bunch of technical things to go through like prosthetics specifically. You get to spend time with your actors as they have all the stuff molded and made to try it on. I think Heath actually had the character very specifically worked out, but I think he pretended not to have it, so that he wouldn't have to just show it. He spoke to me while I was working on the script for months and months and months and he would sort of call me and he talked to me about the type of things he was thinking about. I remember one conversation where he told me he was thinking about how ventriloquist dummies would speak and I genuinely hung up the phone and thought, God, I hope that's good. I just have no idea, but it was really exciting to hear somebody that passionate really exploring character. He worked with his voice coach a lot on how he was going to create this voice that was unpredictable in his cadences, so it would be high, it would be low, with very random patterns, and it was very specifically worked out, but I saw him adapt that or be formed by the wardrobe choices as well. I remember seeing an interview with Laurence Olivier from years back talking about how for him it's the exterior of the character that helps define how it's going to be played. You know, getting the hunchback and the limp and all that [for playing Richard II]. I saw that very much with Heath because he would find a pair of shoes. Lindy Hemming, our fantastic costume designer, found this great pair of shoes, almost clown shoes, but not quite, with a point at the end. He loved those and he loved the socks and everything. He'd put stuff on and it would affect the way he would move and then we'd look at knives and things. He'd sort of pick up a knife and start to use it in a particular way and develop this body language.

For me, the most valuable rehearsal period is on the set. It's getting there and just blocking it out and trying to retain a degree of spontaneity in terms of how I'm going to shoot things, so I'll give the DP [cinematographer] and lighting crew the biggest angle or something to work with, but then we just want to watch the rehearsal and do the blocking from that. I think that rehearsal when you're actually in the place and almost ready to go I think that's sort of when it starts to come to life with the actors. Every now and again you do hit a road bump where there's something wrong with the writing that the actors are finding. One of the things I've learned in my films is that with good actors and experienced actors if they're ever having a problem remembering a line it's always because I've written it wrong, always because there's a non-sequitur and a nonsequitur is very difficult to remember under pressure because it's illogical. You're just throwing exposition is what that usually is, so if Gary Oldman can't remember the line, it's not Gary Oldman's fault. It's my fault almost always, so you've got to start peeling that stuff out. With actors you've worked with before and with an efficient process, with a crew that you've worked with before, I find you can do that on the set in a reasonable amount of time, so we don't need to work it ahead of time too much.

JONATHAN DAYTON AND VALERIE FARIS, *LITTLE MISS SUNSHINE*

VALERIE: We had a week to rehearse, and in some ways, it was as much for them to see how we worked together so the idea of working with two directors wasn't so frightening. And what we did was just mostly tried to develop the relationships between the members of the family so that they would each understand how all the other members felt about each other so that the family would be sort of up and running by the time we got to the set, and that everybody would stay alive in scenes because if they knew what was going on between the father and stepson dynamic, then when the scene's happening, they're more involved in the scene.

JONATHAN: It was a little embarrassing on the first day of rehearsal. We gave everyone notebooks and then we gave them questions, and we had them write answers to these questions. Like what bugs you the most about one of the other characters, and they would write in character, and then we would have them read. They'd write for five minutes, a paragraph or two, and then they would read sentences from their writings to each other, almost like a dialogue and taking turns, and it just allowed everyone to connect with the history of their characters and understand the whole family dynamic.

VALERIE: We asked them, like, what would you change about this person, this character or this person if you could? What could you maybe do with them to change your relationship? Just questions about the relationship and the person and how they felt about them. And then it also allowed us to understand their take on the character very clearly without having to talk about it. We never really sat down and talked about how do you see this character, and we didn't talk about their history, and a lot of that. It just came out through the writing, and it was great because everyone got to experience it at the same time. Abigail [Breslin who plays the young girl] was amazing. She didn't write like an adult. There were little hearts and flowers in her journal. It was more sort of just getting comfortable with each other. It helped us sort of start with a certain momentum going into the first day.

DANNY BOYLE, *SLUMDOG MILLIONAIRE*

I do two weeks' rehearsal mostly because you definitely lose a week to technical stuff, but you're gaining from that technical stuff. It's sort of mini-rehearsals anyway because people try things out. I tried to get the kids to copy each other really. That was the main focus of the rehearsal apart from trying out the scenes. We'd just get them to see if they could imitate any mannerisms because they were playing each other at seven, twelve and eighteen and that process would go backwards and forwards. The eighteen-year-old would look at the seven-year-old and see something that he did or things like that. So I brought all the kids together. But you can't get the older Bollywood actors because they're out doing adverts for nappy and whisky or doing other movies. Although, I had some separate rehearsal time with Anil Kapoor [who plays the MC on the show], but this was a big thing for him because this was his first film in the English language. He speaks perfect English apart from how he pronounces "millionaire," but he was very nervous about it. I would sit with him and he'd want to go through it with me separately, just reading the scenes, so he's checking out the English and stuff like that. He was very nervous, but he did a lot of preparation on watching the role models like Regis Philbin here and this guy Chris Tarrant in the UK, all the different people and all the stuff about how they cross their legs and they get in their chair and all that kind of technical stuff, which they love doing and it distracts from them actually performing. It's to kind of fuss around about everything else, performance is waiting in there somewhere and they're distracting with all these other little things to concentrate on. I always try to rehearse as much as possible, and even if there's only one actor, I'll rehearse the scene and I'll play all the other parts and I find that in a way, I can push the scene if necessary. If I want them to be bigger, I can push it. It's not a problem there in India because the acting style tends to be very big. They do aspire to be like some of the big actors in the US and they do know that when they're working in Western films they should slightly reduce the style and when they dub it back into Hindi, they put all the performance in it back again that should have been there in the first place because they're not bothered by lip synching. We rehearsed everything and tried to explain to the boys through Loveleen [Tandan who worked in casting and rehearsal with the children], so that they knew exactly what was going on.

Location still for *Inception*. INCEPTION—Licensed by Warner Bros. Entertainment Inc. All Rights Re-served.

5

PRODUCTION DESIGN

TOM HOOPER, *THE KING'S SPEECH*

The last time I filmed at home in London was 2003 making *Prime Suspect* and since then I've had to recreate London in Vilnius, Lithuania, Richmond, Virginia and Budapest, Hungary. And I tell you shooting in London is a fantastic double! Almost all the film is location apart from one set which is the Logues' apartment, which we had to build because the place we fell in love with was too impractical. But when I'm looking for locations I love the serendipity of the process. Clearly you've pre-envisioned your movie, the process of going out into the world and looking for locations allows you to make discoveries that take you in different directions and I like opening myself up to the chances of that. That process of going out into the world and learning from the world, I find really helpful.

The central thing for me was finding that space where Logue and Bertie were going to meet because it was quite intimidating having a movie where you kind of need a half an hour, at least a half an hour, set in one room. I felt like when I had that, then the movie would begin to settle in my head, but we didn't have the money to build much so I knew it had to be about locations. And I was determined to find two things about it. One was to express something about the austerity of the 1930s, meaning the '30s you're coming out of the Great Depression. London was filthy and dirty and not gentrified like it is now. And Logue was not a rich man. And I wanted to, through the choice of that location, subvert a lot of the expectation of a film about royalty where sometimes filmmakers become intoxicated by theatricality and lavishness and gold and gilt and I thought this was a great opportunity to subvert that. But also I wanted to find a space that psychologically allowed me to enhance or comment on the King's condition through the design. I have a wonderful relationship with Eve Stewart [production designer] and this is the third thing she's designed. She designed *Elizabeth I*, *The Damned United*, and now this. And fairly early on in prep she said I found the room and she took me to a house in Portman Place where we just parked ten minutes from where I live and led me into this back room and there it was. That wall was found art. And that room is the product of decades of decay and distress. And I have recci-ed [reconnoitered] London so many times, I mean on films, on TV, on commercials and I never knew this room existed and that's just shows the fundamental importance of your collaborators. And Eve Stewart's contribution, just that thing, of knowing that room and having the instinct that it was right from the moment I walked in. And I started taking stills. I put my line producer up against the wall and started taking stills. I think what was terribly important to me about that space is that I wanted to find a visual analog to what stammering was about, and I felt like stammering was really inhabiting these painful silences. It was about inhabiting nothingness and absence and so I was interested in framing Colin's face in relationship to the negative space in the frame and what this wall offered me was to put his face as that character in communication with this huge negative space that had this kind of distressed and alienated quality which I felt was a sort of beautiful expression of his state of mind. And then I could contrast it when I shot back on Geoffrey [Rush]. I framed him against the domesticity of the fireplace, of the books, of the clutter, so you'd have quite a stark division between the psychology of one angle which expresses alienation and the psychology of another angle which expresses sort of warmth and comfort and support.

I mean the only thing strange about this space is that around 6:00 every shoot day I noticed the crew would really thin out and I was thinking I wonder why this is and you know Day 4 you'd be in the middle and you've got one hour to go and half the crew aren't there, and the last hour is not a great time for crew to leave and I discovered that in the basement of this building there was a lap dance training facility. And much as I thought I was creating something very interesting, which all the crew would love to watch, for some strange reason they felt compelled to go into the basement. And the other funny story, we were told that this was owned by a very grand lord and aristocrat. We started shooting there in November and we had another week to do after Christmas and I discovered reading the Christmas newspapers that this lord had been arrested for property embezzlement. He was not a lord, he was not an aristocrat, and so the entire Christmas was spent battling with the lawyers to see if we could go back in to finish shooting.

Shooting in royal spaces or Westminster Abbey, they point blank won't let you shoot in there, in their spaces, as a matter of rule. If you're making a documentary you can, but if you're making fiction you can't. So you know from the outset that you're not going to get anywhere. I mean the same way that you know, the most natural thing in the world in my terms would have been to go and sit down and have tea with the Queen and say, "Tell me about your dad." But that wasn't going to happen either. So you know the follow up, "Can I shoot in your house?" I didn't get that chance. So the final scene where we are in Buckingham Palace is a house called Lancaster House which is the nearest closest building to Buckingham Palace and it's owned by the government and by some bizarre chance the government seemed very happy to take 20,000 pounds a day off us. Whereas the royal family was quite happy not to take our money. I don't know why that would be!

I come back to relying on the knowledge of my team. There's a wonderful location called Battersea Power Station. Richard Loncraine shot *Richard II* there and it's quite an iconic London building. What I didn't know is that there is a control room in Battersea Power Station which is a beautiful 1920s Art Deco stunning piece of design. It was in the era when people wanted to celebrate industrial design by actually designing it well and actually spend some money on it. And again Eve Stewart said, "I know this place," and we went through this extraordinary building site and there was this absolutely perfect replica of 1920s design and we covered up a few of the signs. But if you look carefully you can see sort of very strange ampage and electricity indicators that are faintly on, which we couldn't quite get rid of and so if you look carefully you can see it's not exactly BBC.

The Empire Exhibition is a matte painting [a painting superimposed on a shot that creates the illusion of an environment that would otherwise be too expensive or impossible to build] for that doesn't exist. I filmed my last year of film school *Damned United*, and it was a soccer movie and we filmed at Leeds United Ground Elland Road and I remember leaving Leeds thinking when am I ever going to shoot in this football stadium again and I remember thinking well, "Goodbye Elland Road," never to be seen again. Little did I know I would be back there shooting *The King's Speech*.

What I enjoyed was having recreated London. The park where they had the argument, I live right near Regents Park, and I've walked through that to Soho to the cutting room for ten years and always thought about how to film it and it's great when you get out of your system a deep familiarity with a place rather than a temporary acquaintanceship with a place and I thought so often about how to shoot Georgian London and that architecture and the house was designed by John Adams who is one of our master Georgian architects and it was great getting out of my system years and years of thought about how I'd want to shoot the city rather than the kind of temporary acquaintanceship.

MARTIN SCORSESE, *THE DEPARTED*

We scouted Boston. It's extraordinary, the place, Boston. I hadn't spent that much time there, but we scouted in the winter. And we shot a lot in Boston. We spent, I'd say, more than half the picture in Boston. That bar or whatever that place is where DiCaprio says, "I'm not going to stay here without getting a tetanus shot," a place like that we found in Red Hook. Red Hook is very good to shoot in. It's good, it's safe, it's a nice area. Go shoot in Red Hook. It's good. But we found, though, that ultimately certain deals were better in New York for interiors, and I felt that the film was generic. In other words, the interior of the police station in Boston that I saw can be replicated in New York with the actors from Boston. Certain bars, for example, are actually in New York. It's the same bar I've been shooting in for forty years, basically. It's the same, the tile floor, it felt homey. But I saw those bars in Boston. We had actually a better deal [some cities and states give financial breaks and rebates to allow movies to be made there] in New York at that point. We built the police station in Williamsburg [Brooklyn] and I think one other apartment. The apartment that has the view of the state capital, that was built. We found places in Boston that looked towards the state dome, but I wanted more of a modern look for Colin's upper mobility, and so we created that apartment in Brooklyn. We were fudging the idea that there would be a modern apartment house that had a view of the state dome. It does exist there, but not in the nature of the angle that we had. I must say sometimes shooting in a studio, you have more freedom. In certain cases and the nature of the closeness of real locations, that sort of thing begins to wear on you and the weather at the time, that sort of thing. But if it's climate-controlled and you can actually move that camera and you can get, like in the beginning of the film, a long sequence with dialogue between Mark Wahlberg, Marty Sheen, and Leo DiCaprio. And a scene like that, to have the control of the set is very nice, it's more comfortable and you can move faster, much faster.

There were other places that were kind of difficult. The big shoot-out sequence in some sort of giant warehouse that we found, an old shipyard that they were about to abandon, and shooting that at night in Boston was interesting.

It's a picture about people and their faces and the paranoia and that sort of thing, their eyes. And so the look of it, the places didn't really matter as much.

MARTIN SCORSESE, *HUGO*

We built most of the sets. I think the only days we had shooting on location were in Paris and that was only one day exterior when the kid's looking at the movie theater and then running away. The other three days in Paris were interiors, so everything was built by Dante Ferretti and the train station was our main set. While we were doing that, we were constantly building the graveyard, changing things, getting a bridge and then I said, "We don't need the bridge," "No, we do need the bridge," back and forth, back and forth, trimming the script, moving things around because it was a rather lengthy process to make the picture in terms of the 3D and the children and that sort of thing. But in any event, the one thing I insisted on is that we had the set built in such a way that we can work with Larry McConkey on the steadicam [a device worn with a harness that allows for fluid camera movement]. Bob Richardson [the cinematographer] could design and work with him on where to place the characters in the scene.

CHRISTOPHER NOLAN, *THE DARK KNIGHT*

On these big-scale movies you sort of find yourself just shooting the film and you want to know how you got there because in prep there's so many mechanical things to take care of. You're building bikes and cars and designs and all kinds of crazy things.

CHRISTOPHER NOLAN, *INCEPTION*

Well, we talked a lot about trying to capture what it's really like to have a dream, to be in a dream. And what I felt like I hadn't seen done in a film is treating the dream world with a sense of reality so that while you're in the dream you think it's real and that's one of the story points. So the overriding design idea was to go all around the world and go to real places. We traveled to six different countries, and staged a lot of things in camera in those places, so even where we get into the more fanciful worlds, in limbo for example, we shot on a housing state in Morocco and you use CG [Computer Graphics] to fill it up. So everything to do with the photography and design was really aimed at trying to make things feel real and never sort of give them over to the sort of straightforward surrealism that dreams are often portrayed within movies.

We tried to construct an idea of the innermost thought of this person, the innermost sanctum of their subconscious, so in the center of this fortress are these huge doors and then you have this space in there that for me very specifically you had to feel a bit like the end of *2001*. That was kind of in my head there. It's sort of a mishmash. It's sort of *2001* and *Citizen Kane* scrambled together. But my excuse for that, and I believe it, is that when I think in terms of dreams, when I think of constructing a dream for example, I tend to relate them to movies. Obviously, I'm a big film fan but I think a lot of people are. It seemed likely to me that you could reference those things and they would have some kind of resonant quality to it even if the reference wasn't completely explicit.

The idea was the whole world is based on architecture. He's been trapped in this world for decades with his wife who is also an architect. So we came up with this idea, really of a sort of sequence of different architectural eras based on Le Corbusier, all the sort of really greats of architecture. My initial idea was to use water, and use the sea as the subconscious: it's the eating away at this world they've created. So they first enter this world on the beach, that's a recurring image in the film. And we shot on a beach in Morocco and then had double negative, basically sort of motion track glaciers, glaciers calving and falling into the sea and then applied architectural forms to that so as they progress through this world they walk through various locations in Morocco and then downtown Los Angeles by the Dorothy Chandler Pavilion, DWP building and all that, but it's all expanded with computer graphics.

Guy Dyas [the production designer] did a certain amount of concept paintings. I don't find them terribly useful. I really use them to sell to the studio. Because to me the way those concept paintings are done, and they're very beautiful, and we've all seen the books of them, but you can't really shoot things to look like that. If you do, it's not going to look real, it's going to look like a painting. And so for me, those were a tool for getting everybody talking, but then what I like to do is get on the road with Guy. We went to Morocco and we were driving in from the airport and I saw these buildings there and I said why don't we shoot it there and put water into that main street and walk them through there and then give that over to Paul Franklin [the visual effects supervisor] to create a more expansive world from that. So we shot aerials there and we shot on the ground there.

We do a lot with models as well. First we build more complicated sets with models and we look at that. But I really like everything to be guided by locations. I like everything to be guided by going to a place and finding what we could shoot there for real and then working outwards from there.

Guy built an incredible set on a mountain in Canada that is expanded through miniature work, obviously, where it's collapsing, but with them running around on the ski chase and running around the building, pretty much all of that is in camera, because he built this set, and what I asked him to do and, he did it very effectively, is finish every side of it, so we didn't build a piece that we would then put into a matte painting [where a real set is finished by a painting and combined in post-production]. Even though it was small, it was finished from all angles so you really had a little playground there to shoot a lot of different material, because we got a lot of cross-cutting of people running around, planting bombs and lots of stuff. So we were able to do a lot of that for real and, fortunately, because when you build a set like that you have to do it months out and it didn't snow until three days before we went up there and then we got this huge dump of snow. I have no idea what we would have done if it hadn't snowed.

In the hotel, it was all based around what we were going to have to achieve in terms of zero gravity. So I latched onto a couple of techniques that I'd seen in *2001* when I was a kid. Stanley Kubrick in a day before wire removals [where an actor is hung by wires and then in the editing these wires are eliminated from the image], or easy wire removals, he figured out how to do zero gravity by hiding the wire behind the person. So he was shooting up at somebody hung on a wire, the wire's concealed, and then he'd invert the set to do that and there was a centrifuges that they put together for the running around the space ship scene. So we based our three sets that we built for that on those techniques. We had an eighty-foot hotel corridor that could rotate. We had another version of it that was vertical and you could hang people on wires through the elevated door at the end. We had a hotel room that would rotate and various other set pieces. And we wanted modernism to all of the design. We wanted also to be able to have slightly padded walls and carpeting and things, carpeting with lines in it so that we could hide the camera track. We had to build because you needed a remote head [where the camera can be moved in any direction] when the thing is spinning. So they're all kinds of technical things that played into the design and I think one of the things that Guy and Wally [Pfister, the cinematographer] and all the different depart-ments, Chris Corbould, our special effects guys, they were able I think to integrate their needs into the design process. So it doesn't feel like it's been designed for that, but it very much has. And that even applies to things like hair and makeup where you're saying to Joseph Gordon Levitt, "It would be really good if you didn't have hair flapping around because we have no way of doing that in zero Gs so let's have a tight narrow slicked back hair style." Those kind of things.

STEPHEN FREARS, *THE QUEEN*

Nothing in the film is right. Everything is wrong. We never shot in the right place. I mean had we asked, they would've said no, so we didn't even bother to ask. And then you just have to set about replicating places and using your imagination, which was in-formed by a sort of understanding of British society and how these very, very wealthy and powerful people live. The truth is if you're trying to find Buckingham Palace, there isn't a place that's like Buckingham Palace. It's simply better or grander or more lavish than anywhere. There isn't a second Buckingham Palace in the kingdom, so we did the best we could. We ended up in houses owned by the Rothschilds around London, so there were large houses that were owned by wealthier families. Balmoral we created out of three places in Scotland. Scotland is a huge country with very, very small roads, so there's a lot of driving involved. There was a castle we found on the east coast. There was a house we found on the west coast. The castles in Scotland were hard to find because a lot of them are owned by friends of the Queen. But this proved a blessing because, actually, it meant that you couldn't use the normal places. If you make a film about the royalty of Scotland, you go to A, B, and C. Well, they wouldn't have us, so luckily, we were forced to go look further afield, which actually produced much better and more interesting and more original locations. And then for the outside, which in many ways was the most important, the landscape, we went to an estate which was very, very near to Balmoral and rented that for a few days, but nothing is right. I'm sorry. You can go to Balmoral as a tourist for ten months a year, so we went there and took a still photograph and then artificially put cars in it, and it always seemed to be quite dodgy, and at some point, there were going to be questions asked about your right to do this sort of thing.

I'm by nature a cheapskate. So, for example, the carpets are absolutely dreadful. I mean the carpets are simply wrong, and we couldn't afford to either replace them or color them all in some electronic way. And many houses are just full of these ghastly things. You can't move the bloody things.

In fact, I was always much more concerned that the elements within the film, the royalty, the Blairs, they should somehow bang against each other. Rather than it being seamless, I wanted it to be seamful. I wanted you to be aware of the cutting between the various elements. But, of course, there were times when, for example, the scene of the flowers outside Buckingham Palace, there we actually use newsreel footage and I think newsreel footage of the real queen. So I guess there we were intercutting these two elements.

ALEXANDER PAYNE, *THE DESCENDANTS*

The Kauai land of 25,000 acres, it belongs to a branch of the Waterhouse family, one of those old families out in Hawaii and it is just as the whole film suggests, it's one of those pieces of land that originally was gifted by the king to a vassal and later, fell into the hands of one of those fancy families and there it stands. And it is in danger of being sold in the years to come.

The photographs of the families are the real McCoy. We had to figure out something about clearance [obtaining legal rights for other uses]. It just drives me crazy. Oh, you want a painting, but the studio wants your movie to look like a Holiday Inn motel because they can clear it, and so to get these. To have real artwork, photographs, the legal department goes,

"Well, we don't know who that is."

"Well, they died 150 years ago."

"Well, we have to find their heirs."

Because some crazy asshole might sue us, which is never going to happen in a million years. Don't get me started on clearance. Some of those pictures arrived to me pre-cleared and others were found in the actual houses of those families where we shot, and we asked, "Can we borrow them? We'll be very careful," and we used them because then we knew we had permission of the families to use them, but I really wanted to surround this story with as much as possible the real McCoy.

I'm so interested in showing the place of a film behind the story and I had started that with my Nebraska films and done it somewhat in Santa Barbara County, a little bit in Paris in a short I did, and now this one, I really feel more confident about going to a new place and having a skill set to get enough of a true sense of a place so as to be able to represent it on film. The diplomacy and the observational skills required, I feel a little bit more like I have a good handle on it.

ANG LEE, *BROKEBACK MOUNTAIN*

I was dealing with open space. It's so open that it's actually private.

KATHRYN BIGELOW, *THE HURT LOCKER*

Geography was so critical to this movie. I just felt like you have these vast sets. I mean that's because bomb disarmament mandates two hundred, three hundred meter containment area, so I also felt there's nothing more unnerving than if you are sort of geographically unmoored in the space. I had the movie boarded [what gets shot on what days] once the script was done and I saw the movie in my mind's eye, but not having known we were going to shoot in Jordan. It was boarded based on the script. Then you go find these locations, and you have to kind of rethink the sequences based on the exact locations. In fact, in some cases, like one sequence was written for a cul-de-sac, and I ended up with all these different elevations because it was much more interesting from the standpoint of the film and the characters. So what I thought was important, the real geography, that's where I would pre-block it [figuring out where the actors and the camera get placed].

BILL CONDON, *DREAMGIRLS*

On stage, *Dreamgirls* was set in this kind of mythical universe. They came from Chicago. They wanted to be as big as the Supremes. They kept sort of not being Detroit and Motown, because they were so afraid of being sued at the time. It was so soon after the events it had depicted. But twenty-five years later, because *Dreamgirls* existed, I was able to really make Detroit a character, and it was such a crucial part of the script. The first peaceful civil rights march that Martin Luther King led were there where he gave a kind of tryout of the "I Have a Dream" speech and then there were the riots of the '60s, the urban decay of the '70s. In prep, I had these amazing pictures. There are still bombed-out streets. That is the one inner city in America, one of the few, that really hasn't come back, and there was just amazing stuff that we always planned to shoot. By the time we did get to go back three months before the film was released, the Super Bowl had come to Detroit, and they'd cleaned it all up, and it was all gone, and it was just a shock to get there. We had to then create it. We had to sort of do the Hollywood thing to it again, you know, pull stuff down. It was hard because of our budget more than anything and also the period. And for me, this was a huge budget compared to anything I'd done before, but it was a real mid-sized studio budget, and so the idea of big exteriors with that period element became hard. The biggest one was the car dealership that becomes a recording studio. John Myhre [production designer], when we first met, brought in all these pictures of car dealerships, and they all looked very theatrical, and that was exactly the point that in a musical, everything's got to be heightened to a degree, so there's neon there. There are signs that make it feel almost as though they're standing under a marquee of a theater. And we went down to Long Beach, everywhere in L.A., to find the perfect place, of course, every place had one perfect thing and then something else that didn't work. So what we did find was an empty lot opposite a brick church on a street that had no palm trees, and that was enough. So we just went and built that entire place there.

DARREN ARONOFSKY, *BLACK SWAN*

New York was a big part of the movie. I always wanted a major ballet company. I guess there's three choices: New York, London and Paris. There's not very many foreign dancers in Moscow and St. Petersburg. So those were our three choices. And it all came down to money. It seems when you do these kind of really tight budget films you just have to figure out what's going to be the best formula. And I think very early on, me and my producer Scott Franklin, dreamt this idea of finding some type of space that could be the rehearsal spaces and be the dressing rooms and be the main stage. And we talked about finding a school. But first we went through the Lincoln Center and all the New York stages, but it's really hard to shoot in New York because the stages are all used and with a movie you've got to take it over.

So we found SUNY Purchase which is the State University, it's kind of the art school for New York State, and they have incredible facilities and it just happened to be their winter break and so we kind of moved in there for a month and that became a big part of the landscape. And it also had those beautiful gray walls which I was immediately attracted to. That was such a huge part of the film, that sort of dictated a lot of the color palette and we sort of built it out of the real locations. I always wanted to go to real locations partly because I couldn't afford to build. Also I wanted that sense of reality, to get that kind of New York 1970s, you know, *Rosemary's Baby* type of sense of the city and bring that out. So we shot in all real locations, which when you're doing a kind of a film that's heavy on kind of bugged out visual effects, it's tricky because you can't really put the camera often where you want to and you have to figure out how to work with stuff. Luckily, we had a lot of mirrors in the film so we were able to bounce and get out of corners a lot, with ways like that. It was all a huge compound that had hallways and dressing rooms and we had to re-dress a bunch and paint a bit, but it was a minimal amount of work to get in there and to work with it.

Her apartment was a real place. I always had this idea of the Upper West Side apartment which I had friends that grew up in them so I had a real sense of them and we actually shot in Brooklyn, unfortunately, because the Upper West Side is actually hard to shoot in once again, because it's kind of a no-shoot zone in New York. There's a lot of restrictions because they don't want your trucks everywhere, so we had to find a place out in Brooklyn and it was a great space but it was tiny because we were basically in an apartment trying to make this high-quality film and there was only one extra room where all of us were kind of squeezed in. And we did all these shots that tracked between rooms and stuff so everything was dressed all the time and it was people walking over each other a lot.

When you're working with locations, it's never what you've imagined, you know. So it's really hard to like fit your brain into it and then there's a turning point, when suddenly you get excited about an apartment and then it's, "Oh, we have to work there because I can go from this room to that room," and you start to see different ways you can work with the space. But when you're reading a script you imagine something that's completely different when you're finding certain locations and then it's a big resistance to actually get over that hump. Then you find, "Oh, actually, we can't have that apartment because we can't afford it," or there's no back-up space, there's no support and then that's when it's really painful.

It's always a combination of creative best options. How Matty [Libatique, the cinematographer] can light it, because when you're in a real location and you're dealing with windows, you have to have roof access to get lights in through the windows, to control certain things and so there's budgetary realities. So it's not ever a fully creative decision. It's often connected to the logistics and reality of shooting in the location.

I've gotten into wallpaper. I never had a sense of wallpaper but you get a lot of stuff, texture. That's always fun and Thérèse [DePrez], our production designer, was just amazing with bringing in the whole ballet into the wallpapers and stuff and she did like sun prints. She took leaves and all different types of forest type of ideas and actually made prints and stuff and then turned it into wallpaper, which I guess you can do these days. It's a lot of fun to do that stuff.

We were designing complexity to Barbara [Hershey]'s character to try make her richer and we came up with the idea of what does a dancer do when they retire and I think with some of our research we ran into some that some went into painting and stuff like that. And so that was an idea and we got into this whole Narcissus idea of you know painting your daughter and painting yourself, sort of being consumed by that. And so then it just slowly evolved into a horror beat. You know everything was how can we scare the audience and freak them out with everything in this film. So it just slowly evolved and then during the freak out, we thought it'd be great if the paintings come alive and start talking to her. We knew we were going to do that when we had the art department, the artists who actually created those paintings, do the different mouth positions like you would do in animated film so that it would have that kind of stop motion feel and not that digital feel and that was just an aesthetic choice.

TONY GILROY, *MICHAEL CLAYTON*

We went to Times Square in pre-production, we looked at all the billboards. We began negotiations with several of the different places. We found the one that we liked the most was the Reuters sign, very dramatic. It was in the best camera position and you take your commercial to them and they have a designer there who panels it all out and it's very expensive.

DAVID FINCHER, *THE CURIOUS CASE OF BENJAMIN BUTTON*

Jackson Square in New Orleans is the beginning; and we filled the skies with digital fireworks and, you know, all kinds of little digitally cloned people off in the distance—we filled out the frame, the father runs through Jackson Square, he runs across the street, Esplanade Street, and then back out and back through Jackson Square. There was one shot in the warehouse district of New Orleans and then, magically we're in Montreal.

DAVID FINCHER, *THE SOCIAL NETWORK*

We went to Harvard and it was a little disheartening because the script was actually so contained. The story takes place over six square blocks and I thought this is too easy. We'll go to Harvard and they'll say "yes" and we'll shoot here and we'll be done in October. That didn't happen. We tried everything. And you know, to be fair, it's a little bit of the hottest girl in the room there's like, "I'm probably going to say no but take a swing." So they tell you upfront there's no chance but let's see you dance. So we tried every kind of inroad and eventually they came back and just said, "Two trees died during the filming of *Love Story* and we would never want to see that happen again." That makes total sense.

So just out of vitriol and a sense of wanting revenge I said, "Fuck these people. Let's go find another place," and we started looking on Google Maps for colonial architecture and as it turns out Johns Hopkins is a stunning example of it. And ironically, one of the things that was so hard when we were in Cambridge and we were wandering around, Don Burt, who was the production designer, kept coming back with these photographs and we would say, "It looks great but can you get back from that building a little bit," and, "I need a little more context for it," and what you realize is it's a very small and vertical, and the streets aren't very wide. So in a weird way, going to Johns Hopkins, who couldn't have been more helpful, they were fantastic to us, we could get these vistas and do little matte paintings [a painting superimposed on a shot that creates illusion of an environment that would otherwise be too expensive or impossible to build] of Memorial Hall and Lowell [places at Harvard] and we could kind of put these little gold domes into things, and it was fine. Ironically, as we were talking about it, we were obviously also talking about *The Paper Chase* [that took place at Harvard Law School], only to find out that movie was shot at USC. "I need that kind of burnished old-world thing that you get in downtown LA!" and really, when it gets down to it, the modern university, they all kind of look like bad post-production facilities [editing buildings] from the 1980s. The reality of the actual place just ended up overshadowing everything that we wanted to bring to it. So half of the film was built sets. The dorm rooms, all the hallways, the iron staircase going up, we built a lot of it. We built a lot of it just for expedience because we could fly [remove] walls and do what we needed to do and you would think, you don't have to get that far back for a close up of somebody's fingers, but you do need to be able to move walls and get stuff out of the way. So it turned out to be a kind of a hybrid of whatever the most effective way to get it done. The Harvard president's office was a location in Pasadena where they filmed the opening of *Being There* and we walked in and the furniture was still there. It's fantastic. The Facebook office was a children's museum that had been constructed and the financing had then fallen apart. It was in the North Valley and we looked at it and it was like, "That looks wonderful." It reminds me of ad agencies. I wanted one of those places you could put a bunch of SEGWAYs in and say, "It's such a happy place to work, look we don't care, we skateboard." So this place had that. It had ramps and stuff, and we could paint it in primary colors. We added the mural and actually hired the graffiti artist who had done Facebook's offices.

There's a lot of back and forth with the production designer but mostly it starts with: this is what a dorm room looks like or this is what the house that Zuckerberg had spent his sophomore year in. Ironically, and sadly there had been a murder there recently. It was a shooting and so there was a lot of reticence to us because there had been a lot of paparazzi taking pictures—so they didn't really want us to take reference photos inside, so we kind of stole pictures of the staircases, but we went to a couple of the other houses and got photographs of what their layout was. We cobbled things together based on what we found. The apartment where you first meet Sean Parker was a location in downtown LA. There was a woman who lived there and had decorated it. We saw these photographs and I said, "That's what it should look like." There was a little porch area and there was a bathroom. So we kind of went in trying to figure out a way to shoot this and where are we gonna put the trucks, how are we gonna cable, and finally we said, "Let's just build it" and we literally built that. That was it. There were two views, looking through this doorway and looking through that doorway and it was a small set and we couldn't possibly match everything. There was still no way to talk to the actors. It was like being on location without all the beauty of downtown LA.

I'm a big believer in blinders, you know, trying to define the things that aren't going to be in the movie. What are the limitations? And I think that there's a tendency when you can build something willy-nilly it should be like this or it should be that or that would be really cool, but if you start with a real location . . . it's so valuable to walk around and see what the place actually is. A rather frustrating reality is, because you spend so little time on the ground and you often work from photographs of places that people have pre-scouted for you and you've made these commitments to a specific city and then you find yourself in the process of shooting over say—three weeks wandering around and finding, "That's a much better bagel shop," and you don't realize that the guy's crazy and his brother owned a commercial production company and he hates filming, or they won't allow trucks but you wish you could spend six months in any city that you were going to shoot in, just wandering around, but I still think it's always best to start with reality and work your way back.

I've made distinct choices on what's going to limit me, and those limitations are actually going to help kind of squeeze the toothpaste in the right direction.

PAUL HAGGIS, *CRASH*

We had no money and therefore, it was basically found art that we were going for. And I love working with a production designer who continually challenges you or reads into the script things that you would never have seen. I'd placed this thing in the middle of winter. I knew I wanted it to be the coldest day in L.A. I remember when I was here in the '70s and it snowed in the Valley, and it was just such a magical moment. And so I knew I wanted to build to that. And then one day Larry Bennett [the production designer who Haggis had worked with in television] came up to me and said, "Okay, it's the coldest day in L.A., Christmas."

"Oh, that's really sick, excellent. Yeah, I want to do a Christmas movie about racism and tolerance. Great."

And so he said, "Yes, no one will ever mention it in the script, but put lights up everywhere because, again, they're cheap. You can get Christmas lights very cheaply." It developed. Our lighting plan and what we wanted to build.

I knew Los Angeles that I remember when I first came here thirty years ago or so. I was always squinting when I first arrived. I knew the light was something I really wanted to accomplish. Unfortunately, most of my film took place at night, where that was going to be more difficult. So I said I wanted to continue to shoot into the light. I wanted that halation. I want us to be squinting even at night. And so we sort of embraced that. We embraced the imperfection of the film, and when we started to embrace those imperfections, I think we found a style. Larry did the Christmas stuff on the garage, which I thought was incredibly lovely and tacky, and then he brought the inflatable Santa. "Oh, that's fuckin' perfect," so we put it in the foreground and shot through it.

We did build on location the store that we had to shoot. The biggest challenge was to continually shoot on the locations that had been written for because people kept trying to push us where it was cheaper and easier to handle. They wanted us to shoot in Montrose or something. I kept saying, "Well, it doesn't necessarily look like Westwood, does it?"

On a thirty-five-day shoot, we had seventy locations and so there were many different moves. I had a terrific AD [Assistant Director] who boarded [scheduled] in such a way that we had the actors for two days and then we'd have an actor three weeks later. We had the same scene but with different actors, so we'd have to go back to a location two and three times rather than shooting it out [completing the scene]. We'd go there once with Don Cheadle and once with Ryan Phillippe so that was tough. I'd written a lot of these things for locations I knew and the things I experienced over these thirty years being here. I knew where they took place and so I wrote for them, and then I'd just sit in my office and say, "We'll go to the such and such a place and that's where we'll shoot it." And they'd say, "Well, that parking lot is now a Denny's." So we'd have to go look for someplace else that's perfect, and once you've got the perfect location in mind, it's very difficult to then find someplace else. I knew I wanted Coldwater Canyon, for example, and they'd said, "Well, it's a $6.5 million film. We can't shut down Coldwater Canyon for you at rush hour." So that we found down in San Pedro. I wanted to be able to shut down a four-lane road there on the top of a hill and we found one block that actually worked. There was a long time, long search for that.

I like to get the locations and then figure it out which people love, the ADs [Assistant Directors] love. And so we'd tell them what general direction we're going to shoot in first and then work around that.

DAVID O. RUSSELL, *THE FIGHTER*

I think you have a feeling for what this world is, you know. You know this world has to feel like this and look like this. And if you don't feel that in a sweaty real way I don't think you're gonna get it right. So we knew what it needed to look like and we had family telling us all about where they lived and they were showing us everything. We used their family photo albums. Their albums were a huge source for the hair too. As much as a sense of place beyond the building was the hair and the clothes you know which we just had so much fun with, which was real. We took it right out of their family photo albums. I like feeling you've gone to another world and another place. It was 1990 in Lowell, Massachusetts. The movie is really about intimacy in that community and it really meant the world for us to be there and to be with the family. And they have so many kids and they have so many cousins and everybody there is related to them, so you feel that you're part of the community when you're there. And it was really a sweaty summer and you're all together in that town and it's a very particular town. It's really one of the first industrial towns in America so it has these weird flat-iron buildings that I feature in the opening shot. These big open intersections and then these weird little narrow streets. Of course there was a brief conversation about going to Canada, and it's nice when you have Mark Wahlberg as the godfather of the project who just says that's not gonna happen, you know. And it was really so personal to the family and it was so exciting to this working-class town struggling, that for us to be there, it was the opposite of what you'd normally expect in New York or someplace else. Everybody was like, "Please film over here" and, "What can we do to be part of this? What can we do to help you?" Everybody was coming up to be in the movie all the time. That shot that zips back through the buildings at the opening sequence occurred to me I think a day or two before that shot because I looked down that street and there was all these little houses that were so symmetrical and I knew it would have a telescoping effect if we shot that and I hoped that that energy would slingshot us into the next section of the credit sequence. And so that was the way we used Lowell. That was the actual gym. It's this weird like industrial building and we shot in there, and when we did the smaller fights we blacked it out [make the space dark] and I realized how Scorsese had gotten away with that in *Raging Bull*, you can make a space look huge. You know you black it out, you take these lights back, and it looks like there's all this space. So we shot those small smoker fights in that gym which is not very big.

I love wide shots with great barren spaces. I don't like claustrophobic spaces too much, you know, unless that's the point of it like my first movie was all about claustrophobia so that was all inside. But on this, you know, I had these wide shots like where you had a factory and smokestacks in the background that are all dead now. And it was fantastic, you could have these apartments that were right next to these factories. I love Amy Adams looking down from that porch at Mark Wahlberg. We actually shot in one house that the family had lived in on 11 Marshall Street and they said that during the Vietnam War, these are the guys that went to Vietnam, working-class guys, and one of their cousins had come back from Vietnam and didn't want to tell the family. They didn't know he was back and he took Uncle Jack's horse. I said how did Uncle Jack have a horse and he said Uncle Jack had a horse in town in the backyard and he took the horse into the parlor of the house that we were shooting in, this little like row house, and the mother just passed out. And they said that then the horse shat all over the floor. How real it was, everything was real.

The crack house was my enemy. The crack house was the perfect location in the Cambodian part of town and it just was in a criminal part of town. There was the criminal part of Cambodia town and the not criminal part of Cambodia town. And it just smelled terrible and it had garbage in the backyard and I hated it, but it was the best location. There was no other location. And I think it was either the real one or it was right next to the real one and it had the porch that you could jump out the window. We used a different interior that was a little more spacious. But that house got me. When I was showing Christian [Bale] how he would run down the front steps, I said, "I cannot wait to get out of this location every time," and I said, "Christian, you come running down these front steps," and there was a nail sticking up and I went down on my back and you heard the whole crew go "Oww!" and I'm thinking I might really have a serious injury and I ended up directing on my stomach for the rest of the day. So, I said, "Okay house, you won this round."

Locations are a combination of what feels right and what you try to find out was true and if you really like what's true, if it's important what's true you stick to it, and if not you move on from it. Judy Becker is an amazing designer with an amazing eye for locations and she's tireless and you're always looking, "What about that place, what about this place?" and the donut shop where Micky goes and sees the cop, that was her favorite donut shop in the hood, and you never take "no" for an answer. The first answer's always "no, no," you know, we're not going to give up on that donut shop and for months you're still, "What's happening with that donut shop? Well the guy said . . ." But that had these big glass windows that looked out on the factories and those iron bridges and there was just this amazing vista that Judy was very attached to. So we're glad we finally got in there.

The prison was an actual working prison. And it's where Dicky actually spent time in prison. And I was really spooked out by that. I just didn't feel comfortable going in there you know. And I remember Mark Wahlberg had been in prison, and Mark Wahlberg's brother, who's a really great guy who's a social worker now and I said "Jimmy, I don't want to go in there." He said, "Just look everybody in the eye and let them know that you're just a regular guy and they're all gonna be really cool to you." And he was absolutely right. And Dicky was a "VIP" in the prison 'cause he was a fighter so he got his own cell without a roommate and so we saw the cell that he had been in. We did have to rebuild the set near the cell because we couldn't really shoot in the cell. That was one of our two set builds.

STEVEN SPIELBERG, *MUNICH*

Originally, I wanted to shoot the film on all the locations where the events actually occurred, so Rick Carter, our production designer, went everywhere. He went to Germany. He actually went to the Olympic Village in Munich. He went pretty much everywhere that the film was supposed to take place. He took pictures of England. He took pictures of the places in Paris, in Italy, Germany. Then we just realized that we couldn't possibly afford to tell this story of going to the actual places, and we had to figure out some economic compromise that would allow the illusion to occur that we were in all these places but, in fact, we weren't. So Rick found in Budapest, the whole city is like a Hollywood back lot. You leave the Four Seasons Hotel and you walk ten blocks and you're in London. And then you go five blocks another direction and you're suddenly on the Champs-Élysées. It's an eclectic city of mixed and matched architecture from architects all around Western Europe. So we basically wound up shooting London, Paris, Frankfurt, Germany, and Italy, in Budapest. But then I really wanted a beautiful farmhouse, and there were no farmhouses that looked French anywhere in Budapest. So I used that as an excuse to shoot my first movie in Paris. I've always wanted to go to Paris. And, yeah, I was pretty apparent when I started the shot on the Eiffel Tower and I pulled back, but I couldn't help myself. I asked Mathieu Amalric, the actor who played Louie, would he stand, please, in front of the Eiffel Tower, and he looked at me like I was some kind of a stupid American who wanted to shoot a postcard, which I did. But that was my proof that I was at least in one of the countries the film claims to have existed in.

Now, here's the other amazing thing. We also went to Malta. We began in Malta, and used Malta for five countries. No one ever uses Malta for the city itself, so we were able to go to various sections of Malta and substitute the actual countries from the Middle East for Malta, and that worked out really, really well. Cypress we used it for Lebanon. We used it for Jerusalem. We used it for Tel Aviv. And then, of course, we shot Brooklyn for Brooklyn because there's only one Brooklyn.

The most challenging location was in Malta, and it was the scene that was supposed to take place in Beirut, Lebanon. It was three, four nights of night shooting. The film was shot in about sixty-eight days and nights, and I think that was the most challenging because the sun kept coming up before I needed it to come up, and it was a real scramble to get all the shots.

The challenge when you shoot in a practical location, the ceiling and the walls become your prison. Where do you put your equipment? Where do you string your cables? How do you get your crew in there? It's very, very difficult shooting on practical locations, but there's nothing more rewarding than doing it that way because somehow the truth speaks louder than the manufacturer. And yet at the same time, you've got to take your hats off to the production designers that we've all worked with, and that we all will work with, when they can make something look like you've actually gone 7,000 miles and it is actually in North Hollywood. That's the magic of movies.

We built just a couple of sets. We built the safe houses, and we built part of the Olympic Village. The corridors, the rooms of the Israeli athletes, the coaches, the referees, that was all built by Rick Carter in Budapest in an ice skating rink that the

TIMELINE

1972

September 5 Munich Olympics massacre (scenes 1-19A, pgs 1-10)

Sept 6 The "Committee of Ten" meets in Jerusalem and decides on targets
        Avner and Daphna at home watching the bodies return (scenes 20-34, pgs 10-16)

Sept 11 Avner recruited (scenes 35-37, pgs 16-20)

Sept 12 Avner visits his father (scene 38, pgs 20-22)

Sept 14 Avner's briefing with accountant and Ephraim (scenes 39-40, pgs 22-27)

Sept 16 Avner and Daphna last night in Tel Aviv (scene 42, pgs 27-28)

Sept 17 Avner goes to Geneva (scenes 43-51, pgs 29-30)

Sept 18 The team assembles, Frankfurt (scenes 52-54, pgs 30-36)

Sept 20 Avner meets Andreas and Yvonne, Frankfurt (scene 55, pgs 37-39)

Sept 25 Avner meets Tony in Rome (scene 56, pgs 39-41)

Sept 26 Wael Zwaiter killed (scenes 59-67, pgs 42-46)

Sept 26 The team re-gathers in Latina (scenes 68, pgs 46-47)

October 22 Avner meets Louis in Paris (scenes 69-70, pgs 48-50)

Nov 15 Team arrives in Paris for Hamshari hit (& 3 surviving fedayeen arrive in Tripoli)
    (scenes 71-72C, pgs 50-52)

Nov 17 Robert interviews Hamshari (scene73, pgs 52-53)

Nov 19 Mahmoud Hamshari killed (scenes 74-94, pgs 54-62)
    That night Avner calls Daphna (scenes 94-98, pgs 62-64)

Nov 20 Avner goes to Tel Aviv & Israeli Embassy bombed (scenes 99-108, pgs 65-67)

Nov 22 Geula born (scenes 109-111, pgs 67-70)

Nov 24 Avner returns from Tel Aviv to Geneva (scene 112, pg 70)

Shooting timeline for *Munich*. Courtesy of Steven Spielberg.

Russians built in the '50s and never finished. It was this huge ice skating rink, and we basically built everything on the flat concrete.

We were always on the balconies when we were in Malta shooting the night-for-night exteriors, but when I saw the footage, I wasn't happy with the performances, so we just built the façade in Budapest and months later came back, and what looked like we were on a crane, we were actually about five feet off the ground.

I happened on a room where kids were practicing. And it was all that wonderful warm-up thing you hear before an orchestra performs. And I just thought that that would be a wonderful backdrop, this kind of chaotic mix of Mozart and Schumann and Schubert all together for the first assassination, and that was an idea I got in another location but then we went to the conservatory, got the students to suddenly play very well, but against each other.

I didn't storyboard any of this particular film, and part of the reason I don't storyboard is that I want to get to the set in the morning and let the set sort of tell me what needs to be done with it. I mean there are certain films that I need to storyboard, *War of the Worlds*, which I had made in the same calendar year, I storyboarded everything on that film, not by sketching. This time it was electronic storyboards, meaning making all these special effect sequences come to life on the laptop, and everybody looked at that, and those were our storyboards.

ALEJANDRO GONZÁLEZ IÑÁRRITU, *BABEL*

Originally, the story was written for Tunisia, and you don't want to be in Tunisia, but I traveled to Tunisia, and then I traveled to Morocco. I had been in Morocco when I was seventeen years old. I went there without any money, and I spent like fifteen days there, and it made a huge impact on my life. Then I wanted to have something that really attached me and oddly, Morocco has, production-wise, a lot of facilities now. So in the south of Morocco, crossing the atlas in the south, there's this town called Ouarzazate, which many, many filmmakers are going to. Ridley Scott has been going there for the last three films, I think. And there's now two back lots, huge studios, so it's like a huge city of production now, and I think 90 percent of Bible stories in Europe are shot there because the deserts are very fascinating. The landscapes and mountains, you have black desert, white desert, yellow desert, red desert, any kind of desert you want around there, and towns and communities, so it's fantastic. Ouarzazate is not a very nice place, but around it, there's everything you need. So basically there, I found everything. I think after spending several weeks finding the right spot in terms of the light to shoot, the hour of the day and all that, then the DP [the cinematographer] said, "No, this is worse," and then you have to find the shade.

I remember when I spent one week in Tokyo the first time, I said, "I would love to have a camera here." It's huge, aesthetically. So, I find this film to have a great justification for having a story there, to stretch the idea that anything so far away can really create ripples around the world, right? And that was a perfect spot to make that metaphoric kind of thing. And I started one year before to cast locations. One year after, I was completely another person. I wanted different things, I was in another kind of rhythm and my brain had changed and my energy was completely on other things. I was riding the wave of the film. So when I arrived there, I began to change some things. We rented that club and then, for example, the apartment to shoot that is super-expensive. To rent an apartment in a good place in Tokyo, that apartment belongs to a super-rich people there, so the costs are really insane. The cost is very expensive and the facilities are really hard to get. Nobody cares. So if you say, "I love this restaurant. I want to shoot an exterior shot," even if the guy wants to, he has to ask permission from all the neighbors, and if one guy says "no," you can't shoot there. So it's extremely difficult to find locations in Japan.

JONATHAN DAYTON AND VALERIE FARIS, *LITTLE MISS SUNSHINE*

JONATHAN: Originally, where we first were set up, they wanted us to shoot the film in Canada, and we really fought that for many reasons. There's nothing that looks like the Southwest in Canada. It was very important to us to shoot on location, and so we found this house in Burbank that was the Hoover House, and it was just this incredible timepiece that was just good to go. All the couches had plastic covering them, and it was this amazing thing, and we just removed it, and we wanted kind of this cluttered world . . .

VALERIE: . . . because we needed a house that was big enough that we could shoot in it and not just be locked into shots that we didn't like, so we found a house that had a lot of openings. It had an opening from the dining room to the kitchen and you could get depth in a shot instead of just shooting into a wall and then what's the point of shooting on location. And we also just really wanted to see all the details of a real location, the plugs in the wall and the power lines outside the windows, so this house was just the perfect house, and we shot for about ten days in there out in Burbank, and the whole film was really shot in L.A. because really L.A. is a desert, and Highway 14 was where we shot most of the dialogue in the car.

The convenience store scene where Steve Carell runs into his former lover, the guy he had a crush on, we needed to find a convenience store that had an incline on it, and we found the perfect place way out in the valley, but Shell Oil didn't want us. They don't sell porn magazines in their stores, and they didn't want it known, and we swore we would change everything, but they turned us down at the last minute.

JONATHAN: We had to always find a location that was close enough to the second location that could sort of get us what we needed. The hotel was in Culver City.

VALERIE: The exterior was Ventura, and the interior was Culver City.

JONATHAN: Although what happened is a couple days before we were due to shoot the arrival at the hotel, we had scouted a place in Long Beach that was perfect, and we had done all the stunt coordinating and storyboarding, this elaborate thing of them getting off the freeway and not being able to make a left turn, and they had to do all this stuff. And the City of Long Beach turned us down at the last minute, so we had

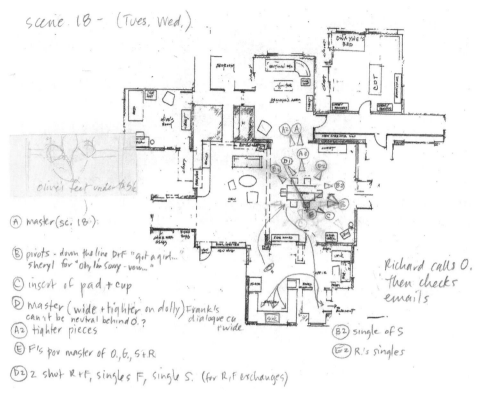

to completely rethink that whole sequence, and so we went up to Ventura, which was another place that we liked, and we videotaped a loose version of it. Then we sat down with Michael Arndt, the writer, and kind of worked out a whole different sequence of them being on the wrong off ramp.

VALERIE: Yeah, it was frustrating. We had a half a day to scout it and a half a day to plan and it was sort of like an action scene. It involved the car and trying to tie it all together. We were shooting in like five different locations and having to make it feel like it was all one route.

GEORGE CLOONEY, *GOOD NIGHT, AND GOOD LUCK.*

We had thirty days to shoot it in. I started looking at things as to how do you keep things confined, how do you create an external fear. I mean the minute you sort of let the air out of the balloon, the pressure's gone. So I started looking at films like *Fail-Safe* that was really close down and *12 Angry Men*. You look at a couple of [Sidney] Lumet films, who was very good at closing a room down and then everything you talked about existed outside was scarier but you didn't see it or it was more important because you didn't see it. So I went to Jim Bissell [production designer] and I said,

"Okay, I want to build this all on one set. Period," and he sort of sketched something out on a piece of paper. And I was like, "Okay, but it's got to look like it's several stories high." So we had to use some tricks. We built a rotating elevator instead of one that goes up and down and so that we'd be in the back of the elevator talking, you'd see people getting on the elevator. Then we would close the doors and rotate it while we were still talking, then open it up, and you'd see Frank Langella get on, and then we'd close the door, and then we'd drop a wall down inside it again, and then we'd open the doors up. So our theory was once you start from the very beginning establishing the idea that you're on several floors, then it won't feel like a stage. It won't feel like it's been built. It's like when you first meet somebody who's wearing glasses. Even if it's the only time they've ever been wearing glasses, you just sort of think of them always as someone who wears glasses.

We went to CBS Radford [a small studio in North Hollywood]. I'd actually shot there when I was on the first season of *Roseanne*. First time I met Roseanne she goes, "You're really good-looking. Why don't you take me out behind the stage and make me stink." Who would've thought I'd be back there shooting a Murrow piece, and it still smelled around there.

We made a cut-out model. Jim does this great thing with the computer. He built a model, and then he has a little tiny pencil camera that he can sort of go through it, because we shot every inch of that set. We had to build swing sets [sets that can be shot at different times according to schedule conflicts] of their apartment. We wanted to create everything with glass so that you could shoot on a long lens all the way through. We wanted it to feel like a Pennebaker documentary in that sense [Richard Leacock and D.A. Pennebaker were innovators of handheld documentary camera work] and we knew that we wanted to be able to reflect things and we were going to mic [having hidden microphones on the actors] everybody and shoot two cameras, which was always going to be a problem because we were going to get in the way.

I storyboarded 980 drawings, every shot, every scene. And there was one where I thought, well, I can't make the camera a character in this one. The camera has to be a fly on the wall. So we would go in and let the actor sort of dictate where the camera would go.

BENNETT MILLER, *CAPOTE*

This is a movie about a desperate person and what the desperate people will do to get what they want. It was not possible to shoot this movie in this country. I love this country and wanted to shoot the movie here, but circumstances were such and my desperation levels were at a place that I was willing to go to this location, which had so much to offer in terms of its locations. We looked all over, and we ended up in Winnipeg, Canada. Nature conspired with us and did not snow for the first time in fifty years in the month of November, so that was a thankful thing. What the movie was about is subtle and it is internal, and the production design was conceived to give emphasis and to sensitize what needed to be felt. It is a period piece, but the objective was never to hit you over the head with a period or to sell the period. There's not one frame in the movie which labors to sell the period that this is when it's happening but rather to respect a responsibility to preserve a level of veracity to the period, but to really use it to communicate tonally.

We modified locations, but the jail cells were really the only things that we built in a drafty warehouse in Winnipeg, but the place became very important, in that there's these two worlds. There's New York City and Kansas. And the idea is that there is a character who, beginning with the charismatic façade, is going to venture out and discover something dark within himself. There's New York City in comparison to Kansas and how that's meant to work and how these landscapes are meant to communicate.

The exterior of the jail is a working jail. The whole prison system was on strike when we were up there, and so we couldn't get in. I was just desperate to get inside those prisons and was about to commit an act to actually do it! But, finally, the strike lifted at the deadline before we could possibly get in, and we got to go into all these places, and there was nothing. The only thing that we found was that portrait of Jesus Christ that's used in the Clutter house. I found that in the prison, but that's it. When you look at the script, there's a lot of pages inside a jail cell, and two things that we thought was as much as shooting widescreen makes sense for these beautiful landscapes, it makes more sense even for being inside these cells and just the permutations that are possible.

There was this incredible warehouse of '50s furniture and Jess Gonchor, who was our production designer, came across this, and he literally showed up with a catalog and threw it on the table, a period catalog from the '50s. And I said, "Well, what's available?" He says, "Everything." It's just an enormous warehouse in Winnipeg. Spain was done up here in Malibu.

ANG LEE, *BROKEBACK MOUNTAIN*

Annie Proulx, the original story writer, took me to Big Horn Mountain, which is in the northeast of Wyoming, and said, "This is what I was thinking when I was writing." It was very pretty and everything. And then during the script rewrite process, I worked with even a bigger master of American West, Larry McMurtry. He sent me back to Idaho and the border along the Rockies because supposedly sheep have to be above tree lines and munching on those nutritious grasses and drink their still water. So it's way up there, that's why it's Brokeback. Okay, I chug along Rocky Mountains on this side. And then I went to a place called Wind River, somewhere just east of Yellowstone. It's prettier, it's more romantic, it's more like the lost paradise. So, that's kind of what I had in mind. And then I realized for economic reasons I have to shoot in Canada for a small budget like ours. They have the tax break, and Wyoming has nothing, no film industry. Have to bring everybody in under those circumstances, and Calgary has a very sophisticated infrastructure for filmmaking. Great film community. So there is your one-third of the budget. There's just no choice. When I went there to check the location, I realized something that bothered me for the last twenty, thirty years. How come American westerns look different now? Then I realized it's all shot in Canada. They're very good at faking American. They do better than Americans themselves, certainly than the Chinese. So it's actually quite perfect because if I shot in Wyoming, I don't know how to fake Texas, where a lot of scenes happen. About four hours from Calgary are mountains, prairies, small towns. Of course, no small town that's perfect, so it's just pieces and bits and we add them up. It's all real location except the tent where they make out.

DESIGNED BY ANNA SHEPPARD
ILLUSTRATION BY ROBIN ARCHER

Costume sketch for "The Basterds" in *Inglourious Basterds*. Courtesy of The Weinstein Company LLC, Universal Studios Licensing LLC, Quentin Tarantino, Anna Sheppard, and Robin Archer. All Rights Reserved.

6

Costume Design

TONY GILROY, *MICHAEL CLAYTON*

In choosing wardrobe, Sarah Edwards who did a great job, came in and she was eager in the beginning, with George Clooney to dress him and put him in a suit. He hasn't been in a suit in a color film in a while and he said, "Look, this guy wouldn't buy a suit with a price point over two thousand dollars, so you can't go to Brioni." And she got it right away.

Well, for Tilda [Swinton], she's the kind of actor who is very much about Halloween and getting dressed up and finding the character and I mean she had never been into an office building before and I took her into an office building and had her meet these women and it was like she was on a zoological expedition. "This is fascinating. Unbelievable." So when she had her earrings, the earrings and that uniform and that final outfit, that horrific thing she wears at the end, for her that was just everything. We chose it together. That was the attention that she wanted. I mean I wanted to make everything available to every actor as possible and answer every question as possible, but I didn't really feel any mastery over getting inside somebody's performance and taking it apart and putting it back together again. It's not something that I really feel comfortable with and that was what she really wanted. That was the energy. She didn't want to talk about where she came from, she wanted to talk about that. What she wears. That's what she needed and that was easy to do.

ETHAN AND JOEL COEN, *NO COUNTRY FOR OLD MEN*

ETHAN: It's kind of like for us in this movie, as in most of ours, it's always not a glamour thing. It is a period thing. This movie technically takes place in 1980, but you know what people are wearing in West Texas in 1980 and what they're wearing there now isn't that different. I mean that was actually a concern whether people would know that it wasn't a contemporary movie and we thought if we put a ring tab on a beer can, that'll do it. We've worked with the same wardrobe designer for many, many movies, Mary Zophres, and like good wardrobe designers she likes character stuff. She likes thinking about wardrobe as a way of thinking about character as opposed to thinking about how to make actors look good. Javier's [Bardem] wardrobe and his haircut as well came from a lot of research to kind of see what things really did look like that. His wardrobe and haircut are largely derived from a picture of a guy in a bar or maybe a whorehouse in Texas in 1979 with that alarming haircut and kind of like tight late '70s wardrobe.

JOEL: Yeah, I mean we saw the photograph and then we showed it to Javier and he was on board. We have worked for years and years with a guy named Paul LeBlanc who approaches what he does just completely from such an original perspective in terms of getting in the character and finding the sort of haircut and he sort of modified a little bit from this photograph, so it was sort of that discussion.

ETHAN: There's a woman who's the manager of the trailer park who has a kind of great hideous print shirt with like Leaning Tower of Pisa it seems from Old Italy on it and Paul complemented it with this weird beehive hairdo.

JOEL: The weapons are meticulously, almost fetishistically, described in the book and in fact when Cormac [McCarthy, the novelist] did come to the set a couple of times, he likes to see the guns, but it was Keith, the propmaster, who would look at the description of the gun in the book and it was described you know this gun has a Parkerized finish or it has a certain kind of stalk or it has a, you know, silencer or a sweated barrel as round as a beer can. You know those are things were all copied from the descriptions in the book.

ETHAN: We told Javier, who had never touched a gun before, I don't think before this movie, we told him we were going to get him on the cover of *Guns & Ammo* magazine. He again, to an alarming degree liked it, and was good at it. Keith took him out target shooting and actually Javier's pretty good at it.

JULIAN SCHNABEL, *THE DIVING BELL AND THE BUTTERFLY*

I pick everything that someone is going to wear all the time. From their socks to their tie to their plaid shirt to the doctor's dyed jackets, the color of the wall in the hospital, because I want the wall and the bodies in them to become like a swimming pool at some time. A very good costume designer went shopping a lot and showed me basically what I'd tell him I wanted: Chesterfield jackets from London because this guy was a Beau Brummel, he was the editor of French *ELLE*, so I wanted him to have red, velvet corduroy pants. I thought, "We need a hat." So when Isaach de Bankolé comes in and gives him the hat, then he puts the hat on top of the camera, so all of a sudden the frame has this furry corner and it was one way of this thing transmitting love when it's something like that. He was his friend and he could read to him. I made the dress that Emma de Caunes is wearing. I had seen images of nineteenth century dresses that were there, so I picked a color of cerulean blue and the lace and all of that.

PAUL THOMAS ANDERSON, *THERE WILL BE BLOOD*

I've worked with a terrific costume designer for fourteen years, Mark Bridges. On a film like the one we were making, there were so many photographs and research materials to work from. We had costume meetings with Daniel [Day-Lewis] and Mark and myself, and it can be a long thing, so I'll be there a little bit and look at things, but we did it over a couple days because you get kind of burnt out looking at stuff, looking at too many hats. You know, you just sort of narrow it down and do it like that. Daniel had a lot of different things to wear, but we never really had a situation where, you know on some films you kind of have to pick one or two main things to wear. We had so much for him to wear that we just sort of tried to pick a good bunch of stuff, probably the same size wardrobe as Plainview [the protagonist] would have, and we brought it out to Texas with us and we were kind of free to make it up as we went along.

CRASH STORYBOARD SEQUENCE & RELATED MATERIALS

Introduction by Jeremy Kagan

**CRASH STORYBOARD SEQUENCE WITH CORRESPONDING
SCRIPT PAGES AND DIAGRAMS (PAUL HAGGIS, DIRECTOR)**

These are the pages from the script of *Crash* with related storyboards and diagrams created for the key scene in which the car turns over and Christine Thayer (played by Thandie Newton) is trapped upside down and is being rescued by Officer John Ryan (played by Matt Dillon) who, in an earlier scene, mistreated her.

Script pages corresponding to storyboards for "Crash Site" sequence provided courtesy of Paul Haggis, Lionsgate and CRASH Distribution, LLC. Screenplay by Paul Haggis and Robert Moresco.

Storyboards for "Crash Site" sequence provided courtesy of Paul Haggis and Jonathan B. Woods.

"Upside Down Jeep" shooting plan courtesy of Paul Haggis.

Notes and diagram of camera setups for "Crash Site" storyboard sequence courtesy of Paul Haggis and Jonathan B. Woods.

64   CONTINUED: 64

THEIR POV

Over the tops of the cars they see a Hummer with a mangled
fender and a piece of shit Dodge with its engine on fire,
driver and passenger doors open. A white Jeep sitting wheels
up in the middle of the road.

BACK TO SCENE

                    RYAN
          Call it in!

Ryan takes off at a run toward the Jeep. He covers the
distance in a few seconds.

65   EXT. CRASH SITE -- CONTINUOUS   65

A couple of motorists stand near the inverted Jeep, unsure
what to do. The roof on the driver's side has been crushed;
the car lies tilted forward with its hood on the ground and
trunk in the air. Gasoline streams down from the ruptured
tank.

                    RYAN
          Get that engine fire out!

Ryan gets to the car and drops to the pavement on the
passenger side of the car. The window open. He sees the
driver, scrunched upside down, still belted into her seat.

                    RYAN (CONT'D)
          Ma'am? Ma'am can you hear me?

No response. Ryan puts his head through the window. Sees
the gasoline dripping down into the car. Hears the soft
voice of a woman crying.

                    RYAN (CONT'D)
          Ma'am? We're gonna get you out of
          there.

Gomez runs up, looks in.

                    OFFICER GOMEZ
          Paramedics are rolling, they'll be
          here in two minutes.
               (sees gas)
          Jesus.

                                              (CONTINUED)

3/18/04   68.

65   CONTINUED: 65

                              RYAN
                    Get an extinguisher, get that fire
                    out.

Gomez runs back to the patrol car.

                              RYAN (CONT'D)
                    Ma'am, are you hurt? Can you move?
                    Ma'am?

Just quiet painful sobs. Ryan looks at:

THE POOLING GAS (THROUGH THE CRACKED WINDSHIELD)

running out under the Jeep, in the direction of the car fire.

RYAN

realizes she may not have two minutes, makes his decision.

                              RYAN (CONT'D)
                    It's okay. I'm gonna get you out.

He snakes his torso into the passenger seat, leaving his
feet dangling out the window.

66   INT. UPSIDE DOWN JEEP -- CONTINUOUS   66

Ryan feels around for the seat buckle.

                              RYAN
                    It's okay. It's okay.

Drifting out of shock, the woman turns to see Ryan's face
right in front of hers and SCREAMS. It's Christine.

                              CHRISTINE
                    No! Stay away from me! Get away
                    from me!

She flails at him.

                              RYAN
                    Lady, I'm not gonna hurt you.

                              CHRISTINE
                        (still swinging)
                    Don't touch me! Don't touch me!
                    Get away from me!

                                        (CONTINUED)

66   CONTINUED: 66

                              RYAN
            LADY! I'm trying to help you!

Anger is taking over from shock:

                            CHRISTINE
            Fuck you! Not you! Not you!
            Somebody else! Not you!!

Ryan ignores her, reaches across her lap to find where the
belt is snagged. She flails at him again, striking his back.

                         CHRISTINE (CONT'D)
            NO! Keep your filthy fucking hands
            off me!

                              RYAN
            Stop moving! I've almost got it!

                            CHRISTINE
            NOOO!

Ryan screams in her face:

                              RYAN
            Lady, I am not going to fucking
            hurt you!!

And she starts to sob uncontrollably. Ryan throws a look to
the window: gas flowing away from the car. Looks back to
her.

                            CHRISTINE
            Please. Please. Don't touch me.

And Ryan looks into her face and sees her pain and
humiliation, and knows he was the cause of it. Finally:

                              RYAN
                (quietly, kindly:)
            Ma'am? Ma'am, there's no one else
            here yet, and that's gasoline there,
            so we have to get you out right
            away.

She looks, noticing the dripping gasoline for the first time.

                         RYAN (CONT'D)
            Your seat belt is caught on
            something, it's jamming the buckle.
            Can you feel where it's caught?

                                          (CONTINUED)

3/18/04   70.

66   CONTINUED: (2)   66

She tries.

                              CHRISTINE
                    No.

                              RYAN
                    I need to reach across your lap.
                    Can I do that, please?

She nods, fear starting to play on her face.

                              RYAN (CONT'D)
                    Thanks.

He reaches across her lap, tugging her skirt down a little
to cover her bare leg. He can't get it loose.

                              RYAN (CONT'D)
                    I need you to move a little, can
                    you do that?

She nods, tries to move. He jams his hand in again and works
the buckle.

                              RYAN (CONT'D)
                    Are you hurt, anything broken?

                              CHRISTINE
                    I don't think so.

                              RYAN
                    That's good.

                              CHRISTINE
                    Are you going to get me out?

                              RYAN
                    Yeah, I'm gonna get you out.

                              CHRISTINE
                    Okay.

                              RYAN
                         (cuts his hand)
                    Fuck! Sorry.

                              CHRISTINE
                    That's okay.

Ryan reaches into his pocket and pulls out a jackknife.
Christine reacts instinctively. He notices.

                                        (CONTINUED)

3/18/04   71.

66   CONTINUED: (3)   66

                              RYAN
            I'm going to cut the belt, okay?

She nods. Ryan saws away at it with the dullish blade.

67   RYAN'S POV: THROUGH THE WINDSHIELD   67

Gomez gets to the flaming Dodge with the extinguisher.

68   UNDER THE DODGE -- THE FLAMES   68

Catch on the trail of gasoline.

69   GOMEZ   69

Runs to try and beat the flames to the Jeep as a FIRE TRUCK
arrives.

                         OFFICER GOMEZ
               Ryan! Get out of the car!

70   INSIDE THE JEEP   70

Ryan works to cut the belt. Suddenly they both notice:

71   THEIR POV - THROUGH THE WINDSHIELD   71

The fire rushes toward them.

72   CHRISTINE   72

shrieks, Ryan keeps cutting, just an inch to go when...

THE FLAMES

burst into the Jeep, enveloping them. Ryan cuts the belt
loose. Suddenly, he's yanked out by the feet! He makes a
grab for Christine.

CHRISTINE

grabs for him, misses.

73   RYAN   73

is pulled from the flaming car by Gomez and a motorist.
Ryan kicks at them and crawls right back in.

74   CHRISTINE   74

sees him coming for her, reaches out.

                                       (CONTINUED)

CRASH

SCENES 62-69 - RYAN, CHRISTINE AND THE CRASH SITE

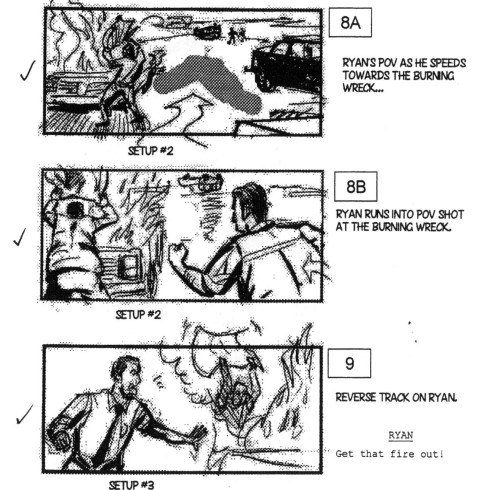

8A

RYAN'S POV AS HE SPEEDS TOWARDS THE BURNING WRECK...

SETUP #2

8B

RYAN RUNS INTO POV SHOT AT THE BURNING WRECK.

SETUP #2

9

REVERSE TRACK ON RYAN.

RYAN

Get that fire out!

SETUP #3

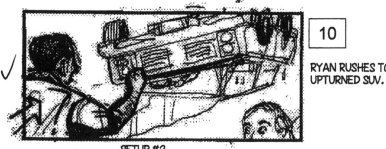

10

RYAN RUSHES TOWARDS UPTURNED SUV.

SETUP #2

CRASH

SCENES 62-69 - RYAN, CHRISTINE AND THE CRASH SITE

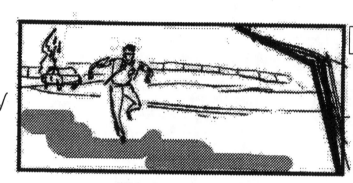

11   ④

WE SEE RYAN RUSHING TOWARDS CAMERA - TO THE RIGHT IS THE FRONT OF THE SUV.

SETUP #5

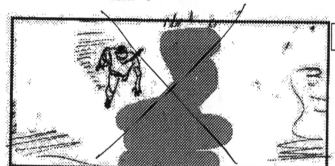

12A

CRANE SHOT OF RYAN RUNNING TOWARDS THE SUV...

SETUP #4

12B

CAMERA LOOKS STRAIGHT DOWN AS RYAN MAKES IT TO THE SUV.

SETUP #4

CRASH

SCENES 62-69 – RYAN, CHRISTINE AND
THE CRASH SITE

Pg. 6

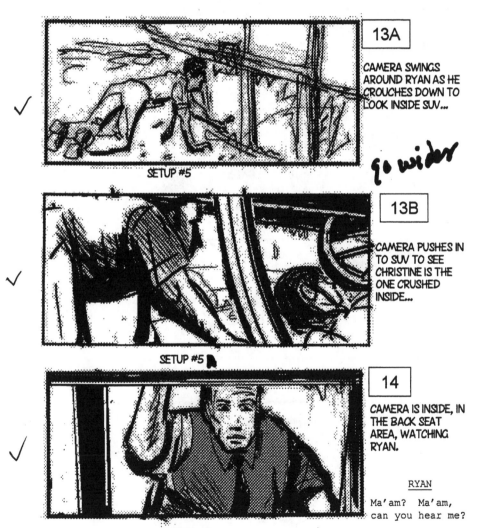

13A

CAMERA SWINGS
AROUND RYAN AS HE
CROUCHES DOWN TO
LOOK INSIDE SUV...

SETUP #5

go wider

13B

CAMERA PUSHES IN
TO SUV TO SEE
CHRISTINE IS THE
ONE CRUSHED
INSIDE...

SETUP #5

14

CAMERA IS INSIDE, IN
THE BACK SEAT
AREA, WATCHING
RYAN.

RYAN

Ma'am? Ma'am,
can you hear me?

SETUP #6

CRASH

Pg. 7

SCENES 62-69 - RYAN, CHRISTINE AND
THE CRASH SITE

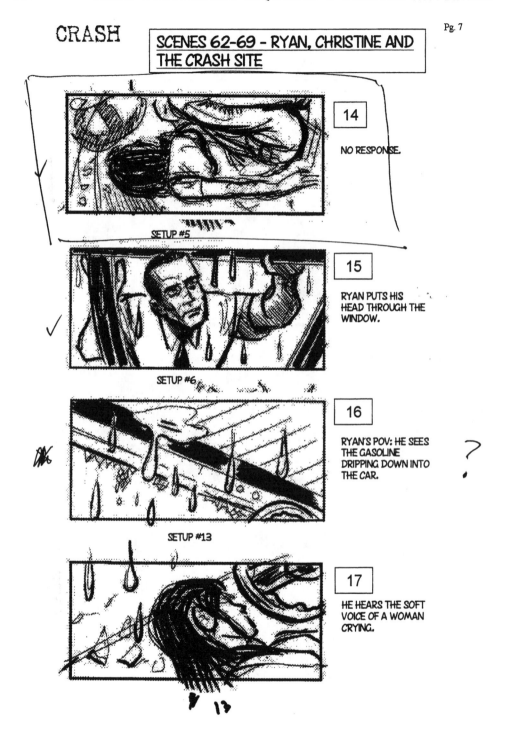

14

NO RESPONSE.

SETUP #5

15

RYAN PUTS HIS
HEAD THROUGH THE
WINDOW.

SETUP #6

16

RYAN'S POV: HE SEES
THE GASOLINE
DRIPPING DOWN INTO
THE CAR.

?

SETUP #13

17

HE HEARS THE SOFT
VOICE OF A WOMAN
CRYING.

CRASH

SCENES 62-69 – RYAN, CHRISTINE AND THE CRASH SITE

Pg. 8

SETUP #6

18A

RYAN

Ma'am? We're gonna get you out of there.

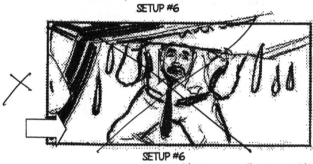

SETUP #6

18B

CAMERA PANS TO GOMEZ, WHO RUNS UP AND LOOKS IN.

OFFICER GOMEZ

Paramedics are rolling. They'll be here in two minutes.

GOMEZ RUNS OUT IN THIS SHOT.

SETUP #8

19

RYAN

Ma'am, are you hurt? Can you move? Ma'am?

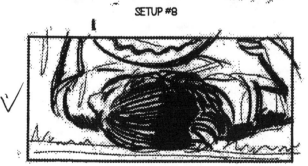

SETUP #7

20

HE HEARS JUST QUIET, PAINFUL SOBS.

CRASH

Pg. 9

SCENES 62-69 - RYAN, CHRISTINE AND
THE CRASH SITE

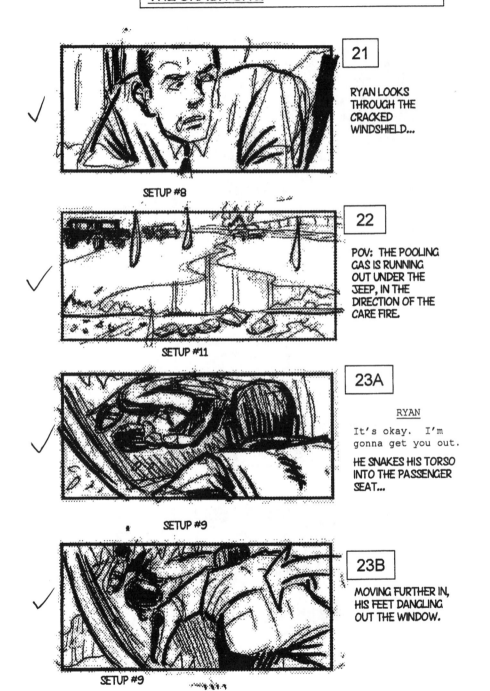

21

RYAN LOOKS
THROUGH THE
CRACKED
WINDSHIELD...

SETUP #8

22

POV: THE POOLING
GAS IS RUNNING
OUT UNDER THE
JEEP, IN THE
DIRECTION OF THE
CARE FIRE.

SETUP #11

23A

RYAN

It's okay. I'm
gonna get you out.

HE SNAKES HIS TORSO
INTO THE PASSENGER
SEAT...

SETUP #9

23B

MOVING FURTHER IN,
HIS FEET DANGLING
OUT THE WINDOW.

SETUP #9

CRASH

SCENES 62-69 - RYAN, CHRISTINE AND THE CRASH SITE

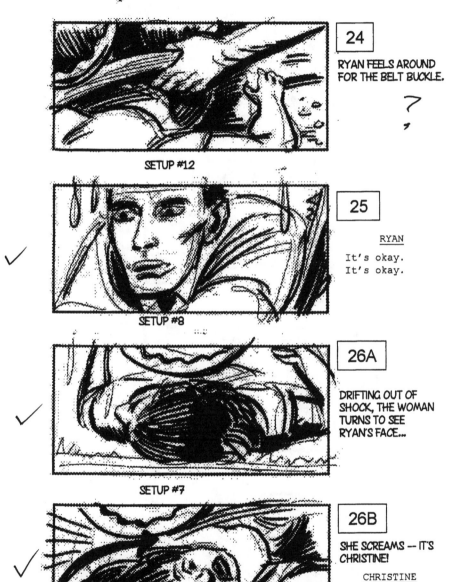

24

RYAN FEELS AROUND FOR THE BELT BUCKLE.

SETUP #12

25

RYAN

It's okay.
It's okay.

SETUP #8

26A

DRIFTING OUT OF SHOCK, THE WOMAN TURNS TO SEE RYAN'S FACE...

SETUP #7

26B

SHE SCREAMS -- IT'S CHRISTINE!

CHRISTINE

No! Stay away from me! Get away from me!

SHE FLAILS AT HIM.

SETUP #7

CRASH

SCENES 62-69 - RYAN, CHRISTINE AND THE CRASH SITE

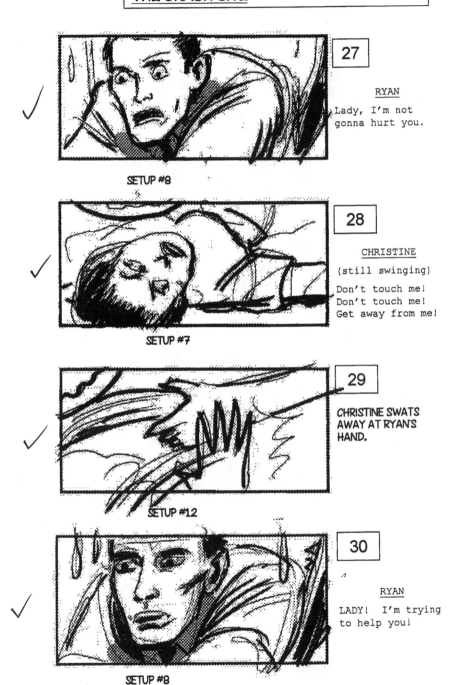

27

RYAN
Lady, I'm not gonna hurt you.

SETUP #8

28

CHRISTINE
(still swinging)
Don't touch me!
Don't touch me!
Get away from me!

SETUP #7

29

CHRISTINE SWATS AWAY AT RYAN'S HAND.

SETUP #12

30

RYAN
LADY! I'm trying to help you!

SETUP #8

CRASH

Pg. 12

SCENES 62-69 - RYAN, CHRISTINE AND THE CRASH SITE

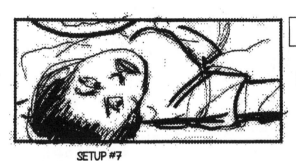

SETUP #7

31

ANGER IS TAKING OVER FROM SHOCK:

CHRISTINE

Fuck you! Not you! Not you! Somebody else! Not you!!

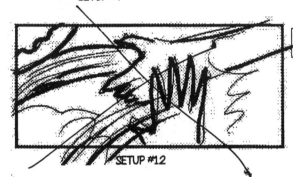

SETUP #12

32

RYAN IGNORES HER, REACHING ACROSS HER LAP TO FIND WHERE THE BELT IS SNAGGED. SHE FLAILS AT HIM, STRIKING HIS HAND AND BACK.

SETUP #8

33

RYAN SCREAMS IN HER FACE:

RYAN

Lady, I'm not going to fucking hurt you!!

SETUP #7

34

AND SHE STARTS TO SOB UNCONTROLLABY.

Pg. 13

CRASH

SCENES 62-69 - RYAN, CHRISTINE AND THE CRASH SITE

35

RYAN THROWS A LOOK OUT THE WINDOW:

SETUP #8

36

POV: GAS FLOWING AWAY TOWARDS THE FLAMING WRECK.

SETUP #11

37

RYAN LOOKS AT CHRISTINE'S FACE...

SETUP #8

38

WE SEE HER PAIN AND HUMILIATION.

SETUP #7

39

RYAN KNOWS HE IS THE CAUSE OF THIS.

SETUP #8

CRASH

Pg. 14

SCENES 62-69 - RYAN, CHRISTINE AND THE CRASH SITE

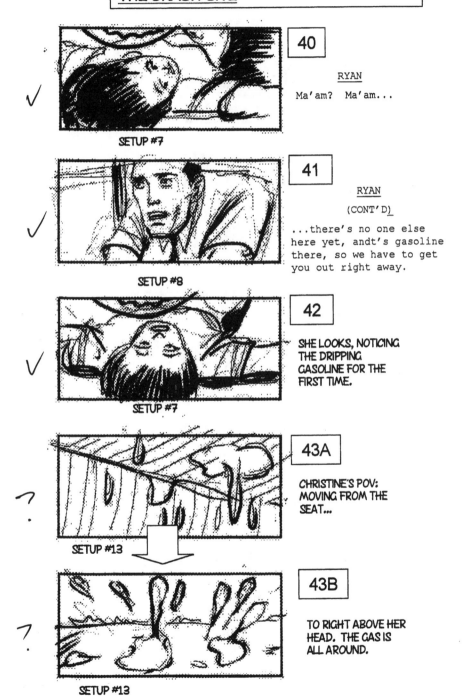

40

SETUP #7

RYAN

Ma'am? Ma'am...

41

SETUP #8

RYAN

(CONT'D)

...there's no one else
here yet, andt's gasoline
there, so we have to get
you out right away.

42

SETUP #7

SHE LOOKS, NOTICING
THE DRIPPING
GASOLINE FOR THE
FIRST TIME.

43A

SETUP #13

CHRISTINE'S POV:
MOVING FROM THE
SEAT...

43B

SETUP #13

TO RIGHT ABOVE HER
HEAD. THE GAS IS
ALL AROUND.

CRASH

Pg. 15

SCENES 62-69 - RYAN, CHRISTINE AND THE CRASH SITE

44

HER EYES WIDEN.

SETUP #7

45

RYAN

Your seat belt is caught on something. It's jamming the buckle. Can you feel where it's caught?

SETUP #8

46

SHE TRIES.

SETUP #12

47

CHRISTINE
No.

SETUP #8

48

RYAN

I need to reach across your lap. Can I do that, please?

SETUP #7

CRASH

Pg. 16

SCENES 62-69 - RYAN, CHRISTINE AND THE CRASH SITE

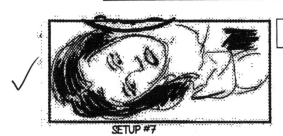

SETUP #7

49

SHE NODS, FEAR STARTING TO PLAY ON HER FACE.

SETUP #12

50

HE REACHES ACROSS HER LAP, TUGGING HER SKIRT DOWN A LITTLE TO COVER HER BARE LEG. - BUT HE CAN'T GET THE BELT LOOSE.

SETUP #8

51

RYAN

I need you to move a little. Can you do that?

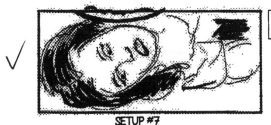

SETUP #7

52

SHE NODS, TRIES TO MOVE.

SETUP #12

53

HE JAMS HIS HAND IN AGAIN AND WORKS THE BUCKLE.

CRASH

SCENES 62-69 - RYAN, CHRISTINE AND THE CRASH SITE

54

RYAN

Are you hurt --
anything broken?

SETUP #10

55

CHRISTINE

I don't think so.

RYAN

Are you going to get me
out?

SETUP #9

56

RYAN

Yeah, I'm gonna
get you out.

SETUP #8

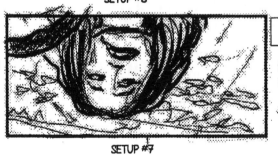

57

CHRISTINE
Okay.

SETUP #7

CRASH

Pg. 18

SCENES 62-69 - RYAN, CHRISTINE AND THE CRASH SITE

58

SETUP #8

RYAN
(cuts his hand)
Fuck! Sorry.

59

SETUP #7

CHRISTINE
That's okay.

60

SETUP #9

RYAN REACHES INTO HIS POCKET AND PULLS OUT A JACKKNIFE. CHRISTINE REACTS INSTINCTIVELY.

RYAN
I'm going to cut the belt, okay?

SHE NODS.

61

SETUP #12

RYAN SAWS AWAY WITH THE KNIFE.

CRASH

SCENES 62-69 - RYAN, CHRISTINE AND THE CRASH SITE

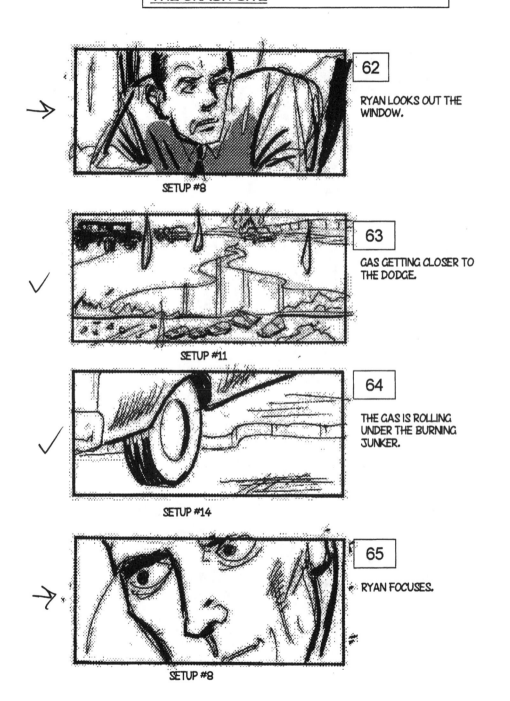

62

RYAN LOOKS OUT THE WINDOW.

SETUP #8

63

GAS GETTING CLOSER TO THE DODGE.

SETUP #11

64

THE GAS IS ROLLING UNDER THE BURNING JUNKER.

SETUP #14

65

RYAN FOCUSES.

SETUP #8

CRASH

Pg. 20

SCENES 62-69 – RYAN, CHRISTINE AND THE CRASH SITE

66

RYAN CONTINUES TO CUT AT THE SEATBELT.

SETUP #12

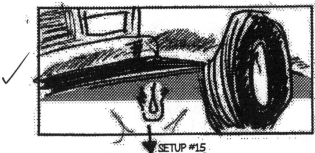

67A

BURNING SHOT OF FLAMING OIL DRIPPING FROM JUNKER...

SETUP #15

67B

FLAMING OIL ONTO PAVEMENT UNDER CAR... GAS POOLS IN ... CATCHES FIRE...

SETUP #15

67C

CAMERA PANS WITH FIRE AS IT SHOOTS OUT FROM UNDER JUNKER...

SETUP #15

CRASH

SCENES 62-69 – RYAN, CHRISTINE AND THE CRASH SITE

68A

GOMEZ GETS TO THE FLAMING DODGE WITH THE EXTINGUISHER...

SETUP #16

68B

RYAN SEES THE GAS CATCHING ON FIRE...

SETUP #16

68C

CAMERA PANS TO POV OF GAS BURNING...

SETUP #16

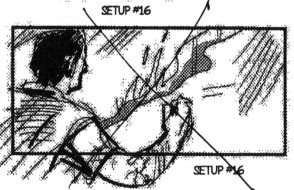

68D

GOMEZ RUNS INTO POV AND CHASES FIRE AS IT BURNS UP THE TRAIL OF GASOLINE.

SETUP #16

CRASH

SCENES 62-69 – RYAN, CHRISTINE AND THE CRASH SITE

Pg. 22

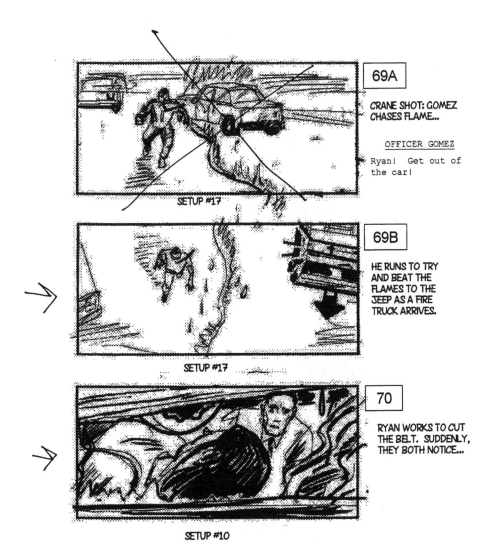

69A

CRANE SHOT: GOMEZ CHASES FLAME...

OFFICER GOMEZ

Ryan! Get out of the car!

SETUP #17

69B

HE RUNS TO TRY AND BEAT THE FLAMES TO THE JEEP AS A FIRE TRUCK ARRIVES.

SETUP #17

70

RYAN WORKS TO CUT THE BELT. SUDDENLY, THEY BOTH NOTICE...

SETUP #10

CRASH

SCENES 62-69 - RYAN, CHRISTINE AND THE CRASH SITE

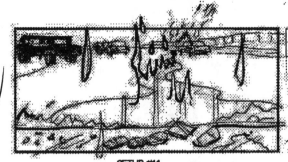

71

THEIR POV THROUGH THE WINDSHIELD:

THE FIRE RUSHES TOWARDS THEM.

SETUP #11

72

CHRISTINE SHRIEKS.

SETUP #7

73

RYAN KEEPS CUTTING, JUST AN INCH TO GO WHEN...

CLOSER

SETUP #12

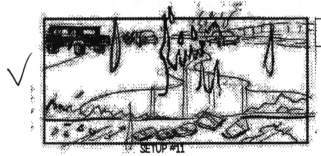

74

THE FLAMES REACH THE SUV...

SETUP #11

CRASH

Pg. 24

SCENES 62-69 – RYAN, CHRISTINE AND THE CRASH SITE

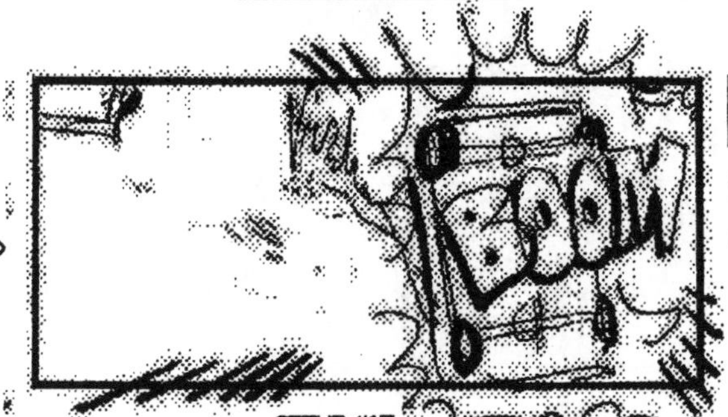

75A

CRANE SHOT LOOKING DOWN: THE FLAMES BURST INTO THE JEEP, EVELOPING THEM...

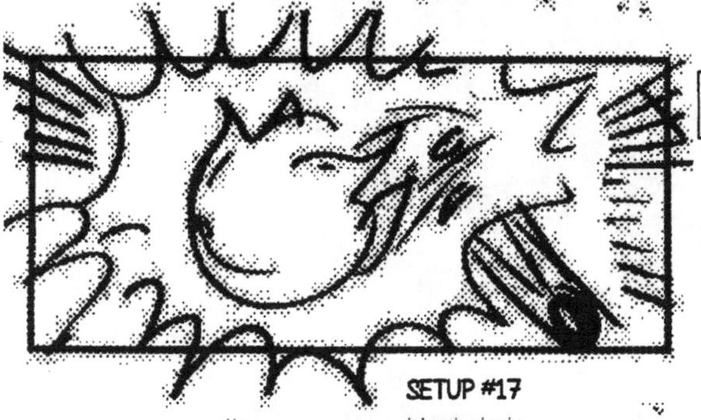

SETUP #17

75B

A FIREBALL FLIES TOWARDS CAMERA.

SETUP #17

76

FLAMES SURROUND RYAN AND CHRISTINE...

SETUP #10

77

LONG LENS OF GOMEZ REACHING THE FLAMING SUV. GOMEZ ENTERS FROM CAMERA RIGHT, AROUND THE FIRE...

SETUP #18

CRASH

SCENES 62-69 - RYAN, CHRISTINE AND THE CRASH SITE

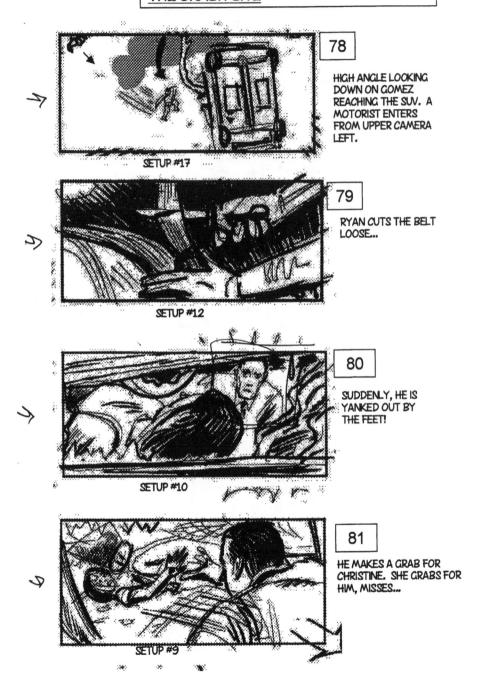

78

HIGH ANGLE LOOKING DOWN ON GOMEZ REACHING THE SUV. A MOTORIST ENTERS FROM UPPER CAMERA LEFT.

SETUP #17

79

RYAN CUTS THE BELT LOOSE...

SETUP #12

80

SUDDENLY, HE IS YANKED OUT BY THE FEET!

SETUP #10

81

HE MAKES A GRAB FOR CHRISTINE. SHE GRABS FOR HIM, MISSES...

SETUP #9

CRASH

SCENES 62-69 - RYAN, CHRISTINE AND
THE CRASH SITE

Pg. 26

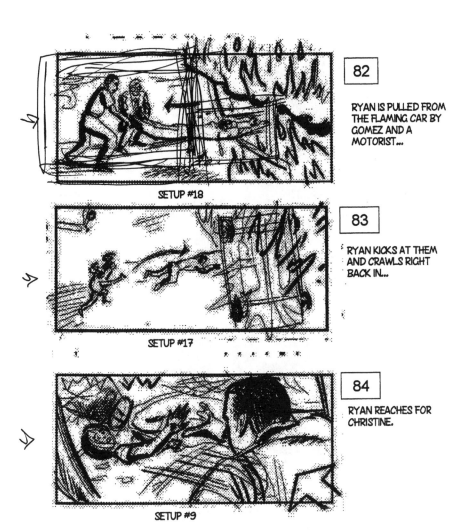

82

RYAN IS PULLED FROM
THE FLAMING CAR BY
GOMEZ AND A
MOTORIST...

SETUP #18

83

RYAN KICKS AT THEM
AND CRAWLS RIGHT
BACK IN...

SETUP #17

84

RYAN REACHES FOR
CHRISTINE.

SETUP #9

CRASH

SCENES 62-69 - RYAN, CHRISTINE AND THE CRASH SITE

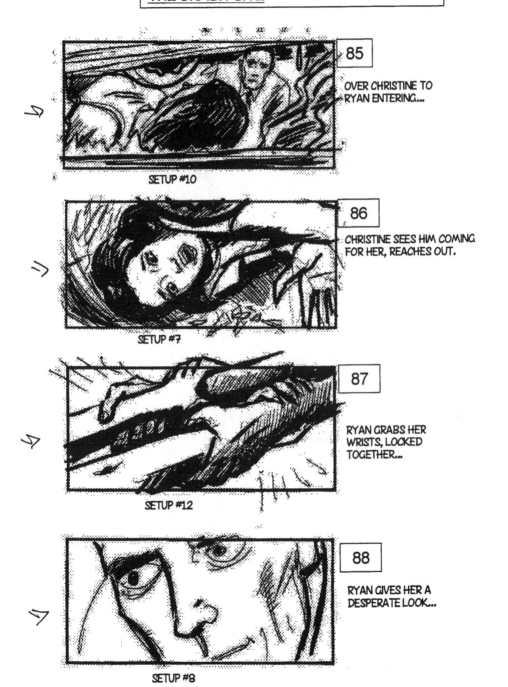

85

OVER CHRISTINE TO RYAN ENTERING....

SETUP #10

86

CHRISTINE SEES HIM COMING FOR HER, REACHES OUT.

SETUP #7

87

RYAN GRABS HER WRISTS, LOCKED TOGETHER...

SETUP #12

88

RYAN GIVES HER A DESPERATE LOOK...

SETUP #8

CRASH

Pg. 28

SCENES 62-69 - RYAN, CHRISTINE AND THE CRASH SITE

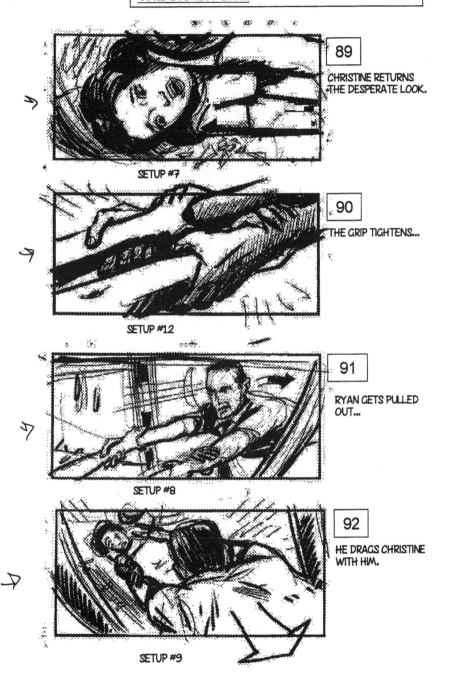

89

CHRISTINE RETURNS THE DESPERATE LOOK.

SETUP #7

90

THE GRIP TIGHTENS...

SETUP #12

91

RYAN GETS PULLED OUT...

SETUP #8

92

HE DRAGS CHRISTINE WITH HIM.

SETUP #9

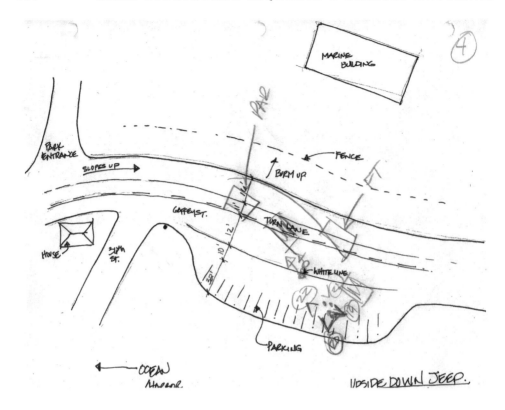

CAMERA SETUPS:

1) ESTABLISHING SHOT OF RYAN'S SQUAD CAR AS IT PULLS INTO FRAME, CREATING A MEDIUM CU OF GOMEZ AND RYAN.

2) RYAN'S POV AS HE RUNS. RYAN RUNS INTO THE POV AS HE REACHES THE BURNING WRECK.

3) REVERSE TRACK ON RYAN AS HE RUNS TOWARDS THE WRECK.

4) CRANE SHOT - STARTING ON RYAN RUSHING FROM THE BURNING WRECK AND TILTING STRAIGHT DOWN ON HIM AS HE REACHES THE SUV.

5) SHOT OF RYAN RUNNING TOWARDS THE SUV - STARTING FROM THE FRONT OF OF THE SUV, PULLING BACK AND AROUND WITH RYAN AS HE ARRIVES, CROUCHES, AND LOOKS INTO THE SUV. CAMERA PUSHES IN TO CHRISTINE.

6) REVERSE ANGLE OF #5 -- MEDIUM SHOT OF RYAN FROM THE BACK SEAT OF THE SUV.

7) THROUGH FRONT WINDSHIELD - CU ON CHRISTINE.

8) THROUGH WINDSHIELD - CU ON RYAN

9) WIDER SIDE SHOT BEGINNING WITH RYAN ENTERING THE SUV.

10) MATCHING SHOT TO #9. STRAIGHT ON THROUGH SQUASHED WINDOW OVER CHRISTINE TO RYAN.

11) CLEAN POV OF GAS DRIPPING AWAY FROM SUV.

12) MEDIUM SHOT ON SEAT BELT.

13) PANNING POV OF GAS DRIPPING - ALTERNATING FROM RYAN TO CHRISTINE.

14) GAS ROLLING UNDERNEATH THE JUNKER.

15) GAS CATCHING FIRE UNDERNEATH THE JUNKER.

16) STEADICAM ON GOMEZ CHASING THE FLAMES.

17) HIGH ANGLE CRANE: GOMEZ CHASES FLAMES TO SUV.

18) GOMEZ APPROACHES SUV, THEN, PROFILE SHOT: RYAN GETS PULLED OUT OF SUV BY HIS FEET.

19) COVERAGE OF RYAN AND CHRISTINE OUT OF THE SUV.

20) ESTABLISHING OF RYAN AND CHRISTINE, THEN CU OF CHRISTINE. BURNING SUV IN THE BACKGROUND.

21) TRACKING OF PARAMEDICS TAKING CHRISTINE AWAY.

22) RYAN AND CHRISTINE GETTING PULLED OUT OF SUV. THEN, RYAN'S CU.

23) CU OF CHRISTINE LOOKING OVER HER SHOULDER.

24) WIDER SHOT OF SETUP #22.

25) INSERT OF FIREMEN.

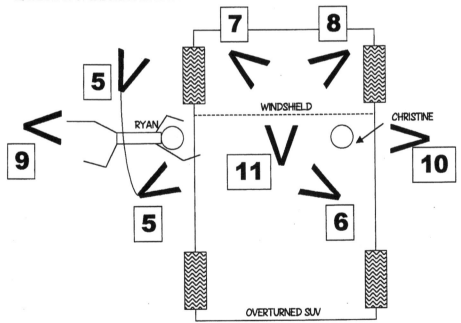

Part II

PRODUCTION

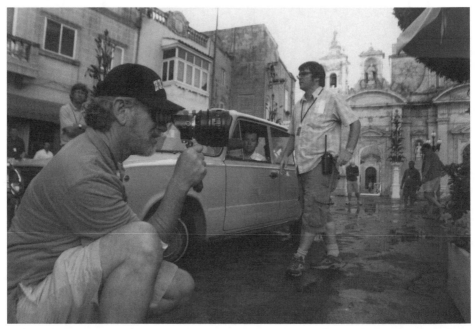

Steven Spielberg on the set of *Munich*. Courtesy of Steven Spielberg and Universal Studios Licensing LLC.

7

THE SHOOT

GEORGE CLOONEY, *GOOD NIGHT, AND GOOD LUCK.*

We wanted it to feel like a Pennebaker documentary in that sense [Richard Leacock and D. A. Pennebaker were innovators of handheld documentary camera work] and we knew that we wanted to be able to reflect things and we were going to mic [having hidden microphones on the actors] everybody and shoot two cameras, which was always going to be a problem because we were going to get in the way. So we had the crew dress up in suits, in '50s suits. Thirty times you'll see our dolly grip [a crew member who moves the equipment that holds the camera] and everybody has a cigarette. That was a frightening time. And just for that opening sequence, we didn't tell them we were shooting. We just gave everybody cigarettes and some booze and had two long-lens cameras and just started shooting sort of behavioral stuff. The minute someone says "Action," everybody sort of like stiffens and it works so much better if you just shoot.

It's hard because you're trying to tie yourself to other people's dialogue. In some ways we get to cheat because I'm not trying to *Forrest Gump* this [with Tom Hanks in character, blended into real news footage]. I'm not trying to force Ed Murrow into a scene and match film stock with [Joseph] McCarthy [Republican Senator who accused people of being Communists]. I always had him either projected by a 16 millimeter or on a kinescope television set. He was always projected. So we had a bit of an advantage in that way that we weren't having to force anything. We weren't stuck in something that would sort of create a lot more problems.

When you have one set, basically, for an entire film, you have all kinds of problems because you go, well, how do we make this different or make it more interesting. You try to shoot it differently each time. We did things to try and help the actors. We made all of [William S.] Paley's [head of CBS] office, his walls, everything twice as tall, to make [Edward R.] Murrow look smaller in there. Frank [Langella who plays Paley] is a big guy. He's like 6'3", you know. We built the set bigger to make David [Strathairn who plays Murrow] look smaller in it.

We stole some of this from some tricks that [director Sidney] Lumet did with *Fail-Safe*. As the pressure got more and more onto Murrow, it became more and more about going to McCarthy because McCarthy's coming at us, and as the McCarthy broadcasts came in, we pushed all of the set pieces, the backdrop pieces, everything in closer, and we just literally physically made it smaller so that it was choking. I talked to Sidney Lumet and he said he did that in the bunker room with Henry Fonda in *Fail-Safe*, where he would literally, physically, move the walls in just to make it more claustrophobic. So we were cheating in a good way.

The most difficult stuff was the Liberace scene [where they used real footage of an interview with Liberace with the actor playing Edward R. Murrow in the same shot] because it was using playback of Liberace actually talking to Murrow playing on a screen behind Murrow where you had to find shots that he could match exactly where he sat and only use these pieces. It was balancing monitors and actually matching things exactly.

TONY GILROY, *MICHAEL CLAYTON*

Ellen Chenoweth [casting director] suggested a coach and we sent Austin [Williams, who plays Clooney's son] to a woman who is a coach and he came back after one or two sessions and he was comfortable and your learning curve goes, out of desperation, it goes up really quickly and the first day I realized if he's not doing something in every scene I'm fucked, so I mean if you look at the film, he's either eating or I give him his cards. The moment he had something to do he would lock in. The moment he was thinking about where he was, he was screwed and the other big benefit was George [Clooney]. George said to the kid, "Did you ever watch the television show I was in? I was a pediatrician! I've done like a million scenes with kids." So they would be locked in that Mercedes for hours and hours and hours cranking the radio. He kept Austin loose.

I'll say one thing that I got that I stole from Paul [Thomas Anderson], I watched a making of, I think it was *Magnolia* because Robert Elswit [the cinematographer who worked for both directors] was shooting and I was watching the thing and I was shocked at how few people were on set. There was nothing on set just Paul and the actors and I went back to Robert and I said, "What is that?" He said, "Well, Paul doesn't let anybody . . . you know there aren't any final touch ups [when makeup and hair and costumes are redone on the actors between takes], there's none of that." I said, "Can we do that? I've never been on movie sets," and he said, "We can do whatever you want." We didn't fully get there. It's a little hard to fully get there with George and New York and whatever, but we had no makeup, no final touch ups, we didn't care. I think it took like a week or two for hair and makeup and costume and everybody to realize what we were doing, but once they got into the rhythm of it, just as long as stuff matched [continuity between takes so the actor looks the same from shot to shot.] I didn't give a shit. I mean it's not that kind of movie.

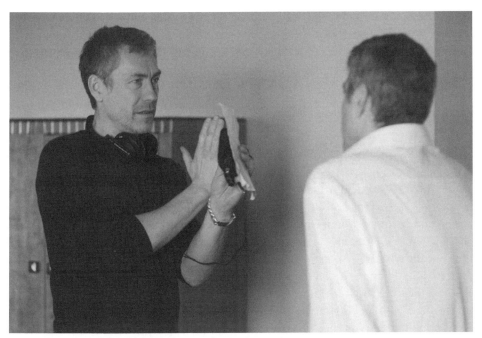

Tony Gilroy with George Clooney on the set of *Michael Clayton*. MICHAEL CLAYTON—Licensed by Warner Bros. Entertainment Inc. All Rights Reserved.

I will never again write a scene just before dawn because I mean you get five minutes in the morning and you get five minutes at night. Literally, that's all you got. The scene with the horses, it was a very, very mapped out, military operation to get all of that covered. I think we went up there five, six times. We ended up videotaping all the pieces. We had a cardboard horse that we put up on the hill. There's a very comical video that's been edited together of Assistant Director playing George [Clooney] and we made the coverage [various individual shots of actors in the scene that will be edited together to comprise the scene] to the absolute minimum. We knew exactly what pieces we needed to get every day and we had five days, five mornings and five afternoons to get everything, that whole sequence. We knew exactly what we were going for and then we had a few extra pieces that if we got lucky, we'd try to get and we got a few, but you know we would have been saved if we would have gotten one day that would have been overcast for the whole thing, but we never got that break, but we also didn't get skunked because we were in the middle of the winter and the whole thing would have fallen apart if it had snowed. The horses, I mean, you have the big panic meeting, you have the horse team that goes out, you have the car guy and this and that and the crane. We had someone in production who was a really great horsewoman, so she absorbed that project and she started going up and she found the horses, the horse people and it turned out that the trick was to have the horses live there on that hill for that week because they were like on the other end of the hill and they built a corral and they lived there and they got really comfortable. There's some very comical gag reel footage of a guy lying on the ground shaking a rattle as George is standing there emoting. You know it's like you talk it to death and you pray to God it's going to work.

The day before, you know, they tell you, "It turns out that the more times you scare them and run, the first shot is the one that's going be the only one that looks right." Great, so we don't have any other horses and we're locked in here and so now we have not only one shot to blow up the Mercedes and one shot to do this and one shot to do something, so basically we've got one shot to scare these horses. You just throw all the prep you can throw at it and we just scared the shit out of the horses and they ran and we had two or three cameras.

I knew what I was going for. The U/North commercial [which is the corrupt corporation in the movie] that is sort of geeky-interesting. We really wanted to create this commercial and really have an identity and one of the things I learned from making movies with Taylor Hackford [director of feature films including *Ray*] was that if there was something that was not supposed to be part of the movie, he really pushes it off to the side and has it exist on its own. We sort of took that to an extreme here. I wanted to have a corporate identity. I wanted a corporation to have a history and I also wanted to have a thirty-second spot that we could use as an artifact however we wanted to use it. I wanted to have a real plastic thing that however we wanted it to be we could do, so we took it away from the movie and long before the movie started, we started conversations with a commercial production house in New York called Fluid and we looked at all those spots that they run on Sunday mornings and we said this is what we want. I took a long time to clear things obviously. The only thing we shot for that commercial is we shot the sort of beatific shots of the children. My daughter's the girl with the seeds going through her hands and the little black boy we shot and we gave it to them and we did a jingle and they came back with a real thirty-second spot that we could legitimately run. We could use it however we wanted to and it didn't smell like the movie at all.

That's about my favorite thing in the movie. I mean seriously that moment of them killing Tom [Wilkinson]. I knew I wanted to do that all in one [single shot, no cuts]. I put the actors with Jerry Hewitt [the stunt coordinator] about a month before and at first they had a stunt man who was Tom Wilkinson's size and then finally Tom came in at the end. We would go back and visit them every week and say, "You've got ninety seconds from the time he comes in the door to the time he's dead." This is all the stuff you have to do and at the end of it, they got really good at it, but the moment of waiting I was really dependent on them and it's hard to say to somebody, "Wait, really wait, but don't wait too long." I wanted a moment as professional, clinical, and awful. I wanted some like smell of shame in the room if that was possible to have them do, so I told them imagine it's like taking a shit in the same room with somebody. There's a moment when they don't want to look at each other when they know what they're doing, but I was really dependent on Terry Serpico [one of the actors] to call it. I didn't want to be off camera going, "Now's the time" and Terry is just a dancer and his timing, he's standing there waiting and everything else is really good, and you know you say, "This one is just so great and, oh God, he's waited too long, no he hasn't." It's just, you know, he called it.

I was going to live or die on what happened in the scene of the confrontation between George and Tilda. I sort of squander a lot of traditional storytelling along the way, it's kind of a wandering kind of thriller because I knew I was living or dying with that scene and so it's sort of all the logistical stuff and it makes you nervous and you figure if you fuck it up they're going to have to let me come back or else we don't have a movie, but I can't come back and have that last scene come alive if it doesn't work. I think that was the real nail-biter. We set up an environment where it was all pre-lit [the lighting crew comes to the location and puts up the lights before the actors arrive, usually on another day] so we didn't have to relight or anything. It was just an environment that the actors could work in and we had a couple days to shoot it. It's a "Ferrari" camera team that just really tuned up and everybody really pulling and at that point really in shape. That's not a scene you would tackle early on in the shoot.

In pre-production in the camera tests we went out on a bitter cold night one night when it was very few people down there in Times Square and I stood in for Tom [Wilkinson] and we worked out the moves for the whole thing. I've never been an actor before and I had never been on camera before and I am just standing there that night for like an hour and half working out these camera moves with this camera running around me, it gave me more insight. It was so valuable just to just stand there and pretend to pretend. We got to work out the moves, but there was something really fundamental that I got out of the vulnerability of being an actor and standing there, something I hadn't really stepped into before.

We were a very, very precise and tidy shoot and yet it doesn't seem that way leaving the opening to the end, but everything else that we did was really pretty buttoned up and there were a lot of people watching me making sure I knew what I was doing and so we built up a lot of goodwill. We were at the Hilton and we were in midtown and we didn't have the final shot and I couldn't find anything that was worthy and we shot a couple shots like the boring Sixth Avenue shot of him in the crowd walking. Everything was just really tedious and I went home one night in the middle of shooting and I don't know, I wasn't watching any movies, I didn't have any time or anything, but for some reason the movie, *The Piano Teacher*, was there. For some reason, I put it in and I got sucked into it and the ending of that when Isabelle Hubert stabs herself and she walks out and I thought, "Wow, there has to be something that raw, it has to be there." I live in cabs, I don't know, I sort of just said, "Let's just try this." Everyone was sort of looking at me for about a week going, "We're coming to the end, we have everything else what are we going to do now?"

"Let's put the camera on George in the back of the cab and see what happens."

And we did it once and it was one of those things where you try it and you go, "Wow, we've got to go back and really get this," so we really went at it. We had no permission, we had a great relationship with the cops by that point and that's the big benefit of having George. We got air traffic moved around and if George comes out of his trailer and takes a picture we can like change the traffic pattern at LaGuardia [Airport] and get the shots. Seriously. So, short of having somebody killed on Sixth Avenue we could kind of do what we wanted as long as we could clear the paparazzi, so we went back the second time and I don't know how many we shot. I bet we did six or seven takes. Clooney's in a cab alone, the camera's fixed, there's a driver. We're in the police car in front.

There's one lead car, a patrol car, that's trying to clear traffic because we didn't want to stop. We wanted to come down Sixth Avenue, come down Fifty-Seventh, then we want to come back down and we've worked this whole route out. We can't control any of it. George is in the back alone. We've got the monitor and it's staticky. It's going in and out because you're moving. We did it three or four times and various things would fuck up. Someone on the street would see George and wave or we would get stuck or something, but he was killing every one of them, he was fantastic. So we're resetting and we're in front of the hill and I lean in the back of the cab and I said, "This is great, what is this?" This is my directing style it's, "What are you doing?" Forensic directing. And he says, "I'm just replaying the movie in my head." That's what he's doing.

DANNY BOYLE, *SLUMDOG MILLIONAIRE*

One of the dangers with India, cinematographically, is that you just go, "Oh, my God!" You go, "Look at that." So we never wanted to try and do that. We kind of wanted to hurdle people in through close-ups to begin with and then through this chase through the slum in the beginning.

We did some tests on film in a slum called Dharavi and I hated the tests. They were kind of classic film tests. They were kind of static, it was very observational and objective. We moved then to a digital medium, which were smaller cameras, silicon imaging 2K camera set-up, which we shot about 80 percent of the film on and that allowed us to move very flexibly, which stopped us being a target for attention and also allowed us to move better geographically through smaller areas. Those were huge challenges and the guy who helped me do it was my first AD [Assistant Director] called Raj Acharya. Raj taught me how to film in Mumbai really and it was very frustrating. We took about ten crew from the West and I think it was a bit frustrating for them sometimes because they expect the first AD to always be beside you, but Raj would work the streets and I knew what he was doing. He was making the film for us out there rather than obeying the rules in the conventional way because it's not a conventional city, it's not a conventional population and it's an extraordinary place to work. We tried to capture some of that and let the narrative free on it.

We had huge issues at the Taj Mahal where we had submitted the script about what we were going to shoot there. We hadn't been quite exactly honest about what we were going to do there and I like to steal things and these kids were stealing shoes because they didn't have any. When the local tour guide saw that, you know because there's a big mafia there, it runs everything, and they got annoyed and drove us out of the Taj Mahal. We hadn't quite got our footage. We sent back another crew later who were disguised as a German documentary crew to shoot the footage that we needed to complete the sequence. They got the high speed shots outside of the Taj Mahal.

The stunt guys there are amazing. I mean they really are. I know it's a cliché to say that the stunt performers are in the stunt arranger's hands, but there they really are. If anybody is hurt, there's a tradition, he will look after them for the rest of their life. They really do become a part of his family and he was this guy called Sham and he just basically built a confidence with the kids and it was clear that he knew exactly what he was doing. The equipment's a bit unconventional sometimes compared to some things you see here, but it's just as good. He's a brilliant guy organizing it and I was terrified of them running beside the train. That's what I was most terrified of, but then they start running and they're that tall and the wheel of the train is that tall. But he had them wired and we spent our CG [computer graphics] budget taking out those wires so if they did stumble, which they didn't thank God, he would whip them out of the way.

It's kind of a mystical thing to do with being in India and what you learn about your-self. I'm a control freak. That's part of the job, that's what we do and you can't really work like that there because there's so many forces that have to work that you kind of have to have respect for, that you might not conventionally understand, but apparently seem to work in our favor throughout including Warner Brothers as distributor, which was one thing that just looked like a disaster because I'd had a film in America that hadn't done very well and you know the next one wasn't going to do very well either. It was going to be even worse, and you thought well that's it, that's the end really. It's just extraordinary the way these things work out you know and people in India say to you, "Go, that's Providence working for you now." If you trust it, the good and the bad, and you go with it, these things will move in your favor eventually or you will learn something about yourself which is much more valuable than what you wanted to achieve anyway. That really struck me.

LEE DANIELS, *PRECIOUS*

The most difficult fantasy scene to do was the Italian scene, Sophia Loren, because I don't know Italian, Mo'Nique don't know Italian, Gabby don't know Italian. I had this Italian guy who was sort of translating, but then I didn't believe him and I said, "Hold up." I had to get my ex-boyfriend on the phone who was in Vienna, who on the phone was telling me and I was saying you know, "Are you hearing it? Are you hearing it?" That was sort of the hardest fantasy.

I drove my cinematographer crazy because we don't believe in rehearsals so we would block it in the moment. I said, "Come on guys, let's walk. Tell me what's going to happen here." I say to the actor tell me what you want to do and I'd make small adjustments. For example, Mo'Nique didn't know why it was that she was dancing. I said, "Because I want you to dance," and she said, "Okay, Mr. Daniels," so that was unexpected for my cameraman. He was trying to figure out what to do there and then when she kicks the TV tray up that was last minute. He really had to follow her with the camera. He didn't know what the fuck was going to go down because I didn't know what was going to go down.

CHRISTOPHER NOLAN, *THE DARK KNIGHT*

I use a single camera and I always stay by the camera for everything and I squeeze into whatever little room when we're shooting. I've found, for my mental process of blocking, figuring out how everything's going to fit together, I've realized that I have to view the film as a three-dimensional entity, as a three-dimensional scenario that's actually going on and put myself into the different points of view. Then, in the edits, it becomes a two-dimensional representation of that, but I like to know what's going on for real.

We shot the film in as aggressive and exciting a style as possible and my frame of reference very much from working with film was to look at Michael Mann's *Heat* and say, you know that's a movie that feels real when you watch it, but it's incredibly exciting, it's incredibly stylish in what feels like a very contemporary way to me with a lot of great textures and so forth, so we found some great Chicago locations where we could shoot for real and luckily the main bank location had this flat marble floor, so we could do dolly shots with these very heavy cameras, but we did a lot of it on steady cameras as well, which if anyone has ever seen an IMAX camera, it's almost impossible to lift on stage. We did break one, the arm just sheared off and fell off, which I don't think ever happened before, but we were really able to get a lot of the shots we wanted in very much the way we wanted.

About the opening shot of the film and I liked it a lot, Heath [Ledger who plays the Joker] and I talked a lot about how we would frame it and everything and then Wally Pfister [the cinematographer] when we set the shot up and rehearsed it, he was a little confused as to why I wanted to shoot it exactly the way I did and then we did the first run through closing in on the mask and then I think he actually turned to me and said, "Oh, that's why you are the director." He suddenly saw that the light on the road came through the eyeholes of the mask so as you come in on the mask, it sort of comes to life in this slightly odd way and the way he stands there is a very peculiar thing, but there was only one take that we could use and if you look at it on an IMAX screen in particular you can see that there's a mistake, the background [actors, sometimes known as extras, who don't speak] was actually cued late, so people aren't moving in the background and then literally into the shot they start moving, so we tried to use other takes and there's something about the way he's standing in that one first take that just works and no other version would work.

Preparation is the thing you worry about, what every department is worried about. Things like flipping a truck over on South Street in Chicago or blowing up a building. Those things go very smoothly because people are so attentive and they put so much effort into it. The things that I find difficult, like the end scene with the little boy being threatened by tooth fairies and everything, that was a very difficult scene to do for a very specific reason. When you're dealing with a smaller, more intimate scene and it's two characters speaking across the table, I find it very frustrating because you want it to be real, but at the same time, you've constructed this and you've worked with the script yourself, so you've only got yourself to blame. You've constructed this impossible labyrinth of blocking to get from A to B to C to D and I think it's very specific to this sort of action element. You get it in thrillers as well with this sort of Mexican standoff and who's pointing the gun at who and how did they get into the room. I find those scenes to be frustrating to work out and it takes a long time to work out particularly when you want to shoot them on location and I love working on location and you never do find the building that had the exact this, that and the other. In the scene with the boy hanging off the edge, it's like you shoot one corner of the building for looking up and a different corner of the building for looking down and another corner for the stunt. That becomes sort of arduous because every department as well is looking to you to figure out how that puzzle is going to work, to tell them what they need to know to make their piece work.

The hardest thing by far was shooting at night with kids. We had a great child actor, but the limited working hours for kids at night in England is incredibly restrictive. They are very concerned to monitor child welfare over night shoots and it's kind of impossible, so what you really have to do is shoot the kids close up, send them home, and then shoot everybody else using a stand-in. That makes it very tough on everybody, but great film actors like Gary Oldman and Aaron Eckhart are incredibly versatile in terms of giving a truthful performance with all these peculiarities in the way they have to be shot and the order they have to be shot in.

I find inevitably when you're shooting a scene and some little thing happens, somebody knocks something over, they do it and everything's wild, that's just terrific. When you get into the edits, it never works. It never works because you're always making the film in a slightly theatrical way. That's what movies are. They're not documentaries. When you try to mix in that little of what happened after you know a certain action, after I've said cut and everything fell over, it never seems to fit.

With *The Dark Knight* I knew exactly how I wanted it to end from before we wrote the script or even the story. I had this ending in mind, the feeling of it in particular, and we went to shoot it at Battersea Power Station, all that stuff at the end, and we were building this big set of the stacks of containers that you see and in the original script I had them sort of running over these rooftops. We were going to get a helicopter to do these massive helicopter shots and I began to realize over the course of shooting the film that Batman doesn't really run very well. It's the costume, it doesn't work very well and then trying to run him over with a helicopter, it wasn't going to work. As we got into it, I began to panic and I realized we had actually shot what was going to need to be the ending already, just in a different context. While we had been doing all our car chases and stuff, we shot this shot with his huge motor bike and we shot it from behind running, in a car behind it, running up this ramp and we had these massive lights on a crane very low down to shoot like down the ramp and at the tail end of the take, he just flares out the camera, his cape is flapping. It flares out. When we watched it in dailies [referring to screening what was shot the day before] and we were watching dailies on IMAX screens in Chicago, it's incredible. We would go in there at six in the morning and just watch these enormous images and everybody, when they saw that take, were very struck by it and said, "Oh it'll be in the trailer." It's a complete accident. It was just shooting into a movie light and I realized as we were planning to film this big shot that we already had the shot we needed. We could just cut it right there on the flare. You know, very unusually I think for my process, that's a complete accident. But I think it was exactly what I was looking for.

CHRISTOPHER NOLAN, *INCEPTION*

The first thing I do on set is call the actors and when they're all there, we rehearse and then I send them away and start lighting. In the rehearsal I start with just myself and the DP [cinematographer] and the actors. And then when we've got something we're happy with in the blocking, we'll bring everybody in who wants to see it. Even the sound guys, who kind of look over the corner, but we let them look at it and then we get on with it. For me, it's very important that on the day, if it's a 7:30 call, we're rehearsing at 7:32 and figuring out what we're doing and then we get rid of everybody and let the DP start lighting. With staging we'll walk in and figure it out on the day. On the tech scout [where the crew goes to locations before shooting to figure out what will be shot and what is needed] I'll look at it with my DP [cinematographer] Wally Pfister and we'll say, "Okay, what I'd like to be able to do, because it's five, six people, if we shoot coverage [various individual shots of actors in the scene that will be edited together to comprise the scene] on this, if we shoot a master, if we go in close up, we'll be here four days." I've got no interest in that. I want to treat it as a real scene. Let the actors move around as they would, get a handheld camera and shoot the thing. And then you start cleaning up [getting the other shots needed], once you've done a moving master [the shot which is often the widest and includes all the actors and what they do] then I need a left look on this guy for that line. That's very much the way I try to do any kind of scene where there's more than really two people because I find the formal grammar of conventional coverage [master shot, over-the-shoulder shots, and then close-ups] to be extremely slow and it lets the actors be lazy because when you're shooting a two shot they don't put everything into it. They do it in close up. And so what we started doing, I think *The Prestige* was the first film where we did it aggressively, we would just literally, every take, we would just change where the camera was positioned so that none of the actors could ever sit back and go, "Okay, I'm not the close up in this," and you'd sort of swing around and suddenly Michael Caine's in a huge close up, and he goes, "What are you doing?" And they got used to it after a couple of takes and it just keeps it interesting, frankly, and it's quicker too. And there's a real dance that happens, and every now and then somebody falls over, and you gotta be careful and the first thing you do is you say to the still photographer [responsible for shooting photographs that will be used for publicity], "Okay, get off the set." You have to set everything out because I don't use a monitor, I'm sort of running around behind the camera as well, so it gets very crowded at times, but there's a great energy to it and I think the actors respond really well to it. It's something we've maintained from smaller films and really tried to keep that spontaneity.

Every day we're screening dailies for a half hour. So every day you're seeing the day's work from the day before. It's interesting it's being done less and less though when I started doing student films it was absolutely required. But we always maintain that, because for me it's a great refresher to jump back to something the day before. It sort of cleanses you from the horrible day you've just been through. So, I get we have this on screen, we've got this in the can [meaning film can where the shot film would be kept]. And then I just go to bed. I don't do anything more than that and then in the car in the morning I read the scenes we're going to do. Sunday night for me is always just horrible. Because as I look at the schedule a week ahead, I suddenly realize that somebody's made a dreadful mistake and on the day I absolutely can't make it ["make the day" means do all the work planned for the day]. The thing I've never managed to figure out is I'm not a bad scheduler and I can go to prep on a film now and I'll go through the one-liner [what is to be shot each day], and I can be pretty efficient figuring out how to help schedule, but somehow once I'm shooting I can't look ahead more than one day. So Sunday night I'll get in and look at the week ahead and my producer's there, and unfortunately my producer has to be there on Sunday night [his producer is his wife, Emma Thomas] when I realize that everybody's screwed up and I don't know what I'm going to do. And then we try to reschedule the week, and shift the days around. It doesn't happen every week obviously but in every shoot there's been some horrible oversight on my part where I've realized that, I've allowed I can shoot two days' work in half a day or something like that. And I have to shift that around. Usually these things just fall between the cracks. It's hard to explain, they're just things when you do these films in a hundred twenty-eight days there are seven months basically so it's very difficult with certain areas literally just looking at the calendar, and going, "Okay, we need about five days to shoot this chase," or whatever it is, then as you get into the specifics of how things are going to be done, it's a rolling prep. So you prep for say fifteen, sixteen weeks before you start shooting. But on a shoot that long where you have that many different moving parts you're prepping about six weeks ahead so things are still being determined as you shoot and it's very, for me one of the big challenges in doing a large-scale film, but it really applies to small films as well I think. When you're wrapped up in shooting and watching dailies, shooting, watching dailies, you're in a sort of fourteen-hour-day cycle that you don't really have time to prep properly. You don't really have time to look ahead. I have a big advantage because I've written the script myself, so it's kind of in me pretty nicely and I've got a good memory for it. That helps a lot, but you know you have the odd sleepless night on a Sunday.

In the scene in the hotel room, as far as the directing goes, it was a little strange because for various location reasons we used the same window for both sides, and so on the wide shots I'm in the other building shouting across to the actor, and then as we got closer and put the camera onto a cherry picker and got three feet closer for the close ups, then I go over to the other building and sort of sit below the window, talk to them from there, but a lot of that, that energy of the location and sitting on a window sill eight stories up, that kind of thing, I mean I think it makes it real for them. We had them on a wire obviously.

One of the first experiences I had making a big movie, for me which was *Memento* which we shot in twenty-five days, was that it was very tight, and when we were shooting the exteriors of the motel, we had to do everything in one day, all the dolly shots, because we didn't have any steadicam [a device that holds the camera making it fluid].

So it was incredibly tricky. We were losing the light [the sun was going down] and then there was some talk about which cars were parked for continuity and I just screamed, you know, absolutely shouted as loudly as I knew how, "Stop fucking around we got to do this," and I turn around and my mother was standing there. She had this look on her face that I've never forgotten, and I said, "Okay." I did realize at that point that that wasn't probably the best way to do it. But the flip side of that is we then made the day, because everybody did get the seriousness of what we were dealing with and we managed to get all the shots we needed. But the person I chose to shout at was actually doing a very good job and didn't forgive me for a long time and held it over me as people can. And so I think what I come away with is a feeling that, if you lose control of yourself, you certainly lose control of the people around you, because they're only doing what you've asked. If they're not actually contributing to what the film's going to be and they're not giving their best, for me the attempt is to not get angry and not lose control of yourself. Go home and punch the fridge.

ALEXANDER PAYNE, *THE DESCENDANTS*

I have found that when you are preparing for an emotional scene, or the ending of the movie, and you overdo it with, "All right. We have to clear the set. All right. We're shooting the end and we're shooting a very emotional scene." If you overdo that, it backfires and the scene gets kind of goopy somehow. I had learned to treat emotional scenes not quite, but almost, as workaday, as everything else. Of course, we all know what's going on. And certainly when George [Clooney] says his tearful goodbye to his wife, we have as few people as possible on set and had it be fairly quiet, but not too much. Everyone knows what's to be done.

When the legal proceedings around him melt away and we go inside Matt's head and we transition to his thoughts, George Clooney has been around cameras most of his adult life, so obviously, he's able to do that and be aware and unaware of that Cyclops careening toward him, and then he did a verbal cue as to when to space out now. He looks like Marcello Mastroianni in that shot. That's when the DP [cinematographer] and I turned to each other and said, "Yes, very Cary Grant and Clark Gable, he's like Marcello." I think once I read the voice-over aloud to get the timing right because you're dealing there with the dolly grip too and when he needs to move with respect to what I hope the rhythm of the eventual voice-over will be.

There's about a six or seven minute sequence without dialogue too when he's jogging on the beach and he finds the lover and then he chases the lover and then he waits lurking to see if the lover, hours later, is going to come out of the house. That's the best stuff to shoot. I love shooting figures in space with no dialogue and, as dialogue-heavy as my pictures are, I'm really thinking about figures moving in space and about telling the story visually. And having really just one actor, a single actor, and shooting no dialogue, I'm in heaven. That's the best stuff.

I've never storyboarded in my life and I just thought it should look a certain way and we were very lucky that day because I wanted it to read as the crack of dawn, and the sun in Hawaii, because it's so close to the equator, rises very quickly and it becomes very sunny very early, but the film gods smiled that day and we started at that early hour. We arrived there before daybreak, before the sunrise, and it was an overcast morning, so there was a lot of fooling around with putting the camera up and having it go in front of him and behind him and all that kind of stuff, up and down the beach, and erasing as much as we could, tire tracks and all that kind of stuff.

Nailing that final scene toward the end where Julie Speer shows up at the hospital with flowers and then has a discussion with Clooney and then berates the woman dying, getting that timing right and having those quick tonal shifts, that took a while. It took a while and I pretty much use all the angles. I'm a three to six [the number of takes on a shot] kind of guy.

At the family gathering, I just wanted to create the world of those casually attired, upper class of Hawaii, and I would say about half of the actors, the extras, in that scene are from those families, and I just said, "Have a party, hang out," and then the cameramen and I and the assistant just walked around and basically shot a little documentary of their party. I used one casting person from the stars down through handpicking every extra. Often in filmmaking, you have three different people. You've got your person in New York or in L.A. who casts the top speaking parts. Then you move and you have a local casting director, and then you have a third person who is an extras wrangler and I got very tired of that division. I didn't want to keep explaining myself to different people, so I found a casting director now who's in charge of all of the flesh in front of the camera from top to bottom. And extras can wreck your movie. A bad extra is a torpedo. And my long-time assistant director, George Parra, knows if I get distracted watching the actors in the foreground, you're on torpedo patrol for bad extras, and as the cameraman used to say, "If you only find it in dailies, you've been hit." But it's not just zombies, they paint the picture of the world you're creating more than the production designers in my book, or at least equal to the production design. At least, they're moving. You look at them. I do. I look at extras constantly. I have my favorite extra in any movie. In *The Last Detail*, there's a fantastic extra wearing a corduroy jacket walking down the street past [Jack] Nicholson and every time I see that movie, I say, "There's my favorite extra." So when I made *About Schmidt,* I'm very proud, it's an okay film, but the extras in that film really paint the picture. It's like the opening of *Dog Day Afternoon.* You're out in the street shooting and then assistants would run up and get releases [from the real people photographed in the scene] signed most of the time.

For the interstitials, I'm always enamored of Ozu [Japanese director of films like Tokyo Story] pictures and how he separates his dramatic scenes with shots of Tokyo, typically trains, and I thought, because part of this film, at least the way I was approaching it, one is the narrative story, but the other is this sort of documentary feel about Hawaii. I was very keen on getting not just a pictorial sense of Hawaii accurate, but a sense of the human landscape and the rhythms. So some people see the film and say, "Oh, it's so mellow and it just sort of lopes along and it's not as sharp as *Election* was." And I say, "Well, that's Hawaii." That was really the feeling of life on the islands seeping into the film. And one is struck there by a constant and vivid sense of nature surrounding you and how puny that nature makes you feel, but also puny in a kind of noble way. You're so happy to feel so puny against that grandeur of nature. I wanted to get a sense of that across. So, I had a very dedicated and beloved

second-unit director curating while we were shooting. He got a crew for about a
month curating those interstitial shots.

LEE DANIELS, *PRECIOUS*

When you're in the work, you're in the work, you're in the moment and God and truth
speak, so it's just there innately, but this whole process has been something that has
been very unique for me and very terrifying for me. I was a wreck at the beginning
and I was told, "Lee, embrace it and enjoy it and don't be terrified," and that really has
been the best advice that any director has given me. When I'm in the moment, God is
working and I'm just in the moment. I'm looking at truth and knowing truth. I didn't
come from the business. I come from my heart when I'm working, and I don't have a
technical background. You stay in your truth. You know what's honest like you know.

The only thing that wasn't sort of rehearsed was the thing I whispered to Gabby,
"Hit her. Punch her. Punch her lights out." And so no one knew that was going to
happen and Gabby just like "bam" and Consuelo, that little Puerto Rican sassy mama
came at her like she was like Godzilla, and it was really an intense moment and all the
reaction shots were very honest. We had three cameras.

MICHEL HAZANAVICIUS, *THE ARTIST*

The point is when you tell people, "I will tell a story with no dialogue," what you say for
real is, "I'm going to tell a story with the images." So I think even if it's not conscious,
people want to see images that you don't use usually. I trust the audience, so you have
to make priorities, you have to say, "This is the main information," and sometimes,
that's something that's really funny, but you have to believe that because it doesn't tell
the story, and especially in a silent movie, you have to really take care of everything,
because I watch a lot of silent movies and the good ones are really masterpieces.

There's three shots in all the dancing and I said to them very quickly that there would
be three shots and I didn't want to over-cut that sequence because of the style of the
movie, and I remember a sentence Fred Astaire would say once to a director, "You
choose. I dance or the camera dances, but not both of us." So I said, "You dance and I
do as little as possible." So I think we did like seventeen takes [versions of the same shot].

It was the last day of shooting so they were very excited and they wanted to do it
more and we were very tired on this day and they took the energy shots and they never
take that. They don't use drugs, they are very healthy. I believe it was the adrenaline
of the dancing with the excitement and the small caffeine plus from I don't know what
they put in those little bottles, but I think the eleventh take was perfect and I say,
"Okay. It's good, it's really perfect," and they came to me and say, "No, it's not good.
It's—da, da, da." So I said, "Just smile, just smile."

We shot some exteriors of the cars, when she drives her car, in the back of Paramount and you can't shoot everywhere, so you need to fill the space with some ac-

curate houses and buildings and everything. So, we used CGI [Computer Graphic Imaging] there.

It's a movie about loving cinema, so the preparation of the shot at the end seemed to me something that could be touching and moving for people, and also I'd like to finish with a silent place, silence and action. So I wanted something very quiet and a very slow crane shot. It was not so difficult to make.

Sometimes when an actor says something, he says a line and it's almost perfect, but you know that if he can change something, it would be better, it will be better. If you wait for the end of the takes and you say, "Cut," and you have ten people come through and you talk to him and then you have three minutes for people to clear the frame and you forget everything. So, if during the take, you say, "Do it again, but just add . . ." you gain time and I think it's more efficient. But for this one, I spoke to them during the shots and also during the takes, and also what I did is I put music almost all the time and they really loved it because usually when you put music, you have to cut it before the take. And here, I was asking for the music and then the action, and so they were surprised for the first takes because they didn't know that music would stay, so that created an emotion and it helped them. They really loved it and at one point, I decided to stop a little bit because they were becoming a little bit lazy. They were waiting for the music.

Bérénice Bejo knows how to cry very easily and actually, the mood on the set this day she was to cry was very, very teenager. I mean, we are doing jokes and I say to her, "Okay. This is a tracking shot and I need the tears at the end of the tracking shot," and she said, "Okay." And we did it maybe nine or ten times and almost every time, the tears were there. I don't know how she does it really, but now in our personal life [he is married to her], when she cries, it doesn't work anymore. "Try something else."

When Jean Dujardin is destroying all the films before the fire, I put some music on. Really, the music helped me very much for that kind of sequence. For him, it was very pleasant to destroy things and to throw everything. The fire sequence was more difficult because all of us had the oxygen masks and he didn't, and for the first shot, I tried not to put the mask on, to be just nice with him and say, "Okay. I'm with you." And for the third take, I said, "Okay. I'm not with you anymore and you have to, I don't."

There's one sequence I realized that nobody understood what was in the script and I thought it was clear, but when we had to do it on set, I realized nobody got it. It's the sequence when we see the dailies, take after take, and we understand that it's like a behind-the-scenes sequence and we see four takes and the way the actors don't make it through the takes, we understand that they are falling in love. *The Artist* is a movie about cinema and I thought that it would be cool for people to see some behind-the-scenes and I'm showing some dailies, some other kind of thing that you don't see in the movies usually. And I realized that nobody understood what was going on and so for them, it was not so easy, because there was me saying "Action." "Action" means that he was waiting for the next "Action" [from the scene within the scene that was showing how scenes are shot] and then there was another "Action." He was acting, not succeeding and then I say "Cut," but it was not the real "Cut" [it was the "Cut" in the scene within in the scene] and then there was the real "Cut." So it was a little bit confusing and I don't know if I'm clear now. But once he got the trick, he really played with it. And what he does with his eyebrows, his eyebrows declared their own independence, they do what they want. So sometimes, I talk just to the eyebrows and said, "Do this or this." It was like maybe 3:00 in the morning because we have another system in France, and we don't have to wait twelve hours between the end of a day and the beginning of another day. So you do close-up of an actress at 4:00 in the morning. That's really strange for us.

Every sequence is different. There's a sequence in the building and they meet and they haven't seen each other for a long time and she's talking a lot and she's going to succeed in the talking movies and he doesn't say anything because he's a silent movie actor. And actually, I really don't care about what they are talking about. What was important was she's full of life, she's smiling and she's talking and talking and talking and he's taciturn and he just looks at her and what's important is the way he looks at her and how he listens to her, and also the composition of the frame because she's going up and he's going down and she's up and he's down and that was important. And actually, for that kind of sequence, if you had the sound, it would be, I think, much less efficient. And when you put out the dialogues, what's become important is what you see and what you show to people. I always try to think of how to put the audience in the process. What I mean is, it's not just about how the actors are feeling the situation and how they make the dialogues and everything, it's about how people will get there. And sometimes, I mean, sometimes an actor can be very intense and it can be too much or not exactly because it doesn't affect the audience, it's not always connected with the performance of the actor. And I try to trust the audience always and sometimes, you really ask the actors, "Don't do anything. Just look, just be playing neutral," and this is the best. I always think of the Kuleshov effect [an editing experiment done in Russia in the early twentieth century that showed how combining shots creates an emotional reaction in the viewer]. It's the main lesson of everything. It's not about being lazy. It's just the less I do, the more people get involved in the process and it will be better because every single person will do his own story and that will be better because they will do it with their own imagination, with their own fantasies, their own ghosts. And silent movie is really about that.

The most important thing for me was the story. I have to tell the story the most efficient way and if I can be elegant, it's better, and if it can be entertaining or clever, it's better, and if I can respect the style of the '20s, it's better, but first of all, if you look at the Murnau [German expressionist director of *Nosferatu* and *The Last Laugh*] movie or the [Frank] Borzage [American director of more than 100 films], you have some very, very sophisticated shots. Really, in *Seventh Heaven*, there's a shot that raised to the seventh floor. They built a lift to make it. The tracking shot in *Sunrise* is incredible. They were very sophisticated shots and their point was to tell the story and so what I did is I watched really a lot of movies, silent movies. I tried to immerse myself in the vocabulary and I'd give to the main collaborators a bunch of movies, like ten or twelve movies, *City Girl* and *Sunrise*, *The Crowd*, *Seventh Heaven*, *The River*, also Lon Chaney and *The Unknown*, John Ford's *Four Sons*, *The World*, *Foolish Husbands* and *Greed*, just for them to understand what could be a silent movie. And once they did it, and they thought they understood everything, I said to them, "Now, we forget everything because now we have to make our own movie and we have to tell what's important is the story, not the reference. So we have to tell our own story." What I did in the movie, and actually, I did it in my two previous movies, which were comedies, but period pictures, the first one was in the '50s and the second one in the late '60s, and what I did is when people do period movies, they re-create what they are filming, what they are shooting, their haircuts, the costume, the location, and everything, but they usually don't re-create the shooting device, the way to shoot it. And that's what I did, actually, I like to re-create the entire process.

There's something I learned, and it was doing the promotion of the movie. The way people adored the dog and I mean, he's the star of the movie and it's a dog, okay. And actually, the way I wrote the script I could not expect that to me, it was just a funny, like a gimmick, a funny thing, a flavor of the '20s and something to change the profile of the main character. So I tried to think why people are so in love with this dog because he's cute and everything, but I can't say he's an actor, okay? He doesn't care about situations created and the story and everything. He doesn't have feelings and everything, and I realized that the main character, the human character, when you think of him, is very selfish. He's egocentric. He's afraid of the future. He's not a very positive character. He could be very negative. And because he has a dog and the dog follows him during all the movie and the dog trusts him, I'm sure that people trust the dog, and people think if a dog loves the guy, the guy has to be someone. There's something positive and the fact is he does that, the dog, by instinct with no words and it puts him in the very center of the whole device in a silent movie. So I really know something about how you can tell something about a character with another character and, yes, I really learned something about that, but I'm not sure I would tell the truth to another director. I would keep it for myself.

DARREN ARONOFSKY, *BLACK SWAN*

It's weird because every film I've become more and more relaxed on the set. ∏ [*Pi*], I think, we shot sixteen days straight at one point. We just gave up weekends and we kept shooting and eventually we didn't stop shooting until dawn of the last day when the producer had to come and take the camera away. Me and the DP [cinematographer] were up all night shooting with a macro lens like close ups of Hebrew letters and stuff, going, "Wow, that's cool," and then shooting math formulas all night and eventually the producer literally pulled the plug on us. And I used to have that type of complete surrender to the job. As I've gotten older and become a family man and have other responsibilities, I've tried to find balance, and you know people like Spielberg who have a family, you know these older directors, you know there must be a way to do it where it's more of a job. More than anyone, I approached this film very relaxed. Of course, there's moments of complete terror and pain and frustration and rage, but I just try to be as present and easy as possible and it's turned into my biggest financial success. There's some lesson there.

I didn't really shot list the film [each day have a summary of all the shots intended], which I don't know if I should admit. But you know my first four films were really shot-listed but I kind of wanted to create the energy for the whole film to be a ballet, and so I was looking for ways to choreograph every scene as a dance, so the ballet scenes were really worked out beforehand, but the kind of dramatic scenes and the acting scenes, I just let the actors go on set, breath, feel. I had a sense of it you know, and me and my DP [cinematographer] would walk through the set and sort of have ideas but we'd see where the actors would lead and sort of improvise with them and create the shots with them.

I usually get stressed out, when there's more than two actors in a scene, about what I'm going to do and block [where people move] and I come up with a few ideas and I maybe sketch a few possibilities of blocking but I try to go, and this is definitely from the Mickey Rourke school of filmmaking, just try to be as open to what's going to happen with the actors as much as possible and then adapt as it happens.

Actors come to the set. You know, you pull them from makeup, wherever they are, get on the set, clear the set, usually me and the DP Matty [Libatique, the cinematographer], in this case, and we just have them start to warm up and then see what they do. If they have a great idea, run with it. If it seems to be not working, suggest an idea. Or if they're doing something a little too complicated that I know is going to be too much coverage [various individual shots of actors in the scene that will be edited together to comprise the scene] try and say, "Hey, what about this idea?" Don't tell them it means two or three less shots, because they're not interested in that, but try minimizing shots. And definitely with this film and *The Wrestler*, I got into the idea of using this handheld master a lot and trying to do as much as I could in one shot and then, once again, cleaning it up and taking up where the coverage, where cut points would be natural and not really destroy the fluid nature of the shot.

What's always hard when you have two actors in one space for a long time is how to make it visually interesting. *Requiem for a Dream* kind of had that ten-minute centerpiece. The whole reason I did the film was the scene between Jared Leto and Ellen Burstyn when they have the conversation he realizes that Mom's on drugs and it was two people sitting at a table and that was a big challenge about how to use the camera to cross the line [a reference to the screen direction actors look in for their closer shots] and try to change the look of it and you want to do something like that but then again you have one day to shoot a five-page dialogue scene so you don't want to over-complicate it, but it was about movement and trying to get them through different spaces in that one space and moving the camera to different sides which adds, when you're in a place like that, you're adding complexity because you're in a limited space and you want to keep it visually interesting.

The mirrors were placed in certain places so I had a sense of where people were going to go but I had to work it out with the actors. I think I actually went in with an idea what was blocking but they came in and in the moment on the day it was about finding those shots and finding those angles which I've kind of been sold on. I joke about Mickey a lot but he's not the type of actor that finds his mark [where he is supposed to stand for the camera]. And so, it's about just being free to allow that to happen and sort of letting that go. And that's kind of really exciting especially if you have a handheld camera which both *The Wrestler* and *Black Swan* had, you can really work with them.

On stunts, I'll bring in a second camera but it's all about just a single camera. Because I also work without a monitor. Sometimes I'll have a handheld monitor next to me, just to check the framing, especially handheld because you're really working, collaborating with other artists and they have different aesthetics, but hopefully you find someone who you trust that's going to get the right shot and find the right frame, but definitely I'm really anal about the frame so I'll have that, but usually I'm just watching the actor and standing and following behind the camera. This one was hard because there were mirrors everywhere because it was part of the language of the film because you can't escape mirrors in a ballet studio and because the film's about doppelgangers and losing your identity and we knew we were going to be playing with that a lot. So there was a lot of crew removal [taking them out of a shot using computer graphic effects in post production] and every time I was there it was another three thousand dollars. So I knew I had to be ducking a lot. And so I was on the floor a lot, you know just watching. I mean there were mirrors everywhere.

To deal with your actors in sex scenes is always awkward. For the famous Natalie [Portman]/Mila [Kunis] scene, we actually had two days scheduled because there were a lot of visual effects in it, not because I'm a pervert or anything. Natalie had to be making love to Natalie and there were all these skin things happening and so we thought it would be hard. But it was so awkward and so uncomfortable. It was, just get through it as quick as possible, is how I feel about the sex scenes. You do without the full contact at first. You clear the set, of course, and you make it just the most intimate situation you can and so it's a very, very closed set with no videotape or anything. There's no replay, so you're sort of just going off your own instincts, so you try to make it as comfortable as possible and then you just walk through it. You say, "Okay, here's what is going to happen." It was all about economy, trying to figure out as few shots as possible, and trying to limit it as much as possible so that I didn't really have to make them go through that uncomfortableness. It's just a continuing conversation and it's funny because if you get the right spirit on the set then people really start pushing and people will come up with ideas, "How about I do this, and how about I do that," and you just try to be open and honest and straightforward with the actors as much as possible which is like, "How do you feel about that?" Usually people are more relaxed. I mean I get really uncomfortable in the situations. It's always tricky. I just ran into the actor who played in *Requiem* and I remember before he had to make out with Ellen Burstyn he was sitting at the craft services table eating burritos the whole time and I'm going, "This is really going to limit how many takes I get. Get him some mouthwash please." There's always funny things that happen like that. It was very interesting because Natalie never did these types of things before on screen. But she was totally game. I remember there's the masturbation scene with the mom in the room and I came up with the idea that maybe she could roll over or something. Just to make it more interesting visually and I was terrified to ask her and then I said, "How about you try that?" and she said, "Yeah, sure, no problem." So the actors are really more comfortable than I find the crew and everyone else. And definitely I think the scene with Natalie and Mila it became very jokey. Generally they were just making fun of me the whole time. So I think all their pain was coming toward me and I just let it happen. Roll with the punches.

Looking at dailies [material shot the day before] I actually find it pretty brutal. The regrets just come up and all the things I missed come up but you know then it's usually my editor playing shrink and saying, "It's okay, we've got it." And then it's just really reading the script as much as possible to figure out where you are in the scenes tomorrow. This film, *Black Swan*, was really tough because we really just had way too much to do with way too little time. And so many times I was fooled by the one sheet [of what is to be shot on the day]. I'd say, "Ah, that's not so bad," and then I'd realize there'd be two more pages to shoot. And every single day was brutal. Most of my other films you get one a week that was like a brutal day. This, every single day, it was just ridiculous. We knew we weren't going to make the days [finish the work of the day], every day.

STEVEN SPIELBERG, *MUNICH*

There's really no challenge in having a monitor and playing some tape through it, but the biggest challenge is when you're outside and the sun's really bright, how do you get an exposure on the monitor and how do you balance it with all the ambient light coming in from the open window? I guess the only real challenge in synchronizing a monitor with action is we had the most famous image from the 20th Olympiad in Munich, Germany, the image where the Black September Fatah man comes out to the balcony with a mask and looks over the side. And I wanted to see what that might've looked like from inside the room, so I actually set up the camera with the actual footage from ABC on the monitor. And then the actor had three monitors that were hidden on the balcony that he could watch the actual movements of the ABC news footage, and he could time his footsteps and time his head turns. And when he looked over the balcony, there was a second monitor just on the other side of the balcony, which our camera couldn't see, that he could look down and make that final little lean forward in sync with the monitor. And that was many, many takes, ten, eleven, twelve takes to get it.

I give a lot of credit to what happens when I wake up in the morning and I go on the set and the set tells me all sorts of things that I should know. I mean in the early part of my career, I planned everything out and I came to the set and there were no surprises. It became just like making hamburgers, that I had already written the recipe for, and they tasted pretty good, but I had written the recipe and there was no surprise. And I just feel that on certain films, I love the surprise. I love to be able to wake up in the morning not knowing what's going to happen that day, how I'm going to be creatively informed of how I should approach a scene, what lens to suggest to put on the camera. I mean to me that is what makes it fun to make pictures.

The crews love me in the morning because I get up in the morning and I walk around. I'm not quite sure what to do and they have time to have some coffee and they have time to kibbutz and I'm getting some ideas going. And then when the scene finally clicks and I know what I'm doing by 11:00, the crew hates me in the afternoon because we're racing to finish the day's work, and it's the second half of the day that's brutal, trying to get everything captured before we have to go home.

I didn't quite know how to shoot that sequence of the planting of the explosive in the phone and then later on with the girl, I didn't quite know how I was going to do it.

I began shooting the scene basically starting with the very first shot of the car pulling up, the phone booth, you zoom back, the car pulls up and stops, so you geographically know where everybody is situated at the beginning of the sequence. And then when I got my idea for the second shot, which was across the street and up a flight of stairs, the whole crew had to run across the street and shoot one angle. And then I said, "Oh, I know what I really should've done." And then we go back outside and we go back to the phone booth, and Ciarán Hinds is in the phone booth. And then I got another idea. So I basically cut the film in my head, but unfortunately, the crew was doing a marathon, literally shooting the cuts in continuity of coming up with the ideas. And that was one of the first times I ever shot a movie that way and it would be certainly the last time. It wasn't worth it.

I was trying to do a lot of these scenes in one [without cuts] because I think it's more realistic. Violence for me is more real when it's not cutty [having a number of separate shots edited together] because when it's cutty, the violence for me is fake. It looks like it's been manufactured to appear violent. But when you can do something in one extended master and you've got people shooting each other and you've got the squibs [that create gunshot effects] going off on the walls and it's very complicated. It's like when documentary cameramen happen to be running inside this apartment building photographing this as it happened, and that's the most complicated way to shoot a picture, because if you don't get it on the first take, you've got to re-squib the entire room, and it takes three, four, five hours before you're ready for take two, so that's the most risky part.

Part of directing is it's psychotherapy, and you're sitting there with a lot of very talented patients and you're trying to make sure that your movie doesn't just blow up in your face and anarchy reigns, and this has happened to me on many movies, but it didn't on this one.

In the story, the Israeli coach was so strong he was actually able to hold back seven of the Black September Palestinians from getting the room for a number of seconds, an inhuman number of seconds. And we actually asked the actor, I said, "Do you think you can actually hold back these other seven actors, or do you want to do something else, should I tell the guys to pull their pushes [not hit as hard as they can]?" And he said, "No, let me see if I can hold them back." His endorphins kicked in, and he was able to hold the door closed until the point that they couldn't get into the room and I had to say, "Cut," and say, "You've got to let him into the room." But he held them all back. It was amazing.

I didn't know quite what was going to happen when all the Israeli actors came into the same space with all the Arab actors, and that was the unknown factor in all of this. And I remember when we began shooting scenes together, the first time the Arab actors and the Israeli actors came together was in the re-creation of the Munich murders at the Fürstenfeldbruck Airport, and that was the first time they faced each other, and they faced each other with Kalashnikovs and hand grenades. And it was really brutal because I didn't know what was going to happen. And after the first take when we had full loads of blanks in two of the guns and in the first helicopter the Israelis were machine-gunned to death and then the grenade went in, none of us expected this to happen, although I knew it would because that's the way the world really works, that when I said cut, the Palestinian actors dropped their guns, ran to the helicopter, picked up Israeli actors, and they all began sobbing in each other's arms. And we stopped shooting. And the actors who were Arab actors who weren't involved in the scene and the other Israeli actors who were not involved in that shot all came running in from the monitor and they all began hugging each other. I just remember we were unglued by this. And I said, "Peace is just around the corner waiting to happen over there." That's how I felt.

And I think the nice thing about the movie was we had a chance to not just make friends with each other during the actual photography, but we were able to have dinner at night sometimes. And we had a couple of parties. We would just get together. I remember we had a party for the crew and everybody showed up, and that's when we really began talking about the problems in the world today, and it was a wonderful time to come together and get to know each other a little bit better, which I think smoothed some of the later scenes when we were having to stage the tragedy.

DAVID O. RUSSELL, *THE FIGHTER*

After a day's shoot, I spend most of my time weeping and then try to arrive early, throw up, and then bring everybody in for rehearsal. I don't watch dailies. It's just watching the same take so many times that makes me hate the whole thing. I see them as they're being shot and then give them to the editing room and then I'm watching a cut the next day. Everybody has their cross to bear. I've pretty much preconceived an idea what the movie is before we do anything and then you have to kind of have this little voice saying, "Shut the fuck up, just let it happen, respond to it." I made a movie ten years ago where I literally pre-vized [pre-visualized] the entire movie and could show it on a DVD to any of the actors, not only where they would stand but where the camera would be and what it would see at any given moment. And it didn't work out. I think it's ultimately demeaning to actors, if they walk into rehearsal and they have marks already on the floor where they're supposed to go. And it's debilitating and it's also boring for the director because you're sitting there going, "Oh, could you just get to that mark at the right time," because I got to be able to cut to this. It didn't work out. So now I find myself reading the script a lot, and you've sort of broken down the script and you know what each scene is about in terms of its narrative, you know why it essentially needs to be part of the chronology. Why it has to fall where it falls and then it's just strip-mining whatever you can squeeze out of it, whatever you can get and that's a lot of being open, I mean you know you're hiring incredibly talented people to come and run away and you want to fall in love and go in whatever direction. You know it is kind of *Mutual of Omaha's Wild Kingdom*. You do want to like see where they lead and you have to be able to have those conversations where you go, "I love it. It's not this movie. It's not leading me narratively toward where I need to go, so I don't feel we can do that." But for the most part now I try let the actors decide. I shoot two cameras all the time. I do like a lot of masters [a shot that cover everything that is to happen in the scene], a roaming master is what I call it. And I like a steadicam a lot. And I like handheld a lot. And then you find your other angles to complement that.

I work very hard on the homework. You want to make sure these things happen. If you have a shorter shoot, that's it. And I like that creative pressure and there was an immediacy to that in *The Fighter*. We only had thirty-three days. We shot the fights in three days so preparing for the fights, Mark [Wahlberg] wanted to do the fights in the first three days, which scared me a little bit because that means you're shooting the ending of the movie on the third day. There was a lot going on in those fights. And we were shooting the fights from outside the ring. Other fight films do it from inside the ring but I didn't consider this really a fight film. I consider it really more of a family character story. We had six cameras from an HBO crew and then we had two additional cameras. And we had seventy-nine hours of footage. But key parts of each fight had been choreographed, you had to know exactly what you wanted those poor actors Melissa Leo and Jack McGee and Amy Adams and Christian Bale sitting there all day ringside waiting for their moment and being in character all day. And then the moments come and you want to make sure you get the angles and the money shots [the most important shots in the scene often on a lead actor]. You make sure you're always getting those. I do have a shot list and then there are discoveries. You have to be open to discoveries that are wonderful and amazing. I like working on a shorter schedule. I think it makes people more focused.

I like more than three or four takes, you know six, seven tops. Just very different. And it's a different way to work. I can convey the feeling of what I want, I just have to ramp the cast up to what we've all been talking about. Getting them into a flow, how you want the rhythm of the scene to go. Getting them off of anything they preciously prepared in their hotel room. Because to me that's six different people with six different performances that they did in their hotel room that wastes a lot of time and they're not relating to each other. And one of the first things you got to do is just forget about that. And they have to trust you and feel safe with you to say, "Okay, I'm going to put that down and we're going to get in the pool together and everybody's just going to see what happens." And I say, "Just say the lines. Forget about it. Just say the lines." And go again, again, again. Rehearse it a few times and then they have their rhythm and then we have it and you can really start. I know the moments when you really want to feel something and you can kind of convey that to them. You have a way that you feel the scene has to be.

I think you get a rhythm. It's like a song, you know. And everybody starts to learn the song that you're all singing, hopefully within the first couple of weeks. I mean that's what the language is, it has a rhythm, it has a feeling to it. The bumpiest part is getting everybody learning that melody of how this rhythm and the feeling of this film goes. Once they have that everybody relaxes, and they feel okay. And they kind of know what they're doing and then they go more this way and more this way but they know the song goes like this. And every day it's a fun experience of Christian [Bale] or somebody saying to me, you know, "Did you like it, should I go a little more, a little less?" In many scenes they can then improvise. Things happen. Because they have the boilerplate down. So you know Mark, some of the greatest lines in the movie were improvised. Mark saying, "You come running in here like a silverback gorilla." You know he just said that to Jack. There's a bunch of examples of where people just started improvising lines.

The argument scene, you know, I have been in that kitchen many times with my own mother. And some of those lines are from my own mother who's an Italian American woman who was tough. Like the daughter line is from my mother. So I know what it feels like. So you know there's just things that people do and you say, "Don't do it so much that way. I feel it's more this way." And if they really want to do it that way, then in take six, they can do it that way. And sometimes, you know, you get into the editing room and you go, "That was a better way. I'm glad she did it that way."

I like doing old-fashioned practical stunts like the cowboy switch [where a stunt person does something and then there is a cut to the actor they are doubling], I was very proud of that. I get excited about that. Like when Dickey would jump out the window we didn't cut. When we did the stunt there's no cut. The guy jumped out of the window, we panned over to Wahlberg, we paned back and Christian [Bale] who then got out of the garbage. He was hiding in the garbage the whole time. And with Amy with the high jump. You know I was very excited about that. She knew how to run like that high jumper and then pan over to Mark and then pan back and she's like, "Oh, jeez, that was such a high jump."

And the sex scene is very interesting to me because I've grown, like I'm very familiar with that terribly uncomfortable feeling, and I remember after I did *Flirting with Disaster*, I was watching these people in their underwear all day, and I said I don't want to do that, so I did an army movie where there was no underwear, you know. And I decided it was a drag for me to be watching these people have sex all day. It was like, I'm on the outside looking in, you know. So what I do now is I feel that my comfort makes them more comfortable and gives them permission. Like the best thing Amy Adams said was, "As long as it happens between 'action' and 'cut' I can do anything." And that was a great turn on to any man who's going to have his hands on her. And so that was great for Mark. Mark felt very free then, very good chemistry. I choreographed pieces of that scene in my mind, and with my girlfriend to try things, like what is hot, you know. I wanted that to be hot in the way I thought was cool. I wanted to have heat in this movie and I thought shooting through that door frame in a voyeuristic way, and I wanted her to wear as little clothes as possible and him to wear as little clothes as possible and I liked her having that confident attitude of crawling on that bed and turning around and looking at him over her shoulder. It's kind of nasty, and they're really enjoying it, you know. Then with the sound of the fight. That was the revelation to me. How am I going to put this in there when we're going to keep the sound of the fight that's about to collide with them? You know, this incoming storm is about to hit them. And so, they're uncomfortable. I say it's almost the inverse of they're uncomfortable but if I say to them, "You have to do this because I'm saying it," then they have permission to be nasty. So then they're freer. Because Mark is very shy and he's very particular about his wife and the shock to me that Mark and Christian, they said, "Can't do, can't do sex, and kiss in a scene, because I'm married." I said, "Does your wife know you're not a plumber? You're an actor, you know. Maybe you should tell her you're an actor." They got tough women at home. I don't know how they're going to work it out. With Christian Bale literally we had a big thing about him kissing that girl in that opening montage walking down the street of Lowell and I said, "You got to find some way to kiss the girl. You know Dicky's kissed a lot of girls in that town." And the way he did was he did it blocking his face and it works and technically he can say to his wife, "I never kissed her on the mouth," because you can't see what's going on. And he did the same thing on the couch. He's sitting, he's on top of that Cambodian girl and he comes away with the lipstick and we don't know how so he can say to his wife technically, "I was never really kissing her." Anyway, so when I let them know that I was all comfortable with sexuality and them being sexy and nasty, that made them a little freer and so they felt it wasn't them doing it in a lecherous way. It's me doing it in a lecherous way. And they can blame it on me and so then they're free.

The scene where Dicky was having his whole sweaty meltdown we were swinging the lights to make it seem like time was going by and days were going by and then we ended up not using that. We had a whole complicated thing going on with lights, day light, night light, day light, night light, as he was sweating. We tried to do it practically. I like doing stuff practically.

The thing about anger moments, you know, is that they are terribly embarrassing and they become representative of more than what they are and so that ain't me, you know, and that ain't how I like the set to be. I don't go, "Gee, that's just my crazy Caravaggio creative process, you know, live with it." I look at that and say, "Oh, that was really embarrassing and let's never have that happen ever again." You have to keep a sense of humor. You have to work with people you have a good vibe with. And you have to just have a very positive attitude. You take any of that emotion and sometimes you just have to go and take a minute and breath or be quiet. Mark would always walk by me, because you know things are tight on that schedule and Mark, he's a big prayer. Mark would sometimes just put his hands in prayer and the two of us would just go, "Yeah, yeah." Because you feel a lot of pressure when you're losing the light [when the sun is going down] or there's something you're not going to get and everybody's about to blow a gasket. I just redouble my efforts to keep a positive vibe.

GUS VAN SANT, *MILK*

We had two months, thirty-six days, I think, to shoot.

The kissing and/or sex scenes the actors bought into it from the beginning and so it became like the easier thing because it was already a given. There was one technique I had heard Gary Clark had used on *Another Day in Paradise*, which was to use a prosthetic penis for naked scenes that would free the actor, so that they weren't really embarrassed on the set, so we had these made up for the characters Diego Luna, James Franco, and Sean Penn. They really dug them actually. They kind of wanted to do these scenes because they wanted to have these things on. As far as the penis goes, one came off. That was an accident.

Everything seems to sort of be an accident in general. It's sort of the whole thing, because you're projecting your expectations on the project and yet you're seeing it come together before your eyes. There's always one time on every film where I'm asking the first AD [Assistant Director] usually, "Who are those two girls standing right there?" because they're presenting themselves to you and it says right here in the script, two girls walk in front of the shop and you realize it's right in front of you. It's part of your

Gus Van Sant. Courtesy of Universal Studios Licensing LLC.

story and in fact you've forgotten, because you've focused in on all of these other things that you've forgotten this extra little bit and you have to deal with where they're going to walk in front of the shop, but the whole thing seems to sort of just be an accident right until the very end even.

Our biggest challenges were crowd scenes and it wasn't really the execution of the crowd scenes as much it was where we were going to get the crowds and since we didn't really have the money to afford a crowd, we were going to have to put them in digitally, so we spent a lot of time. One of my answers was to use archival footage of marches and of crowds marching on the streets we were going to shoot on and sort of like use that somehow to alleviate this need to have a lot of people and then we had help from volunteers, people showed up. Like 2,000 people showed up on the day, so all of our planning and our need for archival footage or our digital effects were all of a sudden not necessary because we had actual people. They came in pretty much wardrobe and we had like our 200 extras that would be in front, our own people. I'm sure there are mistakes in the crowd scenes, but it pretty much became not as difficult as we thought and there was a whole issue with the 16mm footage that we wanted to be using. We wanted to shoot in 16mm the whole film and we were persuaded by the delivery department of Universal Pictures to shoot in 35mm and it kind of undid our entire philosophy of how we were shooting. We were using documentary guys, camera operators and I was kind of unaware that just the size of a 35mm camera, even though it's like it's big, still isn't quite what the 16mm guys do. We had to sort of shift our whole idea and it really started with the 16mm archival footage. We got rid of the doc-camera operators and just shifted our whole like philosophy of how we were shooting.

In a church scene where you could see a lot of detail from the ceiling, in this shot we had a lot of imagery above the heads, I think Harris Savides, our DP [cinematographer], I had worked with him long enough, he had framed higher like that before in some of the things we had done before, and this was halfway through the movie when he started to frame like that, which we liked because you could see the ceiling of the church and unfortunately we had sort of discovered this halfway through and we kept doing it, I thought, it was a metaphor for their lives. It was just a framing choice of our DP that I liked, that we liked that we started using and it was just sort of something that you didn't see too often, so it was visual and then it had other ideas behind it, but I guess it wasn't really an accident. It was just his style. It was only applied when Dan [White] and Harvey [Milk] were having their discussions usually.

QUENTIN TARANTINO, *INGLOURIOUS BASTERDS*

The scene with Landa and Shosanna, the strudel scene where they eat the apple strudel, okay that was one of those scenes that you know it was a big scene for me because they've got to have this interior life that we the audience know what they're going for, but it can't be on the surface or else they're going to rust, and so finding actors, actresses with that kind of balance is a special thing, so I got used to very much playing Landa, doing those sequences with the actresses and in the course of doing it a bunch of times I kind of really almost started rewriting the sequence just with how I was doing it and all the different times I got to do it and stuff came up with this whole thing that was different from what was on the page. You know, months later, now I'm shooting the scene in the restaurant with Christoph [Waltz] and that was one of the scenes I never auditioned Christoph on. So we got down to do it and I go, you know, all that shit that I had almost set into stone in the audition process, that's me, that's not Christoph. I've got to throw all that away. That's me playing the role. Now I want it to be Christoph. So I completely decided to go 180 degrees different on the actual day, on the actual moment, and I hadn't talked to Christoph about it and it was literally he's sitting down at the table, there's a strudel there, we're getting ready to shoot the scene and I just like, you know, went up to him. I always talk to them privately and I just said, "Christoph, eat the strudel. Eat the strudel all the time. Just do your scene, talk, you can talk with your mouth full, but just concentrate on that strudel, you eat it and you love every raisin." I actually think that if you're doing a scene like that, a strudel scene kind of thing, if the audience isn't hungry for strudel, you have not done your scene right.

We built that little house in the beginning and I mean the fact that we were making it a western was palpable. From everyone on set. My script supervisor who's worked on every movie I've ever done said, "God Quentin, this is your first western." We felt like we were making a western and the kind of gallows humor of the second chapter where they're torturing the Nazis and stuff you know that's very spaghetti-western kind of cynical humor going on. But then when we got to the third chapter, the French stuff, I wanted that to be like a French movie, play like a French film, but then starting with the fourth chapter, starting with the Mike Myers scene then it's supposed be like a '60s, mid-60s Mirisch company [producers of major American films including *The Great Escape*], bunch of guys on a mission movie. If it had been one of those movies, the Michael Myers scene would be the first scene in the film and so it was just stylistically changing.

The thing about this movie for the first month, most of it was a lot of the big, big acting scenes and so I was getting kind of self-conscious about the fact that I wasn't giving Bob [Richardson the cinematography] enough sexy shit. For a month it was just two shot, over the shoulder, medium close up. You know they were just acting scenes and I actually went to him and said, "Bob, I'm kind of getting self-conscious that I'm just doing acting crap with you," and he said, "No, that's all we needed for these scenes. We got a lot of stuff to do don't worry. We got a lot on our plate, this is just about that and it's not about anything else."

Actually one of the proudest moments of my directing career in the very early days was in my first week of shooting *Pulp Fiction*. It was all the diner stuff, the stuff that begins the movie and ends the movie. That was all the whole first week and I was stuck on one side of the line [the position of the camera to the actors so that when they look at each other the viewer feels they are in the proper relationship to each other], you know, basically shooting the dinner table from this direction and when I figured out on my own how to get to the other side, which was basically just cut to a neutral shot of Amanda Plummer up there and then I can go anywhere I want, I go, "Oh, my God, I figured that out." Because crossing the line was always my Achilles' heel. It's like the thing that was going to make me an amateur and I still don't quite understand the line. I intuitively get it. My script supervisor, that's one of his main jobs, he goes, "Quentin, there's three kinds of ways you can do this: there's the wrong eye line, there's the right eye line and then there's, well, not really the right eye line, but I think you'll get away with it." That's where I live.

The last shot is so specific. The thing about it was it's a replay of another shot that happened minutes earlier in the movie when Eli Roth and Brad [Pitt] are looking down at the Nazis that they carved the swastika in and I was just always seeing Wes Craven's *The Last House on the Left*. There's this famous shot, on the poster of the movie too, of the point of view of the victim looking up, and grinning over her and the trees in the background and it was always kind of in my mind, but when we actually did it the first time in the middle of the movie, when we put the camera down there and they just lean into the camera, it was like, Oh, my God, this is so *The Last House on the Left*. This is so cool. This is so groovy. I wanted to end it that way, use that as a closing image. I just thought that was the payoff.

Jonathan Demme [director of *Silence of the Lambs*] was in this documentary about Roger Corman [famed producer and director of low-budget movies] and he says, put your characters up-close to the camera, get them in the foreground a lot so the audience gets to know who they are, look for interesting background shots. Okay, we'll look at this flower that's a good foreground piece, put that in front. Think about the background there. That could be a nice little flower pot or that curtains could be really nice in the background you know, so look for that whenever you can. Move the camera when you can, so that when there are people talking have them walk and talk, right, so that camera movement stimulates eye retention. And while you direct, sit down, because what's going to happen is you're going to be standing, you're going to be all excited about filmmaking, you're going to be up for eight hours, nine hours standing up and when your legs get tired, you get tired and you crash and this was before monitors. Now everybody sits down way too much, but back then people didn't sit down at all. The advice I didn't take is the advice that he swears by, "What happens in movies is you shoot a shot, you finally get the take you want and it's really good and everyone pats everybody on the back and everybody shakes hands and you have a little party and it's great and then you get around to setting up the next shot." Okay, well that's just ten minutes pissed away on just like patting yourself on the back, well that turns out to be like an hour and a half or two hours at the end of the day, so no matter what happens, when the take is over and you've got it, "moving on" [an expression used to get everyone on set to the next shot].

Part of the process of working is when I'm done making a movie, it just goes all out of my head. Boom. I don't remember any lens size, I don't remember nothing. It's just erased and then I remember it as I go into the next pre-production and I remember how to work.

TOM HOOPER, *THE KING'S SPEECH*

When I directed *John Adams*, I worked the American system for the first time and it's utterly startling to have a day where you begin on Monday at 6 am and by Friday you're starting maybe at 2 pm and you're ending at 2 am. And the truth is in that system by the half of the week you're just exhausted by the time you get home. Whereas in the English system you work eight till seven every day and it never slips. It's nice having the evening. The major battle of every shooting day is letting go of the pain of the day. Because I become very obsessional about certain things I want to capture. And almost invariably you go home in the car feeling like you didn't catch the one thing you wanted to achieve and it's taken me years to learn to let go of that quickly.

I don't watch rushes [what was shot the day before] and the reason is that all I do if I watch the rushes is relive everything I felt at the time I was doing it. So everything I didn't like when I was shooting I still don't like. And everything I liked I still like. And to relive that pain I find very not helpful. So I go in and watch the cut [edited version, which with digital editing machines can be done faster than it used to be] of the previous day and I find that most helpful. I would say in terms of my prep it's almost all physical, logistical. I want to see every single prop in advance. I want to see every costume in advance. I want to see any piece of gear that's unusual, I want to know it's there. I want to see every extra that's going to be on set. So I want to know going into tomorrow that there's not a single thing that arrives on set that I haven't approved or that I haven't seen or haven't just checked hasn't been fucked up. And that's more important to me in the end than thinking about how I'm going to shoot the next day. The very first film I made I was thirteen years old. It was called *Runaway Dog* and I storyboarded [sketches of what each shot might look like] the entire thing. And I shot the entire storyboard and what was my shooting ratio? 1.5 to 1. So I shot four minutes for a three-minute movie. I've never done that again.

And certainly when I started working professionally I always used to plan, but actually I've come to love the process of not planning everything. You know, I normally do have a feeling of how I'd like to shoot it or a pre-conceived idea, but I find with the level of actors I've been working with, it is much more exciting actually to go with a blank slate and hear what their thoughts are and to create in the moment of the day. And in the end when I used to pre-plan, shooting days became a little executional. It became about just doing the plan and matching the plan. And I think the change for me was my collaboration with Helen Mirren. We worked twice and you know if you work with Helen Mirren and you say, "Okay, Helen, actually you got to stand by that window. On this line you got to cross and then you got to turn." She'll give you one of those looks. And you realize that's not going to necessarily happen. And then you actually start to listen and you realize that someone like Helen is a complete asset to you, because she has a filter about everything she does and if you pay attention to that in terms of blocking ideas and in terms of staging ideas, in terms of what other people are doing in the scene, there's so much you can learn. So now I enjoy the freedom of each day creating in the moment and, therefore, I start each day with quite long rehearsals. I mean, even on *The King's Speech*, sometimes I'd rehearse up to three hours before I'd start shooting. And I don't mind compromising shooting time to get the rehearsal time. I'd rather spend the time rehearsing.

With Colin's stammer, it's different slightly every time because he did it in a very, very physical way and he accessed it in a very physical way. I mean, towards the end of the shoot he had pains on his left side and numbness because if you do that kind of block it involves a lot of muscles and so it's not something that just repeats itself from take to take.

Once I walked into the space that was to be Logue's room, I put my line producer up against the wall and I started going in on a wide lens and I started putting him in an odd corner of the frame and if you look at my location photos from the same day, that was when I decided how I wanted to shoot it, so the idea of shooting wider and closer came as a response to the location. And I think the more I work the more I enjoy that process of having a film in your head and then discovering that your film becomes something different when you go out into the world.

The key day for me on *The King's Speech* was the first day. I chose to shoot the scene that was a ten-minute scene in a ten-hour day because the budget was a little small. But the reason I chose to shoot the scene was I wanted the nerves of the first day to percolate into the nerves of those two men meeting. And you don't have nerves on a film set very long. They're normally gone by the third day. And I also had this idea that I wanted to start not on a wide shot, but on a close up of Colin. And I was also shooting on a wide lens so the camera was probably eighteen inches from his face and so Colin was facing on first day, the first set up, a ten-minute close-up. My theory was: That is what stammering is like, having the ultimate performance anxiety. It was like being under so much incredible pressure, and so I designed everything on that first day to put him under more pressure than he would normally be as an actor. You know he wasn't walking down the street and even the choice of having the camera that close and shooting wide was partly visually so I would have more of the wall and more of his relationship of his face to that strange wall, but it was also so that he would feel incredibly vulnerable and exposed and I think it worked, and Colin said later that it was incredibly helpful to be thrown in the deep end in that way, because I thought there was a psychological link. And I think it's fascinating about how you get a performance and how the placement of the camera reflects the psychology of an actor.

So, by shooting that close in the case of Colin, it helped him feel hunted and over-whelmed and scrutinized and exposed and then when I came round to Geoffrey [Rush] and also shot that way, Geoffrey said to me it immediately made him understand that I wanted an incredibly minimalistic performance, because if the camera was that close and locked, then he knew he had to bring everything down. Now the irony is we all know you could be twelve feet away and just as tight [by using a long lens rather than a wide one]. It's not the camera being close that makes it close, but what fascinates me is the psychology of that decision in terms of the actor. And you know those decisions, when an actor walks on the set, even there's things about the art direction and place-ment of the camera, they all give people clues about what's important. And then the other thing that happened the first day was just working on body language. Geoffrey's brilliant on his body language, he was trained at Lecoq, which is the famous mime school in Paris. Geoffrey uses his whole body and anyone who saw *Exit the King* on Broadway will see how brilliant his body is. And so when you have one actor in this two hander [two actors working together in a scene] who is so aware of the silhouette that his body makes, I became interested in pushing Colin to think about the way he used his body and the whole way he sits on that sofa, the way he uses the corner of the chair as his defense mechanism and he collapses into the corner of the chair and he sits small rather than tall. And breaking down the way that Colin actually stands, he's a big strap-ping lad of six foot three. You know all those things are happening and I think what's so interesting about first days is often you effectively set up so much of the movie and that first scene I felt became emblematic of so many of the choices that would follow.

Tom Hooper with Geoffrey Rush and Colin Firth on the set of *The King's Speech*. Courtesy of The Wein-stein Company LLC. All Rights Reserved.

I've never lost my temper ever apart from once when I did it strategically. I did it because I wanted more time and I decided to get angry because you know it's 7:00 and I need five more minutes and the first AD [Assistant Director] or the producer is saying I can't have it and I decided to get angry to win that moment. But you can't do that very often. I think possibly the people who work with me are more cut up by my disappointment, rather than my anger. I mean, if a key prop is not there and suddenly you can't shoot or if a key aspect of organization hasn't happened, because I care so much about the work that these kinds of things just feel like ridiculous tragedies to me. But, I don't get angry; I just get incredibly pained. I think it helps to work with people more than once. I mean, Danny Cohen [the cinematographer], I've worked with three times and the long-term collaborators forgive you some of these emotional patterns, or they put it in context and they know that you're not always like that. But I think it's also possible to keep your sense of humor. I always like working with a producer who is very funny.

We shot the Empire Exhibition with the same two thousand dummies that had been my crowd a year before. It was a trick I got from Ron Howard that one of the best ways of handling crowds when you have absolutely no money at all is to use inflatable dummies and you mix in one human being for every nine dummies so there's a little bit of movement. And you know you put a hat on them and some kind of dark top and it's fantastic because you don't have to feed them. You don't have to transport them. And I don't believe they get paid.

ANG LEE, *BROKEBACK MOUNTAIN*

I had to shoot even though physically I don't think I was prepared for it with sheep, weather, and mountains mainly, but we had to shoot at end of May waiting for the snow. Just schlep around and try to get sheep this way, 1,000 of them this way and that way. They're not the smartest animal. It's always raining.

If I compare making movies to cooking, I think that's where cooking happens for me, and shooting is just buying groceries. Of course, the most exciting part is shooting. Months of thinking, years of preparation, all the elements have come to one spot, and it's happening, it's fresh. You talk about accidents, happy or unhappy accidents, and I think you should set up in such a way you're covered. So I was mostly thinking about coverage [various individual shots of actors in the scene that will be edited together to comprise the scene]. The more fresh you get this grocery, the better the chance you will cook a good meal. So it's more like cover this way, that way, and one of this, one of that. That's what I was thinking. And full of potentials. I think you can't set up a way a director directs in such a way that freshness might happen, because that's something you cannot plan. You just set it up so you allow it to happen.

What I was shooting, the more movies I make, sometimes you get a feeling it might end up on the editing floor, but painfully I still have to go through it, and usually they are the most difficult scenes to shoot. It's very strange. Like I spent a couple days on this hippie scene, like these two cowboys in the mountain hideout and they're running to a guy and two hippie girls and they offer to share bread and share sex and everything, and this guy has no interest, a true western hero. It's a pretty funny scene. Just won't fit in. And I have to do a very small montage [an editing technique] to get over that time phase quite painfully.

Sex scenes are difficult for me. I'm a shy person, so this is uncomfortable. Usually in the rehearsing time, inevitably you talk a lot, intellectualize it. What's the dramatic purpose, how that fits in their overall character development, what is this scene doing, the elements of psychology, this and that. You just go on and on, now. You go at length so you don't have to like having them touch each other, just avoid that moment. I think the uncomfortableness needs to be dealt with first, so usually I will design some shots. On the sex scenes, it's technically incredibly difficult. If they screw up, they have to apologize. Technically, the tent scene, was a one-take thing. They had to carry the whole scene. The momentum of this or that when you're struggling, and have to recapture it is technically quite difficult and then I want spontaneity. So I distract them from embarrassment, and it's very easy to screw up technically, and they would apologize, like, "Oh, I didn't do well, so I say we do it again." So after you do a few of those, you're into business. I think in the beginning for shy people, they just want to get it over with after the first day, whatever it is, but once they get on with it, technically you're there and they even get to the perverse. Now, let's do this, do that, and you can get into the details. Then they forgot about their discomfort being watched, and that's the way I deal with it. The first six takes maybe just rehearsals. So that's the way I dealt with that because I think if you rehearse it, you lose the freshness. I mean, the fear factor, the uncomfortable, you can use that. You can divert it as a plus energy. The only way they can get out of embarrassment, for example, the gay lovemaking scenes, is it has to be like really good to be recognized as a good performance. And there's the last barrier I think you need to break through. Sex scenes remind me of those news reports back when somebody gets captured, and they speak, "The Taliban are treating me really well." But somehow the eyes tell you, "It's not really me. I'm doing a performance. I'm supposed to do this. Save me." I think actors have this kind of a thing. Either they do awkward stuff or they do something extremely beautiful. They could be exposing themselves, but still not open to privacy, which I think is the hardest thing to get into lovemaking scenes. You want to see private feelings that they're willing to give. How they externalize the internal feeling, that's blocking. Through blocking, then you see it and you can work on it. "Push this way, turn him around this way, go down there, and pull down his pants." I think that's technically among the hardest thing to acting. So I guess sometimes I try to help them by not helping them and put them in awkward position and get over with it then. Then you're getting to the detail and perverse part, and somehow, hopefully, one or two takes, they show you their private feeling they're beside themselves. If you get one of those takes, I think that's a gem. I didn't really get into detail until quite a few takes into it because you want them to pour into it. It's not like I can do it for them. You have to let them get used it. It takes a little bit. Sometime maybe the first take is perfect, but your cameraman misses it or whatever. After three, seven takes, all the technical side's good. By then, they're tired. You lose the freshness then. It's like doing action scenes. The sequence where the wife spots them kissing, it was quite dramatic because that was the first kissing scene we did. We blocked everything privately so nobody sees them kissing, then shot two handheld single camera angles. They felt very brave but they were exhausted after six, or seven takes on each side. Then we do her point of view. And then we turned around [meaning the camera is turned in a new direction] to shoot the wife. And Michelle was going out at that time with Heath [Ledger], and when we turned the camera, I used two cameras, on her. She could hardly see them because there was a small doorway, and the guys just kind of hung on each other like that for her and she said, "You guys got to do it for me." So the guys start sort of whatever, and she got really angry and yelled at them. "Come on, guys, I need it." And then we got that expression of hers, because they had to like really go at each other for her to see and react.

JAMES CAMERON, *AVATAR*

Because I like to shoot, operate myself, I'm right there with the actors while we're doing the scene and because we're shooting in HD, we don't cut and I think the more that you can keep the pit crew back, because to me that breaks everything. The second you say cut, you know, all the energy, all the magic kind of leaves the room. You have to then recreate it, so I like to stay in and I'll usually say to the actors, "Why don't we just do the whole scene three times in a row without stopping," and they love, for the most part, unless we get to the end of the day and it's a long scene. Probably by then we're in pick-ups, anyway, but the kind of actors that I like to work with, you know Sam [Worthington] and Zoë [Saldana] and Sigourney [Weaver] were all pretty much the same, which is they build on what they've just done. They'll lock up a bit of it and know what to do and from that they'll push a little further maybe on a certain beat. They can refine it. You just stay in the moment and I'm keyed up you know because now I know when they're going to make their move, the operating is better. It's not just about getting the performance. It's about getting the shot. The performance is useless if it's out of focus or if it happens off camera or if you're panned off to the other person when the magic's happening over here, so it's about creating that dance.

You know actually the performance capture [a computer process transforming what is photographed into whatever creatures are being created] stuff is the easiest. The shooting part of it is harder because you've got to do two things simultaneously. You've got to get that actor to the point of perfection or brilliance, because brilliance doesn't have to be perfect, and you've got to get it on film or on tape if it's HD and it's got to be lit nicely as well and those are two kind of separate problems. One requires a lot of iteration to get right and the other one sometimes needs a certain spontaneity, so the question is how do you keep it fresh when you're on take four, because you know the focus wasn't right or the light wasn't right and so on, which is why I don't like to over-rehearse, because you need to keep every scene a process of discovery, of working toward an idea and when an actor just does something on take three that's exciting. I'll come in either without cutting and say, "That's really cool, let's go down that path, let's go further that direction, right now. Boom. Just back up four lines, just go," and that's why I like to find out if that give-and-take is possible with the actors before the fact. The funny thing is everybody thinks this motion capture is an anti-acting process when it's actually quite the opposite. I've taken away the lighting, I've taken away the dolly track, I've taken away the makeup, hair

James Cameron with Zoë Saldana on the set of *Avatar*. AVATAR ©2009 Twentieth Century Fox. All Rights Reserved.

and wardrobe. I've taken away getting it in focus, I've taken away all of the artifice of photography and of blocking all the background action and the cars moving and whatever it is you want happening in that frame behind you and the actors. That all gets put in later, so now you're focusing just on the core of the scene. As a director, I'm 100 percent focused just on performance and the actors don't have to worry about having to go again, because it wasn't in focus or because somebody blew something in the background you see what I mean. All that stuff, it's all uncoupled, so now you're in a pure performance mode and that's why I say it's the easiest.

When Neytiri is confronting Jake Sully is a really crucial scene and interestingly it was actually done in four takes and the best take was take three, but I used a little bit of take four editorially. The first two takes were basically the rehearsals and they were so in character by that point about halfway through the performance capture part of the shoot. They were just so in character with just a couple of small adjustments, but it was really just them being their characters and everybody was there. We were able to capture up to twelve people at the moment, so we had the mom and the dad and all the others and the Tsu'tey, the adversary warrior, they were all there you know so they had the eyes upon them and Sigourney [Weaver] was there. So you know that was actually a pretty amazing thing. I mean some scenes you struggle with. Some scenes just appear magically. The trick is to know when it is the magic and when the accidents are wonderful, if there are accidents, and Zoë just kind of went off and she stayed totally in character and totally in accent and everything.

There was a scene where we had Sam Worthington's head in the matte box of the camera. It's when he does the video logs and he's just kind of talking to the lens because the camera has a beam splitter, it actually has a kind of large matte box and to get him feeling like he was talking right in the camera he was actually in the matte box of the camera and he couldn't see anything, and he was in an interior space just kind of rambling anyway and I was like a foot and a half away operating the camera. He didn't want to talk to the crew and he had these kind of long rambles and he literally wanted to do the whole thing that was bits of voice-over that would appear over a twenty-page sequence. He wanted to do it all together. We just wanted to go non-stop. We'd go for twenty minutes, you know, and he'd go up on the line [miss a line in the script] and I'd just talk to him while he was working and he'd get himself worked to a place that felt real to him and then I'd just give him the line and he'd say the line. Sometimes he was struggling with the accent because he was trying to be very real and not get hung up on the words. Then the accent would start to go Aussie and I'd say, "Okay, you just went Aussie," and he'd say, "All right, give me the line" and I'd give him the line and it was a very intimate thing and I find that more thrilling than, you know, blowing up a building, although that's fun too.

Here's the thing about directing, I think, it's like those two things are not mutually exclusive and doing the most technical shot in the world is not mutually exclusive of understanding and enjoying the process of the simplest moment in which the camera is really not really intrusive and I try to make the camera nonintrusive to the actors. I try to make it not, "Okay we're going again because we have to hit this mark to get this effect," and sometimes there's a bit of a tap dance there. I may know I'm going again for a largely technical reason, but I always know there can be something cool that the actors haven't explored yet, so I'll just throw them something new to try.

Directing is about learning and I go after films that are going to teach me something. So after I finished *Titanic*, I did six deep-ocean expeditions. I was dealing with scientists, space scientists, and oceanographers. I was seeing shit outside the viewport that not only had I never seen before, but nobody had seen before and I was having a blast. For me to come back to filmmaking, it had to be that fun and challenging and I had to learn, so I set myself a project that I knew I was going to learn a whole lot. So for about the first year I was standing around after twenty-five years as a director when you're supposed to have all the answers. You're supposed to have all of the answers all the time. That's your job. And I was standing on a set saying, "I don't know what the fuck we're doing," but you know what, nobody else did either and we were making it up, and that was cool.

KATHRYN BIGELOW, *THE HURT LOCKER*

We would never arrive and have no idea what we were doing. It was either pre-blocked the day before or we would have gone through all the locations with the DP [cinematographer], with the crew, and with the cast and we'd know exactly where everybody's going to be positioned and so all four cameras are positioned based on that pre-blocking sequencing and then I know where all the cameras are and then during the shoot I'm with a camera, but I'll move from camera to camera and also I move the cameras like every two to three takes, so that the actor is never anticipating a camera, not playing up to the close-up or not playing to a particular camera. They're absolutely in the zone. They're covering James [played by Jeremy Renner] with a car bomb, whatever it is they're doing, or from the roof looking down, so geography is really, really critical, but I find that in the storyboards, I have that logistical kind of framework storyboards, and then I adjust it to the shooting, I mean to the actual location, but the other thing that was interesting in this piece was I wanted to feel very spontaneous as if it was unfolding in real time, so my cameraman Barry Ackroyd would not look at the rehearsal, he would not look at my pre-blocking, he wanted to discover it for the first take. The second take he obviously knew where people were going. I mean he had a rough, rough sense. Obviously you read the script, you read the scene, you know the protocol, but those adjustments or slight snap zooms, it's almost like you're shooting a cheetah in the wild. In other words, you don't know where that animal's going to go, but you shoot it nonetheless, so it's that kind of photography. There's an honesty to it and I think that worked for us. I mean I would just kind of jump from camera to camera and probably log ten, twenty miles in any given day.

I staged with the actors and obviously with pyrotechnics because that's a cheat in camera. There's nothing done after the fact, so I had to be very careful with the blast blowing in a way that the character, the military doctor played by Christian Camargo was walking, so he could not be in any way impacted by the explosion. You can't get Fuller's Earth [a powdery substance that looks like explosions, but is not dangerous] in the Middle East. You get marble dust, so he would be hit by marble dust. There's a logic to the sequence. They're in the Humvee. But you're not going to be in the Humvee and you're going to be outside the Humvee close to the door of the character you're following, so you know there is a certain rationale, but from the point on, it is finding it through the dust and the haze of the marble dust. Finding it with other cameras. My fourth camera, I always put him in a vantage point of capturing stuff so we get that sense of the observed, the observational position, so in editorial I can move back and forth between the micro you know like a face or an eye, a hand on a gun, and then macro, so you could go in to that fourth-floor window. What was great about that cameraman was not only does he have a great eye, but he spoke Arabic.

I would walk the actors through all of the movements and their choreography, this is down range, this is up range, but I was very careful not to burn them out on performance. I really wanted that to feel very like a taxi is suddenly driving into your bomb disarmament containment area. You know I wanted that surprise. I wanted to actually feel very, very genuine and they were frightened. I would shoot these scenes in their entirety from up range to down range, twenty minutes long. You know we would shoot them and we would go through the entire movement from up to down and then we would do it all again and change all my camera positions and do it all again. Obviously you know after three or four takes they know what they're doing, but at the same time those probably predominantly in the movie are those original one, two, or three takes where there's a sense of surprise and suspense.

We walked everybody through all the movements of the piece and then looked at it, keeping it very pragmatic. The great, great, great benefit of this film was shooting it in chronology, so they had just literally come from that sniper sequence the week before and they were now in the barracks and so you knew they could bring so much to it.

Kathryn Bigelow with Screenwriter/Producer Mark Boal, Actor Christopher Sayegh, and Script Supervisor Aslaug Konradsdottir on location, *The Hurt Locker*. Courtesy of Summit Entertainment, LLC.

I made sure everyone was comfortable in any particular sequence and at the same time, you know, I gave them, not the kind of freedom for improvisation, I don't mean it that way, but where they could own it, where they could absolutely make it theirs.

We chose not to use subtitles because the soldiers are not given any language skills whatsoever. They would never have known what others were saying, since the whole piece takes place through the soldier's perspective.

With our Iraqi actors, I would then go through this lovely man and ask him to tell them either dial it up or dial it down.

As we shot chronologically, that scene with the man chained to the bomb comes at the end of the movie and I think people were also exhausted, but it was a very emotional scene and I remember at the end of the day I'd said, "Wrap," you know, "cut, done, we're done," and nobody moved and they had tears in their eyes. I mean the actor elicited so much emotion, just raw, innate emotion, that was kind of inescapable, and also in that scene I think we all saw sort of an allegory for Iraq at the same time. Here you have this innocent man who is strapped with these bombs against his will, just like the country.

DAVID FINCHER, *THE CURIOUS CASE OF BENJAMIN BUTTON*

We pretty much pre-produced the movie within an inch of its life.

With the makeup, we did it literally in six weeks. In the morning they would have rubber glued on their faces. In the afternoon, we would meet with Eric [Roth the screenwriter] and talk through stuff with rubber still on their faces. They would play with it and we would give them mirrors and they would go into the other room and take a look at what it is and then we'd tear it off, put something else on and then we'd go in and shoot tests. No one could have prepared us for this, though. Brad [Pitt], I mean, at one point, had close to eight or nine weeks where I think he had a six-hour turnaround [time from finishing work one day and starting the next]. He was hammered shit for awhile, he was destroyed.

I always find that the irony of this work is that the things you plan for weeks and weeks and weeks go off like clockwork and the stuff that you take for granted is always the stuff that makes you want to take your own life. The World War I stuff was easy, the train station went off like just checking shots off a list and then you get to two people in a diner saying, "I want to have this baby" and you go, "Err . . . oh, God how are we going to fix this?" We shot it against a blue screen and we shot the exterior in the French corridor and then we'd come back to LA and we built the thing, but it was hard to get. It was one of those things that you just took for granted because the writing was so lovely and then to have to actually find that thing where she can say, "I really want this and I want this in spite of you," and for that to work.

I will pre-viz [a pre-visualized video sketch of scenes] if you let me, but at a certain point it doesn't make sense. I've worked it all out with "wooden Indians" and brought the actors in and said, here's a videotape, here's what you'll be doing tomorrow and then had them go, "Agh." But on this movie, so much of it was on location, and it was a very simple style . . . It was so staid and I think we only laid track [for dolly shots] maybe five or six times and maybe had five crane shots total in the movie. It's a very simple movie.

In the beginning, we had references to other films, like the shadow on the wall. A little *Third Man* [classic movie directed by Carol Reed in 1949] there. I just liked the idea of this guy running and trying to visually single him out. We actually set up a 20K [large movie lamp] and made the light as small as it could be to cast this deep a shadow. Then we had another guy off-camera running and we had to match the two runs, but I just liked the idea of this baby screaming as you see this guy cut out from the rest of the crowd, just an enormous shadow on the wall.

The lightning sequence was designed around the notion that it was the kind of footage you might find in the Library of Congress which is really early turn of the century material and it was all transferred to paper and then re-photographed off paper, so we shot this footage out on a farm in Louisiana and we went out there for one day and we just shot ridiculous stuff with the guy who had like flash paper in his armpits and a little battery and he would just walk over and 'poof' and he'd fall over and we'd go, "Great, we're done," and on to the next one. The poor dog was so schized-out at the end of the day, he wouldn't go near anybody, but we shot all that stuff and we got back and we step-printed it and then we took all the images and xeroxed them and re-photographed them with a digital camera and took those files and played them back.

We tried to do all the head replacement stuff in wide shots as much as possible. It was that kind of old-fashioned "make it as wide as you can and never go to big close ups. We can't afford this." Those are the moments in the movie where you might think, "He looks a little odd," but if we stayed two Ts, [a medium shot] we were okay.

We had three cameras; a production 4-4-4, HD camera which is your high color bandwidth and then you have your HD 4-2-2 cameras that would record where the actor's head was in space so we could erase where that head was, based on all the markers, but we knew exactly where the face needed to be. We needed the performance of the person on-set to be looking in the right place, but he didn't have to say the lines in the same place and then we'd take his head off and Brad would look at a monitor and just respond. We had five or six cameras on the facial capture set. I paid attention to two. The others were witness cams. I like to be next to my 23-inch HD monitor seeing everything, so sometimes when we were shooting in Louisiana we used a Mo-Sys head [where the pan/tilt is remotely controlled] so there'd be the dolly grip and the focus puller all in the room with the actors and everyone else is down the hall, but I actually like being out of the room. I mean I think if it's something we're shooting in close-up I like to stand next to the camera and see what it's seeing, but when you're talking about HD [high definition digital] and workflow-wise, you can play what you shoot back as many times as you want and you can see focus and you are never surprised.

As much as you can test makeup and wigs and wardrobe and all that stuff when we finally got to the Murmansk Hotel and we saw Brad Pitt and we had all the snow machines going on and he came in, you were finally able to say: "Ah, that's what he's going to look like." It is kind of a happy accident when it all comes together and because that was the first time we actually had Brad in the movie—it was interesting. The first time you see him in the movie and the first time Brad's on set is in the boat where it's snowing and Jared Harris says, "Either I drink too much or you've gotten bigger" and he says, "Well, you do drink a lot."

You don't realize how frail someone is when they're eighty. You don't realize what a ten-hour shoot day is for an eighty-year-old. There were days when we had people who were trying so hard, but they would be dressed in wool period clothing and you know sometimes Louisiana can be hot and they would just faint. You would be like, "What happened to the guy that was standing . . . oh, good heavens."

We were shooting til three one night and we had put these tape marks on the floor. This older woman never gets to her mark [where an actor is to stand for a particular shot]. She'd always be blocked by Taraji [who plays Queenie] and Taraji was such a trooper. But she was exhausted and we had the radio-controlled baby going, "Weeee." It's just absurd and then we have this eighty-four-year-old woman who has to hit this mark and I can be a stickler about that stuff and so take forty [the number of times the shot was redone] she's asking, "What do you want?" I said, "I want you to hit the mark." "I've been on that mark every time," and I said, "Come here, I have a high def monitor to show you," and there she was like half of her and a piece of her ear and she was like, "Okay, I'll do one more." I said, "Okay, thank you very much." We ended up having people out of frame just drop sandbags on her feet. Boom. "You're now on your mark."

We reshot the first scene that we then cut from the movie. We reshot when they meet on the lawn. We shot that three times.

DAVID FINCHER, *THE SOCIAL NETWORK*

The first scene in *Social Network* with Mark and Erica, we knew we wanted to set this day three or day four of the shoot. We wanted to say to everyone "Here's Sorkinese [Aaron Sorkin, the writer]. Here's what it is." They're both very photogenic young people and so we could do the over-the-shoulders [cameras set up over one character shoulder looking at the other one] simultaneously and we knew that we were going to have nice light for this. So we parked two cameras over their shoulders, and shot sixty takes, one right after the other, faster, overlapping, cutting each other off. You want to be able to get this pace where they can finish each other's thoughts or try to digress and go back to whatever they were just trying to formulate.

You have the sword and an anvil and a piano hanging over your head so you're scrambling, you're treading water as fast as you can and a lot of times you're saying something that doesn't make any sense, and luckily they're agreeing with you. I have ideas for every conceivable way that something could be said and how it should be grouped together, though sometimes when you're directing people, if you need them to be more natural at the beginning, and you want a nine page scene in under five minutes, part of it is the direction—as irritating as it may be, is: "Great, now faster." I shoot a lot of takes. I don't know if you've heard that, but I'm not doing it to antagonize people. I'm doing it to let them know that we have the time for the happy accident to take place, for it to be incrementally better. Because they're skilled, there's muscle memory and then there's also when you respond to something that you've said twenty times, you know how to say it, it's water off the back of a duck. And so you're trying to kind of create that environment where they can just, you know, fall off the truck in the right way.

The scenes in the Facebook office where Eduardo learns he's been left out of the deal, I wanted to be as private as an attorney could make something that was this public, so I wanted it to take place in a fishbowl. I wanted it to be a conversation that's happening way over there. And I wanted Andrew [Garfield] to be able to see Jesse [Eisenberg] and to be able to have some time in which to go, "Oh!" To have him recall the last three years, mull them over. I also knew that I wanted to have Justin [Timberlake] be one of the people who knew that this was coming down or have a sense that this was IT. So I knew I wanted him in proximity. But you know most of it is we had this great conference room in this place with all these light bulbs and I was like, "That's kind of a great place to take somebody quietly aside—into the brightest room in the whole place." And you can't not see those guys talking back there, even when they're not moving, so I could have Jesse typing away in the foreground and see all that silent drama happening. And then I knew that I wanted to do this long tracking shot which gave him a chance to stalk Mark, and you want to be able to say, "Let's build to it." Andrew, he's a thoroughbred. You know he's built to deliver this stuff. And it was very exhausting for him. He was absolutely shaking. I know it was weird because they were very uptight with each other that whole day. It was nice. They'd done their homework.

I try as much as is possible to bottle rage and bottle bile. You're under a lot of stress and you're under a lot of pressure—not the least of which is that you want *so much* to give everybody who's in front of the camera support. You want to create a world where they can lose themselves and be somebody else. I've had a couple of contentious relationships with actors and a couple of crew people. I just don't understand their thought process and get frustrated and I've behaved badly—But as long as I feel you're working toward something and you can be honest about frustration and disappointment and also be honest about stuff that's a contribution where you go, "I wish I'd thought of that. Awesome." You just want move this thing another twenty yards down the field. It's not just about the ability to smite. I mean, you want big things for *everybody involved*. You want everybody to do their best work, so it becomes debilitating when something gets in the way of that.

DAVID FINCHER, *THE GIRL WITH THE DRAGON TATTOO*

The last shot, it was actually simple, very simple to shoot. We shot it in one night but the biggest problem was motorcycles on cobblestones on hills like this that were wet, even the stunt girl had a couple of face plants that night. It didn't occur to me. I was like, wow, this location is so beautiful and these cobblestones are so amazing, and when they're all shiny and slicked down, they're so photogenic and then you see somebody going sideways down the hill on a motorcycle and, "Oh, this could take a while." I didn't have to ride the motorcycle, so it was fun. We just lined it up and shot. It's Lisbeth's moment, it's what she sees. There's no reason to see what the other two are going through. You want to see how she interprets it and why she interprets it the way that she interprets it. So you have to see it inside her shoes, so it was fairly simple. The biggest problem was trying to get the idea of this jacket. It's one of those things where you say, "Oh, yeah, and then she has the jacket on the back of the motorcycle. That's easy." And then, of course, they fold it up and all of a sudden, it looks like a tennis racket and people're saying, "Was she going to play tennis with him?" that's a terrible ending. Why would she go to play? It's night time. The veil between you and intention is always there, always complicated. As soon as you take the camera out of the box, everybody starts asking, "Why does she have a tennis racket?"

The rape scenes are scenes that aren't fun. Those are scenes where we shot for two days. We talked about it a lot. Obviously, Rooney [Mara] knew what she was going to have to go through to be in the movie and you try to muster as much human dignity as you can in a scene that we're photographing people being relentlessly inhuman to one another and so that was tricky. You block through the whole thing very, very rigorously. This is going to happen, and then this is going to happen, and the panties have to tear away, so those have to be pre-scored [prepared to rip] and this has to happen. Then he has to pull her shirt over her head, so we have to make sure that the shirts have to be ready. So you walk through all that stuff, but there were things that we had never talked about. I never knew what her scream was going to sound like and I said, "Are you working on your scream?" And she was like, "Yeah, my scream," and when we heard it, it was like a child's and, of course, that's the incredibly powerful thing about it.

David Fincher. Courtesy of David Fincher.

I was watching over the camera and you could just see the hair on the back of the first assistant's neck stand up when she screamed and everybody on the set immediately was in a bad mood. Everybody was like, "The coffee sucks," and you're thinking "it might be something else. You might be upset about something else." We shot fourteen or fifteen takes of the master from the back on like a 21-millimeter lens [a wide angle lens] and then over the backpack that she brings in, and we had all that stuff marked out where it was going to be and we shot just how his pants were going to drop and how he was going to sort of "Liberace" his robe and all. We're talking through the whole thing. And we got to the last take and I walked up to them and I said, "Yorick [Yorick van Wageningen], go ahead and get ready, and Roon, you guys: I have what I need, so let's do one more and just have fun with it." That was the take I used.

I think that there's a kind of focus that the actors have in the back of their eyes and I think that when you can erase that, when you can husk that like corn, or you can just tear away at that thing, so that you're just left with them, they know exactly what it is that's going to happen and they can concentrate just on how they want to time their response. I'm more comfortable with the idea of, we've done it, we've done it. We've committed it to sense memory. You know exactly when he grabs this article of clothing and twists it. I can show you the takes and you look at them and you go, to me, take twelve looks better than take eight because it just feels to me like it's happening and that can happen faster. The more they do it, the quicker it can become. Not to say that there shouldn't be a high percentage, double-digit percentage points of awkwardness about any time somebody sexually assaults somebody, but it was the ballet of it, of knowing where somebody was going to be and how they were going to work together. We didn't shoot fifty takes. We shot twelve, fifteen, something like that. We shot with three cameras: a RED [a high-end digital camera] production camera with a fisheye [very wide angle lens]; we shot with an actual little spy camera, and we shot with one of those little disposable HD cameras. So we tried a bunch of different stuff and the stuff that ended up looking the most real was actually the real security camera. It just felt crappier. And then probably at the end, because there was one piece that we had to match, we had to use one of the pieces of the RED footage and we just stepped all over it [film slang for degrading the image] and made it look like the crappy camera. You just look at it and "Wow, that looks awful and I hope we can make the point that we need to make." You don't want to lose the forest for the trees. You don't want to suddenly ask "Who are those people?" When she puts it up on the television, you have to know, "Oh my God, that was there the whole time? She was aware of this?" And you want to be able to see it.

Oh, and though I don't believe in wearing fur, if you're in Sweden in the middle of the night in the winter, you might want to think about it. Maybe you buy a used fur coat.

ETHAN AND JOEL COEN, *NO COUNTRY FOR OLD MEN*

ETHAN: The first images are of Texas. We weren't there. Actually, it was Roger Deakins [the cinematographer]. It was a second unit thing [material that is photographed separate from the principle actors and director] that was shot before we even started shooting the movie. Although we scouted and went to a bunch of places with Roger, he went back with his assistant and shot a lot of dawn and dusk stuff before we started principal photography.

JOEL: We found the spots where we wanted to shoot for those images and then Roger went out, but we didn't want to wake up that early in the morning. But the sense of place was so fundamental to the story, to Cormac McCarthy's novel that it was logical to sort of establish that in a simple way at the beginning of the story and the other part of it was sort of this idea that the character that Javier [Bardem] plays might feel like *The Man Who Fell to Earth* [Nicolas Roeg's 1976 movie], that he comes out of the landscape. You don't know where he comes from, what he's doing out there in the middle of the highway being arrested. All that was sort of what we were after, that he just comes out of the landscape.

ETHAN: And we also wanted to withhold him to a certain extent when we see him at first; we don't see much of him. We pretty much just see his hair, which is pretty much what it's all about.

JOEL: We didn't want to see his face until the strangling. In the fight, they were making a lot of scuffmarks on the floor so we looked at them and went, "Well, that's great." The only problem was the continuity problem obviously because the scuffmarks were there from the beginning and we kept shooting. Other angles that were supposed to be the

Ethan and Joel Coen on the set of *No Country for Old Men*. NO COUNTRY FOR OLD MEN ©2007 by MIRAMAX FIRM CORP. and PARAMOUNT VANTAGE, A Division of Paramount Pictures Corporation. All Rights Reserved.

beginning of the fight, we attempted to clean them up for about five minutes and then said, "Aw fuck it, we'll do it in the computer."

The end is just word for word Tommy's [Lee Jones] saying what's in the end of the novel. We actually weren't sure when we were shooting the movie exactly what we were going to do there, how we were going to end it, and we had at one point scripted a visual representation of the end of that monologue, so we thought we would start with him in the kitchen with his wife and then go to that, but when we shot the scene with Tommy which was midway through the shoot, I think we both realized there is no way we are going to cut away from this, so that was that.

We do storyboard everything and that accident at the end was storyboarded and that was a combination of process photography and shots that were done on the location in New Mexico where we shot that scene. Everything leading up to that, that's a side angle sort of medium close-up of Javier in the car is shot on a stage with the background composited in a computer. He was sitting in a rig that was on basically a big spring that could pitch the whole thing toward the camera and it was tied to an air cannon right off-camera that then blew the sort of bits of rubber glass and dust at Javier. We kind of gradually keyed it up as we did successive takes to see you know what the threshold was for Javier before he got a whiplash!

For Javier's operation on himself, we met with a trauma surgeon before we started shooting and we said, "If you got this kind of wound and you had to treat yourself, what would you do, basically?" We knew there was going to be this scene where he was going to go into the pharmacy, he sort of gets what he needs, but I think that was basically it. We asked this doctor, who was great. He just kind of said I would do this and I think there was some description of him picking the fibers out of the wound that was in the book.

ETHAN: It was a latex appliance over Javier's leg. You know the flesh blended and Christian Tinsley [special effects person] is really good at what he does and Javier was doing it and none of it was doubled.

JOEL: Except for the injection, the last injection.

ETHAN: That's the prop guy.

JOEL: Keith said if you don't want to do it, I'll do it, and Javier said, "Great!" All you're seeing is a little bit of his thigh.

The scene with the dog—that was not a movie dog. We had pictures of other dogs that were movie dogs. This dog swims really well, but they all didn't look right. The one we used, that was a real, that was a mean dog. The dog was trained as an attack dog, a guard dog to go after people. The dog was all the same dog up until one shot where Josh [Brolin] falls on the ground with the dog next to him, which was a different dog, a latex dog.

ETHAN: It was all very low tech and there's no effects or anything. I mean it. It was Josh and the dog in water and Josh would take this agitating toy, show it to the dog so the dog knew Josh had it. Josh would then stuff it into his pants, jump into the water and he would start swimming like hell and they would let the dog go. Chasing the dog and water and everything and the pressure of dawn and dusk. That was the one in pre-production we thought, alright, this is going to be hard.

JOEL: I have to say in addition, while he was doing this, Josh had this thing with his collarbone because he broke his collarbone a week before we started shooting, so when he was swimming in the water, he could only really use one arm and he didn't realize how fast that dog could swim. At the end, basically, the dog was essentially in a harness on the leash, and the leash was painted out and that was composited with the hand firing the gun, which was shot against the blue screen [a method where shots made separately can them be combined].

ETHAN: The thing that was a pain in the ass about this scene was that we decided part of the drama was going to be day arriving, breaking day, and this was exhaustively storyboarded, and we had to shoot each of these at dusk and dawn within twenty-minute windows over the course of many nonconsecutive days.

JOEL: The scene where Javier strangles the deputy was actually a very difficult technical challenge from the point of view of anchoring the two bodies together, protecting the two actors physically. It looks quite simple, but you can't actually put handcuffs on someone and have them exert any pressure without having them completely tearing up their wrists and the weight of one person on another when you're having someone around. There were all these kind of infrastructure in that scene that you don't see under the actors' costumes that took a lot of experimentation to work out, but that's one of those things that goes by fairly fast and you go, "Well, they're tossing each other around on the floor," and in fact there's quite a lot that's going on. We didn't spend that much time shooting it, but we spent a lot of time with the stunt man and the makeup people and the special effects people actually figuring out how do you have one guy fall on top of another and heave him around with a pair of handcuffs on, where you're not injuring Javier and even so Javier got very, very beat up doing that.

JULIAN SCHNABEL, *THE DIVING BELL AND THE BUTTERFLY*

I guess I needed to figure out how to shoot the movie and shoot a movie where they are talking to the camera and the camera is the guy, so when you read the script it says something, but it doesn't really mean what you have to do, so you sort of have to physically break down the text in order to understand really what you're going to tell somebody to do and so if Mathieu [Amalric who plays the lead Jean-Dominique Bauby who is paralyzed] would have had the camera, so if he would have sat near the bed, the eye line of the girls would have been screwed up. We just had to figure out a way really to tell the story according to Jean-Dominique Bauby. It was really great working with Janusz [Kaminski, the cinematographer].

When my father died, I went up into the room a few moments after bile was coming out of his mouth and his eyes were flickering in his head and I thought maybe with that little bit of air still in his brain, I could say, "Dad" and he could maybe see me, but I didn't want to shoot what I saw. I wanted to shoot what my father saw and so that's one shot that we're doing where we shoot at different speeds all these people that are talking to him. The beginning and the ending were one shot. Very little was done in post-production.

For me, it's really about freedom. When a cameraman says to me mount the camera on the side of a car, and I say, "Why is the camera mounted there" and he says, "Well, there are four ways to shoot a car scene," and I said, "Well, if there are four ways to shoot a car scene, we can all go home right now." So he said, "Well, what do you want me to do?" I said, "I want you to take the camera off the car and I want you to lie on the front seat of the car with your head where your feet would be. Start shooting from there." He said, "You kidding?" I said, "No." It's in the movie, but you know, to get people to unlearn what they've learned and just to keep it fresh is a challenge.

The first shot in the movie is Marina Hands's hair flying around. Basically I put her on the back of the pickup truck and then the hairdresser and other prop men they had fans because people's hair doesn't fly even if you're driving in a very fast car, and I had driven up from Contamines years ago before we married listening to "Baby Light My Way" on the CD player driving in it at about 150 mph, and I had that in my head, so that was the first shot of the movie. That wouldn't be a bad poster but it's a little late.

There were no convertibles in the original script, but I wanted to show the landscape and I like convertibles, so there were always convertibles in the movie and I spent a lot of time shooting the trees in Paris and then we were fortunate to have the music from *Les Quatre Cents Coups*, you know, *The 400 Blows* [directed by François Truffaut] and so then he's listening to this and I just wanted him to veer off the road a little and I wanted it to look like, "Okay, it's a ride in the country." Usually you think this is a beautiful thing, you know, you're out in the country with your kid, but if there's nobody around and you're having a stroke, that's not such a good thing. So with the camera I wanted it to pan over to the right and to the left and the cameraman obviously asking where is that camera? Is that God's eye view or whose is it? I mean I wanted the agitation of him shooting and getting closer to Mathieu [Amalric] and Mathieu was stepping on the gas and that's what made that revving sound, it sounded like a tree that was getting cut down, so it was really a guy running alongside the car with the camera and then getting high up on top of him and it was pretty free form. He was getting on the car and he was holding it above. I did it twice.

In Ron Harwood's script it says a day at the beach, but we're supposed to shoot it in four days. I said, "It doesn't say four days at the beach, it says a day at the beach," so the first AD says to me, "How are we going to do that?" I said, "We can do it," he said, "Want to bet?" I said, "Yeah," and Janusz said to him, "You shouldn't bet with this guy," but anyway, we did shoot it in one day. I mean instead of having ice cream they had sandwiches. It's a lot less messy and there's different kind of actresses and actors and Emmanuelle Seigner [who plays Celine, the wife] is somebody that you just say something to her and she will do it. The building can fall down, you can have a hurricane, whatever will go on, she will do what you ask her to do. Marie-Josée [Croze, who plays the mistress] on the other hand is more nervous and somebody said, "Well, how do you feel acting directly to the camera?" and Marie said, "Oh, well it's very complicated," and Emmanuelle would say, "There's nothing to it, but to do it," but then you use those things that each of these people have as ticks or whatever.

I built the room. I put black and green linoleum on the floor and florescent light on the ceiling. When I came to the set, for example, there were no flowers there and

Julian Schnabel and cast on the set of *The Diving Bell and the Butterfly*. THE DIVING BELL AND THE BUTTERFLY—Licensed by Miramax, LLC and Pathé Pictures International.

in Jean-Do's room there were not a lot of flowers, but my friend Fred Hughes, when he was sick he had lots of flowers, so I basically just stopped on the way and bought as many flowers as I could to fill the room up with flowers and I also brought what I thought should be on the walls.

We had great makeup people. It never looks right with a prosthetic thing just stuck on the face, so what we did was we had a patch over one eye, contact lens that was bloodshot on his other eye, a piece of plastic stuck in his nose, a bite plate on his bottom lip and we glued his lip to his face and then his hand were on piece of foam and you could take that off quite easily, but most of the time just so the rest of the actors would never have the feeling that he was a normal guy, he stayed like that all of the time.

I put the bloodshot lens in the eye because when you get sick your eyes get screwed up. I took a piece of latex and I put it over the eye and the prop man had worked in a hospital before and he sewed the eye up. When you take a light and you get it closer, you see the red that's on the inside of your tissue. But basically if you see all that or you're trying to see through it, it's very hard to see anybody or anything, and the one thing that Mathieu said to me is, "You know when you don't move, people think you're not there," and you're not. You're invisible and that whole idea of being invisible informed his humor and that's why Jean-Do didn't have any self-pity. But also if you close your eyes, all of a sudden the landscape gets much bigger and you can have these crazy conversations with yourself that everybody's locked out of.

We had more than one fly [referring to a scene where there is a close-up of a fly]. There were a bunch of flies and they were all frozen and then the fly wrangler, the same guy who sewed up the eye, took the fly, stuck it on his nose and as he got unfrozen, he moved around more.

Mathieu got inside this diving bell, it's a real Medieval device, they bolt this thing onto your torso and you have weights on your feet and I definitely wouldn't get in there. I mean it's brutal and also the radio was broken and I could hear him through the air hose, so if he had a problem, he had to just say my name. I was in the water with him. One moment when I wasn't, all of a sudden the cameraman, not the normal cameraman, this underwater cameraman grabbed him and started to pull him out of the water and you know if you get water in that, water can go inside the helmet and you could drown. So we got him up in the thing and I've never seen Mathieu angry ever. They took this thing off and he says, "What are you doing, I'm acting." The guy just didn't know the finger signs! Everybody else did and then we went back under the water and did that and now you know why Jean-Dominique picked that metaphor. I mean it is brutal and for someone who has claustrophobia like me that was one of the things that really drew me to this because I always thought if I had locked-in syndrome that would be the worst thing that ever happened to me, but the thing I found out in doing the movie was that Jean-Do actually felt selected, he told his friend Bernard Chapuis, "I am not the same guy. I've been reborn as someone else," and I think he really felt that this was a good thing and that's what really changed my process.

I wanted to see what Jean-Dominique Bauby was seeing, not what he would see if we were watching him in a hospital, so I used a swing and tilt lens that could make one part of the image clearer and the other part fuzzier and you can make it more fuzzy if you wanted. We did things basically in the camera. We had to crank the camera where we would wind and rewind on top of our own film, so you could get super imposition sometimes but essentially the blink is this two fingers over your eyes going like that. That was the most natural blink. Other blinks, you know people always talk about a blink being the shutter, the cut. Well, it looks very mechanical, so every time I think about the blinks I think about Chris Walken talking to Dennis Hopper [from the dialogue in the movie *True Romance*] where he says there's fifty pantomimes, seventeen for men, but fifty for a women. "You're trying to tell me nothing, but you're telling me everything." Anyway, I figured out all these different ways to blink. And if you shoot more light on it you will see red the way you see red at the bottom of your eyelids. Once your eye gets sewn up, everybody can close your eye, you see part of your nose. So, I actually had a nose that I put on the lens at one time, then I cut the nose off of it and had a whole face that was on the side. I mean, I had to decide who was going to hold the camera, if it was going to be me or if it was going to be Mathieu Amalric [who plays Jean-Do] or it was going to be the camera man. But obviously the idea that he would be very, very close to the people that were talking to him was essential to me.

There was a wide shot of him in the bed, right before he has his epiphany when he says, "Had I been blind and deaf, or did it take the harsh light of disaster for me to find my true nature?" That's when you see the glaciers falling into the Alaskan Sea. I thought this is a good time to see him. I mean he can't stay in that diving bell anymore and I thought, "Okay, now it's time to turn into a butterfly."

PAUL THOMAS ANDERSON, *THERE WILL BE BLOOD*

We went to the bottom of a fifty-foot mine shaft that had a horizontal entrance and a vertical entrance, so we were able to get our camera gear in one way and be down in there and it was terrific because there were no directing, no directorial choices to make. You had an opening of about three feet to put the camera in, and that was kind of it. You knew just where the camera was going to go, it was dictated by this abandoned mine shaft which is down in Shafter which is the Texas/Mexico border about forty-five minutes where we shot the main portion of the film. Daniel Day-Lewis was in Ireland preparing for the film and I know he was chopping wood in his backyard for months and months, which is really all he could do to practice for it, I suppose. He looked like he knew what he was doing. In the opening he was on a harness so that he could fall, but we did a few takes and I said something that you should probably never say to Daniel Day-Lewis, which was that it looks fake. So then he fell down a fifty foot mine shaft and hit his back and broke some ribs and it looks pretty good. That minute we kept shooting, you know, there was nothing else to do. He looked to me and he said, "Keep going?" and I said, "Yeah, keep going." He just had to then moan and wail at the bottom and act like he was hurt, so it worked out really well.

It's a horrible situation to have a baby out there in that kind of environment. They were twins as you normally have. [When working with babies you use twins or triplets to provide more time to shoot with them as the laws limit how much a baby can be photographed under lights.] But the parents were more concerned because their

Paul Thomas Anderson with Daniel Day-Lewis on the set of *There Will Be Blood*. THERE WILL BE BLOOD ©2007 by Paramount Vantage, A Division of Paramount Pictures and Miramax Film Corp. All Rights Reserved.

babies were crying as they should have been crying, and they were feeling that the babies weren't giving a good performance, and we were saying whatever the baby does is fine. We really were okay and there was no performance we needed from the child. And, of course, they were crying, it was hot and dusty and it was horrible. We were pouring oil on their faces. I have a baby myself. I thought, wow, I should just bring my own baby in here and do this.

We just got very lucky with Texas where the weather is wonderful and horrible at the same time and we just got wonderfully lucky with a rainstorm that came in. We had a derrick out there and we had to light it on fire. There's a terrific Special Effects Coordinator, Steve Cremin, that was responsible for it. I remember actually we were really testing stuff and so we just had a lot of diesel fuel and very, very dry wood to be really simple about it. You can get away with a lot in Texas. To shoot that in California would have been impossible. You can't even shoot a campfire scene in California without a Fire Marshal shutting you down, but in West Texas there really is no adult supervision at all. For the oil, that's not colored water. There's methocyl, and then there's the chocolate stuff that that they put in milkshakes at McDonald's. You know these are all the things that special effects guys love, this was the sort of stuff to make oil, and then we would pour some alcohol in there to get it to rainbow, that sort of thing. The boy being thrown off the roof, we'd actually tried to do that once the traditional way with a young person, but it looks like a really big, small person, man-child being thrown through the air. It was really an embarrassing three days throwing this poor man around and it never really worked. I said this looks really fake and we built a harness and devised to pull the boy through the air and that kind of thing. He was a real tough kid, but he was terrified to do it and then the special effects guy's little ten-year-old daughter did it to show him and once he saw that he was like, "All right, I could do it."

The shot where Daniel picks him up and runs was a steadicam [a device worn with a harness that allows for fluid camera movement] on a golf cart, so the steadicam is sitting on the golf cart and Jeff Kunkel's dolly grip is driving the golf cart and Colin Anderson [the camera operator] was filming. Shots like this evolved as we were on location. We kept talking about in off hours or at official meetings about effects how we might do it once the derrick was built. The official meetings with just everybody are paralyzing because you kind of have to know what is going on and then it happens. Generally, it's the side meetings that splinter off where all the work seems to get done and you come back for another official meeting so you can then describe what we need to do, but more or less everybody's just sort of talking and talking and talking because we're so terrified of this thing that we ultimately have to do, which is burn this thing to the ground and once it's gone I mean that was it. Steve Cremin was the Special Effects Coordinator and it was his obligation to say, "I can light this thing on fire, but there's a chance I might not be able to put it out," and you know, I just sort of assumed he has to say that. Of course, we can put this out, he just wants to cover himself, but we had five or six cameras and the whole thing planned out and the second it went up I thought, we're in the middle of West Texas, the driest place on earth and there's 50,000 gallons of diesel fuel. There's no way we're going to turn this thing off, and it lit up like a Christmas tree, so we had to shoot the whole thing in forty-five minutes. We turned the nozzle off, we tried to pour some water on it, reset a few cameras and just said, "Let's keep shooting till it gets dark," so we did it in forty-five minutes, so it was great because we probably would have still been there planning it right now.

We made most of the film outside and by the time we got to the end we had two very long scenes that were inside and there's not a lot of joy in either of the scenes, so I can remember feeling kind of depressed that they weren't outside.

We hired an interpreter, someone who is an interpreter for a living, not an actor, to teach sign language. He came down just about two weeks early before filming and in the off hours we'd work with him and teach the boy sign language and then for the older boy at the end we cast a deaf actor, a terrific young actor name Russell Harvard.

The bowling alley is in the basement of the Doheny Mansion where we shot the movie, and some of the stuff in the film is based on the life of Edward Doheny, and I first knew about the bowling alley because in looking at the research about his life he got in a ton of trouble, the Teapot Dome scandal, and so he hired a team of lawyers and there was this great picture of this bowling alley he had of his desks lined up the length of the bowling alley for his lawyers to help him and so it became a great place to put this showdown between the two of them and we refurbished it. It was just in repair, it used to actually just be the home of the AFI [American Film Institute] and we went back with Robert Elswit [the cinematographer] and he remembered shooting student films down in this bowling alley. Anyway we refurbished it, and it was just two insane days. I remember it was such a hilarious sight because we all had booties on so we wouldn't mark up the floor or we were in our socks and it was kind of nice, it just seemed like we were operating or something. We could only shoot with one camera. I mean we did it piece by piece. We started at the beginning. We more or less knew what the end was going to be, but we didn't do a full blocking rehearsal of it all. We knew where we were going to start, you were going to sit over here and you're going to get up to start throwing bowling balls, but we tried to not talk too much about it and do each piece as it came to us. And then it was time to throw them and as it progressed down the bowling alley it became something that we had to become more serious about because Daniel [Day-Lewis] was throwing these enormously heavy bowling pins at Paul [Dano], so at that point we had some adult supervision. We did have some lighter pins too. We had real ones mixed with the fake ones, but you know you throw a fake one and if it hits the wall it's just going to bounce back.

Quite honestly, it's horrible to shoot in the city of Beverly Hills. They want you done by 10:00 and it was about 9:45 and it was the end of the film and I knew I had a good shot. "This is fine, here we go," but then they really kicked us out, and the kind of insecurity that you have about, "I know this is the last shot of the film," but it's incredibly hard to commit to for me, "Do we have this? Is this it?" And then we sort of convinced them to allow us to come back the next day with just a few of us, and Daniel, and we spent about two hours shooting. Really it was just fear, just doing this close-up on Daniel saying the end and I was just terrified to shoot the last shot of the film. That is really what it was and we were rushing with five minutes left.

RON HOWARD, *FROST/NIXON*

I make shot lists and I'm very dutiful about that, but in this case, we would just go in with two handheld cameras and just start shooting, so the actors would roughly know where they were going and instead of starting with a wide shot and sort of working through it, I went ahead and had our guys go in and start shooting not so much in an aggressive faux-documentary way, but in a kind of spontaneous, organic feel and the actors loved it. Every take mattered from the beginning and slowly things would fall into patterns and I would be double-checking my list and sort of saying, "Not quite what I imagined, but we did get this pan [a shot from moving from left to right or right to left] from here to there," or "No, I really do need this thing I always had in my head. We're going to fall back and we're going to do a pass for that."

The interviews were shot a little more like a television show, but you know the surprise of this movie is what was going, the drama behind the scene and what it took to actually get there and what was motivating people and the range of motivations and the sort of paradoxes of all that, so there was an energy in that and there's an energy in David Frost, so I felt like that restlessness, tempo and pace was something that I wanted the actors to feel very free to work with. There were four rounds of interviews basically and it was the question of how to differentiate them enough, how to build the intensity. I was trying to make each one feel different rhythmically, stylistically and also try to let the audience understand there were some interviews I kept the cameras in the background a lot, so that they would never forget that it was a television show. Other times I wanted to start with that and dolly around and then move into close-ups that would exclude the video camera so that the interactions would become personal. I kept worrying about the interviews and thinking about it and talking about it as we went along and I also wanted Nixon to have this kind of subtle, but adversarial relationship with the camera, so I wanted places where I could take a moment and have him look up and then cut to the camera and push in on it. There's another one where Nixon's just pummeling Frost and he's completely controlling the interview. That one has a lot of movement and it's steadicam [a free-floating camera on a device worn by the camera operator]. It's kind of Ali in the ring to me. I did keep trying to use these boxing analogies.

It was always sort of encouraging to discover things and suddenly something cool would be happening and Michael Sheen would walk here and suddenly walk into a close-up and you know in the next take you'd say, "Well, if he does that again, I'm just going to just rack [focus] to him in the foreground, and so there'd be this sort of visual style that was getting discovered."

Endings always terrify me. I'm confident shooting. I love shooting. Challenging stuff is exciting. I don't lose sleep over that. The day we're going to shoot the ending, whatever it is, it doesn't matter the movie, it doesn't matter how confident I am with it, I'm always anxious about it and in this case I was very confident, but we just had a limited amount of time to shoot it because it was a sunset thing. The idea as written was that David Frost had given Nixon a pair of old shoes that Nixon had always admired, loafers. Nixon had earlier talked about men should wear shoes with laces, but he was

Ron Howard and Michael Sheen on the set of *Frost/Nixon*. Courtesy of Universal Studios Licensing LLC.

clearly intrigued by these shoes and in the play they hadn't really had time to deal with it. It was a joke but he didn't even show you the shoes and the play ended very differently with the focus on Frost. Peter Morgan [the playwright and screenwriter] had written that he tries the shoes on and walks around awkwardly in them and I thought that was just beautiful. I thought it was just great, but on the day, Frank Langella mentioned they had gone round and round and round about this with the play and they decided to not even show the shoes, but I loved this and he was very excited about it. This planted a question in my mind, so as the sun was going down, I didn't know what else it could be but I started shooting other things: him looking out across the balustrade, him wandering around, and him putting his shoes on and walking off into the sun as scripted, him taking the shoes out and holding them. Ultimately, I had two different versions. I had a version where he takes the shoes out, but doesn't put them on. Three actually. One where he doesn't take them out at all and one where he puts them on and walks away.

ALEJANDRO GONZÁLEZ IÑÁRRITU, *BABEL*

I make these strange cards, big cards. It's only for me. Nobody seems them, right? It's like when I was a student, I always made my notes, because as all of us know, when you are on a set, there are more problems than the film itself. A hundred people are bothering you about everything, but not the film, and, you know, everything happens. Life is moving, and you are trapped in this bubble, and there's no time, and that bubble is affected by life. And so I don't lose concentration, I always use this little card divided into seven, eight pieces, and I put very specific notes on them. I have a big ADD problem, big one. I can't concentrate on one thing. So I need this card, because without the card, I will be in a panic attack. I need to remember all the rehearsals and all that thinking I did in the two years before I'm here. If I lost that [card], maybe I will have it in my memory, but maybe I will not remember it. I put in the facts: where these guys come from, where I will put this in editing because with this film specifically these characters will never be linked physically. They will never see each other's faces. And I will be shooting scenes a year apart and they will have to go together. So I have to hit the point thematically, tonally, and I was very aware that I will have to create the grammar in order that these diverse cultures, stories, all will be together and will not be four short films of National Geographic, but will be a film. And so I was trying to build the grammar that can make sense. So, I was trying to find key elements visually, emotionally—objectives, points of view—that I knew that I will be cutting from these little goat-faces to Tokyo. I didn't want to forget one year after, when I will be in Tokyo, you know what I mean? So I was just trying to memorize that.

The toughest thing, it was very hot, and then, it's funny because when I think of one of the most difficult scenes sometimes, you see these two kids with 300 goats there, and just to put 300 goats in a mountain with two kids, it's like a nightmare because you say, "Okay, rolling," and then the goats are not there. You're like, "Okay, cut. Okay, somebody get the goats." You can't complain, you know what I mean? The goats are goats, so you can't negotiate with them. So that's a very tough, stupid thing, but it can be a nightmare just to have 300 goats with kids, to have them in the frame, you know?

Tokyo, I think, is one of the hardest places for any film director in the world. There's no film commission. So it's almost impossible to shoot anyplace there. So literally we start at 6:00 am on the freeway to shoot that scene of the father and the girl having a conversation, and we decided to be there at 6:00 am on a freeway. It was almost empty. And ten minutes later, literally I stopped the traffic one minute, while we were shooting. Ten minutes later, the police were chasing us. And they pursued us through Tokyo trying to cancel the film because somebody called. The society's organized on some level that is so collective that if any ant does something wrong, you cannot go out of the system, you know? It's very, very strict. For example, the underground train, all that scene, we have to plan like a robbery, like one week in advance. So, we were just jumping in the train, then from baggage, we pull out the cameras. "Okay, ready!" And we were right at the station. "Okay, keep all that!" So everybody was wrapping equipment because the police were there. I will say that 70 percent of that film, it was like a university film, like student film. So it's very difficult.

The last shot, the pullback shot from the apartment in Tokyo, that was something I came up with at the end. I said I want this to happen like that, so everybody was getting crazy, and Rodrigo [Prieto, the cinematographer] and I were trying to figure

out how we will do it. And we thought about helicopters. Well, no permission. Then
to fly a cable from one building to the other, well, we will kill somebody for sure. And
then we found the solution. Because we were on the last floor of the building, we put
a dolly with a crane on the rooftop of the building, so the first 10 meters, it's real, and
then from there, we have some stills shooting from different angles and then in the
computer, so it was a combination.

I shot in two parts of Mexico. One is Tijuana, really the crossing, and then this community that is like one hour and a half south of Tijuana. And it's an amazing community. We literally had a wedding for six days. Everybody was drunk and everybody was
happy and nobody complained. "Just bring the beer!"

So, that's it, okay? 6:00 am and we were having fun, and that was there. And then
all the deserts, we went to Sonora, which is one of the toughest and hottest places
on planet Earth, and we shot there. So we shot desert in Sonora and the wedding
in south.

I think Morocco was tough and Mexico, the desert, was really tough. Because in a
desert something happens to me. When you put the camera in the desert or you want
to find an angle, it becomes this big and you become like, where do I shoot, what is
the right thing to do here. It's overwhelming. You're exposed to the weather and the
wind. So that is a difficult thing, the desert. I will say that in terms of logistics, at some
point I thought that I will have a heart attack, but it was Tokyo because the reason of
the permissions, that was the toughest part.

And then there was the sign language. I'd ask something, and the Japanese boys
would look at the translator. They would respond with sign language. The Japanese
goes to English, the English to me, and when it returned, the answer was completely
different from what I have asked. So it was like—Babel!

And the difficult thing, I think, when you are dealing with cultures, my challenge
was that I was very conscious that I didn't want to fall into my own temptations or traps
of putting in characters or locations that are attractive to me because I'm a foreigner,
and my point of view will be a point of view of a tourist, and I will make it a cliché or
stereotyped character. So I try always to be as faithful as possible, trying to understand
what is real, what is important for the characters, and what is important from their
point of view.

I always question what the point of view is that I want to tell at this moment, right?
And when you have two, three characters, I always find where I should put the camera. Normally, I shoot only with one camera. I don't like two cameras. So I have to
be very, very clear which point of view it will be and how the camera can enhance the
emotion that I want to create. So I question every frame, everything. Even one extra
[someone who is in a scene and has no lines, but acts in the background] in one single
scene, if there's one extra that is doing something, I can just lose my mind because
I know that particular little cancer, I call them the cancer cells, that cancer cell can
impregnate the body and suddenly the film with that extra will create the death of
the body. So I am kind of neurotic in that way, and sometimes it's true that the actors, even when they're great collaborators, don't always have great ideas. Sometimes
they can be completely wrong about what they have created. You say "No." So, then

Alejandro González Iñárritu with cast on the set of *Babel*. BABEL ©2006 Babel Productions Inc. All Rights Reserved.

you have to negotiate again, "Do yours and then do mine, right?" You know that you will be using yours, but at the same time, you have to relieve them in a way. So, I cannot trust them all the time, and sometimes I think that the actors need you to put limits on some things. When Brad Pitt arrived in Morocco, things changed. Originally, there was a fateful reason why they were mad at each other, that this marriage was breaking up because he had an affair. And I thought that was not a good idea and since it was Brad Pitt, it will be kind of distracting. So I thought that losing the child will be even more profound and more complicated, with a lot of guilt for both parents, and when Brad arrived, he hadn't read that change, so we had to understand all over again who these guys were.

MARTIN SCORSESE, *THE DEPARTED*

I see certain editing patterns in my head, and that's the way the picture is designed on the page. I usually go away for about a week and a half in a hotel somewhere and just spend time with the script and draw pictures and notes or whatever. There's a sequence in the film where Matt Damon's character is sitting behind a desk and he's orchestrated a situation which is turning into a catastrophe where Martin Sheen falls off a roof, splatters in front of Leo [DiCaprio]. People come out. The bad guys come out. The police start firing guns. The intercutting of the shooting was worked out in advance, what the size of this shot would be, the size of the frame and also the sound.

When there are sequences, two shots, singles, the problem is who's in the two-shot and how many people are in the background, and it makes a big difference. And very often when you think it'll be a simple two-shot, it turns out that there are many, many other layers involved.

The rat at the very end. I'm reading the last page of the script. Bill Monahan writes after Colin is shot, he writes the phrase, "Then a strange thing happens. A rat comes out and starts chewing away." I said, "That'd be too much, but it's interesting, interesting." But then translating the phrase, "A strange thing happens," visually without it looking like a rat coming out, just that, I mean, a rat is walking into the frame, but it can't just look like a rat walking into the frame. And we tried many different ways, and ultimately the shot at the end of the movie was done the last two-and-a-half weeks of doing the answer print [the final product which is ultimately projected in theaters]. We went back and Rob Legato [visual effects supervisor] in LA built part of that set a little bit and Warner Bros. was kind enough to give us a little extra money because I figured out maybe we'd have to get it from another angle. I tried it with different audiences, different ways the rat would come into frame, and it just wasn't the right tone. Then I started to realize maybe we should shoot over Matt's [Damon] body onto the golden dome because then I thought the golden dome. I said, "Let's go back. Let's go back to the references of *Scarface*, 'The world is yours,' when he gets shot." It's kind of corny, but it has the element of that and "Mother of Mercy" as the last stand of Rico from *Little Caesar*, but primarily from the end of *Scarface*, which tilts up as Paul Muni gets shot or from *White Heat* "Mom, top of the world," that sort of thing. So you see his state house. Then Rob Legato and I were fooling around with the rat, and we were saying we had it on a computer in New York, and Thelma [Schoonmaker, the editor] and myself were working on the computer, and we were tied in with them in LA here [so he could direct long distance], and they had a double down there for Matt and that sort of thing, and we had a really great rat. The rat was eating croissants. It had a great time. And Rob Legato says, "Why don't we put him on the railing?" I said, "Yeah, let's try him on the railing," and that's when it worked, and he actually took his own time there, took his own cues. He then stopped and he exited the right direction. I said, "Beautiful," because it was the last thing, it was the last stroke. It was only three weeks before the picture was printed.

I'm doing one scene there with Jack [Nicholson] and Leo at a table, a long scene where they're talking, and Jack is beginning to become Costello, getting to become unhinged, and he's getting a little edgy. And Leo's character, you sit down and the guy behind you locks the door and only you and him are in the room and this guy says, "I smell a rat," and you are the rat, and you have to make sure you get out of that room alive. It's a very interesting scene. We shot it two cameras simultaneously. We worked on it for quite a while that day, then just shot three or four takes that night, and it was a good scene. There was one line in it that worried me, though, where DiCaprio tells him, "Listen, Frank, you accuse me once, I'll put up with it. You accuse me twice, I'll quit. You accuse me three times, I'll put a fuckin' bullet in your head like anybody else." And I said to myself here's this young guy who he is taking sort of advantage of, the character of Costello liking him like Costello's son, so to speak, his other son being Matt Damon, but I don't know if he would ever say,

"I'd put a bullet in your head like anybody else." I was a little nervous about it. They did it very well, and we were working on this, Bill Monahan [who wrote the script] and I and the actors were working on it, working on the script as we were shooting. I said, "I still feel funny. I think for the guy it's out of line to say that to him." And so after we shot four takes, five takes, whatever it was, it was pretty good, and I said, "Let's break." And they say what do you want to do? I said, "Well, we have the scene for tomorrow. We have another half day in this place." We were shooting actually in the village, downtown in a small bar, and I said to Jack, "Is there anything you could think of, is there anything you could provoke in this scene a little more?" We had the cameras all set up. It's real time. Whatever you do, he's got to respond to it, real. Who knows what's going to happen in the frame? I don't know what the fuck he's going to do. So the next morning, we're going in, and I was in Greenwich Village and it was the summer, and all these people out and Greenwich Village is very happening, all the bright colors, everybody running in the streets and very narrow streets, and all of a sudden, guys come, "Hey, how are you?" You know, people know me in New York, old friends of mine, people coming up. The next thing I know, a guy comes up to me and says, "I have ideas. I have ideas." And it was Jack. I said, "Good. Let's do them." And what happened in the scene, as we were shooting and Leo says that line, "I'd put a fucking bullet in your head like anybody else," and all of a sudden something falls on the floor. And I said to myself, "Well, maybe we should cut." So, Jack puts a gun up and says, "Do you have something you want to tell me?" Well, then it made sense to me. He also had some ideas at that point to try to set the table on fire, and we wanted to do that, but then it got too clumsy. So for me, when I saw things like that and I saw how Leo reacted when he had that gun to his face, I didn't know he was going to take that gun out. I didn't know whether he was going to fire it at him or fire it past his ear, let's say, which could be dangerous. Who knows what was going to happen at that moment? And I said, "This came alive to me." I said, "This is why I do this." I mean, I bitch and moan about making these kind of pictures. But the reality is that suddenly, if everything goes wrong, everything goes right. When something like that happens and Leo holds his own, he says, "I am not the rat," and he's got to get out of that room alive, that's the essence of it, and that's when I'm realizing you sort of make the same picture. And I said, "That's okay. Let's do it again." And we kept going.

In the case of one actor, he had to go do another film, so he had to go away for a few weeks and come back, and when he came back, of course, things had changed. It took him a couple of days to get back up to speed. It was a very complicated way of working.

MARTIN SCORSESE, *HUGO*

I really loved working with the kids. Asa's the heart of the picture. But the 3D changed the performances. And what I liked in the testing in the 3D, Bob Richardson [cinematographer], myself and Chris Surgent [first assistant director] and everybody, we saw in the tests from costume and makeup, we saw that the faces of the actors, Ben Kingsley and Asa and Chloe, Sacha, the dog, all that, all of them came forward in a way. And I started playing with the IO, the interocular, and I said, "Give me more." And they said, "Well, that's going to cost you a head. Your eyes are going to break and your head's going to open." I said, "When that happens, then we'll stop and we'll go back." So we kept pushing forward. I just think for the actors in 3D, and I don't mean a 3D that is showy, where you pick up something and throw it at the camera and then go back to the dialogue, I think this seemed to make things more accessible. So we had to be very careful about pushing even further with the acting because the 3D really accentuates it, and I wanted that to be that way because I felt that since this was a special place that we were creating, like the inside of one of those snow globes or something, that if the audience liked it, okay, we could put the glasses on. They go in there and they stay in there. And you sort of immerse the audience in there, but the actors are the key. A medium shot or close-up was it. I always used to say, "Moving sculpture." It's almost as if you can see around this way and we had to be very careful of working with the boys.

We didn't have any rehearsal with the kids. The reality is once you decide to make the picture, things happen. We're building the sets, we're testing and we decided in 3D. I mean, it's a big gamble. At a certain point, we had no idea. I mean, basically, we didn't know if we could get out of there breathing and while everybody has that problem with a film, this was like everybody said, "Well, they're looking at you because you're shooting 3D." I said, "Oh." So I always tell the story it's like being on a tight-rope and as you start to go forward, you look back, and you can't go back. You've got to go forward. We only had four hours a day with the kids, non-consecutives, and that caused a bit of a problem in that with the 3D at this stage of the game and the big set we had. There were a lot of people on the set, three times, I think the amount of crew. I couldn't see anything and the rig [that holds the camera] is big. It's just that with the green screen and this and that and the costumes and the animals and all the CGI [Computer Graphic Imaging], all this stuff, by the time we ready, very often, we had to stop. One day, the kid had to go to school. They take a break and then they rest and then in one case, he keeps going to school. They keep teaching him stuff on the side there, I don't know. He came back on the set and we were in this small room where the automaton is and there's something about having these sets, but still, I must say even though the interiors of the clocks are sets, they're still metal and the camera is very big and you've still got to get in there, and then there's steam. So it was an arduous shooting for the kids and for the crew. So we're on the set and the steam is coming up in the little scene and he has to go to school. He didn't want to, but, "You've got to. You have to go. That's it. You've got to go." Okay. So he goes. We wait. We wait. We try to do something else but you can't move the camera because it's too big. You can't change lenses on that system. You could change your lens, forty-five minutes, so we had to decide, "That's the lens, man. That's what we're going with. I don't give a damn." I said, "We're going to move in, we're going to move it back." And we did that. We did it. [Bob] Richardson [the cinematographer] got it down to twelve minutes and it was fantastic, his crew. We had a second rig, but we were chasing Sacha [Baron Cohen] with it and we fell, I mean, he tripped over Sacha and that was the end. That was that, for that rig. That was it. Everybody got mad. "Why are you chasing?" That's what we're doing, it's a chase scene, and this happened. It was the first week and then Larry [McConkey, second cameraperson] he fixed it, but it always had a little twitch to it.

"What's happening?"

"Oh, that's the bad one."

"Oh, all right."

So what they did eventually was put the other lens on the other rig, so it was very funny, and this is by way of directing the kids because you had to be aware of all of this, where they would lift the rig, four guys, literally, and I said, "What are they doing?"

"They're changing lenses."

So in the meantime, we do all that, there you go and the kid has to go to school. So we're waiting and we're shooting a storyboard of a lot of the picture in a sense with notated editing patterns and so when the kid came back, this is not a performance thing, but when he came back on set, I said, "All right. All right. What did they teach you?" And he told us something and I looked at him and said, "We could have told you that. What do you need to go over there for?" He was the sweetest thing, the poor kid. Every morning, I'd grab and hug him and he had been coming up the steps and I have a young daughter who's just turned twelve, so I know the sound when he'd be there in the mornings. I'd go, "Oh God, oh God, look at this. What are we going to do? We're have to probably drop that scene because we . . ." and I'd hear, "da, da, da, da," here he comes.

In the station with Monsieur Frick, played by Richard Griffiths, at the kiosk with the newspapers and Madam Emily with her dachshund at the café, what we tried to do was I'd say to the actors, "I'd like you to speak just to yourselves, not necessarily audible for the track." Also gestures, moves, the moves had to be slightly exaggerated because it's almost like a silent film and I said, "However, it's more like, quite honestly, the icon, *Rear Window*." Imagine when Hitchcock shot *Rear Window*, Jimmy Stewart's points of view, you never see the insides of those apartments. You're never inside with a camera. And it's not the thing I'm really comfortable with, but in a sense, Hugo is looking through the clocks. Everything was completely unreal and also, all exaggerated movements. And the actors have to let you know what they're feeling or saying or thinking in an exaggerated way, but it's almost like a different kind of acting, like in silent films where you had a certain style for the '20s. It's almost like that. I mean, there was another style too that Victor Sjöström [Swedish actor and director of over seventy movies] started back in 1915, 1916 in Sweden but that was inherited here too. Sjöström was the mentor of [Ingmar] Bergman [Swedish director of masterpieces like *The Virgin Spring, The Seventh Seal, Fanny and Alexander, Wild Strawberries*], but he did great films here and silent films with Lillian Gish, *The Wind*, and the great film with Lon Chaney called *He Who Gets Slapped*. And his style was such, did you ever see *The Phantom Chariot?* His style was such that the only thing missing was the sound with the actors. It seemed so natural with the actors. So in talking to my actors I would push it more. And then if it was too big, we'd take it down, but it was really in the gestures of Frances de la Tour with the dog and Richard is just trying to get across the set. Richard, he's a bigger guy, so in getting through the people, he already had it. And later at the end, they're at the table when they catch the boy and that was the only time they have dialogue with Sacha. There was this moment when Sacha knocks the boy down and Richard has this facial gesture like he'd been actually hurt and, yes, he did hurt him. I mean, you know, it's interesting because we were dealing with some actors who were . . . I think Sir Christopher Lee is eighty-nine at the time, so it was hard to move them around a bit, so we placed him behind the desk in the bookstore, different things like that. As the picture went on, people had back problems, people couldn't walk, so a lot of scenes were rewritten for some of them.

The first day of shooting for Ben Kingsley and Chloë [Grace Moretz] in the script, it said, "He sees them having a discussion. For some reason, she gets upset," but he gestures and she's upset by it and she leaves, and I said, "We better have some dialogue for that. " So I asked John Logan [the screenwriter] and he wrote some stuff for us and then it became a scene. I said, "I don't want it to be a scene though. I want it to be an observation."

You learn many things. You learn, well, that if you want the dog to kiss an actor or go over and lick, you just pour sardine oil on the actor. Don't tell them until the last minute.

You know, working with 3D, seriously, it's fascinating because you are doing a silent film. You go back. We're kind of stuck in like 1928 or something, 1930, but we're moving ahead with the 3D, knowing that [Georges] Méliès [early French fantasy filmmaker who the movie is about] would have done it and also, the Lumière Brothers [early French filmmakers who worked in the documentary world] did it, and some of their films are being restored in 3D. I've seen them. And I just think the point now is that there's such a change in technology that for any young directors not to be restricted. There's always the storyteller, but maybe the film doesn't have to be always on a flat screen. Yes, there has to be the audience experience, but to keep an open mind to utilize this new technology, because it's no longer cinema, it's a moving image. It's no longer a cinema as we've known the last 100 years of celluloid. It's gone. It's over, and some may say, sad. Yes, I think so, because that's how I grew up with it and I love celluloid, etc., but the reality is this is a new tool and we have to go this way and this is where it's going. One has also to think of where, I guess, young people will be making them for different venues too, for watches maybe, I don't know. Seriously, this is what's going to be happening so keep an open mind about technique, and it's always about storytelling. It depends on how you tell the story in one take or silently. But the main thing is, of course, perseverance, the perseverance to continue.

For the end scene, I said, "We have to start from outside the window." Rob Legato, our special effects person, worked with Bob Richardson and Chris Surgent, my AD [Assistant Director], on off-hours, whatever they were, because we did have a very short day because of the problem of the restricted time working with the children and the boy was in every scene, pretty much every scene, and we only had four hours a day non-consecutive and it was an early day, like 5:00 pm. And we'd talk, we'd rehearse, and that took about, I don't know, two months to lay out and I thought it was too big. Then he changed the walls and I thought it was too small. So then we made a compromise on that. Then they wanted to do it in the hallway and I said, "No, we can't do it in the hallway." So it really went around literally between Chris and the other ADs and Larry McConkey [steadicam operator] working out blocks of areas where the steadicam would go, and then ultimately tracking into the close-up on the automaton who sort of brought everyone together in a sense. One major problem is that it was a 3D rig and it was pretty big. As I understand, they're getting smaller now and it was called real 3D, but Larry had to hold it and he had to move it and hit all those marks, and it was really a physical problem because it was extremely big and literally getting into the close-up at the end, which then was enhanced later digitally. But this was practice and practice and then we did rehearsals and so, first, they used doubles and then they used the actual actors. The dog was fine sitting there, but it was some of the older actors, they couldn't really stand up, so we had Chris Lee sitting down, Richard Griffiths, and Frances had to sit with him. It all literally worked in rehearsal, after rehearsal, whenever I was able to get over there. Larry was able to rehearse it with doubles, and then ultimately, it was the expression on the face of the automaton, which we only got, I think, a week before we finished. It had to suggest it was smiling maybe without smiling and so there were many different faces for the automaton, but it worked out. David Balfour [property master in charge of moving objects on set, like guns] and all the other gentlemen who were working on the automaton in England, the main face for the automaton, it turns out, was taken from the Mona Lisa, that smile. I said, "Hey, that's great." It was so serene. And the problem with the last shot, ultimately, was the lighting on the automaton besides getting everything around it, but when Chloë is seen and she starts her narration, she becomes the writer of the story in a sense. When she sits down, I said, "We have to go around her and come around, and I don't know what we can do." We have a wall there. I said, "No, we can move the walls if that's what it's going to take." And they did. They moved the wall and they also put the chair on a swivel, you see, so all that's real. So when she moves, she's actually is swiveling around, the camera's moving around her and then back through, past the boy, back into the back room and as far as we could get before, literally, Larry couldn't hold it anymore, the camera. We did twelve takes maybe in one day. Setting this stuff up, two months, but again, I don't usually shoot studio pictures, but you had the studio there. You have the sound stage here and you can run over there if you're still awake and work a little bit. The big problem was ultimately lighting the automaton throughout the entire movie because every time you switched the light or put a candle by it, it had a different expression. The shot is that everybody sort of is brought together by the end of the story and so it just seems it has to be one shot. It's not one that draws attention to itself, I don't think. If you look at it, it just seems to be going past people, but technically, the guys who did it were really quite, quite challenged by what was happening there. Then the final touches are by Rob Legato [as the second unit director who gets shots without the actors], the exterior and that sort of thing, and there was a real exterior that we bring through the window. We started outside the window and went through the hallway. We were outside that window and we went through the window from the wall of the building which had some green screen on the sides [which allows superimposition of other images where the green screens are placed] so we just ran into the hallway, see?

There were a lot of special visual effects that became quite intense in trying to get them as good as we wanted, and still make the release date.

The opening stuff is a combination of the actual photography of going past all the people and that gets to the clock with special effects, visual effects. From the Eiffel Tower we go to the back of the train station; we see the trains because at the front of the train station, I said, "Who'll know it's a train station?" You don't know. So if we go through the back way, I said, "Then we see what it is." So we went that way and that meant we've got to go through the trains. So that's how that worked out.

JASON REITMAN, *UP IN THE AIR*

There are no effects in *Up in the Air*, but still the taps [that feed the image from the camera to a monitor] are so bad, that I thought why don't we just have an HD camera, even if you want to shoot on film, that's sitting next to your film camera whose sole purpose is to be zoomed on a face, so that when I'm watching a take, I can have my tap on one monitor so I know what I'm getting and just some HD signal of a close up of their face. We shot in everything. We shot the majority of the film in 35mm [film rather than digital]. You know almost everyone who gets fired in the film was someone who actually just lost their job in real life. We did interviews with real people and did scenes with those real people and we didn't want the limit of mag size [how much film can be shot without reloading] and we wanted it to be a slight sense of reality and I think HD brings that, so we shot them on HD and then when we shot the wedding, we actually held a real wedding. We hired a wedding coordinator, we hired a wedding band, a real priest. I mean for all intents and purposes, those two are married. And it made it feel real and gets little moments, the kind I would never think to create. I hired three guys to be wedding videographers and they basically filmed the wedding and the entire crew hid in another room and I had a mic where I could talk to my three camera guys. I was like, "Just pan right for a second and see what's over there and I had one PA [Production Assistant] dressed as a wedding guest and she had an Earwig too so she could move people out of the way if they were getting in the way of a shot, but in general, I just talked to everyone at the wedding. I said, "All right, we're about to have a wedding. It's going to be an hour, so enjoy yourself and don't look at the camera," and I talked to the actors a little, then we just went in to it and we shot that on kind of lower grade digital cameras. And then I even shot on this new Canon 5D Mark II [which is a still camera that shoots video], which has a great HD chip in it, and that was wonderful because people act differently when you're holding a camera like a still camera. They don't think you're filming them and because of that, they just act natural. You get all the great lenses that you would with the still camera, but it looks fantastic. I really want to shoot a whole movie with one of those.

Shooting time was too limited to come in for a sequence and not have it all thought out, particularly shooting George [Clooney] going through security because we shot that in a real TSA point in an airport. We were one of the first to ever get to do that and we could only shoot from 11:00 pm to 4:00 am when it wasn't being used, so I had a very specific plan. I did storyboards and then I took photos and then we actually got them to let us in in the middle of the night and I did boards of the entire sequence of him going through, shot it on video and cut it together, so by the time we were actually shooting it, it was as specific as possible. What was amazing was George wants to do everything himself, even if it's just his thumb on a zipper, you know, he doesn't want somebody else doing it and he loves being on set and the guy never leaves. He never goes to his trailer and doesn't leave the set until his job is done.

I used to come in more specific. On *Thank You for Smoking* I was very specific every day and I had a plan for everything. I've only made three movies, but over those three, I've started to trust myself more and more and I'm happy that I can

Jason Reitman. UP IN THE AIR ©2009 DW Studios L.L.C. and Cold Spring Pictures. All Rights Reserved.

trust myself to show up on set and know. I'm a good enough director to figure this out today and because of that, things are going to happen in the moment and I'm not going to miss the magic, because it happened in some rehearsal, or I'm not going to force a shot, force an idea because it made sense in my head months ago. You know, I show up on set and I have certain ideas. For the most part, I want to see what the actors do. I want to hear them say the words. I want to see how they would naturally act and I build it around them.

You know my crew is like my family. I've known my DP since I was fifteen years old, so the crew is a family-style crew. Everyone is pretty comfortable. Now, look if it's going to be an intimate moment, and I don't mean like a sex scene, but you know something personal, then yeah, I'll create some space for the actors. You just have to use your common sense.

PAUL HAGGIS, *CRASH*

The scene that was probably the most challenging was because I hadn't realized when we wrote it that I was a pervert, and I found out when I was shooting that, in fact, I was. You'd approach the whole thing as a professional and you say, "Okay, here's Matt [Dylan]. Here's what you do. And, Thandie [Newton] . . ." You talk to the actress ahead of time and say, "This is what we're going to do." And they say, "Yeah, yeah." And then I don't think they really understood what we were going to do and then you sat back and you watch this rape being staged over and over, and you realize that you're the one staging it. And then you're going and say, "Matt, now, you keep putting your hand up between Thandie's legs and you're doing a fine job, but I can't see what's happening because it's caught in the skirt so you have to lift it up, your thumb outside as you're . . ." And you're going, "What am I doing?" And every time I went away and sat down behind the camera or stood behind the camera, my stomach would start to turn as I shot it. And I shot it many times for two nights. And you got to really, really enjoy it. Matt was wonderful about it. He'd be starting to get into character and I said, "Matt, you know, you're doing these people a favor, aren't you?" And he'd go, "What do you mean?"

"Well, you pull them over."

"Oh, yeah, yeah, because if a bad cop pulled him over, boy, they'd be in a lot of trouble here. And so I'm really doing them a big favor by warning them like this and by really making sure. By humiliating them, I'm doing something good."

So, you really got into his head and just let him loose. And then with Thandie, it's pretty easy to see what's happening there and how she's being humiliated and how her husband is being humiliated through her. But the dynamic between them when they were at the car I wanted to have this sort of silent apology from him and, "Please accept me." And her just going, "Oh, you piece of shit." So at one point just as we were doing this, and this is the horrible thing to admit, just as we were about to shoot her close-up when Matt was putting his hands up between her legs, I said, "Thandie, as much as you hate this man, for one flash of a second while he's putting your hand up between your legs, I think you like it." And she went, "Ah!" I said, "Good, let's roll." At least he's being a man in some sort of awful, primeval way and her husband isn't standing up for her in that moment, and so he's not a man in some twisted way. So, you define those contradictions and then you walk back in your chair and you again feel like, what the fuck have I done? But you get it. And so you find those moments. I shot the action first and held the faces for after. I did the close-ups with the hands and everything, and then I went to faces.

JONATHAN DAYTON AND VALERIE FARIS,
LITTLE MISS SUNSHINE

JONATHAN: One of the ways that in working together we can be on a set and just see how shots line up because you can draw anything, of course, but it's really about how the architecture all lines up with the camera, and particularly with a widescreen image, which we'd never worked with before, we wanted to just see how we could use all the locations, particularly the house, and just work with that wide format. So we had a bunch of PAs [Production Assistants] come out, and we just filmed all the key scenes with them using a video camera just working on blocking [where actors move in a scene].

VALERIE: It helps with the consensus, too. Once we've kind of gone through it, because there are two of us, it helps us be on exactly the same page when we shoot.

JONATHAN: We always had to do two big scenes in a day. We had thirty days to shoot it. When we're shooting, we get to talk about what's ahead, and it's more spontaneous.

The night before a shoot day, we've gone to the set and ideally on our own we find all the angles that we like, and even before that, we do a blocking plan, so it's like an overhead view of the dance floor kind of thing of where we imagine, and of course, it changes, but because there's two of us, again, we want to have a battle plan and then that can always evolve, and it does, of course. And then we took little Post-Its and cut them into the widescreen aspect ratio, and then we just do little stick-figure drawings and stick those on our floor plan. And so we'd give a copy of that to the AD, and it basically says here are all the shots.

VALERIE: I think, though, the other part of it is with the comedy, we did a lot of exploration into what makes us laugh about this scene and you just think about in this scene what's going to make it believable and how are you going to kind of get involved in the scene to where you totally buy it, and then if it's real, hopefully, it will be funny. But it's tricky. Like with this film, we weren't laughing a lot on the set. It wasn't like, oh, that was so funny, that's it. It was more about getting the right feeling, and knowing if that feeling was there and it was truthful, then it would hopefully be funny.

We did two days of shooting in Phoenix, the second unit, where it was, I think, hotter than 125 degrees. You could fry an egg on the pavement, and we had all our stunt doubles in the car with their feet in buckets of ice and spray bottles. I mean we thought somebody was going to die in the car because we had no air conditioning in the van, and they had to have the windows up because we shot it with the windows up.

JONATHAN: We had Tom Harper, who's the stunt coordinator on *Fast and the Furious*, which is a little overkill, but it was important to us to have our cast actually do the pushing of the bus. And we talked to Abigail's mother and to Abigail [Breslin] and explained what was going to be required, and in certain shots, we had Tom inside ready to grab her as she jumped in, but they did it all themselves.

VALERIE: It's actually fun if you've ever done it. It's fun.

JONATHAN: We had our offices over in the old Howard Hughes plant, and we had the big area out there where we would practice the best choreography of jumping in. Once the bus breaks down, they have to always park on an incline. So that was really hard to find a place where they could park, and we got just the tiniest incline, and it really wasn't working, but when we added the sound of gravel sort of rolling and . . .

VALERIE: So they've just had their big argument, and they get into the car, and the car kind of just sits there, and it slowly rolls down the hill, and it didn't work till we put the sound of the gravel in.

JONATHAN: We reshot the very ending of the film because we realized that we needed to go back and see the bus one last time, but the really hard scene that we worked the most on was the dance scene and just finding the right crisis. I mean that was probably one of the reasons it took a long time to make the film because it was a fuzzy area. It was the climax of the movie, and we knew that all that had to do with dance that would upset people at the pageant but not upset our audience. And in rehearsing, our choreographer had done the film *Striptease*, and she said, "Well, what if she rips off her pants and does this striptease?" And that was like the perfect answer because for Olive, it could be like, "Look, it's like Superman. I've got a little costume underneath here."

VALERIE: And she's doing it, she's having a great time doing it. She's not doing it in a seductive way. But, actually, that scene did not come together until we got the right song.

GEORGE CLOONEY, *GOOD NIGHT, AND GOOD LUCK.*

Inside the newsroom, we just shot everything. For those kind of scenes, the actors had their information, and I had talked to [Robert] Altman [director of films like *M.A.S.H*, *Nashville,* and *The Player*] about it a little bit. I was confused because we were going to shoot two cameras and we were miking everyone, and I didn't know how much of this you do in the mix [of the sound after the shooting is done] and how much you do with the actors sort of going back and forth, raising and lowering their level [of sound recorded by the mics], and it was sort of a mixture of both going, "Okay, here are the things that we need to focus on. These are important issues. I want to make sure that we talk about John Foster Dulles," or whoever it was, whatever the issue was. But the rest of those pieces you wanted them to feel free enough and confident enough to play, and they did. So you've got actors like those guys. That was something they all came up with once you sat at a typewriter and pulled your story and sort of own it and then you come into that room. I used to sit on the floor and watch my father as a news director and anchorman with all these really talented reporters sitting around, and he would go, "Okay, what's the lead?" and you'd watch them go, "Well, this is the lead." Sort of like the scene in *All the President's Men* when the one guy from Metro keeps trying to get on the front page of *The Washington Post.* They're like, "Metro's not getting on the front page." And you had those guys and you wanted to give each of them a specific belief, like, "You're going to defend this, you're going to defend that," and you give them their stories, but once they own them, they come in there, they're really trying to get their stories. Yeah, that's the un-fun part too, because I'm also playing Fred Friendly, who was the news director, so I could direct it from there. So I actually sit with a pad of paper going, "Okay, Palmer, what've you got?" And then they would tell you a story. So you're literally directing on camera because, believe me, I don't know how actors do it. I don't know how Mel Gibson and Kevin Costner . . . I don't know how the fuck you direct yourself. It is miserable. Now, what do you do as an actor?

"Hey, how are you?"

"Oh, you were fuckin' great."

I had a video playback, but you don't know what you need to do. The two films that I've directed, I've acted in smaller roles in. There's an advantage to that because I know what is required of the character to further the scene, not the actor, and in some ways, that's a good thing. Actors always want to serve the character. That's a good thing. But I don't need to know if you're delivering pizza, the actor will go, "I'm delivering pizza because my parents were alcoholics." You're like, "I know. I need pizza. I need you to say, "Here's the pizza." So you have these sort of battling things constantly between you,

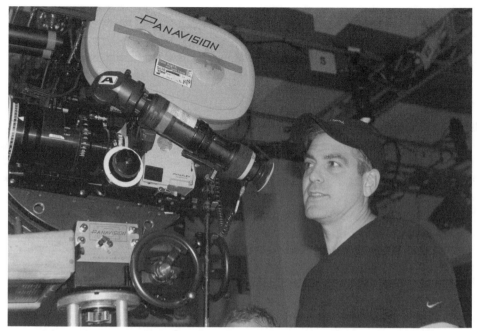

George Clooney on the set of *Good Night, and Good Luck.* GOOD NIGHT, AND GOOD LUCK. Licensed by Warner Bros. Entertainment Inc. and 2929 Productions LLC. All Rights Reserved.

which is the actor going, "Oh, I think I have a problem, and I'm a sociopath, too." So the director wins on those. You know, you go, "Okay, I know what to do to serve this piece," although if we're sitting here doing a scene and the camera's supposed to move in and it's going to get into a tight two-shot of us and I'm talking and it's you and I talking and all of a sudden the camera's here and I know it's here, I'm not acting in the scene. I'm the director going, "Camera's in too soon." And so that's a drag. It doesn't serve the character very well, so I don't know how the guys [like Gibson and Costner] do it. Well, like there's a scene at the end with Frank Langella and myself and David, and I have the first line in the scene, and it's a five- or six-page scene, and you don't ever even look at me, you know? And I don't put the camera on me, and I'm sort of proud of that because it's about those two powerhouses and I'm not part of that. You have two actors who know exactly what to do. I mean, honestly, had I played the part of Murrow, it would've been a fifty-day shoot instead of a thirty-day shoot, you know? David Strathairn, has five-minute scenes, literally five-minute scenes, where we don't cut, and the first time we did it, he did it, the first speech where he goes at McCarthy.

BILL CONDON, *DREAMGIRLS*

We only had sixty-three days. It was pretty limited for something that had this many musical numbers. Musical numbers, every one of them you want to feel different in some way, but often one of the challenges we discovered is that when you've got numbers, many of them with three girls, that they line up when you're looking at it straight, but when they move a certain other way, they're not lining up. And my original idea was to do it here and then we'll refocus it for there, and that didn't work. You often had to make your way around them so that in different formations, there's the right camera angle for it. Three cameras at the same time covering that side of the room getting those angles and then three the other way and then three toward the audience.

I would say it's as close as I'll ever come to making a Hitchcock movie because musicals are almost entirely made in prep, you know? In this case, we had almost a year. We took over a sound stage downtown. The choreography team would work on half of a sound stage, and every Friday, the DP [cinematographer] and I would go down with little mini-cams and shoot the numbers, intercut them with the actors I'd had in to record the script, intercutting it with storyboards and some video scenes, because you really do have to figure it all out before you start, and basically for the sets especially, a huge collaborator were the theatrical lighting designers, Jules Fisher and Peggy Eisenhauer, working out how each set would incorporate the ideas for the lighting design because the movie is really all told through lighting and color. So you have a number like the one in the middle of the movie, "And I'm Telling You," the big number where Jennifer Hudson sings her heart out, that was really all designed around having vast empty spaces, the biggest set we built, a vast empty space that she's trying to fill with her voice and this kind of mothership of light that sort of becomes the power of her voice, that gets pushed up into the heavens. And so that kind of conversation that went on between all different departments continued over months and months and months until we built those things.

There were about six different sound stages. We would re-use them. And then we went to a lot of theaters downtown. The whole movie was made within a one-mile radius of the center of downtown Los Angeles and those great old theaters downtown. We used four of them.

When Deena and Curtis moved to Los Angeles, we wanted a house which was filled with glass, that was that huge kind of glass prison that he had her in. And mid-century houses in Los Angeles, I mean, God knows how many there are, but they aren't that big. That sort of scale, that oversized scale really happened in the '80s and '90s. So we finally found this house that Frank Sinatra built in Chatsworth at the top of a hill. It was his weekend house, which actually isn't that big itself, but it had rooms that were so kind of abstract that you could actually shoot in the same room three different times. Once it's a living room. Once it's a den. Once it's a bedroom. So you never really got the geography of the house, but it was very hard to find a house that had that scale.

I'd show up and something I realized very early on is because of the epic nature of this story, every scene had seven or eight people in it, so it was no easier than doing a musical number. Suddenly it was really figuring out these people in a room and how to tell the story of what's happening with each of those people. So ultimately, I did storyboard or shot list things, the whole movie, before shooting it.

The toughest scene was probably the last one, "And I'm Telling You," the big number. This was the Mount Everest of this show, and I wanted to make sure that everything was cooking the right way. I think we'd worked it out visually in a way that it could build and be exciting and the camera would tell the story as much as Effie was.

And then Jennifer [Hudson], it turned out, again, untrained singer, untrained actress, very talented in both areas, she would sing full-out to the pre-record and after three or four hours, her voice would be gone. She didn't know how to fake it in any way. Once the voice was gone, everything was gone. So we realized that what was meant to take a day-and-a-half was going to take all week, and that was sort of a question of going back and begging for more money to really do it the right way.

STEPHEN FREARS, *THE QUEEN*

In the stalking scene shot from the helicopter, it's a wooden stag at that point because when we were doing CGI [Computer Graphic Imaging], I kept saying, "Well, can't the stag raise its head?"

"Oh, no," they said, "because you haven't taken a shot of the stag from the correct angle." So it is a wooden stag that we shot. There's a wooden stag in the film, and it's slightly embarrassing. The stag would run away when it heard the helicopters. Something's internally wrong with the logic of that.

Sometimes, not particularly in this film, but sometimes it might be going in a certain direction and you just say, "No, no, no, this isn't right. This is somehow going wrong. I always imagined it was going to be like this." So you have to sort of agree on a common language, a common area of how you're going to play it. And I remember I like very much watching very, very good actors change gear in mid-shot. I find that very satisfying. And I remember asking Helen [Mirren] to do it all in one shot because she can, she changes gear, and she did have trouble. After a number of takes, you sort of say, okay, and then I went back a few days later, and she got it right first time. So you're pushing and maneuvering.

In the end, it's how you use the camera in relation to the actors. You could either move the actors in front of the camera, or you could move the camera around the actors. You have a series of choices like that. What I'm really saying is that what makes it interesting is all sorts of intangible things. The actual process of shooting actors talking is quite straightforward. Inside it all are, of course, endless complexities. You really go on enriching it, adding layers, but it's not saying, "Well, let's do it upside down," or shoot it in some particularly complicated way. You actually are making it very, very simple. You're creating something that's very, very complex and then making it very, very clear and very, very simple. I can hear when things are right, so I go on until it makes sense to me. John Huston [actor, writer, and director of *The Maltese Falcon, The Treasure of Sierra Madre*, and *The Man Who Would Be King*] could direct with his eyes shut, couldn't he? He'd look away from the screen. You can hear the truth. So, I use my ear a lot. So when I've got it right, I don't see the point in going on. I mean the actors might want to go on. On *Dangerous Liaisons*, John Malkovich used to say, "I'll go on doing this shot all night," and I used to think, "But there's a schedule," and we couldn't finish the film and things like that. Of course, if the actors have something that they feel they can give you, you should give them the opportunity.

I actually like to be awake for two hours in the night and think about it, and that's when it seems to come to the surface. I'm thinking how do you make the scene believable, how do you make it credible, how do you make it plausible, how do you convince people, "Look, this is what happened," or, "This is what's going on." And you do all that elegantly and gracefully.

It tends to be that people say where should we park the trucks, and I guess you try not to put the trucks over there and then say, "Oh, on second thought, I'll do a shot favoring in that same way," because you're wasting a lot of time just driving everyone senseless, so you know where the sun is going to be. You try and work from that. I do in a sense less and less coverage [various individual shots of actors in the scene that will be edited together to comprise the scene] because you just think I want to show this bit and I want to show that bit and I want to show this bit, and these will show that. In other words, the decisions get taken more and more on the floor. Of course, the more actors you have in a sequence, the more coverage you have to shoot, and I suppose it makes it more complicated. I reshot quite a lot of the film. We rewrote quite a lot of the film, and we went back and shot different scenes. I reshot quite a lot of Blair's part because in a story like that, you're serving two masters, aren't you? You're serving the events, the reality of what happened, and you're serving drama, and I guess you're trying to balance those two things, and dramatically, we got the wrong scenes and the writer went away and re-wrote them and got them right the second time around. And afterwards, you think, well, shouldn't I have known that? But I couldn't. It wasn't things that had ever come up in conversation before. It's the speed with which you identify the problems that are inherent in what you're shooting. I'm always clearing up behind myself like a man who's been sweeping up. I lie in bed, "Oh, I should've done this and that and that. Oh, I'm going to be in the same set. I can sneak that in and not tell anybody." I'm always doing that. I'm a disgrace.

Ang Lee, Heath Ledger, and Jake Gyllenhaal on the set of *Brokeback Mountain*. Courtesy of Universal Studios Licensing LLC.

8

ACTING

ALEJANDRO GONZÁLEZ IÑÁRRITU, *BABEL*

The most important thing for me as a director, was the process that I learned to direct non-actors. Sometimes it's draining, sometime it's challenging, but once you get them, I have never been so rewarded. You know what I mean? And soon I begin to be spoiled by them because, when I was casting actors in Mexico, I was just looking at actors acting, and I was, like, I don't want this. This looks awkward. I was just already spoiled or blessed by the honesty [of the non-actors].

I created a lot of exercises. I had chosen a lot of guys based on physical appearance. Because I didn't understand the language, I said, "Okay, you will threaten this guy and you will justify yourself." And so I put an actual number, let's say, in the room. I said, "Okay, I don't care about the words." For me always it is about the right emotion. I don't care about the words. You can say whatever and still get truth, you know? You can have Shakespeare, but if you don't have the right emotion, I don't care about Shakespeare. So, I went like, okay, just say: "one, two, three." So they were like, "One, two, three, one, two, three, one, two, three." And I saw the guy saying the one, two, three exercise, it was fantastic, and the guy was just there. I began to pair them like couples with the players that I have, and that's the way I begin to find out what they can do.

The father's performance is unbelievable. I did like three days shooting a scene in the mountains, and several set-ups. And it was a very physically and emotionally demanding scene, and that guy was all the time being the same tone, and it was amazing. I have never seen actors, professional actors doing mechanically exactly what you require. Even the little kid, he was conscious all the time I was shooting it, he was in the back, and by himself, he noticed that his microphone was coming out and would be seen, and he covered himself. So he was more conscious than some actors are, and I was really surprised.

There was this guy who sells the rifle at the beginning. He's just a common unemployed guy in the town. He has an incredible face. I want him to break down in
a moment when he's being beaten by the police, and I want him to cry. He couldn't
cry. He was very tough, and he wasn't connected to his emotions and then we find
out that he confessed he hasn't visited his mom in I don't know how many years,
and then he started crying. And he couldn't stop crying all day. And then it was like
a fountain, and he found it like a therapy. He was crying and crying. I said, "Okay,
stop. That's enough."

That scene with the policeman, the young Japanese girl has to cry when she's naked
and she has a breakdown. She was so conscious that that scene was so important that
when we were shooting, she couldn't cry. She did 100 times perfectly the readings,
rehearsing, whatever. The moment that she has to do it for some reason something
happens, and it's terrible.

And then the funny thing is to put non-actors with great actors, like let's say Cate
Blanchett with an old woman of ninety years, that was a woman who has never seen a
camera in her life, or the veterinarian who came from a real dog surgery and his hands
smelled terrible, and in take number seventy-three, Cate is giving everything. But the
non-actors were smiling to the camera. You want to kill yourself, but those little pieces
are gold, and this film has 4,000 editing pieces because it was just kind of capturing,
documenting real moments that make sense, and it's difficult for the actors, and for
you as a director to orchestrate it. It's like playing tennis and putting [Andre] Agassi
with a guy that has never had a racket in his life. "Now, play," and that looks real. So
it's difficult, but it's great.

There was one moment that Rinko [Kikuchi who plays Chieko] was silent in the set.
She was such a disciplined Japanese actor, and she was speaking better than anybody
with sign language and hanging out with all these deaf kids. And between her and me,
we began to have a kind of eye contact and body language communication, and we
were understanding each other perfectly, and that's what was fascinating. You know,
in Japan nudity wasn't a problem. Rinko is a mature woman and at the same time, she
understood that it was not about sex. It was about tenderness. She's not seeking sex.
She's seeking somebody to have some emotional attention paid to her. She understood
the context of the character. The difficult one was, believe it or not, that little boy
in the Morocco looking at his sister naked. That was a huge thing. This is a Muslim
community, yet they were telling me that the girl wanted to do it, but the mother was
worried that the town will throw stones at her or something like that, and I was really
worried. I said, "I don't want to do it with her. Let's bring somebody else that can do
it." But she was stubborn, she wanted to do it until the mother said, "Don't worry. I
will take care of her." So we did, but it was a huge thing.

GEORGE CLOONEY, *GOOD NIGHT, AND GOOD LUCK.*

If you have really good actors, and these kids, all of them, came to work so prepared,
I would give them every morning newspapers of the day, October 4, 1954, and they
would sit down and they would take the papers. Each one of them had their own desk

and their manual typewriter, and they would sit down and type stories that we would later on shoot in the projection room, and I'd sit there and go, "Okay, what's your lead story?" and they would each pitch it. They sort of owned those pieces. But what was great was they would pick up social calendar events out of the thing so that I could say, "Okay, improvise something that's got to get you from here to here while we're shooting. I need you to talk about something about this, and I think you wouldn't like that." And you could give them just very easy notes, and they were so specific and so clean because they owned those pieces of information. That shot that went from the doors opening to rotating to coming out to walking and we also have Dianne Reeves singing live at the same time. We didn't do anything to playback. Everything's done live. We didn't loop a single line in this movie.

I needed to help Frank [Langella who plays the head of the network], quite honestly, playing Paley because if you've only got two or three scenes with someone who is the power, the power in the film, you're not powerful if you go, "I'm big and powerful." You know, you've given it all away. So you need somebody who goes, "How ya doing?" And, it's how you react to everybody.

I think that for me as an actor, in general, oftentimes the best things that happen are sort of accidental. If you've done a play for three months straight and then one night something very funny happens out of it, you go, "Oh, wow, that was different and unusual," and sometimes you're lucky enough to catch it on camera. As a filmmaker, it's trickier because you have such a limited amount of time usually to do things like sometimes letting the camera run a little longer. I'll go until I get what I need, but I don't do a lot of takes because, as an actor, I don't work very well under those sort of circumstances. If I'm working with a director who takes fifty takes, then I don't really start working for the first twenty. I mean, honestly, you get to a point where you're looking at somebody going, "Well, you're not going to print and move on [end shooting the scene and go to another scene] no matter what happens," so you tend to, as an actor, not really get ramped up for it.

I tend to want, as a filmmaker, to say, "Okay, this is your space. I'm going to get what I need first and then let's see what happens from there." First things first, which is I need somebody to deliver the pizza. These are specifics that I need, painting by numbers here. Then let's see sort of where it goes from there. Actors tend to respond pretty well to that because they feel like once they've sort of banked what it is they're trying to do, then they feel like, well, maybe I'll swing a little bit here. I'll say plenty of times, "Okay, we got it. What do you think?" And no actor will go, "Okay, let's move on." Ever. It'll never happen in the history of time. "Oh, good, you got it? Okay, let's move on." Never happen, ever. So as the director, at some point, you've got to go, "We're done. That's enough. Stop acting."

Well, in this film, it was a much different experience than I've done with others. I had just come from doing a television series called *Unscripted* that we'd done basically all improvised, although I sort of had the pretty strong outline to the pieces. I'd sit with these actors, "And here's what we're going to do. This is sort of what we're looking for in the scene." But the trick to it was that you couldn't dictate what it really was going to be because everything changes, including that the star of the show may end up not being the star of the show, and maybe it's this guy over here who is funny or more interesting, and you just sort of have to follow where that happens. So what we would do in all the scenes inside the newsroom was we would let the action of the scene dictate where the focus of the scene would be. We knew we had a structure of what that was, but inside that, each of these guys would come in with information and suddenly somebody could take over the room. "Okay, here are the things that we need to focus on. These are important issues."

David [Strathairn who plays Edward R. Murrow] did this literally five-minute take, and as he finished the take, we moved all the way into his eyes, and he finished it all in one take, and we looked at his first take and I go, "Cut," and we kind of sat there for a minute, and I was like, "Oh, we should probably go again."

"Yeah, yeah, we should probably go again."

And then we said that we didn't need to. And we used the first take, but we would have felt like schmucks had we not done two. But he's that kind of an actor. That's where we got lucky.

DAVID O. RUSSELL, *THE FIGHTER*

Every actor's different you know. Like Christian [Bale] and Melissa [Leo] are super preparation actors. They're super methody [the Method is a style of acting based on the work of Constantin Stanislavski stressing personal affect memory]. You know they go to their workshop and they come out of their workshop and they're all transformed and then Mark [Wahlberg] and Amy [Adams] are more like, it's not that they can't transform but, they're more kind of bringing their authentic selves to what's happening, and they're not as attached. They're both interesting styles of acting. And you needed both to make the cocktail of this movie. You got the quiet people with the really loud people. And one lets the other do it, you know?

Robert De Niro said to me he thought Mark's performance was very underrated because of the quiet, it's very hard to do quiet emotionally carrying the weight of the scene. For instance Amy and Melissa, the big direction with them was: talk like a dude. Because, they had a musicality in their voices. I said to them, "These women are just coming at you from their balls, in a way. And their voices don't go up." Dustin Hoffman was the one who taught me that was legitimate direction, because I always thought that, "Well that's not cool, that's like indication." "No," he said, "The musicality of someone's voice is their character. And it can be the DNA of their character." So I said, "Amy you got to talk down from here." That changed her whole personality from her Disney princess self, you know. It brought out a whole other side of her.

MICHEL HAZANAVICIUS, *THE ARTIST*

I didn't differentiate between silent acting and talking acting. To me, it's exactly the same. And for the actors, I didn't want them to overact because it would be ridiculous very quickly and also, I think people usually, when you think about silent movies, you think of the clowns, the huge clowns like Charlie Chaplin and Harold Lloyd and Laurel and Hardy, and I say that in a very noble way, they were not traditional actors. Even if Charlie Chaplin does have a very modern acting style sometimes, they were clowns in a way that they were overacting, with slapstick and everything. But there's a lot of movies made with very traditional actors and they act very natural, except that it's natural in the '20s, so it looks a little bit like overacting now, but it was supposed to be natural and so I didn't ask to the actors to act in a "silent" way.

KATHRYN BIGELOW, *THE HURT LOCKER*

Probably the most difficult challenge was Anthony [Mackie] putting the knife next to Jeremy [Renner]'s throat and it was something he felt that was very hard for him to do. It's a prop knife, but he felt, this is the man, they're responsible for his life, and therefore it was very hard for him to find that anger even though he's just this spectacular actor, but to find that he put himself in a position where he could potentially harm his teammate or his team leader in this case, so that was kind of working him through that moment and giving him the confidence to do that. You're finding out what he's resisting and what his concerns are and walking through those concerns as much time as he needs. You need to find the right language for him, you know being patient and not rushing through it. He wanted to unburden himself from what his concern was, and once that happened, he worked through his impediment and then felt confident enough to go in there and realize it was a moment in time, they're drunk, a kind of, free for all, *Je ne sais quoi*, that sort of took over and then he was perfect in the moment.

There's nothing more important than making sure the actors are comfortable in any particular moment and giving them the freedom to express to me their concern. You know at times they kind of have to shoulder it, cowboy up. There are moments when that has to happen, I suppose, but on my end I want them to feel the support.

The moment where Eldridge is cleaning the blood off the bullets and Jeremy has to elicit a kind of tenderness that you don't expect from him, it was very important for Brian [Geraghty] not to feel weak, but at the same time he was convinced, the character's convinced, he's going to die. So to translate your being convinced you're going to die and yet, you're not going to appear weak, that's a kind of contradiction in itself. But finding the opportunity to express to me what the problem is, because at first he didn't want to just do the action or give it as much attention that I thought it needed, but then I realized that he didn't want to feel embarrassed, so it's finding that space where the actor can actually become candid. I sensed that was what was going on, what his concern was. We were right there and I saw this kind of a breakdown and I was talking to him and he was kind of expressing this, a bit obliquely, but you knew what was going on, and then Jeremy entered and gave it to him just as he does in the scene. He put the fight back in the soldier and the soldier back in the fight, so basically they worked through it as their characters, and so that was kind of a win-win situation.

I'm listening to tone, pitch and tenor and I'm feeling that it feels right, but then I have somebody who speaks Arabic, speaks all the dialects and that Iraqi actor who is actually speaking in the correct Iraqi dialect for that region and for the region of Baghdad, which is where the movie's set. So I'm relying on somebody else to tell me that she's not saying, "Look, I hate this American production."

DARREN ARONOFSKY, *BLACK SWAN*

That is the most interesting when you run into an actor who wants you to be angry with them, because I have an issue with anger the other way, where I have a hard time expressing my anger. And that was always very strange. You know you run into actors that are looking to be punished, and then how do you deal with that, because they just sit there and they keep punishing you until you confront them about it, which has never been my attitude. My attitude has always been, I'm your friend and here we are, we're just trying to do this creative endeavor, and let's push each other to have a great time and challenge each other to take it to another level. Some performances may have suffered or I've suffered because I end up just taking, absorbing the pain and just sort of rolling with it, letting them get it out that way when it probably would have been easier just to crush it once and then it wouldn't be an issue. But I haven't been able to do that. I've only gotten angry on set twice. I remember both times and they were both to protect actors. And it was something that you've kind of asked for from the crew several times and then something's not there that you know is going to destroy a performance and so you have to be on the actor's side for a second to let them think. So it's just about protecting performance. That is the only time when I've used anger.

ETHAN AND JOEL COEN, *NO COUNTRY FOR OLD MEN*

JOEL: Well, with Javier [Bardem] we had a lot of long conversations where, in retrospect, I feel that absolutely nothing got said.

ETHAN: They were bizarre, and Javier loved to talk. Most of the time I think Joel and I didn't know what he was talking about, but the conversations seemed to satisfy him.

JOEL: And sometimes they ended well and sometimes not so well. He would go off and be upset at the direction that we seem to be pushing him in. Sometimes he wasn't upset at all, but it wasn't a contentious thing at all it was just . . .

ETHAN: . . . all mysterious to us because he would be upset at what he thought we were saying, but we didn't know what we were saying.

JOEL: I think with a lot of those kinds of conversations that you have with actors run the gamut. Sometimes they want to talk about the character from a sort of theoretical view and sometimes it's just about physical direction. And I think actors, especially Javier who has a very, really interesting process, as Ethan said, it was sort of indecipherable to us, but obviously it has to do with his intellect and also his instincts in terms of his physicality. Those things you might say about what you want them to do physically resonate much more strongly and immediately in terms of direction for the actor than any kind of analysis of the character in the context of the text. Sometimes it was about what we essentially knew we wanted to avoid with the character. It ran the risk of being a cliché, you know, the unstoppable killer, the terminator, but how to do that was largely up to Javier and a discussion with him often got into specific things about physicality.

ETHAN: With Tommy [Lee Jones] you just don't talk to too much because, unlike Javier, he might have questions, but you know . . .

JOEL: He's self-sufficient.

ETHAN: He can't be bothered. He knows what he's doing, so it's fine. It's just between the two of us, and the movie set is just a pretty informal, collegial working environment, there's just more of us. Joel says "action" and sometimes forgets to say "cut." Everybody will kind of hold for a take for several seconds when they've run out of dialogue. The AD will say, is that a cut?

JAMES CAMERON, *AVATAR*

Until he is fully embodied as a Navi who cannot go back, who does not have the sanctuary of his human body, I always said to Sam [Worthington who plays Jake], "Don't forget that body's a rental, you know, you crash that car, you're still okay, but the Navi are playing for all the marbles, you know, and there's a fundamental difference," and until he takes that final journey and makes that final leap, which he does at the end, you don't know exactly what he's going to do. It wasn't a slam dunk that it was going to work, and he was taking a leap of faith, and Jake is a character who makes many leaps of faith through the movie, and I also think the audience supports him in those leaps because of who he is. They understand his character, just as they understand the character of Neytiri when she's behind that tree and the soldiers are coming, that she will step out and shoot and she will die because her character defines her destiny unless something intervenes, so when audiences understand your characters, you can do things that are fun. You know when Grace looks up and says, "I need to take some samples," it's a dumb line. It doesn't look like anything on the page. It's the biggest laugh in the film because it's a chuckle of appreciation of who she is, of who she's proved herself to be for an hour and a half previously and it all works in that moment.

Stephen Lang is an amazing actor. He comes so prepared that he doesn't really need rehearsal. I mean that's just his process, because he's a stage actor, because he's done one-man shows. He's very verbal, he's great at memorization. Take one would be amazing, so with Stephen, he was a director's dream to work with. He just made it so easy. We were so simpatico so early on that it was just a joy to work with him and, you know, again I look for actors that have the eagerness and the thrill of the hunt. They really want to find something cool and go after it and pursue it till the end and Sigourney [Weaver] is like that. She's a very iterative actor. She likes to have her definitive close-up done last, so she's got a chance to work the scene, work the scene. Even when you get to her, she still wants to build. I would usually be satisfied by take six and she would ask for more takes and she'd be right, there was something she was trying to find and that she hadn't gotten to yet, and she knew it was out there, and she hadn't found it. I've also worked with actors who take that too far and you know they've been brilliant, but they have some demon, some kind of monkey on their back that they have to go farther and farther, finding something which is elusive and ultimately meaningless. And finally I say it's good, and sometimes you've got to just pull rank, but that's only happened to me once in my career.

GUS VAN SANT, *MILK*

The one that had a very easy job or easiest was Emile Hirsch because the real character he was playing, Cleve Jones, was also our on-set advisor. Cleve is a sort of verbose, magnanimous character, loud and very opinionated. He's the activist on set, so it was really great for Emile to just have this guy all the time.

LEE DANIELS, *PRECIOUS*

With Mo'Nique [who plays Mary], I would go, "Okay, I want you to throw the baby. Did you shave your armpits today, because I told you not to?" How to smoke a cigarette and really smoke a cigarette so that the inhale sucks in and it's honest, so, "When you suck that smoke in, it's real," because she doesn't smoke cigarettes. Her clothing was ill-fitted and wrong. "Mo, how long is it going to take for you to grow a zit on your face, because I want to shoot this one scene with a zit, because I want some zits." She said, "Just give me about four days and some barbeque potato chips and I'll have a zit somewhere," and she did. And she trusted me, you know. We didn't go into this deep like, okay, this is what you got to do. It was just a matter of saying the words, saying the words that I wanted. We talked about the characters so in depth that by the time we said "action," that last scene was one take from her.

Gabby's a genius. She truly is. I mean she says, "Nobody loves me. Beat me, rape me, call me an animal, make me feel worthless." She cried. We did it twice and she nailed it on the first time, but for Paula I was trying to get Paula to do something that I couldn't get her to do, and I said, "Gabby you're going to have to continue to do this," and Gabby cried. We did it ten times, and she did that exact performance, not to take anything away from Paula Patton's performance because it was great, but Paula wasn't giving me what I wanted, so we did it ten times and Gabby gave it to her without the camera on her, ten times. Crying, snot dripping down her nose, it was really powerful.

We shot the end in a sequence, Mary, the social worker-Precious moment. I said, "Mo'Nique, you know she's a beast, she's an animal, she's one note, like we can't change the words, so it has to be something in your performance that makes us not feel sorry for her, but understand her. We have to understand her, because it would help me with the end scene, the end shot." So Mo'Nique delicately, very delicately made us empathize with her by telling her story in a way it was written, "You were on the bed opposite having sex," and it was just written very, very like the character of Mary, mean, vicious, and so she played against the grain, which was powerful, and I can't take credit, though I would like to. And for Gabby's moment at the end with the kids and the last shot of her, that was a woman that I had plucked from obscurity, and that was a woman that was shown love by people. That was a woman that felt like a movie star, so that very last shot of her looking up with a smile was not me directing her. That was the last shot of the movie and she felt great about what she did and she felt loved by people. And the end is up to interpretation. Some people, Gabby and Mo'Nique, think she's going to live. I think she's going to die.

DANNY BOYLE, *SLUMDOG MILLIONAIRE*

Good acting is not really language-based. Certainly we transformed the first third of the film in Hindi, it came alive because the kids' confidence just came straight back again and it just flowered in front of us. It's literally a week out of an executive's life in LA to get to Bombay and back again, so nobody really wanted to come to dispute what was better, you know in Hindi than in English, so we had to transform it into English and there's a couple of the kids that had acted before, but we just went with that. We just thought, well, we'll translate into English. We'll tumble them off the train and they can speak English then. I had a wonderful relationship with this casting director, Loveleen Tandan, and I brought her into the show and kept her on the film virtually for the whole time and she would help me with the kids. She would be working with them in Hindi and we would work with them together then on the set. I mean you just explain to them roughly what it is and they get it, you know, there's a lot of talent there and certainly their performances showed it. I was astonished sometimes about the things they understand, like betrayal. When you abandon someone, you look in their eyes and, you think, how do they understand what it is to abandon someone, to betray someone, to leave them.

Dev Patel was seventeen when we shot and one of the things I was worried about was he wouldn't be intimidated by me, because he would know who I was. I had made a few films in the UK, and I'm very well-known really by most people, who are interested in films, and I was worried. We started to fight. He would fight a bit and I remember when he did it the first time, I wanted to punch his fucking nose off, you know, because we were miles behind already and he said, "I don't think that's right," and you just go, phew, but the other part of you thinks good, because you got to have that, at some point they got to take over themselves and for a young guy like that to do it was amazing, and he was also the only person from London in Bombay. Everybody else was from Bombay, so they were all holding his hand about accent, and culture and stuff like that.

I went back to do some reshoots, some pick-ups and the new actors had learned an enormous amount between the first time filming and going back there. Frieda [Pinto who plays the older Latika] just learned more about it, about what was important in the camera, you know to help the camera, the stillness, the eternal world and, of course, if they work with the right people, you see people flower in front of you. It's amazing.

Azharuddin Mohammed Ismail who plays the youngest Salim is a terrific little actor. I personally don't play many tricks in terms of withholding things from actors. I tend to let them know what's going to happen. The other thing that is interesting is the waiting. The day of filming is the most important thing in terms of rehearsal, despite a whole bunch of time you've done before, because they can be a completely different person. Something could have happened to them the day before that completely transforms them some way which appears in the day's work, so I always have a period in the beginning of the day where we rehearse again, where you let them block it [where they are going to stand or move], but you're secretly manipulating them into the way you really want to block it.

In the hotel where the kids fight with each other, it's just rough and tumble games and I love larking around. I worked with a few kids and I love the whole atmosphere to be kind of loose and very easy. Nobody has to do shouting or screaming or anything like that to freeze up the kids, because that's the worst if they freeze up. You can't unlock it then, because apart from tiredness, you just have to let them go to sleep and let them go home when they get tired. Everything else you get for free from kids. You get this enormous energy. I'm a very enthusiastic director. I tend to encourage actors and so I would always say, "Excellent," and they couldn't understand why having said that, you would need to do it again because that just defies logic, really.

ALEXANDER PAYNE, *THE DESCENDANTS*

The moment when Scottie learns her mother will die, I just lucked out. I didn't say a damn thing to Amara Miller and she was faking it. She didn't even really cry. Somehow her idea of what it was to fake crying looked right. It's not important for the actor to cry. It's important for the audience to cry. Yes, I mean, I was choking up while she was shooting and then I'd say, "Cut." "Where's the candy?"

And she'd run to Craft Services. She has quite a future ahead of her on many levels. She's drunken with the elixir of film acting. We hadn't rehearsed that about how she was going to lie on the couch and say, "Oh, I've seen pornography with my friend and we had guys over to see if they'd get an erection," all that awful stuff. And then how she was flopping around like a salmon on the sofa there, she just came up with that on her own. It's one of those things where someone just does something, and you look at your assistant and that's it! Obviously, with a kid like that, try not to overdo it and that scene, it's a simple little scene and not an emotional scene, but it did require more angles than typically I like to do, a very simple scene, but she just kept doing it. The only thing you lose is continuity, but who cares? She does it slightly differently every time, but I didn't want to screw around with that at all. We'll just cut our way out of it. You want actors who just do it. You don't want to have to say anything and, for God's sake, if it's working, the last thing you want to do is say anything.

When Judy Greer came in for her audition, she was spectacular with zero input from me, so I thought if she did it that well with zero input from me, that she actually wanted more input on the day we were shooting and I didn't want to tell her much. I said, "Just do it." Almost in all levels it is a constant process of discovery, not of execution, and even in directing emotional moments when someone is grieving or learning of a death or saying goodbye to a loved, whatever that is, I try not to have a preconceived idea of what that emotion should look like. We have now seven billion people on earth, which is seven billion ways, different ways, that people cry and grieve and learn news and as long as the actor is doing it pretty truthfully, whatever that means for that actor, I'm happy with what comes out, if I believe it. Sometimes I do give very result-oriented directions. "I really need it to be like this," but with emotional stuff, I want to see what comes. The only thing I like from the actors is that when they are feeling very emotional that I can still say while the camera is running, "Stop, freeze, rotate your head eight degrees to the left," so that I can never lose sight of what's going on technically. I need actors who can roll with that, but as far as everything else, I just kind of let it happen.

DAVID FINCHER, *THE CURIOUS CASE OF BENJAMIN BUTTON*

We re-voiced the performances. I know actors hate to loop [the re-voicing process], but there was no choice. It was like there were leaf blowers, car alarms and it's supposed to be 1906. Brad Pitt started playing as we were looping stuff and we found this thing that we could pitch up [change the sound quality], so we would always start very low and then we'd pitch his voice up.

DAVID FINCHER, *THE SOCIAL NETWORK*

Different actors need different things. I like to nurture actors. I prefer that. But there are also actors that you can't do that with because you are playing into a mechanism that is a behavioral pattern that is set. And you're not going to change it, ever. Sometimes you have to be able to say that to get the best thing out of this person, I have to become that parent that they despise or that teacher that they are looking for the approval from. You know, it's manipulation.

DAVID FINCHER, *THE GIRL WITH THE DRAGON TATTOO*

When Harriet sees Christopher Plummer for the first time after forty years, Joely [Richardson] is rehearsed and you could tell all the actors were primed and ready to weep and I said, "Whoa, whoa, whoa. We're doing *this all day* and I will shoot probably eleven or twelve takes of the master, and I'll shoot over Frode's shoulder and I won't even get to you guys until three or four hours from now. So don't waste it, what we're seeing from down the hallway, we're seeing you and you're tiny. You needn't marshal everything." So that was okay. And then we got into the over-Christopher, over his shoulder, onto Joely and you could tell this was a reconciliation. It was back into the bosom of the family that had been *particularly* dysfunctional. But I said to her, she was kind of welled up, and I took her aside and I said, "You haven't seen him in forty years and he looks terrible and you're part of the reason he looks so bad.

Take a moment to think about that before you . . ." and she was like, "Oh, God, that's so awful. Why would I think that way?" And I said, "Look, he's got tubes up his nose. He's been through a lot." And she came out and she did that in that one little kind of gear-changer, that grinding of getting out of fourth and going back down into second, it was just something that the scene needed. It needed that, "Is it you?" They needed to recognize each other. And I said to Christopher, "Look, how different does she look as a middle-aged woman than she did as a sixteen-year-old? You have to register that. I need to take that moment," because the moment is really before they weep. The moment is really in the moment of recognition, or it was to me. Whatever you want from him, he can do it. He did get tired and he was kind of like, "How many times are they going to wipe my face with a towel and put my make-up back on?" And so that does become a little bit of a planning, strategic issue.

MARTIN SCORSESE, *HUGO*

The main thing with Asa Butterfield is that he was instinctual and he always dealt with the truth of the moment. I hate that word "moment," like if it's not in the script in a sense. But he didn't do something because it said so on the page or even because I told him to. He is very genuine and so even though it was only the four hours non-consecutive, this kid was on and so was she {Chloë Grace Moretz}, you see, and she had a different thing. She worked a different way, but he had this thing where literally, two, three takes, and then Chris Surgent [First Assistant Director] would go over and talk to him a little bit, "A little more, a little less." And in the case of the emotional scenes and his reaction shots very often, especially with Ben Kingsley, I told Ben, the boy is standing there and he says, "You're a thief, get away from here." And the kid's reacting, he's reacting to being called a thief, because it's in the script that he's being called a thief and he's dealing with it. I said, "But you know what? Just yell at him. Tell him some other things." And so we did a lot of off-camera dialogue without them knowing to get these reactions. "You call yourself boy. Look at you. You're in rags. You're a disgrace to human beings," whatever he was doing, and the kid is looking, but that worked out very well with him all the time, with her too, we did that a lot. She did it with him. When she kissed him, she would tell him certain things and he would get a look in his eye and that's a genuinely bashful move that he did because he didn't expect it. With the emotion, since there were two or three times the amount of people on set, a great crew and everything, but it's a set. People, they have coffee, they're talking over there, people are talking, monitors everywhere. I said, "The monitors, we're like at Buckingham Palace. There must be monitors watching what the hell we're doing."

"How come?"

"Well, this is 3D."

"Oh, well, why does there have to be monitors everywhere? Every place I go. All right. Never mind."

I mean, I could walk for miles, I'd have monitors. I thought we were doing *Captain America*, that they would have monitors.

"That's 3D."

"All right. All right. All right."

Okay. So the main thing was to clear everybody away, because it's very sweet in the morning with the kids.

"Oh, look how pretty you look."

"Get away. Leave them alone. Let them think."

I said, "Clear them," nicely, of course.

His mother was very, very, how should I put it, there was no sense of being in a movie in a way. He also was able to live on that set, in a sense. He had the costumes, the same costume, all the time until the ending. He lived in those clothes until he started to grow, of course. We had to make adjustments, but the thing was that he and his mother weren't distracted by a movie star, making a big picture. I say, "Here's what you've got to do tomorrow." So he went home, he'd focus on that. She would tell me and Chris when he was ready. I mean, and we only had those few hours, so we would line up the shot real fast, etc., and literally talk to him. I never had to say much. And, I mean, I would talk to him all the time prior to that or the night before or whatever, but basically, on the set, it was very quiet at that moment. And then we'd do one take and I told Chris, "You think you want to go again," because at a certain point, he would be very far away, the monitors and that sort of thing. And he would give us that second take or that third take, which was full-out and particularly with Ben, when he gets the ashes in his hands, or with Sacha [Baron Cohen], because Sacha was just dragging and dragging and at a certain point, the kid is like being knocked around in a way, and he really reacted very strongly on one take, that was the key take that we used with him, but he was always dependable that way. We knew we could do it, and don't forget, it took a long time then to shoot because of the time restraints, so we got to know him very well. But there were no coaches. I would say, "Come on, let's hurry up. He's going to have a beard by the time we get there." He's very intelligent and I could see it in his face. I could see it in his eyes. He understood. As I said, he may have done things at first because it's in the script, but then he found the reality of the person literally. "I'm coming to buy something, I'm going to give you money, I get change back." That has to be truthful. You don't grab because it says in the script, "You've got to get your change back." It's as simple as that. And if an actor's doing that, I mean, that's the kind of picture I like to make, you're there.

PAUL THOMAS ANDERSON, *THERE WILL BE BLOOD*

Paul [Dano] had the benefit of working with Daniel [Day-Lewis] before on *The Ballad of Jack and Rose*, so he kind of knew what he was in for and Paul's no slouch, he's a very serious young actor. I don't mean humorless, but very committed.

JULIAN SCHNABEL, *THE DIVING BELL AND THE BUTTERFLY*

My technique is to live with my actors. We don't rehearse and I don't make any storyboards. I translated the script into French with each of my actors separately, so really it was each person's monologue in a sense. Mathieu [Amalric who plays the lead Jean-Dominique Bauby] knew me pretty well and my wife is the woman in the hospital who sticks her tongue out so that he will swallow and he says, "Come on, this isn't fair" and she is the one who keeps saying, "Oui" when he says, "No," in the church scene. I knew somebody that had a cerebral hemorrhage and they stopped taking Tegretol and what happened was they were speaking and all of a sudden they get stopped in their speech and kept saying the same thing over and over again and, I told Mathieu about that and he just did that in the car.

I don't want people to act in the movie. I don't want anybody acting. If they just have to get through the day and do whatever someone asks them to do that's fine for me, but young people and good actors are like sponges and they see something and they pick it up.

I built the room in the hospital. The wonderful thing is that Jean-Dominique Bauby played by Mathieu Amalric is in a sound box on the other side of the wall. He can hear everything that they're saying to him and they can't hear anything that he's saying, so whatever he's saying he's saying spontaneously as we are doing it and really he is very funny and he is really bright and he understood the sardonic sense of humor that Jean-Do had.

ANG LEE, *BROKEBACK MOUNTAIN*

I found American actors were the best among actors from England or China in terms of off-camera work [when an actor, not on camera, reads lines and works with the actor who is on camera] and American actors have the best work ethic. They do it for real, so the partner can get a real response, and therefore, I have to shoot, if there are teary scenes, I have to shoot the guy who had the tear first, because I learned from the past if I show the other guy first, the guy will be really crying off camera, and by the time I turn around, he's exhausted. He's cried out. They just want to give. Sometimes even after I have shot them, and we have turned around, now they really cry. I mean they're just marvelous. Only American actors.

Young actors offer a lot because they just try to please you, managing to get it as genuine as it is. That's why I like to use younger actors.

With children, it's kind of painful to see kids crying. Sometimes after you're pretty satisfied, you do one take and see what happens. They know they can torture the adult. They just know. It's psychology. Once they're not shooting, they're always nice. I don't know why.

Over the years, I found out the best thing to do for me and for my actors is you prepare as much as you can so you're available for accidents to happen. You must allow life to happen on set. I think only the best actors, certainly this bunch I worked with this time, and amazingly they're so young, they respond. I think a lot of us directors, we try to be prepared and if things don't happen our way, we get really frustrated and actors do, too. And I found actors, they act, they react. Only the best I work with, if the opponent does something different, then they change. Those are the ones I really love to work with. So I'll prepare a lot and then throw every preparation out of the window and pretend I never prepared.

BENNETT MILLER, *CAPOTE*

When Phil [Seymour Hoffman] watches the hanging, I provided him very realistic execution, and what you see is basically his first time seeing it. We shot the gallows first but kept
him away from it, and then we recreated it for him. We did two takes with one camera.

One of the challenging moments was when he's telling a story around the dinner
table. That came in the beginning of the second week of shooting, and Phil struggled
for the first week, and he just did not kick into gear, and I think we both sort of felt like
we've got a crisis. He had told me that it takes him a while to warm up and that if we
could front-load the film with the easy stuff, that it'd give him a chance to acclimate,
and this was the first scene that he needed to own. And it couldn't be saved in any way,
he had to do it. He needed to jump through every little hoop of the scene and everyone
just says, "Oh, he's so fearless." He's not fearless at all. He's courageous. But there was
a lot of fear there. Phil and I've known each other since we were sixteen years old, and
he was having a meltdown. And I felt pretty powerless about what to do other than to
just stick with it and just not leave the room and just sort of slug it out. We were talking
about *Race with the Devil*, you know, John Huston [that film's director], Humphrey
Bogart. In the beginning of one scene was an improvisation, which is something that
Phil does not feel that comfortable with in rehearsal, and as we got going, we sort of
encouraged him to own the character and just be on his own two feet, and now was the
first time in the film that we began with an improv, all of those party scenes are almost
entirely improvised. There were no high-fives while shooting this thing, but I will say
that the stuff that I would've imagined was going to be the most difficult for Phil ended
up as some of his most impressive scenes, being the easiest and being done in two
takes, like when he says goodbye to the killers at the end and it's an emotional scene.

BILL CONDON, *DREAMGIRLS*

With acting styles, Anika [Noni Rose] works it out by doing it a few times and Eddie
[Murphy] is sort of, "Are we done yet?" Eddie got that about her and respected her
enough that he would hang out for her. He'd do all of her coverage [various individual
shots of actors in the scene that are edited together to comprise the scene], all those
things that he was well-known for not doing. He really went the extra mile to help her,
someone from the stage making her second movie.

JASON REITMAN, *UP IN THE AIR*

You're on set, you're burning time and you go, okay, this is not working, the actor was
only good in the audition, not on the set. So how crucial are they? How much am I
going to shoot around them? Am going to cut their dialogue, is it just one word that's
throwing them off? Is it just one sentence? You go to your other actor that's in the
scene, maybe they can help get it out of them. You know, come at them differently.

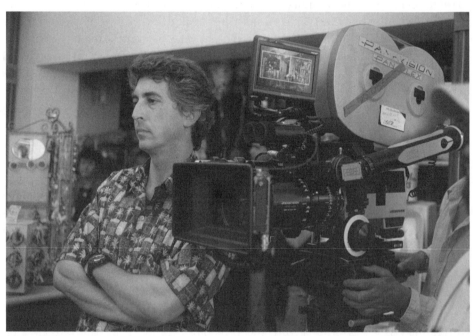

Alexander Payne on the set of *The Descendants*. THE DESCENDANTS ©2011 Twentieth Century Fox. All Rights Reserved.

9

CAMERA

MARTIN SCORSESE, *HUGO*

To be flat out about it, basically, I'm a 3D fanatic. It goes back to the Viewmaster, those little Viewmasters. I always liked to be inside that stereo image. It was a wall that was in there, some wall, not just the depth. It was some other world it seemed to create and, of course, I was eleven years old or so when the first 3D films were out, or that first batch of 1953, *House of Wax, Phantom of the Rue Morgue* and so many others that were made at that time, the sci-fi pictures Jack Arnold directed, *It Came from Outer Space,* pictures like that, and then *Dial M for Murder*, of course. But again, *Dial M for Murder* was not released in 3D. It was shown on 3D later and that was an example that he uses the 3D effect very masterfully in the one scene where she is being strangled, but the rest of it is, again, it's almost like being onstage with the actors, so that the lamps and the tables become part of the story in a way. They're in the foreground a lot. Flowers, and through the chandelier looking down. It's a marvelous film to study or just to enjoy, watch when he cuts to a different angle on which line of dialogue because it's a play. It is a play, and yet, it's a cinema, it's cinema. All but the one shot in *Dial M for Murder*, which has affected me so many, many years, is when he is making the phone call and you see the mechanism of the telephone, whatever. That one shot, you see everything. I want to do that shot, but what it did in my mind is the result, you see every shot of the mechanisms of any kind in *Hugo* is there, and very often, even in *Taxi Driver* and a few other things, it has never left us. But in any event, the 3D, I never thought I'd be able to make a film because of the subject matter and also, because of what I normally do, and it's because of the industry. So when Jim Cameron did *Avatar*, yes, okay, that opened up a whole new thing, but what really got me was when we had to go up to San Francisco I think around 2003 when George Lucas gave a seminar on digital projection and digital filmmaking [as opposed to shooting on film stock]. He was about to release his latest *Star Wars* picture. And it was

Steven Spielberg, Michael Mann, myself, I think [Brian] De Palma, and I'm not quite sure, Oliver Stone, Francis Coppola, everybody there, discussing the pros, and some discussing the cons, of digital. And Jim Cameron didn't show up, but he sent a message on film and a sequence from a documentary he was doing, one of those subs going under water. So in order to see that, we had to go down to this theater that George Lucas has there and it was 3D and it was great. I just said, "This is obviously where he's going and here's what's going to happen." Now, of course, the kind of pictures I make, they aren't known for, I don't think, advances in technology and in fact, I'd rather go backwards. I'd rather get the camera smaller in a way now, but that doesn't mean I couldn't use a small camera that's 3D. I really think so. I just think you have to go back to the beginning of cinema, the beginning of the motion picture, I should say moving images. Everybody immediately wanted sound, color and depth. That's it. They did, everybody, literally, all kind of sound processes were going on that didn't hit until 1927, '26 and they really went with that. Color was being tried in so many different ways until finally came Technicolor. Everybody wanted color, so they painted it. It was fantastic. Those are actual, in the end of our movie, the clips of the gala are the actual George Méliès films with the actual tinting and hand-coloring. Of course, we converted them to 3D at that moment, but the thing about it was the color in 1935, I believe it was *Becky Sharp*, three-strip Technicolor. Everybody accepted it then. They said, "No, the color is true now, the right flesh tones, etc., etc., etc." However, color was always then relegated to certain kinds of pictures, musicals, westerns, comedies, etc. Even [Ernst] Lubitsch [great comedy director] did *Heaven Can Wait* in color. So color wasn't taken that seriously. In fact, the Academy had two categories, Best Cinematography, Color and Best Cinematography, Black and White until about 1970 or so. I always tell the story, Andrew Sarris, the film critic, said around 1968, "In the future, every film will be made in color," and this was a shocking thing for us because we just were, "Oh, I love black-and-white." Yes, I love black-and-white, and we happened to grow up on black-and-white. That's what it was. We had no choice. But basic, when color film came out, it was something else, but black-and-white was the main instrument, the main style, that was being used. So interestingly enough, color, the use of color at that time was so important because with color, you tell a story. Color means something. It just does. And it doesn't matter if everybody is working together, you do certain things. For example, Fellini made his first film in color and it was a big event, *Juliet of the Spirits*. Bergman made his first film in color, *All These Women*, and it had to be a comedy. Oh, Antonioni made his first film in color, *Red Desert*. So color meant something. By the time color was the norm, I think it was pointed out there were only four or five films made in the '70s in black-and-white and when we wanted to do *Raging Bull* in black-and-white, Irwin Winkler [the producer] told the studio, and they didn't want to do it, and he said, "Every picture that's been made in black-and-white in the '70s has been a hit." That's *Last Picture Show*, *Paper Moon* and *Lenny* and *Manhattan*, that's the other one. They said, "All right. We'll go with it."

If you see pictures move, yes, what are we doing, replicating reality or not reality, but life around us or how we perceive life around us. These are made up of different elements, right? Color, sound, for the most part, distance, movement, but primarily, space and so, space is another element to tell a story. It's another way to go. It's another element, I should say, in the mix that we should try to include, and also it can work for us, really can work for us. We thought when this came do it in 3D and [Robert] Richardson [the cinematographer] decided it was real 3D, not converted [a process where you take a film shot in 2D and make it 3D in post-production], I was kind of excited. We were all frightened, of course, but we embraced it and technically, you can go on for hours about it, but basically, they're a different meaning. It all has a different meaning, everything had a different meaning.

Wherever we put that rig, things change, and I designed the picture pretty much because I do storyboards a lot and the storyboards are drawings. That's just the way I know how to do it and very often people are, "Oh, you do storyboards," yes, that's what I did. I was a little kid and doing drawings when I was small and that's what I want to go back to, but to get that drawing to come alive, you have to have a big crew and a lot of money, people. So, okay, but I want to get back to that little drawing that I made before my father came home from work. Okay. So with that, I would design the picture that way for the most part but in some places, I couldn't because we hadn't had the sets yet designed and certain 3D sequences, one of which you can see where the boy points and he said, "I live there." You've got to shoot up the tower. You're going to see the tower, it's going to be a pendulum there. And I was in the tower. I was in the top of the Gare de Lyon, I think it is. There's a tower in Paris and we went up there, but it had no pendulum, but it was quite impressive inside that clock looking out over Paris, but in any event, what we found was whenever we set that camera down, whether it was a designed shot or whether it was a shot we had to improvise, and sometimes compress because of time, we literally had to rediscover how to tell a story because it's about the story and the element of space really helps.

It really helps, what you put in the foreground, what you put there and where you move, but we weren't afraid to shoot very often, as if it was 2D. It doesn't matter and nobody told us and when they did tell us, "You can't do that," we tried it anyway and we found, if something was really hard on the eyes, we could tell right away. It hurt, it was painful. I was wearing glasses and seeing the conversion [how the 3D is created by the amount of separation between two lenses shot simultaneously]. It was so tricky, so when I forego the flip glasses and used the regular glasses, I mean on the set a few times, I would complain bitterly about the damn thing being out of focus. "Look at this," seriously yelling outside the tent like some old man, and they'd say, "For God's sakes, what, he's out of his mind?" and then, "Put your glasses on," and I go, "Never mind, never mind." But the main thing is getting to a point where you don't need the glasses and I think with the encouragement of making the 3D flexible, economically feasible, and then the audience losing the prejudice against the idea of it's a gimmick, it's not a gimmick. It's the way we see life. Use it.

TOM HOOPER, *THE KING'S SPEECH*

I explored the idea of short-siding the characters [where the actor in the frame seems to not have the appropriate spatial relationship], and hunkering down Colin [Firth] in the bottom left-hand corner of the frame so the frame overwhelmed him and he was marginalized by it and I found ways to make Colin feel diminutive in the frames so the frame is almost more dominant than him and he wasn't in a frame in a strong position. And one, of course, of the long-term games I played in the movie is when they first meet, I used the shortest siding, I used the most edgy framing, and over the course of the film they arrive at classical equilibrium. So by the end of the movie there is the one-third, two-thirds balance [the framing of a character on one third of the frame, looking toward the two thirds of empty space]. They are long-sided, the lens lengths get longer, and so by starting in such a jagged place they earn the equilibrium which is a support to their friendship. But everything for me is about emotion and story and how my visual choice can somehow support the DNA of the storytelling, the DNA of the emotion.

MICHEL HAZANAVICIUS, *THE ARTIST*

And there's a lot of shots in the movie that are not period at all. For example, there's a sequence when he discovered the sounds tests. It's in a screening room and he laughed at sound and he decides at that particular moment that it's just a gimmick and he will stay with silent movies, and it's his bad decision. And I wanted to have a very strong backlight from the screen come into the projector and I wanted sharp shadows and I wanted him to start the sequence when he stands up in the light and he says, "Okay. I refuse sound." And then he moves and he is in the darkness because that's his decision. That's what it means. And so I wanted that light as a reference from the screening room in *Citizen Kane*. "Yes," my cinematographer says to me, "That it's not period at all. I mean, it's '40s," and I said, "Yes, but who cares? I mean, this is the story. This is how I want to tell the story." So you make adjustments.

We shot the film in color because in the '20s, the film was full of nitrates and you today don't have that specific gray with very special glowing white and you can't have it anymore with black-and-white. You want to shoot in black-and-white, yes, but it was best to get the color correction. We always talk of black-and-white, but I was talking always of the gray, and that we could only get by first shooting color.

JAMES CAMERON, *AVATAR*

I think it's a challenge to do a fluid camera style and have authentic performance at the same time because they kind of work against each other, but I try to work out something with the camera guys and usually I'm operating so I work out something quietly with the dolly grip and with the DP [cinematographer] that will work through a range of movement and then it's just, we start the scene and I'll feel it and I had a good deal with the dolly grip on *Avatar*. He'd see when my foot would come down off the dolly and I'd start pushing like I wanted to go to the right and he'd try to smooth out my movement because I'd be seeing something in real time. I think that's fun and in shooting a 3D film, in theory it shouldn't change your style much, but there's a tendency to shoot a little closer to the action just on wider lenses and so to give it a sense of art and style and the lighting is sometimes trickier because the lights will get edgy quicker than they would on longer focal lengths you know, but as time has gone on on my films, I've started to get more improvisational with the photography and with the actors, which I really enjoy a lot and that's partly why I enjoy operating.

The other trick to moving camera is that it's all got to cut to itself and so I try not to cut too much in my mind when I'm shooting. Now in some of the stuff that was CG [Computer Graphics] I've got a lot more time to plan my camera moves. The live action stuff is harder, but you know the theory here was that by operating a virtual camera and operating the live action camera I was going to be the only person in both places you know because we had a live action crew, a live action DP. Those guys go on to a different movie and a year later someone's doing the virtual cameras as well. The only thing that made sense to me was to do both myself, so there would be a continuity of style, so the camera moves in the live action stuff would look like camera moves in the virtual stuff. The virtual stuff is not supposed to be thought of as virtual. It's supposed to be thought of as just other live action that just happened to be ten-foot tall blue people in the middle of an alien jungle, but it was supposed to look real and I'm not saying every shot looked real, but I think for the most part we captured a photo-reality, so the idea was let the camera, let the subconscious feeling of the camera's movement connect those two worlds together, so even little things connect like jitteriness and informality and/or organic camera movement, a kind of a handheld style. Sometimes you're even using like little pop zooms, things you would almost do in a natural history context. You know stuff that I did in a few documentary films in between *Titanic* and *Avatar* and you know when you're out there and something happens, you zoom in on it. It's a natural instinct, so I used that stylistically to put emphasis on the film, in both live action and in the virtual stuff and when so I'd do it to a snap reset to a tighter focal point instead of cutting. And the reason I did that was because we found out that in 3D it's better to stay continuously in a shot because if you can stay in a shot and do the job of three, it works better because the eye doesn't have to adjust to it all the time. Now you can also cut rapidly without penalty, but you start to lose the added value of the 3D at that point.

When we were integrating human beings with the Navi, we call it the simul-cam—it's something we created for this film. I was working with the virtual camera in the earlier days before we started live action and I was just getting my head around how it worked and I was standing there and I go, "All right guys, let me get this straight, this is not really a camera. It's a piece of metal with some markers on it, but the computer system sees where it is. The motion capture system sees where it is, knows its orientation sixty times a second, tells the computer to run a real time, and solve what it would look like if it was a camera, right?" Right, but what if it was a camera? What if we did all that and it was actually a camera and it was actually photographing live action actors and we used it to put in real time of the world that they were in, which was CG? I'm seeing in the viewfinder a CG character, Sam Worthington's character, that we just captured an hour earlier in an adjacent volume right off the set and I picked a couple of takes. The guys prepped the takes to feed into the simul-cam system. Now I'm on a live action set. I'm up on a step ladder, handholding the camera, looking down at live actors who are running around pretending that there's a ten-foot tall blue guy there and I see the blue guy. I see Julene run around the gurney and be yelling at him to sit down and

I could, with confidence, pan and tilt off her to Sam, but it's not Sam. It's what Sam did an hour earlier. We called it simul-cam because originally we thought we would do it all together, but it turns out in order to get the eye lines and the timing, it's better if you sort of get one tent peg in the ground while everything else is still flapping in the wind, so we captured Sam so the timing was the same on every take, so that their eye lines would work, but I could correct that. I could see in the eyepiece whether it was working or not. It was an HD eyepiece on the camera that was handheld. It's a monitor and you kind of hold these two handles. Sometimes you wind up balancing it on your knee, the thing only weighed twenty-eight pounds, so you can do pretty much anything and then you would ask from a monitor and I did a lot of operating on a monitor.

BENNETT MILLER, *CAPOTE*

The film has a sort of de-saturated look with no primary colors. There's a little bit of red in the blood and the American flag for a second, but it's meant to sensitize you and work with the cinematography. With just two talking heads, what widescreen could provide was one thing, and the other thing again was to create an atmosphere and a situation where the emphasis is really kind of taking off the specifics of the jail cell and in a way becomes nondescript. And shooting wide open [where the lens lets in as much light as possible], like on a 1:4, for most of those jail scenes, and coming in so tight that you create a new landscape, which really just is the faces and has about as close an experience I think you can get to the experience of listening to something on the radio, which for me is another dimension altogether.

QUENTIN TARANTINO, *INGLOURIOUS BASTERDS*

I actually don't like using more than one camera. I try to keep it one camera all the time. So with the exception of the sequence where we're actually burning down the theater, we just use one camera and even the action stuff, I'll usually only use one camera. One of the things I find is you do some action thing, the car takes a jump does this, and you put a camera here, you put a camera here, you put a camera here and you put a camera here. Well, they all fucking look good and you want to use them all and all of a sudden you've cut up your action as opposed to seeing the thing go from vroom to boom.

I just like actually lighting for one shot and one shot only. I kind of like the me-thodical process of: we're dealing with this side and we're dealing with her and now I'll deal with him and it's all sculpted for that. But this was my third movie with Bob Richardson [cinematographer] and we just kind of create this really wonderful, symbi-otic relationship. One thing about Bob that's really cool also, and I get this with a lot of cinematographers, I actually find cinematographers know more about the history of film than most directors I meet. I'll talk to and they're just rhapsodizing about this movie and that movie and I go, "Ahh," these are my people. I get this guy, all right, but one of the things about this movie was, I wanted to have three different styles as the chapters progressed. You know the first two chapters, that's kind of the western part of the movie, the spaghetti western done with WWII iconography.

Bob is the easiest guy to work with. Like in the case of doing *Kill Bill*, he obviously didn't know as much about Japanese anime or about Japanese samurai movies or Shaw Brothers' Kung Fu films as I did, but he was voracious. I sent him like thirty videocassettes and then the next thing I know, two weeks later he sends me these weird haiku kind of e-mails and then sent me this message and it just said, "Okay, I've seen all thirty, I need more." I'm used to sending people stuff and they never watch them and he was just voracious about it and getting really turned on by the snap zooms that the Shaw Brothers would do all the time so we'd watch shots and we'd talk about this, and what's great about Bob is that you can come up with a cool, big shot and he's going to be excited about that.

STEVEN SPIELBERG, *MUNICH*

Because of the documentary aspects of the whole break-in, I wanted to keep the sequence shaky camera. At the same time, I didn't want it to be so shaky that we couldn't see who they were, what they looked like. And so it was a combination of some styles.

PAUL THOMAS ANDERSON, *THERE WILL BE BLOOD*

The shot where Paul [Dano] gives his first sermon, I didn't really preconceive it. I mean it's always ideal to have something in one shot [without cuts to other shots], because it's hard enough to get it once, let alone get it again in another direction, you know, but something like that in particular where someone's going to have to rise to the occasion and do a lot of physical work, rather than chop it up and ideally, if it can work and make sense, it can be like that, a oner [a scene shot with no cuts]. The night before, Paul had been spending some time in the church and trying things on for size and I came in later that day after shooting and I looked at what he had planned out and it looked really good and I said a few things, which was really nice because I saw how he had plotted it out and I said what's really nice is I could shoot it in one take. It's nice because you're after that one thing as opposed to piecemeals.

DANNY BOYLE, *SLUMDOG MILLIONAIRE*

I've always loved those shifted angles. I always find it amazing when you watch them. You've always got this horizon in the cinema, which is that screen. That's your horizon, so that's stable, so everything's inside it. I've always tried to go cock-a-hoop with it really. It's just my taste but some people loath it. I mean really loath it, and that's fair enough, but that's personally what I love. I love looking at things slightly off balance like that.

Danny Boyle on the set of *Slumdog Millionaire*. SLUMDOG MILLIONAIRE ©2008 Twen-tieth Century Fox. All Rights Reserved.

LEE DANIELS, *PRECIOUS*

Well, I had to shut down production two weeks into the film, which was the scariest thing I'd ever done and I didn't even know that it was cool to do. I did it because I knew my movie was going to suck if I didn't. The first cinematographer and I were not on the same page. Andrew Dunn is so wonderful, my cinematographer. He had one week of prep. I said, "Look, I got to create three worlds." The world which I knew of as a child, which was unsteady. I never knew whether the lights were going to be turned off, whether there was going to be food in the refrigerator, whether or not my dad was going to come home in a fit, so I wanted to feel in Mary's home like I felt, uncertain and in fear, troubled. So I told him how I wanted it to feel and with the week, I gave him images of whatever it was and the production design was a replica of the house that I grew up in as a kid. The second was the learning environment, which was a cocoon. I wanted to feel like she was walking into a safe place. Like every time we saw Ms. Rain we would go, "Ah, ain't nothing going to happen to her now," you know. So it was a safe environment, a warm environment like she was walking into a cocoon, and the third was the fantastical which we use sound and over-the-top colors and just whatever.

I had a storyboard, but I had to throw it out when I got rid of my first cinematogra-pher and we really, really trusted on me having in-depth conversations with Andrew the morning of, "What I'm doing, and what can you do? Do we have all the equipment that you need? Tell me, so are we good," "Yeah," and we prayed a lot.

JASON REITMAN, *UP IN THE AIR*

I wanted the film to begin in Ryan's point of view where you see airports as kind of beautiful architecture and wonderful places to be, so throughout the beginning of the film and this was across every department, a lot of wide lenses, lots of moving camera, lots of dollying camera and the color palette was muted and very cool looking. A lot of half-light, a lot of beautiful lighting. Even the extras were picked for being more attractive and their clothes are more tailored, their movement more specific. Over the course of the film, life becomes more real. We go to handheld, warmer colors more like the *Juno* color palette. Long lenses, handheld camera, even putting some of those snap zooms in to make it feel a little bit more real. Extras were picked because they weren't as tailored, and the idea was for his life to become more real.

Part III

POST-PRODUCTION

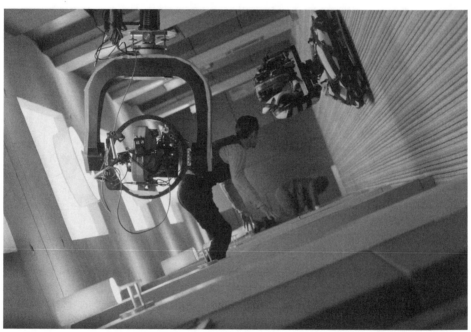

Actors on the set of *Inception*. INCEPTION—Licensed by Warner Bros. Entertainment Inc. All Rights Reserved.

10

Editing

BENNETT MILLER, *CAPOTE*

Mostly scenes got shorter. So maybe we lost a third of the script.

The dinner table scene I ended up cutting and re-cutting with Chris Tellefsen, our editor, for almost the duration of the edit, which was like a four-month edit. I kept on coming back to it because we just slipped through when shooting. I mean it was just like the crisis mentality sustained itself like throughout edit.

RON HOWARD, *FROST/NIXON*

Post-production is ultimately where you kind of finally end up really making the movie and it's a discovery like: "God we could have saved another day of shooting, you know."

Ultimately, I had two different versions for the end. I had a version where Nixon takes the shoes out, but doesn't put them on. Three actually. One where he doesn't take them out at all and one where he puts them on and walks away. I cut it like it was scripted and thought it was beautiful. People liked it and I sort of said well, "What do you like about the ending?" and they said, "Well, it's just great that Nixon seems to have changed." I went, "Oh shit." Nixon didn't change. This isn't about Nixon changing. I thought it was wonderful that he couldn't wear the shoes no matter how hard he tried to be like David Frost and we went back and forth and finally we tried this ending where he just takes them out, and I happened to have shot it in just a panic in those last five minutes, him putting the shoes on the balustrade. I wound up cutting the two versions and I frankly liked him walking in the shoes, but I tried it one more time and this time we actually tested two simultaneous audiences with the score sheets and the whole thing and they both played really well and in my heart of hearts I kind of liked the walking, walking the shoes and we saw the results and our movie tested well every time we screened it, but it tested like five, six points better in the one where he walks away in the shoes and that's significant. I thought well there you go and we got to the focus group and they asked the question about the ending and they all said, "Yeah, we liked it" and he said, "Why?" and they said, "Because it was nice that Nixon changed." I said, "Five points, it's not even worth it. We can't possibly do that." We went with the five points less version, but that was a nerve-wracking one, but I was glad we scrambled around and shot a bit extra that day.

STEVEN SPIELBERG, *MUNICH*

I tend to cut my movies as I shoot them, so I do pretty much have my movie several weeks after I'm done shooting because I've already made nine, ten, eleven passes on each scene on the locations, because what I do is I shoot, then I go to the editing room. And on weekends, I'm in the editing room. In the mornings, I'm in the editing room well before my call [to come to the set to shoot].

We didn't have that much time to tell the whole story and the film was long. I think with the end credits, the film was close to two hours and forty-something minutes, and there was a lot of scenes that were really scenes about Steve and Carl and Hans and Robert and Avner in the safe houses, conversations that they would have. A little more background about who they were, who their families are. There was more personalizing of the team in the early drafts of the script, and I put a lot of that on film, and I found I really didn't need it because they were economically telling you more about themselves in a kind of spareness, which is how Tony Kushner writes. And the minute we tried to, I think, indulge ourselves and speak to what it was like before this mission, the film bogged down. It was a different kind of a movie. It had lost its momentum.

I found a lot of times just because I still cut on film and I'm sitting at the KEM [a flatbed film editing machine no longer in use], the only KEM in town by the way, and we have twenty-five bulbs left before we have to switch to the AVID [a digital editing machine]. So I've got about three movies left before I'm going to be forced to go to the AVID. But a lot of things happen in the editing room, which is interesting, especially when you're trying temp music [temporary music to be replaced by the composer's original] and when you're dropping the dialogue. It's just film is the most malleable art form ever invented. It's the greatest art form ever invented, as well, but it really doesn't pull apart. It's like taffy. You can just pull it and you can go walk a mile that way, I can go walking a mile this way, and there's something still stranded in between, and that's what's great about how you re-tell your story again and again in the editing room.

DAVID O. RUSSELL, *THE FIGHTER*

I do not watch dailies. I'd rather give the editor very specific notes when I'm shooting that are sent to my editor so that she almost knows exactly how I want her to try and cut it and which takes I want her to use. So I'll say, "Take six was my favorite and maybe there was something interesting in take five, if you need an alternative," and then I would cut to this angle for this and I would stay there for this much dialogue and then I would try popping over to this. You know so I'll be very specific about it. Because I think you feel it, I feel it in the moment, how I want the scene to go. Of course, that changes and you learn many things in the editing room. Because one of my least favorite things is to see a rough cut that is nothing of what you had in mind. And you know, it's depressing.

ANG LEE, *BROKEBACK MOUNTAIN*

I think the editing room, the beauty of that is actually you don't have to deal with panic. You're making your movies, everything's put together, and they start to make sense to you. I think editing itself is a process. For me, it's not like you prepare up to that point what you're thinking, and then you're shooting. Then you come to a close. The whole phase of everything is another re-creation. So after you get all this, to me, you start to realize what you're dealing with, and that's a new phase, and it's a process I partake very closely with editor. I come like fifteen minutes after they arrive, leave like fifteen minutes before they leave, so I'm there all the time. I felt I was making a movie with my fellow filmmakers. So the whole post-production, editing certainly is a main part of it, is the most pleasurable thing. That's when you feel like filmmakers instead of angry with the actors, whatever and weather when you're not always in control.

TONY GILROY, *MICHAEL CLAYTON*

I had written the opening monologue in the script and we shot it. The first conversation I had with Tom [Wilkinson who plays Arthur], Tom said, "This is all voice-over, you don't need me," and I said, "No, we're going to shoot it," so that was George's [Clooney] first day at the Queens House of Detention and he and Tom sat down and did it and we shot it because we really didn't know what we would end up using in the end. In the cutting room we really didn't know how this opening would develop. We finished and we hadn't shot the opening. Any of that stuff was all done in post and I had to let Robert Elswit [the cinematographer] go and we were in the cutting room and it was a real science project for about six weeks it was sort of like a mini film school education. It was fascinating what you could and could not put against the voice-over in the beginning for the movie. Because it was a disembodied voice you couldn't show a single face. If anytime we put a face up, your mind would immediately try to make sense of what's going on and say is that the person who is speaking. So we tried a bunch of stuff in a stick-figure, shitty kind of way, and that was such a disaster, so then we were in the Brill Building [a classic downtown Los Angeles building that was also used as a location in *The Artist*] where my brother cut the film and he's in his room and I had all my little digital cameras and I started going back to a lot of the law firms that we scouted and other places we had relationships with and just going back at night with a bunch of digital cameras and making a lot of little movies with the machinery. All these law firms have all these great transfer systems for documents so we were strapping cameras to carts and sending them down things and all the little macro shots of wheels and we gradually over six weeks we kept putting it back, putting it back and putting it back and we sketched together this homemade DV version of all these images so it was all sketched out. Then we went back and grabbed all the hero versions [using professional cameras] of it. But I learned doing that work there for six weeks really was fascinating in what you could and couldn't do.

George and Sydney [Pollack, actor, producer and director of *Tootsie, Three Days of the Condor, Out of Africa*], they made sure I had final cut [the final editing control of how the film will be put together], they did everything to protect me all the way down the line and you would catch their eye across the room. He was the only other person on the set who actually knew about what you're going through at four-thirty or when they're about to pull the plug [when you're told you can't shoot anymore by the financing organization].

JASON REITMAN, *UP IN THE AIR*

At the end, for the first time Ryan Bingham [played by George Clooney] looks up at this airport destination board, we can tell he doesn't feel the same way about it and he goes to take a step and we cut the clouds. The clouds, we added that. I really thought that he was going to go take a step and it says this in the screenplay. He goes to take a step and we cut to black and oddly originally I was looking for something similar to what you experience at the end of *Avatar*, where the eyes open and you realize this is not the end, but rather the beginning of a journey and you cut to black and it's so smartly done but I realized that did not work for my movie. You needed another beat because we're leaving the audience with, you know, a fairly large question about not only George's life, but this is a film that deals with the stuff that we're thinking about on a daily basis. Are we with the right person? Have we found the right person? Could we live alone particularly at a time when people are losing their jobs and they're losing what's most important to them and I realized I needed a moment for the audience to just settle for a second without credits and think about those decisions for themselves and that's where the clouds came from.

GEORGE CLOONEY, *GOOD NIGHT, AND GOOD LUCK.*

We were in Italy, which by the way, I highly recommend if you're going to do it on an AVID [a digital editing machine]. I put an AVID at my house in Italy. That's a good place to edit. You can sucker like the greatest editors to come out and do a film for nothing.

"Oh, we can't afford you? Well, we're going to cut it in Italy for ten weeks." "Really?"

DANNY BOYLE, *SLUMDOG MILLIONAIRE*

We kept cutting and we'd go anywhere. We'd go back in time ten years for one line and then come straight back without any indication. You'd just go for an almost ordinary line of dialogue, which fitted into a present-day scene.

JULIAN SCHNABEL, *THE DIVING BELL AND THE BUTTERFLY*

I had these two archivists and I asked them to look for glaciers. I asked them to look for bullfighting sequences. I asked them to look for certain things that I needed and they came up with this stuff and I was just sitting around listening to Bach for hours, watching it go one way and then it would stop, and then go the other way and like in Elem Klimov's *Come and See* where at the end everything plays backwards. So once the sound goes out after the accident and you hear Claude's voice say, "I had one last thought we were going to be late to the theater and then I sank into a coma," you realize that his body of work, his body, was transformed and we get to partake in what's been accomplished and now there is no fear of death and he can just go back to and be part of the glaciers again and everything is sort of back at peace.

QUENTIN TARANTINO, *INGLOURIOUS BASTERDS*

When I wrote this scene of the theater burning down, I thought that I would stretch it out a little bit more and give the audience moments to applaud and then when I was editing I was like no, no, no I'm not going to do any of that stuff. This fire's just got to be so raging that if a bomb didn't blow up in the next two minutes everyone would be dead anyway. I wanted to not have any disaster movie kind of crap. I wanted it to just be the boom and it's over and so I didn't really give the audience time to applaud. Every once in a while audiences do applaud, but I think they're trying too hard. I don't think that's a genuine applause and when the theater explodes, it's more like, "fuuuck, all right." That's the reaction I want. Then we have the epilogue with Brad [Pitt] and Landa and they are the real protagonists in the film. This is who we've really invested in, so when the audience starts realizing for the first time that Brad truly has the upper hand on Landa and for the first time in the film, Landa does not know the answers, questions being asked, that's the audience's release, that I didn't give them in the fire sequence. When Brad just says that one line about the, "I've been chewed out before," and that's kind of a funny line, but the audience reacts really over the top. It's not that funny, but it is the release they've been waiting for and he's their boy. That last image was just kind of making a hubris comment. It hit me when I was writing but was I going to keep that in and then I was like it seems cowardly not to, so I just had to have the balls to leave it in.

ALEXANDER PAYNE, *THE DESCENDANTS*

Morgan Freeman narrating *March of the Penguins* actually fell off the truck in editing. I came in to watch the editor's cut, after two weeks' break after shooting the picture, and one of the assistant editors had stuck it on and we never changed it. A film needs a coda, not all, but often films, you have an ending and then you have a coda. It's a rhythmic thing. I felt it in the editing that it just needs a little coda. The dissolve to white and then back out of white, that was in editing. On the script phase or in planning the film, we do think of as many transitions, so we can shoot them, and then in cutting, you come up with others. It's sort of an obvious one, but implying death, a dissolve to white sort of makes sense and then out of that, that was in editing.

It was only two or three scenes that wound up on the floor. One of them is the rapprochement between the father and the older daughter and his learning how to become a father and all that kind of stuff. There was a nice scene when the family arrives on the island of Kauai to search for the lover and they arrive in the hotel room. This is before they go out onto the beach to look for him, hope to spot him on the beach. The father gets off the phone with the doctor back in Honolulu and finds his daughter smoking out on the balcony and says, "They just unhooked her. It'll just be a matter of hours, maybe weeks, a couple of weeks. We don't know. So how are you doing?" And it was sort of a heart-to-heart between the two, a nicely written little scene. And they acted it very nicely and it was tricky to cut that because of that growing relationship between father and daughter, but I lost it for rhythm to keep that part of the picture going.

I watch dailies about the first three weeks and then I get too tired and I also lose interest. I think, "Well, I was done when they shot it. I know what we shot and as long as I get that phone call at 1:00 pm every day from Kevin [Tent, the editor] back in the cutting room,

"How does it look?"

"It looks great."

"Did such and such work?"

"Yeah, yeah, yeah."

"Do you think I got everything?"

"Yeah, I think you did, but you might want to get a close-up. Could we do that?"

"Okay, fine."

Whatever that five-minute conversation is, it's the highlight of my day. Then when I get to the cutting room, I don't watch an assembly [the editor's first version of the movie] anymore. It's just too dispiriting. I take the two weeks off to forget all about it and when I get to the cutting room, I really want to work as an editor, not as a director in love with his material. I want to start the whole film fresh. So we'll start at the beginning and I say, "All right, Kevin. Show me what you did," but we do it piecemeal. Don't show me the whole goddamn film, no way. "Let's start watching dailies." So then I begin with him my process of memorizing all the footage. So I'm pretty much there the whole time, and I'm helpless without him. It's really like a co-writer. He is a really indispensable part of what I do. We have done all my five features and one pilot. When I got the financing for *Citizen Ruth,* I called up an editor I knew, [Carole] Kravitz, and said, "You're too expensive and too unavailable for me. Could you recommend anyone?" And she recommended two names. Kevin was one and I met him and that was it.

Usually, if you only had one dissolve in a movie, no one cares, but if you have a wipe [a type of visual transition], you have to have at least two wipes. But I figure I'm fifty years old now and I can do whatever I want, so one wipe. We tried to cut there, we tried to dissolve. Nothing worked. Put a wipe and, oh, it works.

So often in film, you're trying to make an omelet, but it screws up, so you just make scrambled eggs. The scene where the little girl learns the mother is dying was a whole scene where she's walked in and kind of beat by beat is led through that and we tried to make that scene work and it was kind of dragging down that part of the picture and we tried to make it work cut after cut after cut. And finally, it didn't and finally, we just made scrambled eggs and found an appropriate piece of music, a moving piece of music.

STEPHEN FREARS, *THE QUEEN*

For me, the making of the film is the learning what film you're making, in a sense. The whole thing is this sort of journey in which you discover many, many things.

For Diana, I found a woman in France who was a look-alike, and when I was shooting the crash in the tunnel, I actually shot a close-up of her at the moment of impact. And I thought that would be very, very powerful. We got into the film, and the film would just stop at that point because all people were interested in was whether she looked like her or not. In fact, she did look very like her, but the conversation became about that. So in the end, we took out that shot, and I think at one point you see the top of her head or something. But the verisimilitude of the resemblance, the accuracy of the resemblance proved to be a distraction, and so we pulled back and didn't show the death in that way.

The documentary footage is provided by an absolutely brilliant documentary director, a man called Adam Curtis, who made *The Power of Nightmares*, and he's in himself very, very mysterious, so he brings his footage, then he edits it, and then three weeks later, my editor has the courage to re-edit it.

We'd cut it and bits of the film didn't work, and you just thought, oh, I see we actually shot the wrong scene, or it shouldn't be like that, it should be like this. But you couldn't take the material and maneuver it to be like that. You have to just go and do a different scene.

KATHRYN BIGELOW, *THE HURT LOCKER*

The thing that was so critical in that ending is to both feel the futility of the conflict, but also the triumph of the character. Okay, how do you do that? 365 days left and the most critical thing I think is the information in the title. You know it's a different company. It's not Bravo, it's Delta. You realize here we go again, but it's a man who's at peace and there's a kind of triumph. You know he's doing what he loves, he's doing what he's very good at, it gives him a sense of purpose and meaning, unlike anything else in his life, even his family, and so there's a kind of bravado, in a sense swagger and hubris, and he's going down into who knows what, the unknown and whether or not we can imagine he can survive these next 365 days or not, I have no idea but nonetheless, you have to have a sense that there will always at the end of that road, another road. Whatever road, another IED and another one and another one and another one and another one, so it's futility and triumph.

CHRISTOPHER NOLAN, *THE DARK KNIGHT*

In the edits we found out that the opening shot we had done couldn't be the big shot in the film and I don't know why. We tried to make it work for a long time and then we realized that partly I think that because of our IMAX presentations it's such a sort of overwhelming format that you sort of need to open with the big helicopter shot and get people into it, so that a little more eased into the film before you present to them what to us is the more important image. It's a strange example of the more important image needing to come a little bit later.

CHRISTOPHER NOLAN, *INCEPTION*

Certainly when we got into the edit suite, I remember the first time we screened the third reel of the film we thought we'd completely screwed up. I mean we went to lunch and said I have no idea how to make this work. Because it's twenty minutes of people talking with nothing, I mean just nothing going on in a huge action movie. So we spent a couple weeks of thinking, "Okay, it's a little scary." I think it was the most tense we've been in the edit suite actually, but you come out of the experience at the end going "Okay, well, we always had this feeling that whatever happens with the movie, at least we've done it the way we wanted to. At least we've taken the opportunity we had and really run with it," and I think you have a responsibility to doing that if you find yourself lucky enough to have an opportunity.

I never look at cuts. I never look at the assembly. We start from scratch in the editing room. And I don't let my editor use music, so we don't use any music until we've been through the entire film, got all the dialogue ready and then we start layering in some sound effects as we go. I'll look at a scene as Lee Smith [the editor] puts it together and we'll look at all the dailies and start putting it together.

MICHEL HAZANAVICIUS, *THE ARTIST*

I really love editing and my two other movies, I worked with an editor, and the first movie was, okay, I'm in collaboration and the second one was not so good because at a certain point, I decide and you just push the button, so it's not really gratifying for him too. So I know that I'm not a big friend with editors, so for this one, I decide to edit myself and so I just ask for an assistant to work with me. And actually, she was really good and I think, better than the editor, I'm sorry to say that, the editor I worked with before. And for this one, this is maybe the part I prefer, the editing, and actually, I see everybody speaks always about the sets and the shooting and the shooting and the shooting, and if I am honest, I love the shooting, but in a way, I'm always shooting thinking of the editing. And I'm defying sometimes on set, where everybody says, "Oh, it's great. It's so funny. It's really good, it's really good." I know that I will be alone crying in the editing room in four months and what they want is just to make the day [finish the work for that day]. What's true in October on set is not necessarily true in February in the editing room, so I really try to take care of that. There's a first cut made by the editor and we call it in France the monster and I think it's because it's really scary when you see because you don't recognize what you're shooting and what you shot. Your actors, they act terrible and the story is boring. There's no rhythm. It's awful. It's really, yes, depressing and so I take sequence after sequence, or narrative block after narrative block, and I really try to work on the structure first. I want to find the structure, and then we work on the characters and the actors. And once I made that, usually it's way too long and I made that for the three last movies and I predefined the length of the movie and the two previous ones were comedies and I decided it won't be longer than one hour and thirty-five minutes, period. I don't want to argue. I don't want to discuss. That's how it will be. And at one hour and forty-two minutes, even the producer said to me, "No, but it's good." I said, "Yes, but it's too long. We have to cut again and again," and I really try to be very deft, because someone has to do it and for this one, I thought that one hour and forty minutes will be the longest I could do, and the first cut was like more than two hours and I really had to put it in one hour and forty minutes. I tried to cut into the sequences, like the first part of the sequence, we don't need the exposition, for example, so I cut half of that sequence.

We cut with a digital machine, I cut my first movie in film and I went crazy. We almost fight with the editor, but as I say, I'm not friend with editors, so that's okay.

I think it's beautiful, these [title] cards with these letters. For people who come to see a silent movie in theaters now, I think they want to see that. You want to find that kind of a flavor and actually, there's a lot of cuts that are not useful in the movie. They're just here like jokes or just to make fun, but they don't really help for the story. I could take it off, but I decided to keep it. And also, sometimes, I changed the cards in the editing and it's funny because the actors played something and I changed the cards and it was better, yes. I read that Howard Hawks [master director of such movies as *His Girl Friday, The Big Sleep, Red River*] did that. He wrote cards for silent movies and he was always changing because he thought it was like a crappy movie so he changed it to make it better.

MARTIN SCORSESE, *THE DEPARTED*

There are many sequences in the picture that were designed, particularly the opening scenes in the sequence, long dialogue sequence between Mark Wahlberg and Marty Sheen and Leo DiCaprio, where he's sort of taking him down, ranking him down. That goes almost like a one-act play, and we designed all the shots, specifically every camera move and detail, the actors moving a certain way. We knew we'd never use it as one long scene and that was shot all in one and then that actually broke up in the editing rather rapidly. The hardest job of the editing, quite honestly, was balancing the characters in this particular story and trying to keep the story clear, too. I never did that before. I never had a film with a plot. I never did a plot. And then the real process was screening the picture for people, screening it, screening it, screening it, screening it, screening it, constant screening. Friends, enemies. Let's just keep screening it and seeing how the intercutting of certain scenes or the trimming of certain scenes or the replacing of other scenes with others what it does to the different characters. The preview taught us a lot. It was in Chicago. For the first forty-five minutes, we're kind of hiding down in our chairs, getting real nervous and then we began to realize that they were responding to something, responding to the actors, the characters, the story, and so we felt a little more comfortable. And also this element of the woman's story that we hadn't really solved during the shoot, and the studio was graceful enough to give us an extra two days' shooting of a couple of scenes with her to balance her out, but we needed to put the whole picture together and try many different versions with her scenes before deciding what we needed with her.

When we previewed the film in Chicago that gave us a sense of knowing that with the first cut at three hours and five minutes that we had something. If we could pull it out in the next cuts, in the next two or three months with everyone helping, with everyone working, I knew the studio, everything, editors, actors, writers, whatever, we can really make something that might be enjoyable, and give something to people to think about.

MARTIN SCORSESE, *HUGO*

And all throughout the editing, Thelma [Schoonmaker] would ask me, "Should we hear the dialogue," because at times, we thought we should, and I said, "No, let's go back to the idea that you really don't hear it. You get a sense of it," but it was a little tricky to get, without a sense of some murmuring that you could hear, some decibel level that was audible, something like that, to get the kid to react. And it was hard for Thelma and I to find that without it becoming a scene. I didn't want it to become a scene and so that was the first time we did that and I realized, no, we've got to go the other way. They still needed some dialogue, but I don't want to know what it is.

Thelma was very concerned about cutting 3D. We both looked at each other and said, "What do you want to do, cut it in 2D?" I said, "I don't know." I said, "Cut it in 2D?" At the end of the picture, they were looking at *A Trip to the Moon* in the house and Madame [Jeanne] is there. They're hiding this from George Méliès. He's in the other room. And after the film is over, Chloe says, "You were beautiful," and on camera, you see Madame and she's looking straight ahead and Chloe is behind her and says, "You were beautiful." And then we hear off camera, "She still is." And that's a cut to over the shoulder." George Méliès is here and they're over there and they all turn and we're on his back. He's been there. I also want one where we do a head-on the whole group, put the camera on the floor because it feels like you're on the stage. In these wide shots, the lens has to be down there. It was a mirror apparently, it wasn't a lens, but it had to be down there. And so that we had that too and it looked great. He was in the right frame, the table, Michael Stuhlbarg, the kids. It looked great because it had a depth to it and you really feel you could walk into the room and you also feel the tension. So we were cutting in 3D, cutting in 3D, too with glasses and at a certain point, if you watch the film for two hours, you have glasses, okay, you throw them away, whatever, but if you're shooting for a long time and then you're editing for a long time, they gave me little flips. You could just flip the lenses over your regular glasses, but it started to cut into my nose here, because I was always going like that, and I was crushing it down. So, she said, "Why don't we just cut this, recut this scene?" We were already cutting to his back after he says, "She's still beautiful" and then they all get up, over his shoulder. Thelma said "We have to do some re-cutting. Why don't we do it 2D for a little while?" I said "All right. Okay." So we did cut it in 2D and I'm looking at the scene and she says, "You were beautiful," and then you hear him say, "She still is" and it cuts over his shoulder and I said, "That doesn't seem right." It wasn't connected with the 3D, see? "That doesn't seem as effective. It doesn't seem strong anymore." And then it cut to the wide shot and we had the camera on the floor shooting this way the whole scene. I said "Why don't we go to that, for God's sakes? That looks more impressive. Look, he's there. They're there, great." So we did that and recut the whole scene and then about two weeks later, we checked it out in 3D. It wasn't as good. There was something about him in 3D, that's the power. I mean, it's that subtle. You've got to be very careful.

I've been working digitally since 1995, I think, with *Casino*, I think that film we used it, made in '95. This was certainly shot in high-def and cut with the Lightworks [a digital editing machine] that Thelma uses. Pretty much every scene was pretty tough for us and we worked together pretty closely since 1980 and so one of the few times, I think this picture, I asked Thelma to put together some scenes while we were shooting because of the technological issues. The technology was such that it was so complicated ultimately that to make our release date, we had to sort of overlap cutting because normally, I like to cut, be there. So we were doing that in London. By the time we got in the editing room, it was still a day and night situation.

Basically you always look at the first cut. I hate it. As George Lucas says, "If you don't come out at the first cut and vomit, then it's not a good picture," because it gets you just so sick, sick, really, and it's not the work of the others. It's just, what happened? Where's the story? Who are those people? So, it's devastating. So, okay, in this case, we screened the picture twelve to fourteen times during the post-production. First, we start with a small group of people and then we do a bigger, a little bigger, a little bigger. We bring people in, friends of friends of friends, or I don't know who they are. They write our cards [comments] and then there are only a few friends of ours who come and see and we talk to them. The rest are all friends of theirs or people they know of and in this case, we had to bring children. So during those screenings, it took about five screenings before I realized what we had to do, which was start compressing and compressing even more and pulling stuff out. And ultimately, one of the screenings, we had the producers there. Everybody was there. It was all right. I think it started at two hours and forty minutes, and obviously, we got it down to 2:35, then 2:30, 2:25. And I think around 2:15 or 2:19, is when we screened it I realized something. We looked at it, Thelma and myself, and everybody was there and we had a discussion afterwards, da, da, da, okay, but we knew what to do. We attacked it and we locked the door. We wouldn't let anybody in. We didn't answer the phone for about four weeks. It was a siege. They were throwing plague victims at us. I mean, everybody's going, "What are you doing?"

"I'm not talking. Leave us alone. We know what to do. "

So Thelma, she'd look at me and look at the first scene and she'd go, "Did you understand what happened there?"

I'd say, "I have no idea."

She said, "Why don't we drop it."

I said, "What are they saying, the dialogue I hear it?"

She said, "Are you listening?"

I said, "Cut out most of the exposition throughout the whole picture." Somehow, the visual took over. The faces of the people in 3D took over the story. We just kicked it and we just kicked the film and we were laughing and complaining and enjoying it and they'd roll in some food every now and then. My daughter would come by and see me, "See you later, Daddy. Good night."

The audience was telling us that they're not listening to certain things and maybe that's my fault directing the actors a certain way. I don't know, but we were stunned by it, but we were real happy because we knew what to do then, pull it out, take it out, move it here, change that. I mean, literally, we just had a lot of energy and we showed it again and it was a major difference, a major difference. Then we screened another six, seven times. We were lucky to get all the screenings in, but the digital helps that. I mean, it really does.

DAVID FINCHER, *THE GIRL WITH THE DRAGON TATTOO*

We had a little sequence after Stellan [Skarsgård] dies where Steven Berkoff comes and they have a conversation about all of the photographs that were found in Martin's torture chamber and there's this whole discussion about that, but it sort of led the audience to believe that, okay, well, that's the end of the story. And then when you had to rev up the chainsaw for the Harriet story, people were confused and they tended to get anxious. So we lopped that off and tried to craft an ending that was still ballistic. It still made it feel like we're tying up loose ends. We were always building to this emotional cliffhanger between a forty-something man and a twenty-something girl, and to me, the thing that was nice was just falling off the cliff at the end asking: where does she go from here?

DANNY BOYLE, *SLUMDOG MILLIONAIRE*

When we had the first cut of the film it was three hours long and the TV show was like ivy. It was everywhere over everything, strangling everything and it was just like you thought you were just doing a promo for this incredibly successful TV show, because it's kind of got this built-in extraordinarily built-in element, the music, this heartbeat music that you can't cut, you can't stop it and what they do on the show is they bury it with applause and it goes out, but there's all these techniques they have for it and that was one of our biggest challenges in post was getting rid of the show, stripping it back as much as possible.

There's a kind of a hidden spine, which is a love story and we wanted to introduce the heroine right at the start and the other element was she was so beautiful, I thought, you always think back a bit when you go and see movies when you're sixteen and you think and you see a beautiful girl like that, you're going to just stay there and try to see more of her. Ideally she'll take her clothes off at some point, but even if she doesn't, you know, it's a more romantic thing.

TOM HOOPER, *THE KING'S SPEECH*

For the first time in my life I sent Colin [Firth] and Geoffrey [Rush] the cuts of the film as I was progressing and because I felt their taste was so interesting that I actually got editing notes from Colin and Geoffrey. Both of them picked up things I'd missed because actors have a muscle memory from a performance and when they saw the cut they could remember there were a couple of times from their muscle memory of doing a scene and there was a moment I'd missed.

GUS VAN SANT, *MILK*

During the editing, you work on the beginning and you get it just right and then you realize the rest of the movie is in need of attention and you start working on that and then after you get that just right, you realize that the beginning is no good, and then you go back and forth until finally you have to hand it in.

There are happy accidents in the editing for sure. I think one of the things that I've had happen on films is there was a transfer of a lab that had a Jackie Chan soundtrack. The sound imposed over the entire reel for some reason and we really liked it. And we tried to get the rights to this Jackie Chan soundtrack through Universal who had had the US distribution. This wasn't on *Milk*. This was on *Paranoid Park* and we actually did reproduce it. We had to reproduce it. We couldn't get the rights.

JONATHAN DAYTON AND VALERIE FARIS, *LITTLE MISS SUNSHINE*

VALERIE: The dance scene did not come together until the very last days of editing,

JONATHAN: Yeah, we changed the song that she dances to. By changing the song and just continually reducing the scene to its just essential elements, it finally landed.

Cast performing on set of *Dreamgirls*. DREAMGIRLS ©2006 DW Studios L.L.C. and Paramount Pictures. All Rights Reserved.

MUSIC AND SOUND

CHRISTOPHER NOLAN, *THE DARK KNIGHT*

And what we were able to do with the music and the sound as well as what Hans Zimmer [the composer] had come up with was this incredible sort of noise for the Joker. This incredible sort of razor blades on cellos and things. It's a very bizarre slide and it goes on for several minutes and we use it a lot in the film. We opened with it, and that way, it allows us to go quite big with all the sound and then go quiet, so you can hear this very fine sound almost like feedback like on the radio or something. It lets you go very quiet, very small because there's something about the way Heath [Ledger who plays the Joker] chose to play the character and the way we tried to put it into the script. It is quite intimate, so he uses knives and not guns. Everything is very close-up and very personal.

CHRISTOPHER NOLAN, *INCEPTION*

And I don't like to use temp [temporary] music so I get on the phone with a composer, Hans Zimmer in the case of *Inception,* and then just harass him and harass him for demos so the first time we screened the film for the studio it was all new music, it was all his music. I think the problem with temp music for me is that it immediately makes things look better than they are. You can't then replace it with something very easily because you fall in love with it. And Lee [Smith] is a very fast brilliant editor and was a sound editor and knows a lot about sound and music and everything. At first he was very suspicious of this way of working. He didn't really understand why I was saying, "Just don't put any music in." And I think he's gotten to like the method and he's carried it to other directors because you see the film at its worst and you see the scene at its worst. Because music elevates a film. And then what we tend to do is we'll screen the whole film with very very little music in it. And every film I've done really has been exactly the same. You watch the film and at the end of it you go, "This is really working well. I don't think we really need much music in this film." And then four months later every single second of the film has Hans Zimmer with like sixty horns blaring and we don't know how we got there. The other thing we do with Hans is we don't let him see the film. So when he's writing his music for me he's not seeing anything. And then what we'll do is we'll take demos he does. We had him read the script and I'll send him a few stills like you know on the *Dark Knight* I showed him photos of Heath [Ledger] as the Joker and he just sends hours and hours of demos and we'll take odd little pieces and mix them around. The great thing with Hans is he's very free and very easy. When you get to the dub stage [where all the sounds are mixed together] for each cue we'll have a hundred and twenty tracks. So we're free to create with that and mess around with that and he's completely fine with that and enjoys it. What I think he enjoyed working that way for me is I wanted him to do what he'd done on other great films like *The Thin Red Line,* which I think is one of the greatest scores ever done for movies. And when you watch that film, it's not scored to each moment. It's scored over the whole move of the film and how it could build every sequence. And what that lets you do by not making him work to cuts is you can let him flesh out an idea of over several minutes, which is a long time, you know, in a modern movie with the way films are put together. And what that lets you do with a film like *Inception* is connect scenes and bind the film together. A film that could easily fall apart, fragmented into its different mechanisms and different layers. And he's able to help guide you through the film and in *Inception* particularly, I put the demand on him to divide it into the different time scales that the film is working on and so he's working in different time signatures. He's working in 4/4 time, and then it's other time. And so you can go faster and slower in the same precise rhythm, so as you're going deeper into the dream, the music is getting slower, but it's getting bigger which is particularly demanding. He actually did the first brass recording session, the week after we wrapped [finished shooting] before he'd seen anything. So it's a fun way of working.

DAVID O. RUSSELL, *THE FIGHTER*

I very often watch the film and say this is great. It doesn't need a lick of music and then you turn around and there's music everywhere. Only on two films have I really thought of it a lot. A little bit on *Spanking the Monkey*, but mostly on *Three Kings* and on this film I pre-conceived propulsive or interesting songs that I needed to cut to try to shoot to or cut to. And I knew that these guys were classic rock guys and I have very particular taste in that department and I wanted to overlap with their taste and I knew we had no budget for it but I wasn't going to let that stop me. And I have a lot of people to thank for that. So first there's Philip Tallman, an amazing music editor, and he put together an amazing temp score. I wanted to buy that temp score and they said you can't do that, it'll be too expensive. And I knew that wasn't right. And then I saw *Inglourious Basterds* and I said, "Well, he bought his whole temp score," and Quentin [Tarantino] said, "No it's not expensive. It can actually save you money." And in this case it would have. Jon Brion's a great brilliant musician and virtuoso musician/composer who produced many great musicians and he did *Huckabees* with me which I got drunk on the music on that and there's not one square inch of that movie that doesn't have his score all over it. And it's beautiful music. So, I said, "Jon, what do you think of this movie?" And he said, "The songs are your score. They work so fantastic." I said, "Let's try it." And he's Mr. Melody, strong melody, and he always has a theme and I said, "Let's try a theme." And it was a disaster. Because he writes strong melodies and the movie was so gritty and real it couldn't tolerate that. It just was a different movie. And his music is brilliant, but it wasn't the right music for that. So that was heartbreaking, because we're friends and so now it was more expensive because we had to pay him and then we got in Michael Brook [the composer] who did *Into the Wild* and he just never nailed it. And we did want him to pay close attention to our temp score because our temp score was just fantastic. And I would've bought it if I could have bought it. For the songs I had to turn to Sue Jacobs, who's a great music supervisor who helped Julian Schnabel. She knows how to approach someone, artist to artist and never says no. And you can get it for nothing or little, less than you would have. Cameron Crowe helped me with Led Zeppelin. They told me they'll never license that song, it's never been licensed, it's the first song on their first album. And that was a revelation in the editing room to have that sequence play without dialogue to play big plot turns with one big, whole, song. When Jimmy Page and Robert Plant [of Led Zeppelin] are not getting along, it's a big issue. Other filmmakers have been turned down when they're not getting along because they can't agree. And we were fortunate that they were getting along. Cameron Crowe introduced me to their business manager, their guy here in the States and I basically spent three months becoming his friend and working on him to, you know, if you're willing to crawl and grovel. And then he went over to England and he was in our corner and he got it. One came to see the film and loved it. So these guys all made favored nations deals with us [where everyone profits equally] and it was just a blessing. Sometimes songs work great. Perseverance makes all the difference.

TOM HOOPER, *THE KING'S SPEECH*

Before I talk about music I think the key to this was also the use of songs and we do live in a world where increasingly there can be pressure on you to mediate almost every emotion through music and I felt in this it was quite important to have a lot of songs and that was because what existed in the silences were this wealth of tiny effort noises, clicks, exertions of the throat that Colin [Firth] was making which the moment you literally put music in, if you put too much sound effects on, then you see, they get lost. And actually a lot of the work on the sound was about preserving what he'd done on the day in terms of these extraordinary sounds he was making. We did a little bit of ADR [Automated Dialogue Replacement] but we couldn't get back to it because it was such a physical place he'd gone to. And of course there's a slight tendency on sound, people kind of think, "Okay, let's just take the dialogue and then clean up, you know clean out everything else and then re-build everything." My philosophy on sound is I want the microphone to be running all the time. I want the live sound to be always present in the movie. But paying attention to that, we picked up a wealth of detail that even I wasn't aware at the time of being caught.

I do use temp [temporary music] but I do have exactly this problem with sometimes you fall in love with stuff and it can haunt you when you're writing. So I'd quite like to try holding it back longer or getting the composer to be the first person to score. But the music is interesting because part of what's special I think is some choices my editor made and one of the first times I saw the assembly of the final speech in the movie, Tariq [Anwar, the editor] had chosen to put Beethoven's Seventh on it and I found it extraordinarily powerful when I first saw it. There was a logic that was, Logue uses classical music as therapy, so there's the Mozart earlier on headphones that helps Bertie speak, and there was something about the restraint of the Beethoven, the tentative rhythm of the Beethoven, the amount of space that Beethoven created for the stammering when it started that seemed great. When Alexandre Desplat joined as composer I was absolutely ready for Alexandre to explain to me why he could do something much more appropriate than Beethoven. But he actually defended it. He said the reason why he felt the Beethoven was great was that Beethoven exists in our public consciousness. All of us have some vague memory of that piece of music. Some of us know it very well. And it helps elevate the speech to the status of a public event that exists in our public consciousness whereas film score is always internal to the film. It can't ever reach out to remind us of the public at a global level. And I thought that was a brilliant defense and made me even more clear I wanted to use it. And then he also explained that Beethoven was actually the anthem of the French Resistance which I didn't know because you'd think a German composer wouldn't necessarily end up as that. So for him as a French composer it had a particular power. I've always felt when you're working with truly great actors that the difficulty with score is that there's a risk that the composer is saying to you, "What Colin Firth really means is he's sad." That's what they see, he's just sad. And sometimes music, because of its structure, it's hard for music to hold a number of opposing ideas at once. It's hard to dance on a pinhead. I remember, again very much, working with Helen Mirren who's so quick in her mood switches, just thinking, music isn't necessarily that deft at making these very quick sort of switches. And I felt the same with Colin and Geoffrey [Rush] and the brilliance of Alexandre is he seems to be able to write music that enters into this complex dance with the actors and doesn't editorialize the performance. It allows the performance to come first and it supports it and it dances with it and more than any other composer I've worked with, Alexandre really loves actors and takes tremendous care of the unique thing they're doing and realizes he comes second to them and is supporting them.

DAVID FINCHER, *THE SOCIAL NETWORK*

This film was very different from previous films only in that I probably spent six months begging Trent Reznor to be involved. I had been listening to *Ghosts* which is a kind of ambient instrumental record that he'd done and I just thought this is what I think the movie should sound like. I also had, because it was a movie about kids who were unsupervised in an adult world, it's kind of a John Hughes movie [who wrote and directed popular movies like *Ferris Bueller's Day Off, Sixteen Candles*]. I started thinking about *Risky Business* and *Tangerine Dream*, so I went to Trent and said I want you to do this synthesized score because it's about computers and I want there to be this sort of buzz a kind of electricity that binds all these people. And he said, "I'm not ready to do something like that right now." So I just kept in touch and we temped the movie with a lot of pieces from *Ghosts* and finally when he was recharged, because he'd just come off a massive tour I started working on him again—I brought him in and I showed him some scenes. Now whenever you show a composer the first cut of a movie you want them to be excited, to wrap their arms around it and Trent's a very low-key guy, incredibly straightforward and he sat there, a lot like when I was doing music videos and musicians would play me their songs and you kind of sit there and you think, should I be tapping my toe, or what's the proper degree of response to listening to somebody's new single? So he's sitting and he's watching the movie and I, of course, not so secretly watched him watching the movie and we saw about forty-five minutes and at the end of it he went, "Interesting." And then he got up and he left. And "interesting" means a lot of different things to a lot of different people. My mother always used to say, "interesting" when she didn't like something. So "interesting" for me is a kind of buzz word. You mean, "*interesting*, interesting?" or like "interesting, dismissive?" So I called him and I said, "What'd you think?" And he said, "Yeah, yeah, there's something there. I think there's something there." And literally, over the transom, a week and a half later, there were thirteen different sketches that we basically took into the edit room and started moving temp around and placing it under picture and *that's pretty much the score*. I think he thought he had emerged unscathed until: The music under the rowing scene came out of going to Henley on Thames. I'd never been to Henley. I didn't know what the Regatta was. I'd read about it in the script, and it was a very deceptive narrative trap because you know Aaron [Sorkin, the writer] just announces "cut" we're in the middle of this race that we don't know anything about. We don't know what it means to these guys. We don't know whether it's that important. I was like "what is the Henley Regatta?" So we had always thought we would kind of stage the Henley Regatta on the Charles because I had these Googled pictures of it and it looked like a couple of grandstands, some bunting. It's 250,000 people! It lasts a week and it's a mile long. It's huge. A really big deal. So when we finally went there and they explained to us that it was an Edwardian garden party that took place on the longest straight stretch of the Thames, and that it was the Super Bowl of rowing, I said, okay, let's start looking for Edwardian music—and I went to Trent hat in hand and said could you do a little Wendy Carlos with this? I think that took him probably twelve weeks. And he was ready to blow his brains out.

DARREN ARONOFSKY, *BLACK SWAN*

Actually one of the major reasons I did the film was to see what Clint Mansell, my composer, would do with Tchaikovsky. And I remember sitting with him at some music conference way before we started the film and saying that in front of a crowd of people and it kind of kept me through some of the dark times trying to raise money was thinking about what Clint would come up with. And you know Clint I don't think reads music very well and he was a rock star, he was in Pop Will Eat Itself which was some kind of British rock band in the eighties. It's actually very funny, in his videos he had these dreads and just these really cheesy videos of him dancing around and stuff, but he just took Tchaikovsky and spent about six months deconstructing it and ripping it apart and pulling it apart and going to elements and finding kind of signature lines and then sort of building a score out of it. And what I did is I went through and I saw the film as a ballet and we kind of went back to the fairy tale of Swan Lake and then tried to turn it into a real twenty-first century story but where all the characters were related to it and the music was going to be the kind of main transformed element that would sort of drag us through that. So the whole idea was to take Tchaikovsky's score and turn it into a modern horror score. Because you're starting off with music that's been in the public domain for a very long time, it's been everything from under Bugs Bunny cartoons to Volkswagen ads and how do you make that exciting and scary for an audience? So I'd say about 30, 40 percent is original ideas from Clint based off of what he was listening to and then the rest of it is actually Tchaikovsky re-arranged and re-instrumented, if that's a word, so different instruments are playing different parts. Early on I was listening to the music non-stop when I was working on the script and on the subway, everywhere I would go I'd just be listening to it, so I'd get to know all the main cues and then I actually sat with the music starting at the end of the film. I would play the music and I would choose different pieces for different scenes and try to connect the scenes to the ballet. Which was a great process for the screenplay because then the screenplay became more like the ballet. And then Matthew Bourne who did the all-male Swan Lake, he's a great choreographer from the UK and after he saw the film, what impressed him the most was that we kept the score in the same order as the ballet. He said you didn't have to do that for anyone but me. Because no one else would see that you were so orthodox to Tchaikovsky. I think the first cut was without music and because I think the music has to be created for the scenes, I just think if you put temp score over it, it just never feels right. It's just always being borrowed. The seminal theme song from Clint Mansell from *Requiem for a Dream* that's been overused by everyone came from an early thing when he read the script. He created a mix tape and it was nearly lost and we were struggling trying to figure out the music and I went down to New Orleans when he was living with Trent Reznor actually, and we played that early inspiration that came out of the script and there was one bar that was in there and I was like, "Oh, this is great, let's put it over this shot," and then he just developed it into something. A really good approach is having the composer off with the script without image trying to create some sense of it. And the same thing happened with Clint on this one, trying to find horror moments within the Tchaikovsky ballet that he could sort of expand on and turn into something. It was an interesting process because when the score came in, it brought the film to a whole other level of hysteria and I was kind of terrified of it because it changed the film completely and I was thinking of going back to him and being like, "Whoa, this might be too much," and then I sort of said, "Fuck it, let's run with it." And it brought the whole sense of the ballet into the film of the hysterical melodramatic horrific gothic tone. And that all came out of Clint.

With the animation of the paintings, we didn't actually know what they were going to be saying to be honest. That all happened in ADR [Automated Dialogue Replacement where original dialogue is replaced by a new recording]. We brought in Natalie [Portman] early and threw out a few ideas and then we had the other actresses come in, Barbara [Hershey] and Mila [Kunis], and had all of them do different voices so we could layer it and stuff, and we sort of created it. And then we did a kind of a scratch track [sound that is temporary to indicate what will be in the final version] of it that the animators were able to work off of and then we just completely kept refining it and refining it.

STEVEN SPIELBERG, *MUNICH*

The sequence when the men first meet, I decided not to have them speaking, and I was going to let Johnny Williams [the composer] figure out how to speak for them musically. I wasn't going to have to worry about that. So I just had them all talking, and I just said, "We're not going to record sound so just start talking," and everybody talked about different things. I remember Mathieu Kassovitz, who plays Robert, talked about the impact of *Godfather 2* over *Godfather 1* on his career. So if you read his lips, he's speaking about Al Pacino and he's talking about Michael Corleone. So everybody was sort of vamping. I think Ciarán Hinds was talking about playing Caesar in the HBO series *Rome*, and if you read lips, it's the funniest scene in the movie.

ANG LEE, *BROKEBACK MOUNTAIN*

The music part, after I did *The Ice Storm*, it becomes part of a creation. Because they can do the computer thing, whatever the movie needs that doesn't make sense, I can now pull it together, and I glue it with music. So note by note, I will do it up to the last looping, the mixing. It starts to make sense to me.

PAUL THOMAS ANDERSON, *THERE WILL BE BLOOD*

I had heard Brahms before when I was writing the film and I kind of put it to the side and thought you know this might be good. Then I forgot about it for a while and generally when you get to the end of the film you know the editors will put together some kind of a reel of all the kind of insane stuff that's gone on, so it was in the music bin in the computer to begin with since I put it there and the editors put together this thing celebrating the end of the film with that piece of music which reminded me about it again. I said "Oh, okay." So from the kind of a joke reel, it reminded me of that song and I thought well, good. Then we put it in the first time and I thought, "Is this cheating? Are we allowed to do this?" I don't know, it just felt so good. It felt so satisfying. You always kind of chuck yourself if something feels really right or good. You know you're like, "Aw, no, is that fair? Can we do that?"

MARTIN SCORSESE, *HUGO*

At first the boy is never really around the others face to face. So therefore, we have to take everything from his point of view, which is kind of fun actually. It's enjoyable because then you can alter it. However, I didn't want to hear what they said and I remember the way it sounds in characters in Jacques Tati films [like *Mr. Hulot's Holiday*] and so I played that for a number of people. Particularly later in the post-production, I had all the sound crew come in and watch *Playtime*. I said, "You can hear what they're saying, but you really can't hear what they're saying."

I called in Howard [Shore, the composer] as soon as possible. I believe he came on the set a few times and we discussed it. We kept making changes in the cuts and in 13 screenings, you make a lot of little changes and he has to go back and Jennifer Dunnington, the music editor, she had to go back and recut it. We said, "Move that here." So it was an exhausting, until the last minute until he went to New Zealand and even there, we got him. He was working on *The Hobbit*.

The only thing I looked into really myself was music of the period. I listened to Django Reinhardt a lot, and other music of the period. The film has references to Rene Clair films, who used music a great deal in 1930. He was making the transition of sound, silent film to sound in *Sous les Toits de Paris* also *A Nous la Liberte*. So that was the sound I wanted, so we talked about that and Howard came up with this idea almost like a waltz and we chose those waltzes. There were about two or three that I chose specifically and redid them in Paris with a wonderful group, incredible guitar players and that sort of thing, and we used it for the café scenes. And for recorded music, I said, "What were they listening to at the time?" And the two songs that come to mind immediately were done in 1914 or 1915 and they're both used in Jean Renoir's *The Grand Illusion*. The beginning of *The Grand Illusion,* you see the record and you hear "Frou, frou, frou, da, da," and the camera pulled up and you see [Jean] Gabin singing along with it, and I always liked that. So truthfully, it must have been 1914, so if somebody had a record player, they could be playing that. And the other in *Grand Illusion* was where they put on the show and they perform a song called "Marguerite" and that's a song I really liked. That was a big hit. We use it in the film. That was a rights problem though. We couldn't use the original recording because even though it's in the public domain, there was a certain group in America that owns whatever and they said, "Somebody might recognize it." I said, "But everybody else has cleared it," and he goes, "Yeah, but there might be that one person." We had to redo it. And that's the only two recorded songs. We started to work on it while we were editing. It's a matter of having sentiment without being sentimental. That was the other thing, which I'd hoped we'd get. I'm not sure. I think we did. But in any event, it is the sound of Paris at the time.

MICHEL HAZANAVICIUS, *THE ARTIST*

There's no bad guy in the movie. It's a very kind movie. The antagonist of the character is the sound. So I needed the sound at the end of the movie and I needed it very quiet, like a normal, something normal, something back to normal.

The music was really, really important from the very beginning. When I started to write, I was listening to the music of the great Hollywood classical composers, Max Steiner, Bernard Herrmann, Alfred Newman, Franz Waxman, all these great, great Hollywood composers. And I give all these records to the composer I knew I was working with and I asked him to study this music and this very particular sound and how it works, and I asked him to watch the movies as well. Even if it was not silent movies, I'll just leave it, to try to understand how it works with images. And he is not a specialist of some philharmonic orchestra and so he really had to study the orchestration and everything. And when I was shooting, I'd play music onstage and so then when I get back to the editing, I asked Ludovic [Bource], the composer, "Okay. For this sequence, I'll use that," and sometimes it was not period music. For example, in one sequence I wanted a very nostalgic mood. I played "The Way We Were," which is not really '20s, and actually, when you listen to the music in *The Artist*, you recognize the pop music influence. And so we started to work, but he started to work sequence by sequence, and so I said, "No, it can't work like that. We can't have a track for each sequence." So I cut the entire script in narrative blocks and I said, "Okay, Ludovic, maybe there's fourteen narrative blocks, so I want fourteen different music." I mean, every block, I say to him "From here to here, it has to be very charming, very light, very Disney, and here, this is the rival of this character, Peppy Miller, and she has to be full of life and everything and charming, okay. And then there's a problem here, there's a conflict, so you have to play it. But here, when this actor does that, the problem is solved, so you have to be . . ." So I give him all this structure and so it looks simple like that, but actually, it's not really because also the editing is always moving and we are going shorter, and in the structure, even if it's supposed to be the same, it's changed. I wanted to kill him, he wanted to kill me, and so for him, it was really a huge work because he had to respect the story, and I'm the one in charge of the story. And he had to respect the references on all the sound and he did something great. He studied the Hollywood composer. He went back into Stravinsky and into Gershwin. Yes, he studied the references of the references and so he wanted to respect that and also, he had to respect his own sensibility because he's an artist as well. And we had to do it in a very short time, because we wanted to be ready for the Cannes Festival. It was really important for us because of the nature of the movie and so he did it very quickly. We started the editing in end of November and I had to finish the editing in February, early February, to let him time to finish the orchestration and to record all the music in one week in Belgium. Also I used some original music because I had a problem, which is usually, you always have in talking movies some musical sequence. If you want to show that time is going, you make a musical sequence, but when you have music all the time, it's not so easy to make a musical sequence. So I decided to use original music like songs Rose Murphy's "Pennies from Heaven." This is my musical sequence.

ALEXANDER PAYNE, *THE DESCENDANTS*

I had the idea before shooting that I would try to score it with 100 percent preexisting Hawaiian music. Every one of my other films, *Election* is about half and half score and songs. Where you use preexisting music and try to make it work and the editor, the music editor, the music supervisor, and myself, the four of us, have the challenge of working with images, using something from the outside, which seems fairly monochromatic, which is Hawaiian music. You go to Hawaii and you're in the lobby, and you're at the airport and you turn on the radio, it all sounds pretty much the same, and a lot of it crappy, like any genre, but then to ferret out the good stuff and then see how it could be bent this way or that to support comedy, rhythm and pathos took time, and I had the idea of using Gabby Pahinui. He was a slack-key guitar player and singer who lived from the '20s to the '90s. I fell in love with his music and I had the idea of scoring the entire film with his music, like Leonard Cohen in *McCabe & Mrs. Miller*, or Cat Stevens in the [Hal] Ashby picture [*Harold and Maude*], but I found I wasn't able to, but still I used a lot of his music throughout. And even the strumming guitar, is largely preexisting. It was a lot of trial and error. Kevin [Tent, his editor] and I are the ultimate arbiters. We totally respect the music supervisor and music editor. We've all worked together since '98 on *Election*. They're really indispensable, but the Supreme Court is Kevin, in my opinion, and then, confirmed by Congress, confirmed by our screenings.

BENJAMIN BUTTON STORYBOARD SEQUENCE

Introduction by Jeremy Kagan

THE CURIOUS CASE OF BENJAMIN BUTTON STORYBOARDS (DAVID FINCHER, DIRECTOR)

Here we have four Storyboard sequences:

The first is for the WWI battle scene in which the clock that runs backward is shown. We see the people in the station in real time but the war scene is played in reverse because the Clock Maker wanted to reverse what happened.

The second storyboard is for one of the Lightning Bolt scenes in which lightning repeatedly strikes a character in the film.

The third is a longer storyboarded sequence showing the scene on the boat where we meet Benjamin Button grown up for the first time, played by Brad Pitt without head replacement.

The fourth takes place in Paris where Daisy is dancing with a ballet company. The storyboards show the sequence of events that make up the chain reaction resulting in Daisy getting hit by a taxi cab.

Storyboards ©2008 PARAMOUNT PICTURES CORPORATION and Warner Bros. Entertainment Inc. All Rights Reserved.

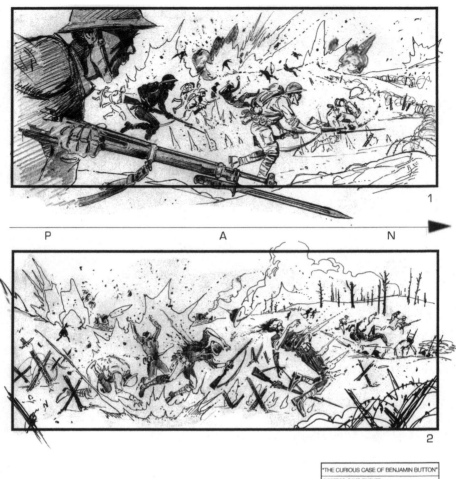

"THE CURIOUS CASE OF BENJAMIN BUTTON"
DIRECTOR: DAVID FINCHER
SCENE: 13   WW1
DRAWN BY: RICHARD BENNETT   09/28/05

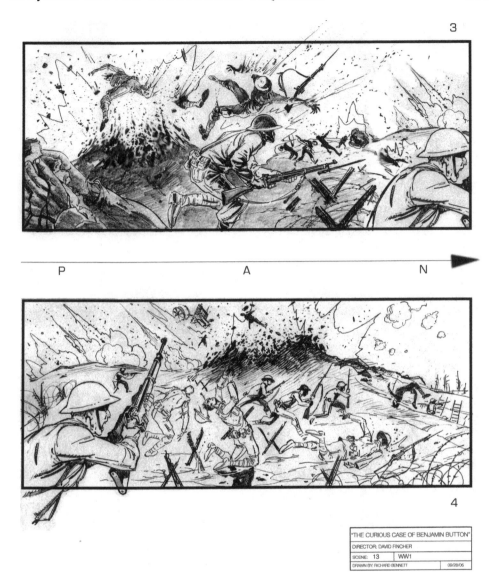

P   A   N

"THE CURIOUS CASE OF BENJAMIN BUTTON"		
DIRECTOR: DAVID FINCHER		
SCENE: 13	WW1	
DRAWN BY: RICHARD BENNETT		09/28/06

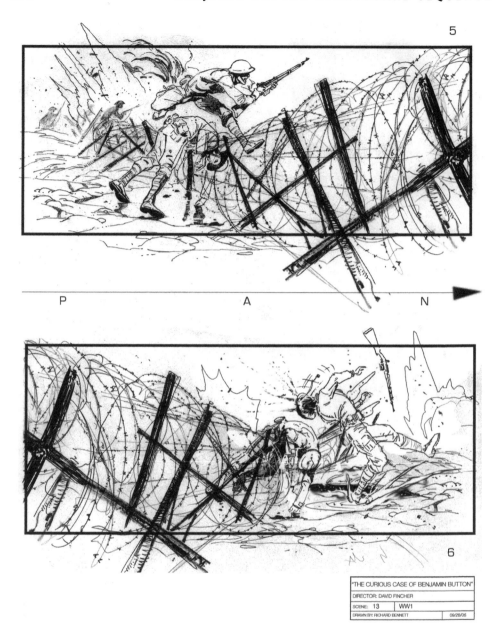

5

P   A   N ▶

6

"THE CURIOUS CASE OF BENJAMIN BUTTON"
DIRECTOR: DAVID FINCHER
SCENE: 13   WW1
DRAWN BY: RICHARD BENNETT   09/28/06

"THE CURIOUS CASE OF BENJAMIN BUTTON"

DIRECTOR: DAVID FINCHER	
SCENE: 107	Dusk/Tug Boat/John Grimm
DRAWN BY: RICHARD BENNETT	09/26/06

14

15

"THE CURIOUS CASE OF BENJAMIN BUTTON"	
DIRECTOR: DAVID FINCHER	
SCENE: 108	Tug Boat/Benjamin/Rain
DRAWN BY: RICHARD BENNETT	09/28/06

16

17

"THE CURIOUS CASE OF BENJAMIN BUTTON"		
DIRECTOR: DAVID FINCHER		
SCENE: 108	Tug Boat/Benjamin/Rain	
DRAWN BY: RICHARD BENNETT		09/29/06

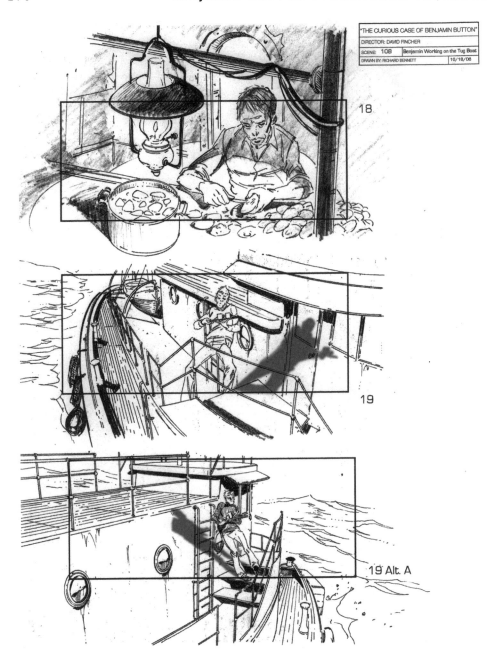

"THE CURIOUS CASE OF BENJAMIN BUTTON"
DIRECTOR: DAVID FINCHER
SCENE: 10B   Benjamin Working on the Tug Boat
DRAWN BY: RICHARD BENNETT   10/18/06

18

19

19 Alt. A

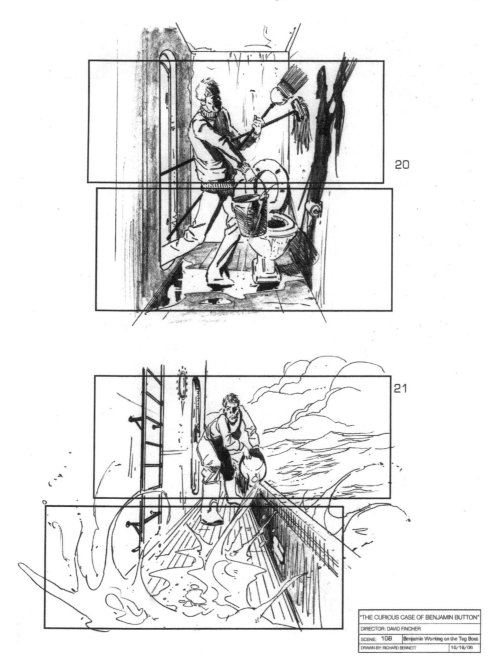

20

21

"THE CURIOUS CASE OF BENJAMIN BUTTON"
DIRECTOR: DAVID FINCHER
SCENE: 108 | Benjamin Working on the Tug Boat
DRAWN BY: RICHARD BENNETT | 10/18/06

Tilt
Down

29

"THE CURIOUS CASE OF BENJAMIN BUTTON"

DIRECTOR: DAVID FINCHER

SCENE: 119   Murmansk Street / Winter Palace Hotel

DRAWN BY: RICHARD BENNETT   09/26/06

29 Alt. A

14
Tilt
Up

15

16

"THE CURIOUS CASE OF BENJAMIN BUTTON"	
DIRECTOR: DAVID FINCHER	
SCENE: 208	Daisy rehearsing/man crosses the st.
DRAWN BY: RICHARD BENNETT	10/12/06

17

18

"THE CURIOUS CASE OF BENJAMIN BUTTON"		
DIRECTOR: DAVID FINCHER		
SCENE: 208	Cab driver breaks	
DRAWN BY: RICHARD BENNETT		10/12/06

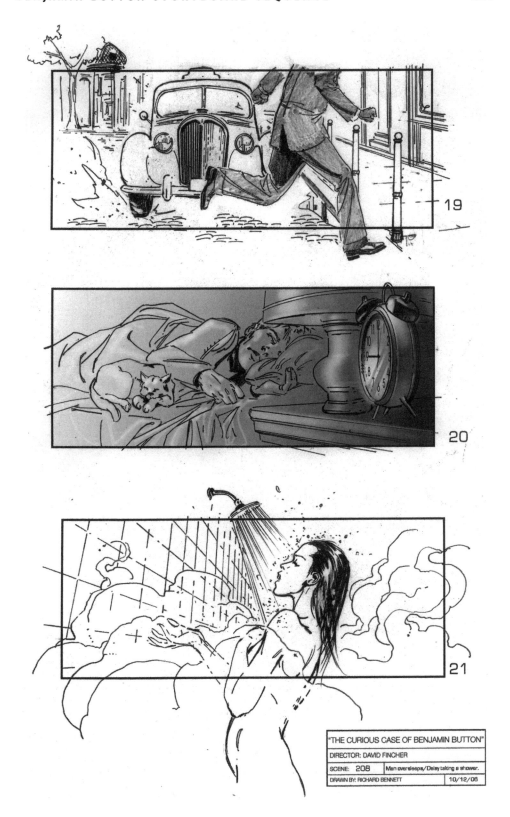

19

20

21

"THE CURIOUS CASE OF BENJAMIN BUTTON"

DIRECTOR: DAVID FINCHER

SCENE: 208 | Man oversleeps/Daisy taking a shower.

DRAWN BY: RICHARD BENNETT | 10/12/06

35

36

37

"THE CURIOUS CASE OF BENJAMIN BUTTON"
DIRECTOR: DAVID FINCHER
SCENE: 208   Truck Taking off/Couple kissing.
DRAWN BY: RICHARD BENNETT   10/12/06

43

44

45

"THE CURIOUS CASE OF BENJAMIN BUTTON"		
DIRECTOR: DAVID FINCHER		
SCENE: 208	Daisy & Friend safely crossing the street.	
DRAWN BY: RICHARD BENNETT		10/12/06

46

47

48

"THE CURIOUS CASE OF BENJAMIN BUTTON"

DIRECTOR: DAVID FINCHER

SCENE: 208   Sun getting into driver's eyes
              Cab hits Daisy

DRAWN BY: RICHARD BENNETT   10/12/06

49

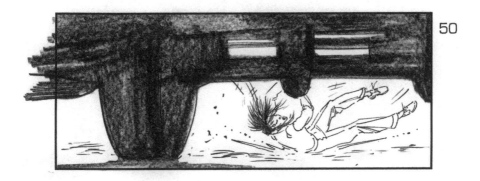

50

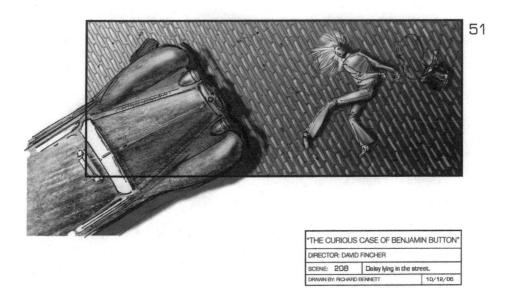

51

"THE CURIOUS CASE OF BENJAMIN BUTTON"		
DIRECTOR: DAVID FINCHER		
SCENE: 208	Daisy lying in the street.	
DRAWN BY: RICHARD BENNETT		10/12/06

Part IV

THE WORST AND THE BEST

Martin Scorsese and Director of Photography Michael Ballhaus on the set of *The Departed*. THE DE-PARTED—Licensed by Warner Bros. Entertainment Inc. All Rights Reserved.

12

The Worst and the Best of Filmmaking

DAVID O. RUSSELL, *THE FIGHTER*

I have to tell you it was a really good shoot, so I don't have any real worst ones. In fact I loved it so much that I wish we were making a TV series up there because we got so attached to everybody and I still have this weird muscle memory like we're going to go back there and hang out with everybody. I learned a lot. I learned that I think I'm best when I'm closest to a raw emotion and a simple story. I like that and I learned a lot of respect for that. And I learned a lot about having the best possible collaboration and vibe on the set from Mark [Wahlberg]. I think I kind of feel it's just the way I'd like to keep working.

ANG LEE, *BROKEBACK MOUNTAIN*

The worst is the weather. Somehow, it was always raining and cloudy. For weeks I thought. I was worried that people would think the sun never comes out in Wyoming. I don't know why, it just kept raining.

The best part is, I will say, actors. I feel I was very blessed working with those actors. It was just lovely. I shared my life with them and we really love each other. I forgot about cinematic ambition and I forgot I was unhealthy and I was nurtured back to life.

ALEJANDRO GONZÁLEZ IÑÁRRITU, *BABEL*

I think the process was fantastic; it was a very powerful human experience that really transformed me, transformed all of us. I think it was just making that in all these countries benefited us from that experience culturally, intellectually, physically, spiritually. It was fantastic.

The most painful moment was when I saw for the first time the assemblage of the film, four hours and a half, and I really wanted to kill myself. It was the most scary, terrifying moment. After all that, you saw what you think you got, and it's not there. You are already exhausted, and then you have to start again, and that was the most terrifying moment.

PAUL HAGGIS, *CRASH*

In pre-production we never had a green light, we were always being shut down because of economics. I mean everyone was fighting to get the film financed, but it just every week, we seemed to get the plug pulled and I'd just show up Monday morning and they'd say, "What's Haggis doing here? We've pulled the plug." And that was hard. We were told we had a green light when we got Sandy Bullock, we were just relieved. But at that point, I remembered Cathy [Schulman, one of his producers] came up to me and said that she was really sorry they had to cut several hundred thousand dollars more from the budget and that I couldn't get this and this and this. And I said, "You know what? Give me whatever—I don't care. Give me a Brownie camera and a pair of swizzle sticks. I'm happy. I want the cranes. I want them all. But I'll shoot differently." And even as horrible as that was because it was so compressed and going forty-five days to forty, thirty-five, just the ability to shoot, it was fabulous. The best was shooting.

MARTIN SCORSESE, *THE DEPARTED*

I have that gene made up in DNA apparently that makes us who we are, and there's a glass that's half empty, there's one that's half full, so I'm the one that's half empty. So I found that the worst part of it was the internal nature of the picture and the actual process of making the film was extremely difficult for me. And also because of the nature, for many different reasons, this may sound funny, but it doesn't mean that I wasn't enjoying the process, but it was a process that kicked me and made me move into different areas. It was like being with your worst enemy and your best friend at the same time.

The best part of it was watching the audience reaction.

TOM HOOPER, *THE KING'S SPEECH*

I think that probably the best was working with those actors. Working with Geoffrey [Rush] and Colin [Firth] I had two people who became incredible collaborators on every aspect. And they've become great friends through it and I think one of the things that gives the film its particular quality is my fondness that was growing for them while making it which you can't fake.

Tom Hooper with Helena Bonham Carter on the set of *The King's Speech*. Courtesy of The Weinstein Company LLC. All Rights Reserved.

The worst moment is always practical and I think I would have to say shooting on the real Harley Street which is where all the medical establishment is. It was a Sunday morning and we were doing Helena Bonham Carter arriving through the fog and we were doing it for real, so we closed the road down. We had the block. We had fog machines everywhere. And we'd set it up, we'd filled the street with smoke, we're going in for the first take and then I heard from every corner of the compass fire engines coming towards us, and I'm talking twenty, twenty-five fire engines. I mean every fire truck in London descended on us. And you have that moment between the first noise and the arrival where basically you have the three minutes to sit there before this happens. And it became quickly clear that the day wasn't going to happen. Of course, I was persistent and then I had it explained to me that there were intensive care patients on Harley Street and it was the legal obligation of hospitals to evacuate the intensive care patients every time there was an alarm. So not giving up, we then spent the next few hours with masking tape and shower caps trying to tape up every window of every key hospital with the help of a couple of runners who the firemen were particularly fond of. And in about four hours we could shoot again.

RON HOWARD, *FROST/NIXON*

I love the whole process.

There are only two sections that I despise and it's that casting area. Like putting people through that, having been an actor, and yet it's crucial, so you have to take it seriously, and I just find it to be uncomfortable. You're making big decisions about leads and key supporting people that are going to influence your movie no matter what you do on the day. Movies do take on a life of their own and a lot of it has to do with the casting, so I find that a nerve-wracking period. The other period is selling the movie. I do it, we do it and we love our movie enough to do it and we care about it and it's being responsible to the folks who've financed it and distributed it, but I wish that wasn't a part of it. I wish you made it, saw what the audience thought and went on to the next thing. The actually making of the movie, there are good moments and bad moments, but to me it's all fascinating and of course I've grown up around it, so I'm comfortable in that environment. I get energized by it.

JONATHAN DAYTON AND VALERIE FARIS, *LITTLE MISS SUNSHINE*

VALERIE: Well, I would say the day we got the phone call that the studio was dropping the movie was probably the worst.

JONATHAN: And then the best, I mean it was all so fun, but the best was the Sundance screening, where we didn't have time to really do any kind of preview, and we had just shown it to a few friends and gotten comments. To have the audience there and our cast there who had worked so hard and for them to see people responding in that way. You don't know how to express your gratitude towards everyone who's worked so hard, and of course, the most rewarding thing is just to sit in an audience and watch the film with people.

BILL CONDON, *DREAMGIRLS*

The worst was the studio insisted that the first preview be to an audience that wouldn't know what they were seeing, so it was mostly kids thinking they were seeing an action movie, who then got shown this musical. That was a hideous way to introduce this movie to the world. And the cards [where audiences fill out reactions to the movie], one kid said, "How did these people know how to rhyme?" And it really bothered him. Like every bit of the convention of it bothered him.

   And the best of it, I have to say, was the next screening, where we did let them know what they were seeing. We did all work so hard that to create an experience that would be as close to musicals that we all loved when we were growing up and also the live experience where you're interacting with the audience, with what's happening on screen and to see the audience react in that visceral way, I think was the most thrilling part.

DAVID FINCHER, *THE CURIOUS CASE OF BENJAMIN BUTTON*

I love everything up until you start shooting. It's fucking horrible. I love meeting actors and imagining what they're going to be clothed in and what their makeup is going to look like and what the sets are and then you get there and you're like, "Can you come back just a few inches? Nope. Okay, fine." You know that's the part I hate.

DAVID FINCHER, *THE SOCIAL NETWORK*

I think that the thing that was the most fun about this was having a studio that wanted to make a movie regardless. They were going to make this movie. They loved it. They loved the script. You're not pushing a rock up a hill. I mean there was no Sisyphus at all in this. I don't want to undercut anybody's idea about how much you have to struggle, but in this case Amy [Pascal of Sony Pictures] wanted to make this movie. Scott Rudin [the producer] paved the way. And we got to cast a bunch of kids that I just know probably I'll regale my grandkids with "I knew them when!" It was so much fun to be able to put together this little troupe of twenty-something's who just wanted their "at bats." They wanted to point over the left-field wall and they wanted to do whatever it took to be as good as they could be. I mean, you know Armie Hammer had never rowed before. He trained for seven months. It was just an amazing thing to see. You know, so often you're working with actors around a schedule for something else that they're doing and all of a sudden we had this Mercury Theatre [Orson Welles' repertory theater]. We could just kind of mandate, "This is what you're doing for the next six months," and aside from the acting and learning the lines and having to do the head replacement, the scanning and stuff, I'll see you in Henley and you better be able to row a mile and a half race in under whatever because you'll tip the boat if you can't pull your weight. It was a great thing. I don't enjoy shooting. I don't like the compromise and heartache but when you have a bunch of faces who want to be there and they want to tear it up, it's so much fun.

JASON REITMAN, *UP IN THE AIR*

The best part is that you get to tell stories using the culmination of every art form and tell them for more people than you could with any other storytelling form. I can make people laugh. I can make hundreds of thousands, maybe millions of people laugh or I could move that many people. I don't know what the worst part is. The best part is that I get to do it.

BENNETT MILLER, *CAPOTE*

Honestly, I think that the hardest part was probably just the anguishing through it with Phil [Seymour Hoffman who plays Capote] and the performance.

And I think one of the most rewarding moments was maybe ten weeks into the edit, I invited Phil in to see like the middle hour of the film, and it was a hard thing to do and making the movie was difficult and a lot of anguish and despair and stuff like that. And I hit play on the AVID [the digital editing machine] and left the room and let him watch

Bennett Miller on the set of *Capote*. Courtesy of MGM Media Licensing. CAPOTE ©2005 UNITED ART-ISTS FILMS INC. All Rights Reserved.

this middle hour, and I just kind of went down a hall to the kitchen just beneath Ang Lee's office on Canal Street and waited for Phil with no idea how he's going to take it. And after an hour, he just kind of leaves the edit room and walks down the hall and sits down at the table, and he just says, "Good for us," like we did it. It was hard, but we did that. Like we went up to Winnipeg, where we didn't want to go, and we did that.

GEORGE CLOONEY, *GOOD NIGHT, AND GOOD LUCK.*

I'd gone through some back surgery and stuff, and they have a very rigid physical test now for insurance that they wanted me to take or they wouldn't bond the film. And it's a $7.5 million film and you're trying to play within these parameters of, "This is how it's going to work and this is our budget and we're really working very hard to get this thing working." We're going to pay $250,000 for the bond [to insure the health of people on the movie and any other unexpected contingencies], which is a lot of money out of the budget, and it's already getting a little irritating, and they were like, "Well, you can't pass the physical, then we're not going to bond the film." And there's this thing in you that goes, "Fuck you, I'm rich." And literally there's that moment where you go, "I tried to play by the rules," and I'm on the phone with them, and I went, "How much is this fucking bond?" They're like, "250." I go, "All right. What's my house worth? Fine, the fucking film's bonded." And it was one of those furious things, like I was going, "Are you out of your mind? I don't feel great, but I feel like I could finish a thirty-day shoot. I feel like if I'm going to bite it, I'll finish the film."

The best was the first night. I'd screened it for my dad. That was the best because, you know, he's a newsman. I did it for my dad. I did it about my dad. He's the guy that sticks his neck out at all the times that it's uncomfortable to stick your neck out, and he's lost a lot of jobs over the years because he said, "That's not correct." And it was about news. And so then my mom and dad came out, and I got them drunk on wine and had a screening at a little theater just for him, my mother and him. You can talk about film festivals or opening night or anything, but there's nothing more nerve-wracking than a newsman watching a film about news who's not apt to give out compliments very well. And he just got up and he walked out, and I'm like sitting there. He just kind of walked by me and tapped me and went, "You got it right." And then he walked out. There was high-fiving then.

DARREN ARONOFSKY, *BLACK SWAN*

There was the day when we had to shoot the prologue of the film, the opening dance number. And it was the last dance and we had to shoot and we had sort of run out of ideas of what to do with it, so we were just going to make it up, so I came in very loose. I knew what the choreography was. I knew the space, which was actually an interesting space at SUNY Purchase, which was where the closing scene of *All That Jazz* happened. So it was kind of hallowed ground to be in there as a dance movie. That day I noticed something was up with Natalie [Portman]. They were lifting her differently and she was hiding from me that something was wrong with her rib, which actually in the massage scene with the physical therapist, she's actually being worked on. She was

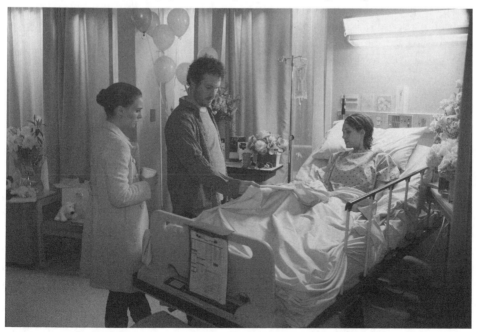

Darren Aronofsky with Natalie Portman and Winona Ryder on the set of *Black Swan*. BLACK SWAN
©2010 Twentieth Century Fox. All Rights Reserved.

a real physical therapist. That wasn't an actress. She was coming to work on Natalie. I was like, "Oh, we can shoot it," and everyone was game with it, so she was actually being worked on, she just had to stay in character while that was happening. And so we made Natalie go off and get an X-ray just to see what was going on and you're sitting there watching the hours go by and for some reason, there was some technicality where we couldn't call an insurance day or something. And it was also at the end of the week so it meant we were going to be shooting at 3:00 or 4:00 am doing a physical dance number. So you're watching your day disappear when you have this incredibly complex thing coming up in front of you. But then out of it when you are suffering, hoping that your actor's okay, you're trying to figure out how you're going to make the day so the invention of turning eight shots into four shots, which is what that sequence was, happened. And it gave us time to work it out. And then to really strip everything down and turn it into a spotlight and a black space. So out of the pain came this sort of iconic look for the opening of the movie. And then when you're on set and it's just happening in front of you and you see the camera and Natalie is healthy because she didn't have any broken rib or anything and got up on point and walks off into a spotlight and it's just like, "Wow, there's the end of the opening epilogue." It's great. So the worst and the best on the same day.

CHRISTOPHER NOLAN, *THE DARK KNIGHT*

Finishing the film, for me, is the best thing and the worst thing. When you go through this process for a few years and you get to the end of it, it's fantastic because you've achieved it, done it, because you've been through all this, but there's also this tremendous sense of disappointment for me because it's done. That's always a very weird period for me before it then gets released and everything, where you sort of don't know what to do with yourself. You're pleased and you're relaxed, but at the same time you really miss it and it's sort of gone, and that's been the same for me on every film, actually.

CHRISTOPHER NOLAN, *INCEPTION*

Best is finishing, especially this film which took me ten years from when I started it to when I finished it. So finishing it was very bittersweet. I was extremely pleased to be able to look at it done, but there's something very sad about that because it's finished. I suppose one thing I sort of re-learned that I think I learned on *Memento* but definitely came back to me on *Inception* is we came into this process with an enormous amount of freedom because my last film had been very successful. We immediately sort of offset that by having an enormous budget that we needed. But we sort of took the decision that we're in a position that very, very few filmmakers get to be in, which is they're going to trust us to do something that they might not ordinarily. And so we just sort of jumped off the cliff and stuck to our guns. We never compromised anything and Leo [DiCaprio], particularly, was a great collaborator in that he really pushed me to try and make the film the most extreme version of what it could be. He never wanted it to be successful. I don't think that was in any way his desire. He was probably upset it was so successful. You know I think that he approaches things from a very pure creative point of view. He just wanted really to explore that character and so he pushed all of us to just do the film exactly how we wanted to do it and to see that pay off was relearning a valuable lesson about sticking to your guns.

LEE DANIELS, *PRECIOUS*

The worst part is having your mother tell you she hates your movie. There's nothing worse than that. *"Why can't you make movies like Tyler Perry?"* The best part is having so many people cry in my arms, telling me that they have been touched. Even greater than that, saying that they're touching their children, and, "How can I get help?"

STEVEN SPIELBERG, *MUNICH*

Well, I think the worst for me on *Munich* was the six years of indecision about whether I should make this picture or not. That was the worst for me. And I was making other pictures during that time and developing this one, but I had a lot to lose. I didn't really have to make this story. There was more for me to lose than to gain by telling this story. I have the Shoah Foundation. I've got 52,000 holocaust survivors [who were interviewed about their experiences during the Holocaust] who think the world of me and depend on me, and I didn't want to let them down. I didn't want to feel like I was betraying any of their beliefs in this story, which touches every single color of the spectrum of how people feel about what's happening today. And so it was six years of really putting it off and deciding for maybe a few months I'm not going to tell the story and then picking it up again and saying this is a story that has to be told. If I don't tell it, who else is going to tell it? I kept looking for other people to tell the story and nobody wanted to go near the subject matter and understandably so. And I think that was probably the worst.

And I think the best part of the movie, which goes along with the story, was after we finished our first day of shooting in Malta, I realized that I was telling the story, and that was the best day I had.

TONY GILROY, *MICHAEL CLAYTON*

The worst part is the finality of walking away from everything and saying that's the last time I'm going to do this. It's the clutch of, "Do I really have it? I'm never coming back here again. This is the last moment I have to get this shot." It's that sort of stunning reality every day, about six times a day. The night before a scene is shot, you know, this script you've been working on for years, all of a sudden you realize it's going to go the next day. You got to get really brave after a while to do that.

The best part is to be in charge, but not really. The best part was sort of this tribal journey through all these different communities that I had sort of witnessed from the outside. You go from the early pre-production community, then you leave the office and you go here and then you shoot. Then you're shooting the movie, then editing, then you're mixing and then it's a world of color. I mean it's all these communities that you go through, and if you're having a good time and you like the process and you want to be around people who really know what they're doing, that was an unanticipated pleasure.

GUS VAN SANT, *MILK*

Maybe the worst thing I can think of is we tested very high on a test score. Our first test in Seattle, I think it was, and then we were asked to test again and we were in the editing room. We were thinking about changing a couple of things, but the studio wanted to test it again and so because we were testing in Portland, Oregon away from Hollywood, we had all these conspiracy theory meltdowns in the editing room, because we had a lot of time on our hands and our imaginations started to go crazy and it was a lot of talk about encounters and executives and so forth.

The best is probably just seeing it into the final stretch and that we were part of the awards season.

QUENTIN TARANTINO, *INGLOURIOUS BASTERDS*

To me, the worst part is getting up in the morning. That is definitely the number one thing I hate about directing. I am not a person that gets up at six in the fucking morning, all right. When you got to do that, I actually find it oppressive at a certain point. I would shoot splits [half day, half nights] or nights all the time, if I was just a selfish bastard who only cared about myself, all right. I should have. I also don't like pre-production that much. I want to fucking get at it. I want pre-production to be as short as possible. You know what I mean? I did a WWII period movie and we had eight weeks pre-production or six or something like that and I wanted less and I realize that I was just being a spoiled brat, but I was kind of, "Let's just fucking do it. Let's just do it, all right," and I know that's irrational, all right, and the other teams need the time to get their shit together, but you know I want to get going right away.

My favorite things are when I've accomplished something that's just been like a sword of Damocles hanging over my head, all right. Whether it be something like, say, the opening scene of *Basterds*. I wrote that scene in '98 and one of the reasons I never gave up on this script when it was giving me problems was, I can't give up on that scene. It's one of the best scenes I've ever written. I've got to do it. So to have a sequence like that in your mind for a long time, it's great, but at the same time, it's mine to fuck up as a director, okay. I did it on the page and then I got to cast the right actors, but I can fuck it up and I'll know that it's me who didn't do it. So when I do the scene and I've accomplished it and I walk away at the end of that week, I'm, "Okay, that's it, I feel this. It's done." I feel a sense of accomplishment. Wow, I did it, it's okay, it's going to be fine. What I've done a lot in this last decade is trying to do wild action scenes, whether it be the martial art fights in *Kill Bill* or car chasing in *Death Proof* or the big fire shit in *Basterds*, I'm literally writing stuff I don't know how to do. I don't know how I'm going to do this. I've never shot a car chase before. I don't know how to do it, but I know that I'm going to learn how to do it from doing it. But also, I don't want it to be okay, I want it to be one of the best I've ever done, so I'm pushing myself that way. However as you get closer to those days, there's a tremendous amount of trepidation. I mean because there's going to be about two days where I'm the dumbass and by day three, you kind of start figuring it out and you start getting the vocabulary for it, but when you finally do accomplish that, you know you did it. Like when we walked away from the burn set, I knew I had my end sequenced. That was like I said, a sword of Damocles hanging by a single thread for the entire shoot. When I knew I got it, it felt amazing.

JULIAN SCHNABEL, *THE DIVING BELL AND THE BUTTERFLY*

I think the prize is doing the work and I think it's all good. Someone can always fuck your movie up later no matter how good it is, but the part I did, I admit I am guilty for all of my sins and I'm happy with all of it. I love working with the actors. It's a privilege to make a movie.

DANNY BOYLE, *SLUMDOG MILLIONAIRE*

The best for me is that each day is a new day, because it doesn't matter how bad it gets, and you do have terrible days on any film, but the next day you just start again. You're building towards something eventually, and people are judging you about that, but in terms of yourself and the crew working, you just got to get up and start again and you've got another chance to get it right again, which you often don't do. You never get quite what you want. It's that opportunity to start again each day, and even if you've got ninety days or twenty days, whatever it is, each day is a new day to begin again really. I suppose the worst thing is that you see some things and you think, "What were we doing?" and you just feel that shallowness and emptiness of entertainers. That's always the worst of it for me.

JAMES CAMERON, *AVATAR*

I think the worst part of directing is having to talk about your movie afterwards, in all its forms. This film should speak for itself really, but you have to. You have to do it. It's part of the marketing and all that and I would probably have a different answer to the best part now than I would have previously. Previously I would have said something like it's really cool when people all over the world react to your thoughts and ideas, your art and the art of all the people on your team and so on, and I would have said that previously, but having done the expedition process knowing that there is a certain situation that you put yourself in, that I put myself in to challenge myself and I do it with a team of people and I know that at the end of that process, I can talk about it for ten years and I still would not be able to convey how difficult it was, how complex it was, how the decisions were made and how luck was a factor and what it took on the part of myself and my teammates to accomplish it. I could never explain it and it's like cops and their partners never being tight because they can never explain to their wives or to their parents what they go through on the street. I know it's the same thing now coming out of *Avatar*, a four-and-a-half year process, people stick a microphone in my face and say, "So how was it done?" It's ludicrous. The world will never understand what it took to make that movie. So the best thing for coming out of the end of the process is the respect of my team for me, and my respect for them as people who did something together. And, if you can make a lot of money doing it, that's cool too.

ETHAN AND JOEL COEN, *NO COUNTRY FOR OLD MEN*

ETHAN: Driving home at the end of the day I go, "Fuck, I am so stupid, why didn't we do this or that." Or, man, those seventeen times a day when you have to admit that you're unbelievably stupid, and again the positive thing is the process keeps changing. It's really stimulating that it's all these different things. I kind of feel fortunate that we're involved in all those things and not just in production or not just in post-production. The fact that it's doing so many different things is just stimulating.

JOEL: The other part is the social aspect of making a movie, which is that you're migrating through these communities, but these communities are all these interesting collaborations. It's very different from sitting in a room and writing, doing a solitary activity. Just that aspect of it is such a fundamental part of making movies that it seems that if that isn't where you derive a good part of the enjoyment, you're in the wrong job.

KATHRYN BIGELOW, *THE HURT LOCKER*

I don't think there's a worst part, but I'd say the best is, didn't John Ford [director of *The Searchers, The Grapes of Wrath, How Green Was My Valley*] say, "Filmmaking is painting with an army"? It's the collaborative process. I love it. I love working with a team. I like the whole process that is really a team effort. You know it's not that hierarchical structure. It doesn't end and begin with a director. I really think of it as a complete team effort, that everybody impacts this result on the screen and no one person does it, and that to me is probably the most exciting. You know somebody has an idea. Somebody is contributing something and giving above and beyond their wildest expectations of themselves and that's amazing.

PAUL THOMAS ANDERSON, *THERE WILL BE BLOOD*

It's great to do it. It's sad when you're not doing it, but I look forward to being able to do it again.

Appendix A:
Additional Materials

SCRIPT PAGES AND NOTES

(handwritten, top) ⑭ H.'s Face / Eyes — move in

2.

He sees...

⑮ A TOY BOOTH. *Boom Down* WIDE H.'s — *TO*

Bedraggled and struggling. A counter filled with windup toys,
dolls and little games.

GEORGES, a grim old man with a white goatee, sits at the
counter of the booth.   ⑯ CU - G.   ⑰ XCU eye

⑱ EYES - H. (Clock)
⑲ Hugo watches. SAME AS ⑭

⑳ ISABELLE appears from inside the booth and talks to the old
man. She has a book under her arm. H.'s P.O.V. THRU Clock.
㉑ I. TIGHTER · H.'s P.O.V. (over shoulder / book)
She is a lively, imaginative girl about Hugo's age. She has
a charming Louise Brooks haircut.

Isabelle argues a bit with Georges. He snaps at her. Upset,
she hurries off.   Dialogue?

Hugo watches her go.   H.'s P.O.V.
                     ㉒ SHE exits - PAN TO COUNTER PAST F.G.
SAME AS ⑭ ㉓ Then he turns his gaze to the toys on the counter.   PANELS
       ㉔ PAST F.G - H's P.O.v.   PAN   TO
He sees the old man aimlessly wind a TOY MOUSE. It skitters   REVEAL
across the counter. The old man crosses his arms. Falls   COUNTER.
asleep.   ㉕ H.'s P.O.V.   ㉖ Tighter
          ㉗ F.G.   H.'s P.O.v.
Hugo stares at the toy mouse. H.'s P.O.V.   H.X. FACE
                                                F.G.
㉘ Then he moves.
OVERHEAD — From Clock To Spiral Staircase (PAN Fw   ㉛ AIR VENT
                        BEYOND)   at ...
He skitters through a series of passages and opens an air
vent. He carefully climbs out, into the station...   #2
㉚ Tighter (?) ㉜ XLS H.'s DOWN | ㉝ |㉙ XLOS up Stairs—PAN Thru
Opens vent.   Climbs out   DOWN HALL TO VENT
3 INT. TRAIN STATION -- TOY BOOTH - DAY ① TRACK H.'s P.O.V 3
                                           H. ENTERS - looks around
Hugo creeps to the Toy Booth.   ② TRACK with H. MCU

The toy mouse is there on the counter.

Georges still appears to be asleep.

Hugo stops.

Waits.

Looks around.

③ Carefully reaches for the toy mouse — 3.D
CLOSER?
But--   ④ MOUSE,
                     MOVE IN
                     GRABS

Handwritten notes on script for *Hugo*. Courtesy of The Martin Scorsese Collection. HUGO ©2012
Paramount Pictures. All Rights Reserved. 2012 GK Films, LLC. All Rights Reserved.

7.

④ Maximilian follows, not quite so agilely, upsetting tables and waiters--

Chaos--!

MOVE IN TO TIGHTER - FAST.

⑤ MADAME EMILIE, the shy older woman who runs the cafe, screams and clutches her beloved little DACHSHUND to her chest--

The dachshund barks furiously at Maximilian--

Hugo loops around a table-- ⑥ *HOW?*
ARCH CAM. AROUND (?) and end on

Where a man who looks suspiciously like James Joyce is having *dd. x DATE*
a demitasse with a man who looks suspiciously like Salvador
Dali--

⑦ They are agog as Hugo races around them ... followed by *HEAD ON*
Maximilian ... followed by the Station Inspector-- *MASTER-OF THE*
Too- All RUN THROUGH
6 INT TRAIN STATION -- GRAND HALL *WIDE* *FRAME*
① Hugo finally sprints away from the cafe. *(CRANE DOWN* 6

Tearing through the crowded terminal again. *S.I. into MCU*

The Station Inspector calls after him: *"STOP!"*

        STATION INSPECTOR
   STOP THAT CHILD! -- APPREHEND! ④ *H·CU*

② *MCU* MONSIEUR FRICK, the shy older gentleman who runs a NEWSPAPER ③ *WIDE TRACK*
KIOSK across from the cafe, makes a half-hearted grab for
Hugo-- *#3*

But Hugo suddenly--

Dives-- *3-D*

⑤ Sliding on the polished floor between Monsieur Frick's legs-- *#3* *Reverse on*

Then he's up and gone--

Monsieur Frick looks up, alarmed, leaps to the side as--

Maximilian thunders past--

The Station Inspector follows -- ⑥ by now Hugo has disappeared
around a corner-- *H. To us - see corner*
m.S.I. Follow past in them

The Station Inspector and Maximilian rip around the corner at *H. gone*
top speed--

7 INT. TRAIN STATION -- CORRIDOR -- DAY ① *S.I. MCU -* 7

But Hugo is gone--! ② *S.I. M. Lens - Dog level*

48.

Two little hammers come down and trail along the edges of the disks... *(22) 3D* *(23) 3D →*

The little hammers translate motion back up through a series of rods. *(24)* *(25)*

The rods silently turn other intricate mechanisms in the figure's shoulder and neck... *(26)* *(27)*   *3D?*

The shoulder gears move... *(28)*

Engaging the elbow...   *TILT TO Elbow*

Setting off a chain reaction of movements down to the wrist...   *(29)(30)(31)*   *in 31 - TILT TO WRIST*

And finally...

The hand. *(32)*

OUTSIDE again:

Hugo and Isabelle watch. *in (10)*

The Automaton's hand moves slightly. Just a twitch. *in (11)* *(33) MCU HAND*

They gasp.

Hugo and Isabelle lean forward, wide-eyed with wonder.

(34) The miniature hand begins, very cautiously, to move. *LO & up on A HAND IN F.G.*

Hugo and Isabelle hold their breath.

The Automaton dips the pen into the ink and begins to write. *(35) Head ON PAN — CU INKWELL TO Hand/pen*

It draws a small line. The hand moves. Another small line. The hand moves. Another small line.

Hugo and Isabelle lean closer.

The Automaton continues to move. Dip the pen. Draw a line. *(41) Tig/HF on Inkwell* *(36) OVER SHoulder OT A. TO Hand PEN.*
Move. Draw a line. Dip the pen. Move. Draw a line.
(42) HEAD ON MCU A But it is meaningless.

A series of scratches and lines without order.

Nothing.   *(37) OVERHEAD*

Hugo stares. *(43) CU H* *(38) Tig/HFV of 35*

His heart sinking.   *(39) Tighter of (36)*
   (40) Tighter on pen point

DICKIE – LOUD BRASH – YOU NEVER KNOW WHAT YOU'RE GONNA GET. YOU WANT THEM OUT OF THE ROOM. IT'S BORING I WISH THE NICE PART OF THEM WOULD COME BACK. DICKIE. FROM BRASH MOMENTS – TO QUIET SOLITUDE IN A BATHROOM AND A FLASH TO THE OLD DAYS -- WHAT'S WRONG DICK? NOTHING I'M JUST TIRED. NEED ANOTHER BEER. AND RETHINK – AS SMOKING CRACK – THIS WAS MY MISTAKE – THAT I MADE –

AT A THEMATIC LEVEL IS IT ABOUT BROTHERLY LOVE –WHAT IS IT ABOUT.

DO BALD SPOTS AND WIDOWS PEAKS – AND SHOOT OLDER FOOTAGE LATER – LOST TEETH. Missing teeth. Find the good person who can do the hair. GETFOTO OF DICKIE WITH THE HAIR.

--BE SURE TO GET ROMANCE OF MARK AND CHARLENE – MAKE THAT COUNT MAKE IT MATTER.
--DICKIE JUST WITH THE CRACK WHORE.
--DICKIE BREAKS THRU EMPATHY FOR HIS BROTHER IN SECOND HALF – AND NO ONE ELSE – NOT FOR HIMSELF -- . THE WAY YOU CARE FOR ME NOW – YOU GOTTA DO IT FOR YOU. YEAH. BUT WE SEE HE DOESN'T. he says my wish that you would come thru for me cam e true. But that was only half my wish. What was the other half. That you can do it for yourself. Take care of yourself. Care. And we see from dick's face that we don't know.
MIDNITE COWBOY. SO END IT IN A FUCKED UP WAY. LIKE ROCKY ENDING BUT WITH FRACTURED STUFF LEADING UP TO IT – FRACTURED ALL THE WAY.
- see brother's training each other and only dickie can push micky. To it.
- WHO IS SOULFUL IN THIS MOVIE AND CHARMING – MAKE MARK CHARMING AND SOULFUL – LIKE ROCKY
- -LET HIM BE TENDER WITH WOMEN
- THE GRADUATE MOMENT AT THE END -- after the victory fight.
- OR SHOW AGAIN THAT DICKIE STILL REMAINS THE STAR OF THE FAMILY – PERIOD –
- OR DICKIE REALIZES AT THE END MICKY IS THE STAR – THE NEW STAR.
- HOW DO WE ROOT FOR DICKIE -- THE BURDEN OF THE TOWN ON HIS SHOULDERS – HE COULDN'T HANDLE IT – THE TOWN THE FAMILY THE MONEY PRESSURE – HE WAS JUST ENJOYING HIS JOYFUL GIFT AND IT'S POLLUTED NOW – IT TURNED IT INTO A JOB – A PRESSURE – WHEN HE WAS A KID THOSE WERE HIS GLORY DAYS AND THOSE GOT TAKEN FROM HIM AND GIVEN TO TO THE TOWN – HE LOVED BEING A KID WITH THE GLORY AND THE HOPE – I went 12 rounds with sugar ray Leonard – why isn't that good enough.

Is it that we quietly disregard mark for half the movie – til he gets with Charlene etc --?

David O. Russell's personal notes for *The Fighter*. Courtesy of David O. Russell.

Dinner scene prep/ pg.6-23
Nugget
This film is about our desire to be winners / Our need to win and the value of
losing

Essentials
1. **The World**
   Diversity/conflict./love

   Competitive
   Passionate
   Absurd

Music-
Scene Prep-Dinner Scene-(from April 5)

Plot Point- The entire family is going to take Olive to the pageant (so Richard
can prove he's a winner)

Feeling Journey-Beginning/middle/end
   Curiousity (set-up) if these people can barely stand having dinner
together how are they going to go on a three day road trip together. Olive wants
to understand Frank, Frank is curious about this family, Dwayne is curious but
buries it. As an audience we have to be interested, and like these people, be
entertained by their differences…
   Anticipation (point of ignition) now what?
   Panic (crisis) Sheryl says "Fuck"   what are we going to do?
   Dread (resolution) Richard's pep talk to Olive. Richard feels if we are
going to do this I am going to use it to show how my program works, how he can
be a winner

Characters
Sheryl-Responsible, open-minded and strong
Richard-dreamer, unrelenting, insecure craves authority
Frank-suicidal, arrogant and curious
Grandpa-tired, hedonistic, out-spoken
Olive-curious, open and excitable
Dwayne-disciplined, passionate and intelligent

Relationship- literal-family / feeling-opponents in a sporting event, debate…

Overall Action-
Sheryl-*create harmony, promote openness and honesty*

Typewritten notes for dinner scene in *Little Miss Sunshine*. Courtesy of Jonathan Dayton and
Valerie Faris. LITTLE MISS SUNSHINE ©2006 Twentieth Century Fox. All Rights Reserved.

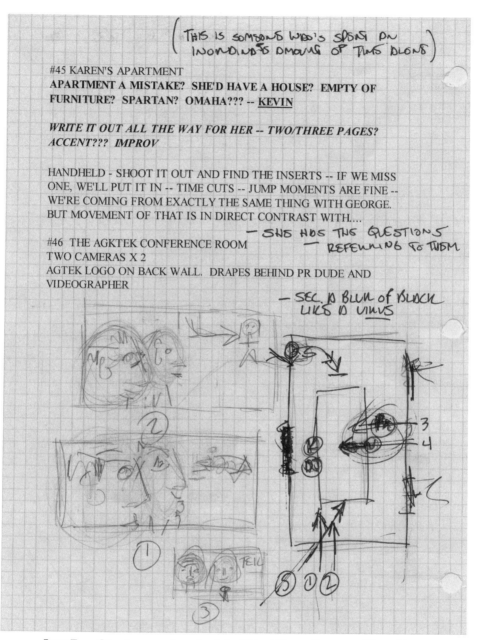

(THIS IS SOMEONE WHO'S SPENT AN
INORDINATE AMOUNT OF TIME ALONE)

#45 KAREN'S APARTMENT
**APARTMENT A MISTAKE? SHE'D HAVE A HOUSE? EMPTY OF
FURNITURE? SPARTAN? OMAHA??? -- <u>KEVIN</u>**

*WRITE IT OUT ALL THE WAY FOR HER -- TWO/THREE PAGES?
ACCENT??? IMPROV*

HANDHELD - SHOOT IT OUT AND FIND THE INSERTS -- IF WE MISS
ONE, WE'LL PUT IT IN -- TIME CUTS -- JUMP MOMENTS ARE FINE --
WE'RE COMING FROM EXACTLY THE SAME THING WITH GEORGE.
BUT MOVEMENT OF THAT IS IN DIRECT CONTRAST WITH....

- SHE HAS THE QUESTIONS
- REFERRING TO THEM

#46 THE AGKTEK CONFERENCE ROOM
TWO CAMERAS X 2
AGTEK LOGO ON BACK WALL. DRAPES BEHIND PR DUDE AND
VIDEOGRAPHER

- SEE. A BLUR OF BLACK
LIKE A VIRUS

From Tony Gilroy's personal notebook for *Michael Clayton*. Courtesy of Tony Gilroy.

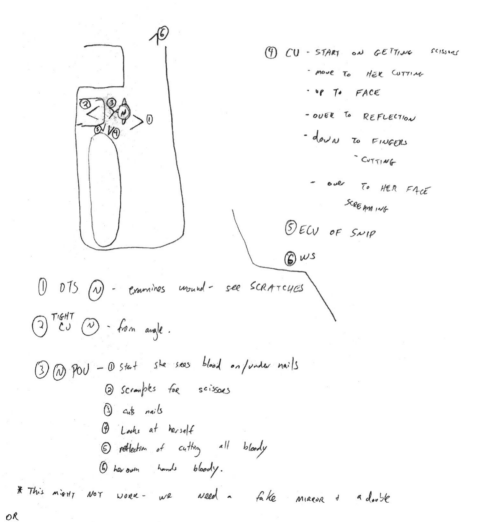

SCENE 528

We need to build the reflection.

④ CU - START ON GETTING SCISSORS
- move to HER CUTTING
- UP TO FACE
- OVER To REFLECTION
- down TO FINGERS
- CUTTING
- over TO HER FACE
SCREAMING

⑤ ECU OF SNIP

⑥ WS

① OTS Ⓝ - examines wound - see SCRATCHES

② TIGHT CU Ⓝ - from angle.

③ Ⓝ POV - ① Start she sees blood on/under nails
② scrambles for scissors
③ cuts nails
④ Looks at herself
⑤ reflection of cutting all bloody
⑥ her own hands bloody.

※ This might NOT WORK - we need a fake MIRROR + a double

OR

Darren Aronofsky's shot list for *Black Swan*. Courtesy of Darren Aronofsky. BLACK SWAN ©2010 Twentieth Century Fox. All Rights Reserved.

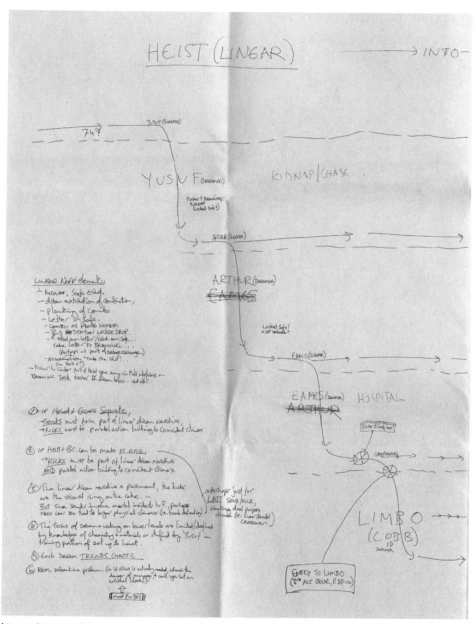

Linear diagram of film narrative for "the heist" sequence in *Inception*. Courtesy of Christopher Nolan.

COSTUME DESIGN SKETCHES

Costume design for Peppy's restaurant interview scene in *The Artist*. Courtesy of La Petite Reine, The Weinstein Company LLC, and Mark Bridges.

Joker character sketch from *The Dark Knight*. THE DARK KNIGHT—Licensed by Warner Bros. Entertainment Inc. All Rights Reserved.

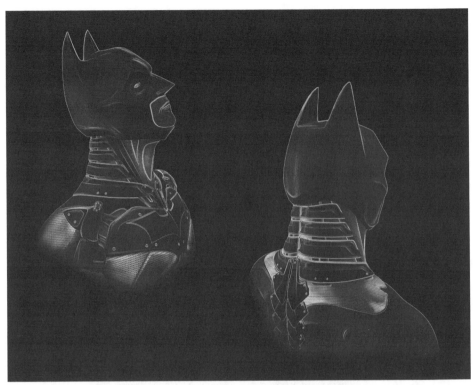

Batman costume sketch from *The Dark Knight*. THE DARK KNIGHT—Licensed by Warner Bros. Entertainment Inc. All Rights Reserved.

Costume sketch for *Dreamgirls*. DREAMGIRLS ©2006 DW Studios L.L.C. and Paramount Pictures. All Rights Reserved.

DESIGNED BY ANNA SHEPPARD
ILLUSTRATION BY ROBIN ARCHER

'INGLOURIOUS
BASTERDS'
DIANE KRUGER
AS **BRIDGET VON HAMMERSMARK**
CINEMA PREMIERE

Costume sketch for Bridget Von Hammersmark in *Inglourious Basterds.* Courtesy of The Weinstein Company LLC, Universal Studios Licensing LLC, Quentin Tarantino, Anna Sheppard, and Robin Archer. All Rights Reserved.

STORYBOARDS

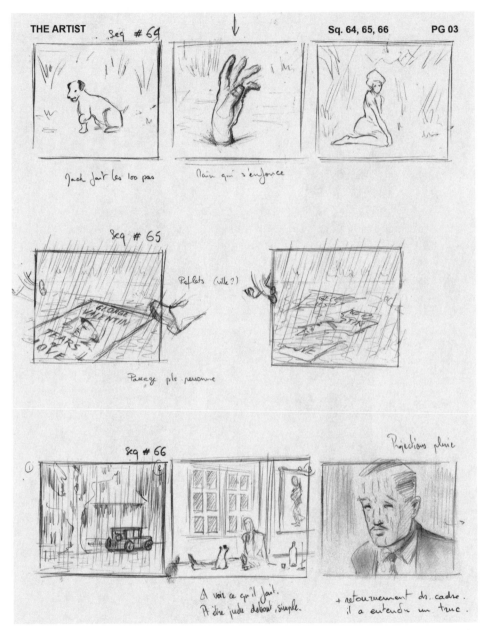

Storyboards for *The Artist.* Courtesy of La Petite Reine, The Weinstein Company LLC and Michel Ha-zanavicius.

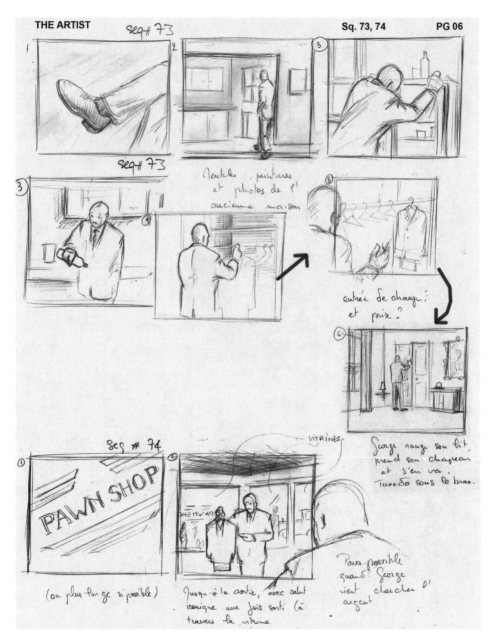

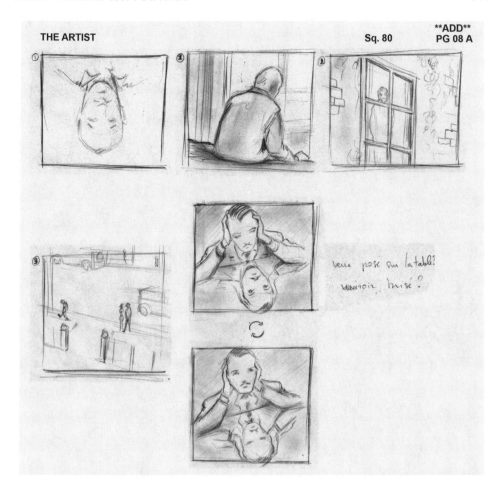

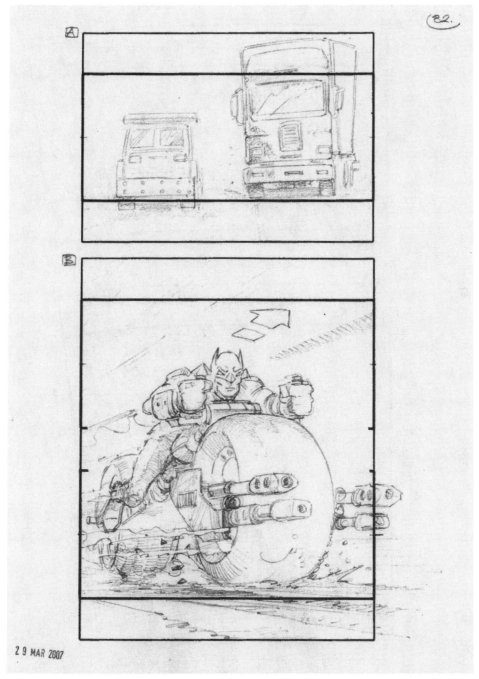

Storyboards for the "truck-flipping chase" sequence from *The Dark Knight*. THE DARK KNIGHT—
Licensed by Warner Bros. Entertainment Inc. All Rights Reserved.

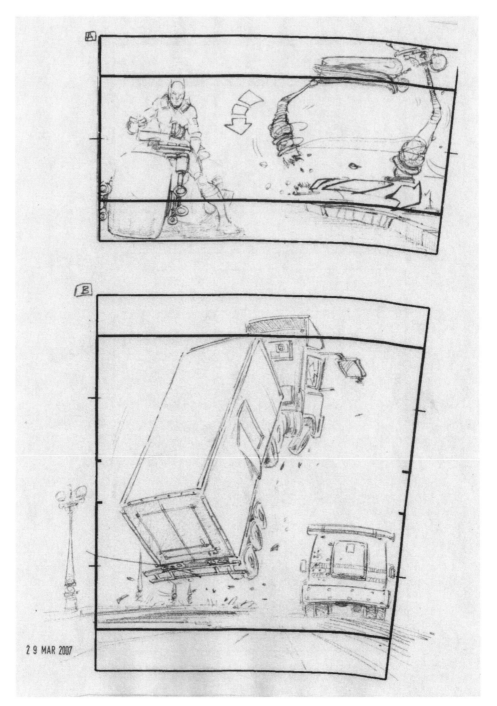

29 MAR 2007

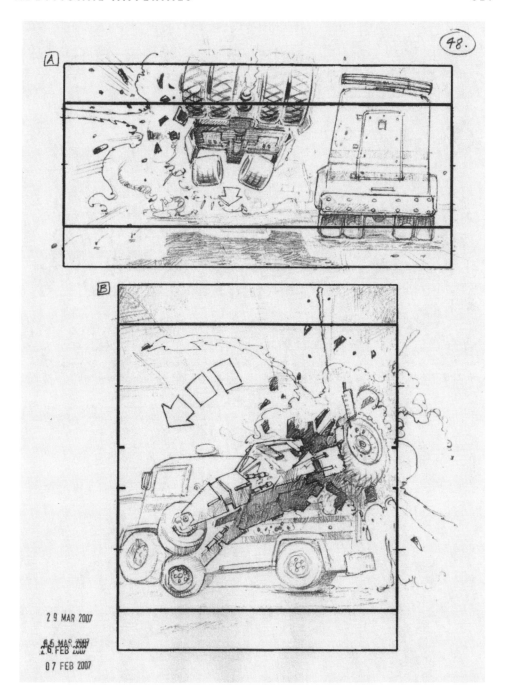

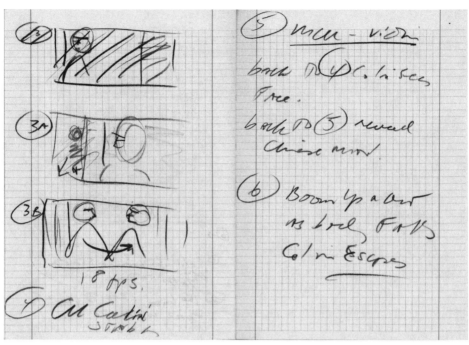

From Martin Scorsese's personal notebook for *The Departed*. Courtesy of The Martin Scorsese Collection. THE DEPARTED—Licensed by Warner Bros. Entertainment Inc. All Rights Reserved.

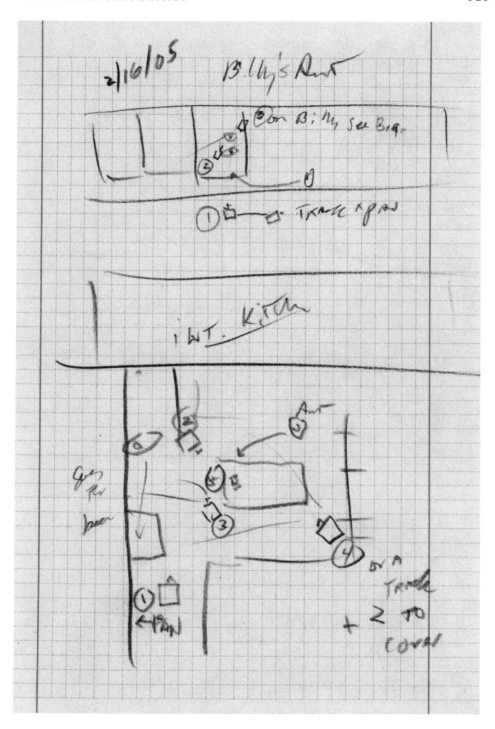

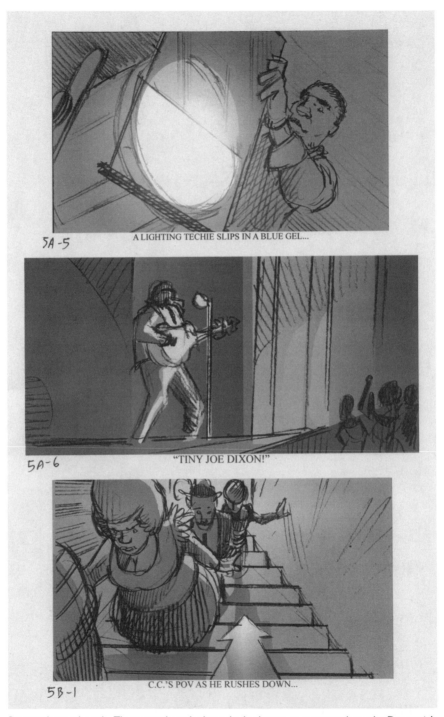

Dreamgirls storyboards. These storyboards show the backstage encounter where the Dreamgirls realize their competitors are wearing the same wigs they are wearing so they decide to flip theirs around, creating their signature look. Courtesy of Bill Condon and Brad Parker. DREAMGIRLS ©2006 DW Studios L.L.C. and Paramount Pictures. All Rights Reserved.

5B-5 "GOD, I NEED TO REST. WHERE'S OUR DRESSING ROOM?"

5B-6 LORRELL: "EFFIE, THERE'S NO TIME FOR THAT!"

"WE GO ON IN TWO MINUTES!"

5B-7

5B-8   EFFIE: "WHAT?"

DEENA: "COME ON, LET'S WARM UP." WITH LORRELL: "MOVE, MOVE, MOVE RIGHT OUT OF MY LIFE"
5B-9

5B-10   THE STEPP SISTERS SLINK PAST...

...WEARING IDENTICAL WIGS!

5B-11

5B-12

5B-13

5B-14

5B-15

DEENA: "OH NO!" LORRELL: "WE'RE RUINED UNLESS WE CAN FIND NEW WIGS."

5B-16

EFFIE: "WHY DO WE NEED WIGS IN THE FIRST PLACE?" DEENA: "BECAUSE WE NEED A LOOK."

5B-17

"I GOT IT! TURN THE WIGS AROUND!" LORRELL: "WHAT?" DEENA: "TURN THE WIGS AROUND!"

5B-18

LORRELL: "OH DEENA, IT'S SO... DIFFERENT." DEENA: "IT'S SOPHISTICATED LOOKING. COME ON."

5B-19

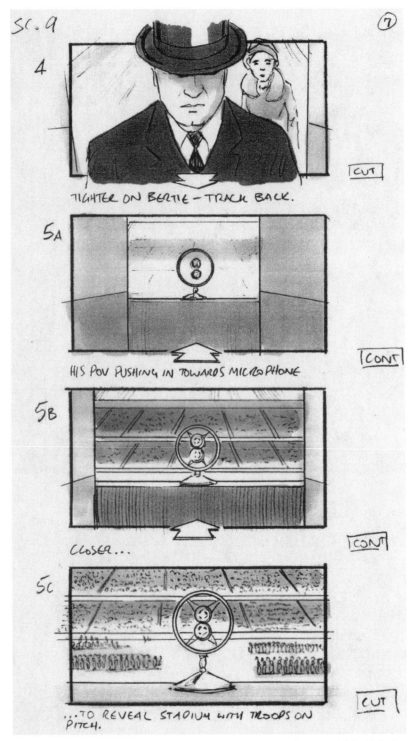

Storyboard for *The King's Speech*. Courtesy of The Weinstein Company LLC. All Rights
Reserved.

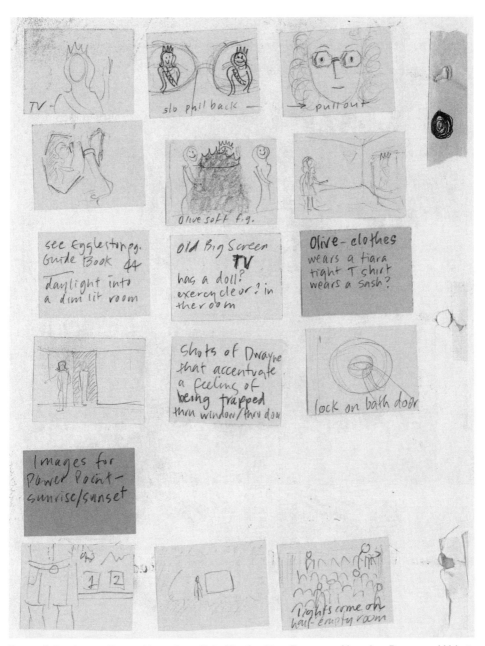

Personal sketches on Post-it Notes from *Little Miss Sunshine*. Courtesy of Jonathan Dayton and Valerie Faris. LITTLE MISS SUNSHINE ©2006 Twentieth Century Fox. All Rights Reserved.

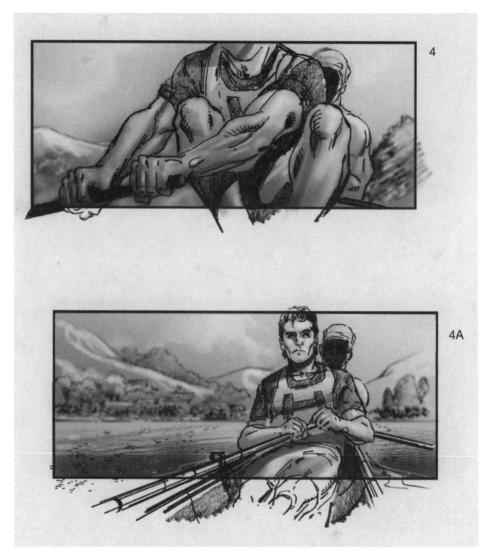

Storyboards for *The Social Network*. Courtesy of Columbia Pictures, David Fincher, and Richard Bennett.

The Social Network

The Social Network

The Social Network

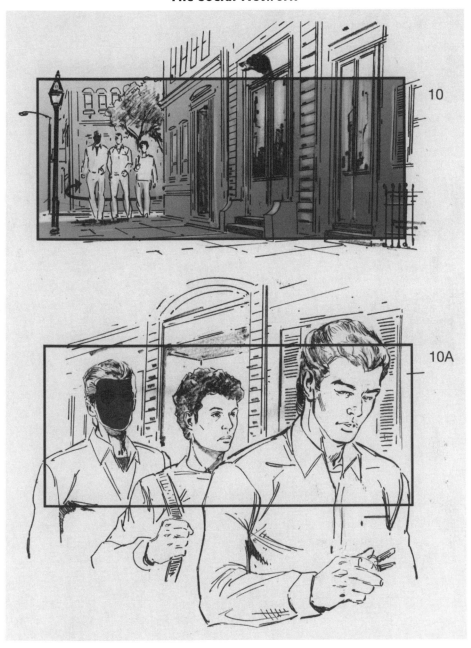

PIX Notes Report   *GDT*

sc001_board_tracks1.jpg

Author	Marker	Note	Date
D. Fincher		Fade Up: Helicopter POV (Could be banking) approximately 25mm lens -- 100 + feet over snow covered valley. High Horizon, VERY soft light. We drop in rapidly -- defoliated trees and rock covered in ice -- make up the landscape... we align with and travel along a train track running like a black zipper...	5.8.11 10:15P

sc001_board_tracks2.jpg

Author	Marker	Note	Date
D. Fincher		...Until we are 10 feet over the tracks, and we are moving at 90 miles per hour. The snow coming in bursts, the lens is finally obliterated by ice...	5.8.11 10:18P

sc024_board_lake.jpg

Author	Marker	Note	Date
D. Fincher		Helicopter POV of a black and yellow passenger train making its way through a mountain pass -- off to one side muted sunlight glints off a frozen lake. This is NOT picturesque -- this is a foreboding landscape, a place where the people must be made of harder stuff... The train movement must have the requisite "rolling" and the camera is moving thru a significant snowstorm.	5.8.11 10:21P

Visual effects boards from *The Girl with the Dragon Tattoo.* Courtesy of Columbia Pictures and David Fincher.

APPENDIX B:
ABOUT THE NOMINEES

WOODY ALLEN

Annie Hall (1978), Manhattan (1980), Hannah and Her Sisters (1987), Crimes and Misdemeanors (1990), Midnight in Paris (2012)

Woody Allen got his start as a writer for such iconic television programs as *The Sid Caesar Show*, *The Ed Sullivan Show*, and *Candid Camera*. He went on to work as a stand-up comic before writing his first feature screenplay for the 1965 hit *What's New Pussycat?* The following year he made his directorial debut with *What's Up, Tiger Lily?* Over the course of his career, Allen has written and directed close to fifty feature films, including *Everything You Always Wanted To Know About Sex° But Were Afraid To Ask*, the multi-award winning *Annie Hall, Manhattan, Hannah and Her Sisters, Crimes and Misdemeanors, Alice, Bullets Over Broadway, Mighty Aphrodite, Deconstructing Harry, Match Point*, and *Vicky Cristina Barcelona*. Among the numerous accolades he has received, Allen won an Academy Award for Best Screenplay for *Midnight in Paris*, Best Director and Best Screenplay for *Annie Hall*, and Best Screenplay for *Hannah and Her Sisters*. In 1978, Allen earned the DGA Award for Outstanding Directorial Achievement for *Annie Hall* and was nominated for three other DGA Awards for *Manhattan, Hannah and Her Sisters, Crimes and Misdemeanors*, and *Midnight in Paris*. In 1996, Allen received the DGA Lifetime Achievement Award.

PAUL THOMAS ANDERSON

There Will Be Blood (2008)

Writer, director and producer, Paul Thomas Anderson received attention for his short film *Cigarettes & Coffee* at the 1993 Sundance Film Festival. He expanded the short into a full-length feature, *Hard Eight*, in 1996, which earned five Independent Spirit Award nominations. In 1997, Anderson directed and produced the three-time Academy Award nominated film, *Boogie Nights*. *Magnolia* followed in 1999, earning three Academy Award nominations and the Golden Berlin Bear Award at the Berlin International Film Festival.

He also served as Executive Music Producer on *Boogie Nights* and *Magnolia*. In 2002, he directed *Punch-Drunk Love* and in 2007 he wrote and directed *There Will Be Blood*, starring Daniel Day-Lewis. The film was nominated for six Academy Awards, eight BAFTAs, the Directors Guild of America Award for Outstanding Directorial Achievement in Motion Pictures, and Golden Globe Awards. In addition to his feature films, Paul has directed many short films, including *Blossoms & Blood*, *Mattress Man Commercial*, *Rituals and Resolutions* and *Flagpole Special*. He also served as the "Stand-by Director" to Robert Altman on *A Prairie Home Companion*. Paul's most recent feature project is *The Master*.

DARREN ARONOFSKY

Black Swan (2011)

Darren Aronofsky was raised in Brooklyn, New York. After high school, he studied film at Harvard University and his senior thesis, *Supermarket Sweep*, earned him the title of National Student Academy Award finalist, paving the way for his career. His first feature, π, won the Director's Award at the 1998 Sundance Film Festival and an Independent Spirit Award for Best First Screenplay.

In 2000, Aronofsky premiered *Requiem for a Dream* at the Cannes Film Festival, and soon thereafter the film was named to over 150 Top Ten lists including *The New York Times*, *Rolling Stone*, *Entertainment Weekly*, and the *American Film Institute*. Aronofsky earned five Independent Spirit Award nominations, including one for Best Director. He also wrote and directed the science-fiction romance, *The Fountain*, starring Hugh Jackman and Rachel Weisz. The film was nominated for a Golden Lion at the Venice Film Festival. In 2008, he produced and directed *The Wrestler*, which also premiered at the Venice Film Festival where it won the Golden Lion Award. *The Wrestler* won Best Feature at the Independent Spirit Awards and garnered Academy Award nominations for Best Actor and Best Actress.

In 2010, Aronofsky directed *Black Swan*, starring Natalie Portman, earning Aronofsky a DGA Award nomination and four Oscar nominations, including Best Picture. Among other honors, the American Film Institute honored Aronofsky with the Franklin J. Schaffner Alumni Medal and the Stockholm Film Festival honored him with the Golden Horse Visionary Award. His next feature will be *Noah*, based on his graphic novel of the biblical story.

KATHRYN BIGELOW

The Hurt Locker (2010)

Kathryn Bigelow's recent directorial achievement, *The Hurt Locker*, was released in June 2009 and became an immediate box-office success. She directed and produced the film, which starred Oscar-nominated actor, Jeremy Renner.

The Hurt Locker received six Academy Awards including Best Motion Picture of the Year and Best Original Screenplay, and Bigelow earned the Academy Award for Best Achievement in Directing. She also won the Directors Guild of America Outstanding Directorial Achievement in Motion Pictures Award for the film, two BAFTA Awards, a Golden Globe, and the Golden Lion at the Venice Film Festival.

She got her start directing films like *The Loveless* and *Near Dark* in 1985, which she directed and co-wrote. *Point Break*, the 1991 psychological thriller about the struggle between two young men, starred Keanu Reeves and Patrick Swayze. When Bigelow's *Strange Days* was released in 1995, the film was highly praised for its energy and unique, intense visuals. She also directed *The Weight of Water*, which starred Sean Penn, Sarah Polley, Catherine McCormack and Elizabeth Hurley. Based on the best-selling Anita Shreve novel, The *Weight of Water* made its premiere at the 25th annual Toronto International Film Festival in 2000. Bigelow's 2002 release, *K-19: The Widowmaker*, starred Harrison Ford, Liam Neeson and Peter Saarsgard, and told the true story of a heroic Soviet naval crew. *Zero Dark Thirty* is her most recent feature film.

DANNY BOYLE

Slumdog Millionaire (2009)

Danny Boyle's first feature, *Shallow Grave*, earned him the Alexander Korda Award for Outstanding British Film at the BAFTA Awards, Best Director at the San Sebastian Film Festival, The Empire Award for Best Director and Best British Film, and the London Critics' Circle Film Award for Best British Newcomer. *Trainspotting*, Boyle's second feature, is one of the highest grossing British films of all time. The film won four Empire Awards including Best Director and Best Film, and was nominated for a BAFTA Alexander Korda Award.

In 2002, Boyle made the smash horror film, *28 Days Later*, which earned more than $80 million worldwide and a Saturn Award for Best Horror Film. His other feature films include *Millions* starring James Nesbit, Alex Etel and Lewis McGibbon; *The Beach*, starring Leonardo DiCaprio; *A Life Less Ordinary*, starring Ewan McGregor and Cameron Diaz; *Alien Love Triangle*; and *Sunshine* starring Cillian Murphy. *Slumdog Millionaire* is his eighth international theatrically released film, which won the People's Choice Award at the 2008 Toronto International Film Festival, eight Academy Awards (including Best Achievement in Directing) and the Directors Guild of America Award for Outstanding Directorial Achievement. In 2010, he directed *127 hours*, which was nominated for six Oscars.

His work in television includes producing Alan Clark's *Elephant*, and directing *Strumpet*, *Vacuuming Completely Nude in Paradise* and the series *Mr. Wroe's Virgins* for which he received a BAFTA nomination. Boyle's career started in the theater with Howard Barker's *Victory*, Howard Brenton's *The Genius* and Edward Bond's *Saved*, which won the Time Out Award. Boyle has also directed five productions for the Royal Shakespeare Company. Boyle is at work on a new feature titled *Trance*.

JAMES CAMERON

Titanic (1998) and *Avatar* (2010)

James Cameron was born in Kapuskasing, Ontario, Canada. In 1971, he moved to California where he studied physics at Fullerton Junior College while working as a machinist and a truck driver. Cameron quit his trucking job in 1978 and raised money from a consortium of local dentists to produce a short film in 35mm. In 1982, he wrote a low-budget, high-impact vehicle, *The Terminator*, which made over $80 million worldwide.

Cameron has subsequently written/produced/directed some of the film world's most successful, highest-grossing action and visual-effects adventures, including *The Abyss*, *Terminator 2: Judgment Day*, *Aliens*, *Rambo II*, *True Lies* and *Titanic*. He also co-wrote and produced *Point Break* and *Strange Days*, and produced *Solaris*.

Titanic literally stormed the globe, ultimately grossing more than $600 million at the domestic box office and over $1.2 billion abroad. The film was recognized and honored by numerous organizations, received fourteen Academy Award nominations and won a record-tying eleven Oscars that include Best Picture, Director, Visual Effects, Music, Song, Cinematography, Sound, and Costume, as well as additional nominations and awards from the Directors Guild of America, Screen Actors Guild, Writers Guild of America, Producers Guild of America, People's Choice Awards, BAFTA, and many others.

Post-*Titanic,* Cameron began exploring several new entertainment avenues. In 1998, he formed a television development and production venture with Charles Eglee.

Their initial efforts led to a one-hour dramatic series for Twentieth Century Fox Television and FBC titled, *Dark Angel*. Cameron also explored his interest in space, which became the motivation for writing and producing a miniseries and an IMAX 3D film focused on the first manned mission to Mars.

Cameron also set to work on a digital 3D camera system that he developed with partner Vince Pace. With the new camera system, Cameron proceeded to make underwater documentaries. His team's historic exploration of the inside of Titanic was the subject of Cameron's IMAX 3D film, *Ghosts of the Abyss*. In May 2002, Cameron guided his robotic cameras inside the wreck of Bismarck, which resulted in groundbreaking discoveries about the sinking of the legendary German battleship, and the Discovery Channel documentary, *James Cameron's Expedition: Bismarck*. In addition, Cameron's team made three expeditions to deep hydrothermal vent sites in the Atlantic, Pacific and Sea of Cortez over a two-year period, which became the subject of *Aliens of the Deep*, also released in IMAX 3D. Most recently, Cameron returned again to the Titanic to complete his interior exploration of the ship, which was showcased in the Discovery Channel's program, *Last Mysteries of the Titanic*.

In 2009, Cameron wrote and directed the box-office hit, *Avatar*, which was acclaimed for its use of advanced technology. The film earned three Oscars and another six nominations. Cameron also received his second Directors Guild of America nomination. He won the DGA Award in 1998 for *Titanic*. Cameron is currently working on the screenplays for the *Avatar* sequels and the highly-anticipated *Battle Angel*.

GEORGE CLOONEY

Good Night, and Good Luck. (2006)

George Clooney and Steven Soderbergh's film and television production company, Section Eight, has produced *Ocean's Twelve*, *Ocean's Eleven*, *Confessions of a Dangerous Mind*, *The Jacket*, *Full Frontal* and *Welcome To Collinwood*. Clooney also executive produced two Section Eight films: Warner Bros.' *Insomnia* and Focus Features' *Far From Heaven*.

Clooney made his directorial debut in 2002 with *Confessions of a Dangerous Mind*, which earned him the Special Achievement in Film Award from the National Board of Review. He executive produced and directed five episodes of *Unscripted*, a reality-based show that debuted on HBO, and he was the executive producer and cameraman for *K-Street*, also for HBO. His 2005 hit, *Good Night, and Good Luck.*, earned six Academy Award nominations, including Best Achievement in Directing for Clooney, three Golden Globe nominations and a Directors Guild of America nomination for Outstanding Directorial Achievement in Motion Pictures. *Leatherheads*, Clooney's third feature film, premiered in 2008 and in 2011, he directed *The Ides of March*, starring Ryan Gosling, Paul Giamatti and Philip Seymour Hoffman.

Alongside directing, Clooney starred in *The Descendants*, *Up in the Air*, *Michael Clayton*, *Syriana*, *Ocean's Twelve* and *Ocean's Eleven*, the Coen brothers' *O Brother,*

Where Art Thou?, among many others. He won the Golden Globe Award for Best Actor in a Motion Picture Musical or Comedy in 2000 and an Oscar for Best Performance by an Actor in a Supporting Role in 2005. Prior to playing lead roles in blockbuster features, Clooney starred in several television series, including his five-year run on *ER*.

Clooney was executive producer and co-star of the live television broadcast, *Fail-Safe*, an Emmy-winning telefilm developed through Maysville Pictures and based on the '60s novel of the same name. In 2000, the film was nominated for a Golden Globe Award as Best Mini-series or Motion Picture Made for Television. He will be seen in Alfonso Cuarón's *Gravity*.

ETHAN AND JOEL COEN

Fargo (1997) and *No Country for Old Men* (2007)

Known as the Coen brothers, Ethan and Joel Coen are Academy Award-winning American filmmakers. For more than twenty years, the pair has written, directed and produced successful films. *Blood Simple*, their first film, earned the Grand Jury Prize at the Sundance Film Festival in 1985. The brothers followed with *Raising Arizona*, *Miller's Crossing* and *Barton Fink*, which won the *Palme d'Or* at the Cannes Film Festival and earned three Oscar nominations. In 1994, the duo wrote and directed *The Hudsucker Proxy* and in 1996, *Fargo*, which received five Academy Award nominations. The Coens won an Oscar for Best Writing, Screenplay Written Directly for the Screen. Their 1998 comedy, *The Big Lebowski*, was nominated at the Berlin International Film Festival and in 2000, *O Brother, Where Art Thou?*, starring George Clooney and John Goodman, earned two Academy Award nominations. Known as "the two-headed director," the Coen brothers share a similar vision in films, which has led to the success of *The Man Who Wasn't There*, *No Country for Old Men*, *A Serious Man* and *True Grit*—all of which earned Academy Award nominations. *No Country for Old Men* received four Oscars including Best Achievement in Directing, Best Motion Picture of the Year and Best Writing, Adapted Screenplay, and received the Directors Guild of America Outstanding Directorial Achievement in Motion Pictures Award. While the brothers often alternate top billing for their screenplays, they share film credits for editor under the alias Roderick Jaynes. Their next feature, *Inside Llewyn Davis*, is scheduled for release in early 2013.

BILL CONDON

Dreamgirls (2007)

Bill Condon wrote and directed the Academy Award-nominated film, *Dreamgirls*, which earned eight Oscar nominations, two BAFTA nominations, and a Directors Guild of America Award nomination, among many others. He also wrote and directed *Kinsey*, for which he won the 2005 International Film Award from the British Directors Guild. The film also earned an Academy Award nomination for Best Supporting Actress. Condon previously wrote and directed *Gods and Monsters*, which won the Independent Spirit Award for Best Feature and was named Best Picture of 1998 by the National Board of Review. The film earned Condon an Academy Award for Best Adapted Screenplay and garnered nominations for its stars. As a writer, he adapted the big screen version of the musical *Chicago*, earning him a second Oscar nomination for Best Adapted Screenplay. The film won six Academy Awards, including Best Picture of 2002. Condon most recently directed the final installment of the *Twilight* saga.

LEE DANIELS

Precious (2010)

After tabling his screenwriting aspirations, Lee Daniels managed actors before stepping into the world of directing. Daniels made his directorial debut in 2006 with *Shadowboxer*, which screened at the Toronto Film Festival. He was also nominated for the New Directors Award at the San Sebastian Film Festival.

Precious, his latest film based on the novel by Sapphire, earned six Academy Award nominations, including Best Achievement in Directing. The film won both the Grand Jury Prize and Audience Award in the US Dramatic Competition at the 2009 Sundance Film Festival. With the support of Tyler Perry and Oprah Winfrey, *Precious* was released by Lionsgate and Daniels became the first African American to be nominated for a Directors Guild of America Award for Outstanding Directorial Achievement in Motion Pictures. *Precious* was nominated for three Golden Globe Awards including Best Picture, Drama, and eight NAACP Image Awards including Outstanding Motion Picture and Outstanding Directing in a Motion Picture, Theatrical or Television. The film also garnered five 2010 Independent Spirit Award nominations including Best Feature and Best Director.

With his production company, Lee Daniels Entertainment, Daniels produced *Monster's Ball* (2001) and became the first African American producer of an Oscar-winning and nominated film. His company also produced *The Woodsman*. Daniels most recently directed, produced and wrote *The Paperboy* and is in pre-production on *The Butler*.

JONATHAN DAYTON AND VALERIE FARIS

Little Miss Sunshine (2007)

Jonathan Dayton and Valerie Faris have collaborated on more than seventy-five projects in film, television, commercials and music videos. They made their feature film directorial debut with *Little Miss Sunshine*, but the duo began their careers creating and directing an MTV show, *The Cutting Edge*. Dayton and Faris also directed videos and documentaries for artists such as REM, The Red Hot Chili Peppers, Janet Jackson, and The Ramones, earning two Grammy Awards, nine MTV Video Awards and a *Billboard* Music Director of the Year Award. Together, they have directed episodes of the sketch comedy series, *Mr. Show*, and produced two feature films: *The Decline of Western Civilization Part II: The Metal Years* and *Jane's Addiction's Gift*. They co-founded Bob Industries, a commercial production company that directs ads for VW, Sony PlayStation, Gap, Ikea, Target, Apple and ESPN. Dayton and Faris's sophomore feature was *Ruby Sparks*.

DAVID FINCHER

The Curious Case of Benjamin Button (2009), The Social Network (2011) and The Girl with the Dragon Tattoo (2012)

David Fincher made his feature film debut in 1992 with *Alien*[3]. In 1995, he directed *Se7en*, the lauded crime drama starring Brad Pitt and Morgan Freeman, and two years later he directed *The Game*, starring Michael Douglas and Sean Penn. He re-teamed with Brad Pitt in 1999 on *Fight Club*, based on Chuck Palahniuk's novel.

Fincher directed *Panic Room* in 2002, starring Jodie Foster, Forest Whitaker, Dwight Yoakum and Jared Leto. In 2007, he directed *Zodiac*, which was named to over 150 ten-best lists, including those of *Entertainment Weekly*, *USA Today* and *The Washington Post*. *The Curious Case of Benjamin Button*, in 2008, was nominated for thirteen Academy Awards, including Best Picture and Best Director, and it won three awards. The film was also honored with five Golden Globe nominations and won two awards, including Best Director from the National Board of Review. Fincher received a Directors Guild of America nomination.

In 2010, he directed *The Social Network*, which received four Golden Globe Awards including Best Picture–Drama and Best Director, and was nominated for eight Academy Awards, including Best Picture and Best Director. The film won three Oscars

(Writing, Editing and Original Score), and Fincher received his second DGA Award nomination.

In 2011, Fincher directed *The Girl with the Dragon Tattoo*, an adaptation of the best-selling novel by Stieg Larsson and starred Daniel Craig and Rooney Mara. The film was nominated for five Academy Awards and earned Fincher his third DGA nomination. His most recent project is the Netflix original series *House of Cards*.

STEPHEN FREARS

The Queen (2007)

Stephen Frears has directed for both film and television. His credits include the low budget hits *My Beautiful Laundrette*, *Prick Up Your Ears* and *Sammy and Rosie Get Laid*. Stephen made his Hollywood debut with *Dangerous Liaisons*, which earned him a BAFTA nomination for Best Director. He gained an Oscar nomination for Best Director in 1991 for *The Grifters*, and directed an array of films like *The Hi-Lo Country*, *High Fidelity*, *Liam* and *Dirty Pretty Things*. In 2003, he returned to British television to direct *The Deal*, which looked at a pivotal moment in the relationship between Gordon Brown and Tony Blair. Stephen went on to direct *Mrs. Henderson Presents* in 2005, followed closely by *The Queen* for which he received Golden Globe, DGA, BAFTA, BIFA and Oscar nominations for Best Director. Frears's most recent project is *Muhammad Ali's Greatest Fight*.

TONY GILROY

Michael Clayton (2008)

Tony Gilroy, the son of Pulitzer Prize-winning playwright and filmmaker Frank D. Gilroy, made his feature film directorial debut in 2007 with *Michael Clayton*, which he wrote and directed. The film earned six Academy Award nominations including Best Achievement in Directing; Best Writing, Original Screenplay; and Best Motion Picture of the Year. *Michael Clayton* also earned BAFTA nominations, four Golden Globe nominations and the Directors Guild of America Award nomination for Outstanding Directorial Achievement in Motion Pictures. His second film *Duplicity* earned Julia Roberts a Golden Globe nomination.

An acclaimed screenwriter, Gilroy spent seven years working on the trilogy of *Bourne* films: *The Bourne Identity*, *The Bourne Supremacy* and *The Bourne Ultimatum*. Gilroy has also written three screenplays for director Taylor Hackford: *Dolores Claiborne* based on the novel by Stephen King; *The Devil's Advocate*; and *Proof of Life*, which Gilroy also executive produced. Gilroy's additional writing credits include

Michael Bay's blockbuster *Armageddon*, Michael Apted's *Extreme Measures* and *State of Play*, among many others. *The Bourne Legacy* was his most recent feature film that he wrote and directed.

ALEJANDRO GONZÁLEZ IÑÁRRITU

Babel (2007)

Alejandro González Iñárritu directed and produced his debut feature film in 2000, *Amores Perros*, which was nominated for an Academy Award for Best Foreign Language Film.

He conceived, directed and produced his second film, *21 Grams*, in 2003. The film received two Oscar nominations and five BAFTA nominations. In May 2006, he completed the third film in his trilogy, *Babel*, for which he received the Best Director Award at the Cannes Film Festival. The film was nominated for seven Academy Awards, including Best Picture and Best Director, and won the Golden Globe for Best Motion Picture (Drama). *Babel* also received six Golden Globe nominations, including Best Director; a BAFTA Award for Best Picture and an NAACP Image Award for Best Director. Iñárritu was nominated for the Directors Guild of America Outstanding Directorial Achievement in Motion Pictures Award. Following *Babel*, Iñárritu wrote and directed the Oscar-nominated film, *Biutiful*. He has several projects in development.

PAUL HAGGIS

Crash (2006)

Paul Haggis left a successful career in television (*EZ Streets*; *Walker, Texas Ranger*; *Family Law*) to concentrate on feature films. In 2000, he turned to F. X. Toole's short stories, one of which became the successful *Million Dollar Baby* starring Hilary Swank and Morgan Freeman. Clint Eastwood directed Haggis's screenplay in 2004 and in less than a year, the film grossed over $100 million in the United States. Haggis co-produced *Million Dollar Baby*, which earned four Oscars, and he received a nomination for Best Writing, Adapted Screenplay. Haggis also concocted a story for an original screenplay that he and his friend Bobby Moresco wrote, entitled *Crash*. He directed *Crash* in 2003 with an ensemble cast and it premiered at the Toronto International Film Festival. The film was acquired by Lions Gate for domestic distribution and upon its release, *Crash* proved to be an independent hit. The film was nominated for six Academy Awards and won three, including Best Motion Picture of the Year, Best Writing, Original Screenplay and Best Achievement in Film Editing; and was nominated for the Directors Guild of America Outstanding Directorial Achievement in Motion Pictures award.

Haggis has written a number of successful stories and/or screenplays from *The Last Kiss* to *Flags of Our Fathers*, *Casino Royale*, *Letters from Iwo Jima*, *In the Valley of Elah* (which he also directed), *Quantum of Solace*, the documentary *Speechless* and *The Next Three Days* (which he also directed). He created and developed the television show, *The Black Donnellys*, with his writing partner Bobby Moresco. Haggis is working on *Third Person*.

MICHEL HAZANAVICIUS

The Artist (2012)

French writer and director Michel Hazanavicius began his directing career in television. He co-wrote and co-directed the television movie, *La Classe Américaine* and in 1994, made his acting debut in the feature, *Fear City: A Family-Style Comedy* (*La Cité De La Peur*). In 1996, he transitioned to screenwriting, with credits including comedies like *Delphine 1*, *Yvan 0*; *Le Clone* (*The Clone*) and *Lucky Luke and the Daltons*. In 1999, he wrote and made his directorial debut with *Mes Amies* (My Friends). He directed the comedy *OSS 117—Cairo* in 2006, followed by *Nest of Spies*, a spy spoof starring Jean Dujardin. Hazanavicius and Dujardin reteamed for the hit sequel *OSS 117—Lost in Rio* and most recently, *The Artist* (2011), which won the DGA Award and was nominated for ten Academy Awards, winning five, including Best Directing, Best Original Screenplay, and Best Motion Picture of the Year.

TOM HOOPER

The King's Speech (2011)

Tom Hooper wrote, directed and produced the short film, *Painted Faces*, when he was eighteen years old. The film premiered at the London Film Festival and was released theatrically and shown on television. Hooper was later nominated for an Emmy for helming the revival of ITV's *Prime Suspect 6: The Last Witness*, starring Helen Mirren, and he also directed Hilary Swank and Chiwetel Ejiofor in the BAFTA-nominated film, *Red Dust*. Additionally, Hooper's television work includes *Daniel Deronda*, *Love in a Cold Climate*, and the multi-award-winning ITV comedy drama, *Cold Feet*. Hooper directed the one-hour specials of *Eastenders*, which received a BAFTA for best soap two years in a row. He received an Emmy for directing *Elizabeth I*, which won three Golden Globes and nine Emmy Awards, including Outstanding Mini-series and Best Actress for Helen Mirren. His television movie, *Longford*, won Golden Globes for Jim

Broadbent, Samantha Morton and for Best TV Film. He directed *John Adams*, starring Paul Giamatti and Laura Linney, which won four Golden Globes and thirteen Emmys. Hooper directed all nine hours of the mini-series, executive produced by Tom Hanks and Gary Goetzman for HBO.

In 2009, Hooper directed *The Damned United* starring Michael Sheen as the legendary English football manager Brian Clough based on the novel by David Peace. The film was nominated by the South Bank Show Awards for best British film and premiered at the Toronto Film Festival. *The King's Speech* premiered in 2010 and earned twelve Academy Award nominations, and won four awards including Best Achievement in Directing and Best Motion Picture of the Year. Hooper also won the Directors Guild of America Outstanding Directorial Achievement in Motion Pictures Award. His most recent credit is *Les Misérables*.

RON HOWARD

Apollo 13 (1996), *A Beautiful Mind* (2002) and *Frost/Nixon* (2009)

From dramas like *A Beautiful Mind* and *Apollo 13* to hit comedies like *Parenthood* and *Splash*, Ron Howard has created some of Hollywood's most memorable films. He earned an Oscar for Best Director for *A Beautiful Mind*, which also won awards for Best Picture, Best Screenplay, and Best Supporting Actress. The film garnered four Golden Globes as well, including the award for Best Motion Picture Drama, and Howard won Best Director of the Year from the Directors Guild of America. He and producer Brian Grazer received the first annual Awareness Award from the National Mental Health Awareness Campaign for their work on the film.

In 1995, Howard received his first Best Director of the Year Award from the DGA for *Apollo 13*. The true-life drama also garnered nine Academy Award nominations, winning Oscars for Best Film Editing and Best Sound. *Apollo 13* also received Best Cast and Best Supporting Actor awards from the Screen Actors Guild. Many of Howard's past films have received nods from the Academy, including the popular hits *Backdraft*, *Parenthood* and *Cocoon*, the last of which took home two Oscars. Howard has served as an executive producer on a number of award-winning films and television shows as well, such as the HBO mini-series *From the Earth to the Moon* and FOX's *Arrested Development*, an Emmy Award winner for Best Comedy that Howard also narrated.

Howard's portfolio includes some of the most popular films of the past twenty years. In 1991, Howard created the acclaimed drama *Backdraft*, starring Robert De Niro, Kurt Russell and William Baldwin. He followed it with the historical epic *Far and Away*, starring Tom Cruise and Nicole Kidman. Howard directed Mel Gibson, Rene Russo, Gary Sinise and Delroy Lindo in the 1996 suspense thriller *Ransom*. He worked with Tom Hanks, Kevin Bacon, Ed Harris, Bill Paxton, Gary Sinise and Kathleen Quinlan on *Apollo 13*, which was recently released in the IMAX format. Howard's other films include the blockbuster *Dr. Seuss' How the Grinch Stole Christmas*, starring Jim Carrey; *Parenthood*, starring Steve Martin; the fantasy epic *Willow*; *Night Shift*, starring Henry Winkler, Michael Keaton and Shelley Long. Howard directed the suspenseful western, *The Missing*, starring Oscar winners Cate Blanchett and Tommy Lee Jones; and *Cinderella Man* with Russell Crowe and Renée Zellweger.

Howard and Grazer first collaborated on the hit comedies *Night Shift* and *Splash*. The pair co-founded Imagine Entertainment in 1986 to create independently produced feature films. The company has since produced a variety of popular hits, including *The Nutty Professor*, *The Nutty Professor II: The Klumps*, *Bowfinger*, *The Paper*, *Inventing the Abbotts* and *Liar, Liar*.

Howard made his directorial debut in 1978 with *Grand Theft Auto*, but he began his career in film as an actor. He first appeared in *The Journey* and *The Music Man*, then as Opie on the long-running television series *The Andy Griffith Show*. Howard later starred in the popular series *Happy Days* and drew favorable reviews for his performances in *American Graffiti* and *The Shootist*.

In 2006, he directed the big-screen adaptation of the international best-seller *The Da Vinci Code*, starring Oscar-winner Tom Hanks, Audrey Tautou, Sir Ian McKellen, Alfred Molina, Jean Reno and Paul Bettany. In 2008, Howard directed *Frost/Nixon*, which earned five Academy Award nominations and another Directors Guild of America Award nomination. In 2009, he adapted Dan Brown's best-selling novel *Angels & Demons* to the big screen. Howard's most recent feature was *Rush*, about a Formula 1 champion driver.

ANG LEE

Sense and Sensibility (1995), *Crouching Tiger, Hidden Dragon* (2001), *Brokeback Mountain* (2006)

Ang Lee was born in Taiwan in 1954 and moved to the United States in 1978, where he received his BFA in theater from the University of Illinois and his MFA in film production from New York University. Lee's first feature, *Pushing Hands*, won Best Film at the Asian-Pacific Film Festival. The film was also nominated for nine Golden Horse Awards (the Taiwanese Academy Award) and won three, including Special Jury Prize for Lee's direction. In 1994, *The Wedding Banquet* premiered at the Berlin Film Festival and was awarded top prize for direction. The film was nominated for the Golden Globe and the Academy Award for Best Foreign Language Film and six Independent Spirit Awards. In Taiwan, *The Wedding Banquet* received five Golden Horse Awards, including awards for Best Film and Best Director. *Eat Drink Man Woman*, the third film in the trilogy, premiered as the Director's Fortnight at the Cannes Film Festival in 1994. It was nominated for Golden Globe and Academy Awards and was voted Best Foreign Language Film by the National Board Review. In 1995, Lee directed *Sense and Sensibility*, which was nominated for seven Academy Awards, including Best Picture, and won the Oscar for Best Screenplay Adaptation. In addition, the film received the Golden Bear Award at the Berlin Film Festival, as well as Golden Globes for Best Screenplay and Best Film. In 1996, Lee completed *The Ice Storm*, adapted by James Schamus from Rick Moody's novel. The film was selected for competition at the fiftieth International Film Festival in Cannes and won the award for Best Screenplay Adaptation. In 1999, he directed *Ride with the Devil* starring Tobey McGuire. Lee's *Crouching Tiger, Hidden Dragon* (2001) won an Academy Award for Best Foreign Language Film, a Golden Globe Award and a Directors Guild Award for Best Director. He previously received a DGA nomination for *Sense and Sensibility* in 1995.

Lee also directed *The Hulk* for Universal Studios, and in 2006, he earned his second Academy Award for his direction of *Brokeback Mountain*. He won the Directors Guild of America Award, BAFTA, Independent Spirit, and Golden Globe Awards for Best Director. *Brokeback Mountain* won three additional Golden Globe Awards, including Best Motion Picture–Drama; the Independent Spirit Award for Best Feature; three additional BAFTA Awards, including Best Film; and the Golden Lion Award for Best Picture at the 2005 Venice International Film Festival. *Taking Woodstock* (2009) was nominated for a *Palme d'Or* at the Cannes Film Festival and in 2012 Lee directed *Life of Pi* based on the novel by Yann Martel.

BENNETT MILLER

Capote (2006)

Bennett Miller directed and produced his first film in 1998, a documentary titled *The Cruise*, about New York City tour guide Timothy "Speed" Levitch. The film garnered the top prize of the International Forum at the Berlin Film Festival. In 2005, he directed *Capote*, after his friend of over 25 years, Dan Futterman, presented him with the screenplay. The film starred Philip Seymour Hoffman, who Miller and Futterman met at a summer theater program in Saratoga Springs, New York. The film earned four Academy Award nominations as well as a win for Hoffman for Best Performance by an Actor in a Leading Role. In addition, *Capote* earned four BAFTA nominations and the Directors Guild of America nomination for Outstanding Directorial Achievement in Motion Pictures. Following the success of *Capote*, Miller directed *Moneyball* in 2011, starring Brad Pitt. The film earned six Academy Award nominations, including Best Motion Picture of the Year. His most recent project is *Foxcatcher*.

CHRISTOPHER NOLAN

Memento (2002), *The Dark Knight* (2009), and *Inception* (2011)

Christopher Nolan began making movies at an early age with his father's Super-8mm camera. While studying English Literature at University College London, Nolan shot 16mm films at UCL's film society. His "no-budget" noir thriller, *Following*, enjoyed great success at a number of international film festivals, including Toronto, Rotterdam, Slamdance, and Hong Kong, prior to being released theatrically in the United States, United Kingdom and France.

Nolan's second film was the low-budget independent feature *Memento* starring Guy Pearce, Carrie-Ann Moss and Joe Pantoliano. Nolan wrote the screenplay based on his brother Jonathan's short story, and he directed the film. *Memento* brought Nolan numerous honors, including Academy Award and Golden Globe Award nominations for Best Original Screenplay, Independent Spirit Awards for Best Director and Best Screenplay, and a Directors Guild of America Award nomination.

Nolan followed *Memento* with the psychological thriller *Insomnia*, featuring Academy Award winners Al Pacino, Robin Williams and Hilary Swank. He was recognized by the London Critics Circle who honored him with the Best Director of the Year Award. In 2005, Nolan co-wrote and directed *Batman Begins*, starring Christian Bale, Michael Caine, Liam Neeson, Gary Oldman and Morgan Freeman. Praised by both critics and fans alike, the blockbuster introduced a re-imagined franchise that has made more than a billion dollars to date.

For his fifth film, Nolan co-wrote, produced and directed *The Prestige*, a mystery thriller starring Hugh Jackman, Christian Bale, Scarlett Johansson and Michael Caine. *Empire Magazine* named Nolan the Best Director of the Year for the film, which also received Oscar nominations for its art direction and cinematography. July 2008 brought the release of the record-breaking and commercially successful *The Dark Knight*, a film that earned Nolan WGA, PGA and DGA nominations and won two Oscars.

Nolan wrote and directed *Inception*, which debuted in July 2010. With a cast comprised of Leonardo DiCaprio, Ken Watanabe, Joseph Gordon-Levitt, Ellen Page, Marion Cotillard, Cillian Murphy, Tom Hardy, Tom Berenger and Michael Caine, the sci-fi actioner was nominated for eight Academy Awards, won four, and Nolan was also nominated for the Directors Guild of America Award. He was previously nominated for *Memento*. *The Dark Knight Rises* was released in July 2012 and he has several projects in development.

ALEXANDER PAYNE

Sideways (2005) and *The Descendants* (2012)

Alexander Payne's feature film directorial debut was *Citizen Ruth*, released in 1996, followed in 1999 by *Election*, which earned Best Screenplay awards from the WGA and the New York Film Critics Circle, as well as an Oscar nomination for Best Adapted Screenplay. In 2002, *About Schmidt* premiered at the Cannes Film Festival and received two Academy Award nominations for Best Actor (Jack Nicholson) and Best Supporting Actress (Kathy Bates). Payne's DGA Award-nominated *Sideways* (2004) went on to win an Oscar for Best Adapted Screenplay and was nominated for four others, including Best Picture and Best Director. His 2011 film, *The Descendants*, was nominated for a DGA Award, received five Golden Globe nominations, winning two including Best Motion Picture–Drama. The film earned five Academy Award nominations, including Best Picture and Best Director, and garnered Payne an Oscar for Best Adapted Screenplay.

SEAN PENN

Into the Wild (2007)

Sean Penn's feature film directorial debut was *The Indian Runner* (1991), which he also wrote and produced. In 1995, he wrote, directed and produced *The Crossing Guard*. His third film as director-producer was *The Pledge*, named as one of the Top Ten Films of 2001 by The National Board of Review and nominated for the *Palme d'Or* at the Cannes Film Festival and the Golden Lion at the Venice Film Festival. Penn also wrote and directed the United States segment of the compilation film *11'09"01 September 11*, nominated for a French César in the best European Union Film category and honored with a Freedom of Expression Award by the National Board of Review. In 2007, he directed, wrote and produced *Into the Wild*, which was nominated for a DGA Award for Outstanding Directorial Achievement in a Motion Picture and a WGA Award for Best Adapted Screenplay. Sean Penn has received five Academy Award nominations for Best Actor for his performances in *Dead Man Walking*, *Sweet and Lowdown*, *I Am Sam*, *Mystic River*, and *Milk*. In 2004, he won an Academy Award for his performance in Clint Eastwood's *Mystic River*, and in 2009 he won the Oscar for his starring role as gay rights activist Harvey Milk in Gus Van Sant's *Milk*.

JASON REITMAN

Up in the Air (2010)

Jason Reitman premiered his first short film, *Operation*, at the 1998 Sundance Film Festival and since then his short films have played at over a hundred film festivals worldwide. He has also directed a number of award-winning commercials.

Reitman made his feature film directorial debut with his 2006 hit, *Thank You for Smoking*, which he adapted from Christopher Buckley's novel. The film earned a Golden Globe nomination for Best Picture–Comedy or Musical, an Independent Spirit Award for Best Screenplay and a WGA nomination for Best Adapted Screenplay. In 2006, Reitman was named Best Debut Director by the National Board of Review.

Reitman's second feature, *Juno*, earned him an Academy Award nomination for directing. The film earned a win for Diablo Cody's screenplay and additional nominations for Best Picture and Best Actress (Ellen Page). *Juno* also won three Independent Spirit Awards and a Grammy Award.

Up in the Air, which Reitman both wrote and directed, starred George Clooney and Vera Farmiga. Reitman won a Golden Globe for Best Screenplay and was also nominated for Best Director and Best Film—Drama. The film also earned PGA, WGA, DGA and SAG nominations. His 2011 film, *Young Adult*, starred Charlize Theron and received a nomination for Best Performance by an Actress in a Motion Picture–Comedy or Musical. Most recently, Reitman directed *Labor Day* for 2013 release.

DAVID O. RUSSELL

The Fighter (2010)

David O. Russell wrote and directed his first feature film, *Spanking the Monkey*, which premiered at the 1994 Sundance Film Festival where it won the Sundance Audience Award. The film was also named Best First Feature and Best First Screenplay at the Independent Spirit Awards. His second film was the acclaimed comedy *Flirting with Disaster*, which appeared on many top ten lists for 1996. Critics and audiences were very receptive to the film, paving the way for Russell to employ a more ambitious scope for his third feature, *Three Kings*. The film starring George Clooney, Mark Wahlberg and Ice Cube was released in 1999. Russell earned a nomination from the WGA for Best Screenplay and the film appeared in over 100 critics' top ten lists. Boston Film Critics Society named it the Film of the Year and selected Russell as the Best Director of the Year. Russell's professional relationship with Mark Wahlberg continued when he made *I Heart Huckabees* in 2004, followed by *The Fighter* in 2010. The film earned Russell a Directors Guild of America Award nomination, seven Academy Award nominations and two wins for Best Supporting Actor and Best Supporting Actress.

Russell joined the board of the Ghetto Film School in 2002 and alongside his industry colleagues, he has helped over 500 teenagers tell their stories. Most recently, he directed *Nailed* and *Silver Linings Playbook*.

JULIAN SCHNABEL

The Diving Bell and the Butterfly (2008)

Before making his mark as a filmmaker, Julian Schnabel established himself as a well-known painter around the world. His work has been the subject of retrospective exhibitions at the Centre Georges Pompidou, Paris; The Whitechapel Gallery, London; The Stedelijk Museum, Amsterdam; The Tate Gallery, London; and The Whitney Museum of American Art in New York. In 1996, he wrote and directed *Basquiat*, a film about his fellow New York artist Jean Michel Basquiat. Schnabel earned a nomination at the Venice Film Festival and recognition at the Independent Spirit Awards. His second film, *Before Night Falls*, won the Grand Jury Prize at the Venice Film Festival in 2000 and earned Javier Bardem an Academy Award nomination for Best Actor. His 2007 hit, *The Diving Bell and the Butterfly*, earned four Academy Award nominations, two BAFTA nominations and a Directors Guild of America Award nomination for Julian. Schnabel won a Golden Globe for Best Director–Motion Picture. He followed with a documentary titled *Berlin* in 2007 and in 2010, he directed *Miral*, which earned Schnabel a UNICEF Award at the Venice Film Festival.

MARTIN SCORSESE

Taxi Driver (1977), *Raging Bull* (1981), *Goodfellas* (1991), *The Age of Innocence* (1994), *Gangs of New York* (2003), *The Aviator* (2005), *The Departed* (2007) and *Hugo* (2012)

Martin Scorsese's first feature film, *Who's That Knocking at My Door* (1967), caught the attention of producer Roger Corman, for whom he directed *Boxcar Bertha* in 1972. In 1973, he co-wrote and directed *Mean Streets*. Scorsese's 1976 film *Taxi Driver* was awarded the *Palme d'Or* at the Cannes Film Festival. He followed with *New York, New York* in 1977, *The Last Waltz* in 1978, and *Raging Bull* (1980), which received eight Academy Award nominations including Best Picture and Best Director. Other feature directing credits include *Alice Doesn't Live Here Anymore* (1974), *The King of Comedy* (1983), *After Hours* (1985) which won the Best Director Award at the Cannes Film Festival, *The Color of Money* (1986), *The Last Temptation of Christ* (1988) which earned him an Oscar nomination for Best Director, *Goodfellas* (1990) which received six Academy Award nominations including Best Picture and

Best Director, *Cape Fear* (1991), *The Age of Innocence* (1991) which was nominated for a DGA Award, *Casino* (1995), *Kundun* (1997) and *Bringing out the Dead* (1999).

Scorsese's *Gangs of New York* (2002) earned numerous awards including a Golden Globe for Best Director and ten Academy Award nominations, including Best Picture and Best Director. His next feature, *The Aviator* (2004), received eleven Academy Award nominations, including Best Picture and Director, winning five Oscars. In 2006, *The Departed* was released to critical acclaim and Scorsese was honored with a DGA Award, four Academy Awards including Best Picture and Best Director, as well as a Golden Globe, and Best Director Awards from the New York Film Critics and the National Board of Review. More recent features include *Shutter Island* in 2010 and *Hugo* (2011) which earned eleven Academy Award nominations, including Best Film and Best Director and winning five, as well as a DGA Award nomination, a Golden Globe for Best Director, and National Board of Review Awards for Best Director and Best Film. Upcoming feature releases include *Silence* and *The Wolf of Wall Street*.

Among Scorsese's documentary credits are the 1973 Oscar-winning *Woodstock* for which he served as editor and assistant director, as well as *Italianamerican* which he directed in 1974, the 2003 PBS series *Martin Scorsese Presents: The Blues* and the 2005 series for PBS, *American Masters: No Direction Home: Bob Dylan* (2005) for which Scorsese was Emmy-nominated for directing, as well as the Rolling Stones concert film *Shine a Light* (2008), and the Peabody Award-winning *Elia Kazan: A Letter to Elia* (1983). More recently, Scorsese directed the HBO documentary *George Harrison: Living in the Material World*, earning him both DGA and Emmy Award nominations in 2012.

Scorsese also serves as executive producer for the HBO series *Boardwalk Empire,* for which he received a DGA Award and an Emmy Award in 2011 for directing the pilot episode, as well as a Producers Guild Award for Television Producer of the Year in 2012.

Martin Scorsese has received the Directors Guild of America's Lifetime Achievement Award, and has also been honored for his career contributions by the American Film Institute, the Film Society of Lincoln Center, the Kennedy Center Honors, and the Hollywood Foreign Press Association.

STEVEN SPIELBERG

***Jaws* (1975), *Close Encounters of the Third Kind* (1977), *Raiders of the Lost Ark* (1981), *E.T.: The Extra-Terrestrial* (1982), *The Color Purple* (1985), *Empire of the Sun* (1987), *Schindler's List* (1993), *Amistad* (1997), *Saving Private Ryan* (1998), and *Munich* (2005)**

Steven Spielberg is one of the most influential filmmakers in the industry, a principal partner of DreamWorks Studios, and a ten-time DGA Award nominee. He is a three-time winner of the DGA Award, for *The Color Purple, Schindler's List,* and *Saving Private Ryan. Schindler's List* garnered Oscars for Best Picture and Best Director. His other DGA Award-nominated films are *Jaws*, *Close Encounters of the Third Kind*, *Raiders of the Lost Ark*, *E.T.: The Extra-Terrestrial*, *Empire of the Sun*, *Amistad*, and *Munich*. Spielberg has directed, produced or executive produced seven of the top-grossing films of all time including the *Indiana Jones* franchise, *Jurassic Park* and *Transformers*. A three-time Academy Award winner, Spielberg took home his first two Oscars for Best Director and Best Picture for *Schindler's List*, which received a total of seven Oscars, seven BAFTAs and three Golden Globe Awards (Best Picture and Best Director). Spielberg's 1998 film *Saving Private Ryan* was nominated for eleven Academy Awards and won five, including Best Director. *Saving Private Ryan* also won two Golden Globe Awards for Best Picture and Best Director, in addition to the Best Picture Award from the New York Film Critics Circle, and Best Picture and Best Director Awards from the Los Angeles Film Critics Association and the Broadcast Film Critics. In 2005, *Munich* earned five Academy Award nominations (Best Motion Picture of the Year and Best Achievement in Directing), two Golden Globe nominations and Spielberg earned his tenth DGA-Award nomination. His other films include *A.I. Artificial Intelligence*, *Minority Report*, *Catch Me If You Can*, *The Terminal*, *War of the Worlds*, *The Adventures of Tintin* and the six time Academy Award-nominated film, *War Horse*, among many others.

He is the recipient of the Lifetime Achievement Award from the American Film Institute and the prestigious Irving G. Thalberg Award from the Academy of Motion Picture Arts and Sciences. In 2000, he received the DGA's Lifetime Achievement Award. Also, after making *Schindler's List*, he founded Survivors of the Shoah Visual History Foundation which became the USC Shoah Foundation Institute for Visual History and Education in 2005. Most recently, he completed the long-anticipated biopic, *Lincoln*.

QUENTIN TARANTINO

Pulp Fiction (1995) and *Inglourious Basterds* (2010)

Quentin Tarantino made his directorial debut with *Reservoir Dogs* which he wrote, produced, and directed. Following the success of that film, many of the scripts written during his time as a video store clerk became hot commodities, including *True Romance* and *From Dusk Till Dawn*. His second film, *Pulp Fiction*, won the *Palme d'Or* at the 1994 Cannes Film Festival, numerous critics' awards, seven Academy Award nominations including Best Director and Best Picture, and won a Golden Globe and an Academy Award for Best Screenplay. His subsequent films include *Jackie Brown*, *Kill Bill Vols. 1* and *2*, and his collaborations on *Grindhouse* and *Sin City*, based on Frank Miller's graphic novels.

Tarantino also served as an executive producer on Eli Roth's *Hostel*. In 2005, he produced *Daltry Calhoun*, executive produced *From Dusk Till Dawn* and *Killing Zoe*. A longtime fan of Asian cinema, Tarantino presented Yuen Wo Ping's *Iron Monkey* to American audiences in 2001 and Zhang Yimou's *Hero* in 2004.

He also directed the season five finale episode of *CSI* called "Grave Danger," which garnered Tarantino an Emmy nomination for Outstanding Directing for a Drama Series and further fortified his place as a true American auteur. His most recent film, *Inglourious Basterds,* was nominated for the *Palme d'Or* at Cannes and Golden Globes for Best Picture, Best Screenplay, and Best Director. The film received eight Academy Award nominations, including Best Motion Picture of the Year, Best Achievement in Directing, and Best Writing Original Screenplay, which Tarantino wrote as well as directed. He also earned his second Directors Guild of America nomination for Outstanding Directorial Achievement in Motion Pictures. He was previously nominated in 1995 for *Pulp Fiction*. Tarantino's most recent film is *Django Unchained*.

GUS VAN SANT

Good Will Hunting (1998) and *Milk* (2009)

Audiences and critics alike have taken note of Gus Van Sant's movies since he made his feature film directorial debut in 1985 with *Mala Noche*, which won the Los Angeles Film Critics Association Award for Best Independent/Experimental Feature Film. He also directed other award-winning features, including *Drugstore Cowboy*, *My Own Private Idaho*, and *Even Cowgirls Get the Blues*. Van Sant's direction of Nicole Kidman in the black comedy *To Die For* won her a Golden Globe Award, and the film was screened at the 1995 Cannes and Toronto Film Festivals.

Van Sant's next feature, *Good Will Hunting*, earned him a Best Director Academy Award nomination. The film was nominated for eight other Oscars including Best Picture. He also received a DGA Award nomination.

Van Sant followed with his controversial remake of Alfred Hitchcock's *Psycho*, which was the first feature shot-for-shot recreation of a film, and then *Finding Forrester* before returning to his independent film roots with *Gerry*. He scripted the latter film with its actors, Matt Damon and Casey Affleck. In return, the experience inspired him to write and direct *Elephant*, which won both the top prize (the *Palme d'Or*) and the Best Director Award at the 2003 Cannes International Film Festival.

At the 2005 Cannes International Film Festival, Van Sant's *Last Days* was honored with the Technical Grand Prize. His next project, *Paranoid Park*, was adapted from Blake Nelson's novel of the same name. The film earned him the 60th Anniversary Prize at the 2007 Cannes International Film Festival. In 2008, he directed the Oscar-nominated film *Milk*, which also earned a Directors Guild of America nomination.

Throughout his career, he has continued to make short films that have won awards in film festivals around the world, including the adaptation of William S. Burroughs' short story, *The Discipline of D. E.*, which screened at the New York Film Festival. In 1996, Van Sant directed Allen Ginsberg reading his poem "Ballad of the Skeletons" to the music of Paul McCartney and Philip Glass, which premiered at the 1997 Sundance Film Festival. His other shorts include *Five Ways to Kill Yourself*, *Thanksgiving Prayer* (a re-teaming with William S. Burroughs), "Le Marais" (a segment of the feature *Paris, je t'aime*) and *Mansion on the Hill*. The latter is part of the United Nations–funded Project 8, which was created to raise awareness about essential issues facing our world today. A longtime musician himself, Van Sant directed music videos for many top recording artists including David Bowie, Elton John, The Red Hot Chili Peppers, and Hanson. He has most recently worked on the feature film *Promised Land*.

Appendix C: Biographies of Winning Directors' Team Members and Key Creative Collaborators

THE ARTIST (2011 DGA AWARD)
MICHEL HAZANAVICIUS, DIRECTOR

Antoine de Cazotte, Unit Production Manager

Antoine de Cazotte served as Executive Producer and Unit Production Manager on *The Artist.* He has also worked as Executive Production Manager on such features as *Dancing North*, as a Production Manager on *Kabloonak* about the making of Robert Flaherty's *Nanook of the North*, and has served as Production Supervisor on the documentary film *Oceans.* Most recently, de Cazotte was the UPM and Executive Producer on the feature film *Maniac.*

James Canal, First Assistant Director

James Canal began working with director Michel Hazanavicius as the First Assistant Director on the spy parody *OSS 117: Lost in Rio.* Other First AD credits include feature films such as *Angel-A, Mr. Bean's Holiday, Cortex,* and *Ca$h.* Most recently, he served as AD on the French comedy *The Players.*

David Cluck, First Assistant Director

In addition to *The Artist*, David Cluck has worked on such feature films as *The Players*, *Carriers* and *Monster*, directed by Patty Jenkins. He began his career as an Assistant Director in the mid-1990s on *Ground Control* and *River Made to Drown In*, for which he also received Executive Producer credit. Other feature credits include *Imaginary Heroes, Believe in Me*, and most recently *The Players* and *Apparition.* Cluck has also worked on television reality series such as *Eco-Challenge Fiji Islands, Combat Missions,* and *Surviving Nugent.*

Guillaume Schiffman, Cinematographer

Guillaume Schiffman is a frequent collaborator of director Michel Hazanavicius, having shot his two spy parodies *OSS 117 Cairo: Nest of Spies* and *OSS 117: Lost in Rio*. Schiffman filmed *The Artist* in color and monochromed it to black and white, earning him an Academy Award nomination and BAFTA Award. Early in his career, he worked with filmmakers like as Andrzej Wajda, Volker Schlondörff, Claude Lelouch, and Jacques Rivette. His most recent feature credits include *Gainsbourg: A Heroic Life* (for which he received a César Award nomination), *The Players*, and *Populaire*.

Laurence Bennett, Production Designer

Laurence Bennett has worked as a production designer on films such as the *The Artist* (which earned him an Oscar nomination, a BAFTA nomination, and a César Award), *Crash* and *The Next Three Days*, both directed by Paul Haggis. Bennett has also worked in television on series including *Grey's Anatomy*, *Once and Again*, and *The Starter Wife*. Most recently, he collaborated with director Robert Redford on the political thriller, *The Company You Keep*.

Mark Bridges, Costume Designer

Mark Bridges is the Oscar-winning costume designer for *The Artist*. He has collaborated on many critically acclaimed feature films including David O. Russell's *The Fighter*, and Paul Thomas Anderson's *Magnolia* and *There Will Be Blood*. Bridges began his career as a Costume Assistant on Joel and Ethan Coen's *Miller's Crossing*, followed by work as Assistant Costume Designer on *The Grifters* directed by Stephen Frears. Other costume design credits are the films *Boogie* Nights directed by P. T. Anderson, *8 Mile* directed by Curtis Hanson, *I Heart Huckabees* directed by David O. Russell, and *Land of the Lost* directed by Brad Silberling. Most recently, Bridges worked with Paul Thomas Anderson on *The Master*, as well as *Silver Linings Playbook* directed by David O. Russell and *Captain Phillips* directed by Paul Greengrass.

Anne-Sophie Bion, Editor

Anne-Sophie Bion was nominated with director Michel Hazanavicius for an Academy Award for editing *The Artist*. She has also edited *War of the Buttons* and most recently, the comedy *Stars 80*. Previously, Bion worked as an Assistant Editor on many films, including *Mesrine: Killer Instinct*, *Mesrine: Public Enemy #1*, *Micmacs*, and *Sarah's Key*.

Ludovic Bource, Composer

Ludovic Bource is a long-time collaborator of director Michel Hazanavicius, having scored all of the director's work since his short, *Mes amis*. Bource composed the scores for Hazanavicius' *OSS 117: Cairo, Nest of Spies*, *OSS 117: Lost in Rio* and most recently, *The Artist*, which won him an Oscar, a BAFTA Award, and numerous additional prizes for Best Original Score.

BROKEBACK MOUNTAIN (2005 DGA AWARD)
ANG LEE, DIRECTOR

Tom Benz, Unit Production Manager

Tom Benz has had a long career in feature and television production. In addition to working as Unit Production Manager on the DGA Award-winning *Brokeback Mountain*, he has worked on many features including *Cool Runnings* directed by Jon Turteltaub, *Rollerball* directed by John McTiernan, *Shanghai Knights* directed by David Dobkin, and *Resurrecting the Champ* directed by Rod Lurie. Benz has also worked on movies for television such as *Roswell: The Aliens Attack* directed by Brad Turner, *Christmas Rush* directed by Charles Robert Carner, and *Family Sins* directed by Graeme Clifford.

Scott Ferguson, Unit Production Manager

Scott Ferguson served as Unit Production Manager and Co-Producer on *Brokeback Mountain*. Other work as a UPM and Producer has included the DGA Award-winning movies for television *Recount* directed by Jay Roach and *Temple Grandin* directed by Mick Jackson, which also earned him an Emmy Award for Outstanding Television Movie. In addition, Ferguson received an Emmy in 2010 for producing the HBO television film *You Don't Know Jack* directed by Barry Levinson. His extensive feature credits include *Man on the Moon* directed by Milos Forman, *Heist* directed by David Mamet, *All The King's Men* directed by Steven Zaillian, *Eternal Sunshine of the Spotless Mind* directed by Michel Gondry, and *Laurel Canyon* directed by Lisa Cholodenko.

Michael Hausman, First Assistant Director

Michael Hausman served as First Assistant Director and Executive Producer on such DGA Award-winning and Oscar-winning feature films as *Amadeus* for director Milos Forman and Ang Lee's *Brokeback Mountain*. He also worked on the DGA Award-winning movie for television *Recount* for director Jay Roach, which earned him an Emmy Award and a Producers Guild Award. Other notable credits include Milos Forman's *Hair*, *Silkwood* directed by Mike Nichols, Steven Zaillian's *All The King's Men*, *Eternal Sunshine of the Spotless Mind* directed by Michel Gondry and Martin Scorsese's *Gangs of New York*.

Pierre Tremblay, First Assistant Director

Pierre Tremblay has worked extensively as a First Assistant Director in feature film and television production. In addition to the DGA Award-winning and Oscar-winning *Brokeback Mountain*, his other credits include Michael Winterbottom's *The Claim*, *Resurrecting the Champ* directed by Rod Lurie, the comedy *Rat Race* directed by Jerry Zucker, as well as the movies for television *Call Me: The Rise and Fall of Heidi Fleiss* directed by Charles McDougall, *Holiday in Handcuffs* directed by Ron Underwood and *The Ron Clark Story* directed by Randa Haines, and the dramatic series *Heartland*.

Rodrigo Prieto, Cinematographer

Rodrigo Prieto is the Oscar-nominated cinematographer of *Brokeback Mountain*. He served as director of photography for the Oscar-nominated *Amores Perros* directed by Alejandro González Iñárritu, and has collaborated with many award-winning directors like Curtis Hanson (*8 Mile*), Spike Lee (*25th Hour*), Oliver Stone (*Alexander*), Julie Taymor (*Frida*), and Cameron Crowe (*We Bought a Zoo*). Most recently, Prieto worked on *Argo* directed by Ben Affleck.

Judy Becker, Production Designer

In addition to *Brokeback Mountain*, Judy Becker has worked on features films such as *Personal Velocity: Three Portraits*, directed by Rebecca Miller; *Garden State*, directed by Zach Graff; Todd Haynes's *I'm Not There;* Lynne Ramsay's *We Need to Talk about Kevin;* and *Shame* directed by Steve McQueen. In 2009, she was nominated for an Art Directors Guild Award for *The Fighter*. Recent credits include the HBO series *Girls* and the independent feature *Ruby Sparks* directed by Jonathan Dayton and Valerie Faris, as well as David O. Russell's *Silver Linings Playbook*.

Marit Allen, Costume Designer

The late Marit Allen designed costumes for features films including *Brokeback Mountain*; Stanley Kubrick's *Eyes Wide Shut; Mrs. Doubtfire* directed by Chris Columbus; *The Secret Garden* directed by Agnieszka Holland; Frank Oz's *Little Shop of Horrors*, *The Weight of Water* directed by Kathryn Bigelow; and Mike Newells' *Love in the Time of Cholera*. In 2008, Allen was nominated for an Oscar for her work on *La Vie en Rose*, which also earned an Award nomination from the Costume Designers Guild. She previously received a CDG Award nomination for her work on *Eyes Wide Shut*.

Geraldine Peroni, Editor

The late Geraldine Peroni earned Editing Award nominations with Dylan Tichenor for *Brokeback Mountain* from the American Cinema Editors and BAFTA, and shared a Satellite Award with Tichenor for Outstanding Film Editing. Peroni was a close collaborator of director Robert Altman, working with him on such films as *The Company*, *Dr. T and the Women*, *The Gingerbread Man*, *Prêt-à-Porter*, *Kansas City*, *Short Cuts*, and *The Player*, which earned her an Academy Award nomination in 1992.

Dylan Tichenor, Editor

Dylan Tichenor began his career as Geraldine Peroni's assistant editor on Robert Altman's *The Player*. In 2007, he earned an Oscar nomination for his work on Paul Thomas Anderson's *There Will Be Blood*, for which he also received an American Cinema Editor's nomination. He shared BAFTA and American Cinema Editors Award nominations for *Brokeback Mountain* with Geraldine Peroni, and also shared a Satellite Award with her. Other credits include Paul Thomas Anderson's *Boogie Nights* (nominated for a Golden Satellite Award for Editing), Wes Anderson's *The Royal Tenenbaums* (nominated for an ACE Award), and was nominated for a Satellite Award for his work on *The Town* directed by Ben Affleck. Most recently, Tichenor edited *Lawless* for John Hillcoat and Kathryn Bigelow's *Zero Dark Thirty*.

Gustavo Santaolalla, Composer

Gustavo Santaolalla won Academy Awards for Best Original Score for *Babel* and for *Brokeback Mountain*. Santaolalla began his professional musical career performing in bands, then moved on to composing cinematic scores, working with directors like Michael Mann on *The Insider, Collateral*, and *Public Enemies*; Alejandro González Iñárritu on *Amores Perros, 21 Grams, Babel*, and *Biutiful*; Sean Penn on *Into the Wild*, and Walter Salles on *The Motorcycle Diaries* and *On the Road*.

THE DEPARTED (2006 DGA AWARD)
MARTIN SCORSESE, DIRECTOR

Carol Cuddy, Unit Production Manager

Carol Cuddy began her career as a location coordinator for Milos Forman on *Ragtime*. She went on to become Production Manager on films like *Little Man Tate* directed by Jodie Foster, *The Scout* directed by Michael Ritchie; and *Illuminata* directed by John Turturro, for which she also served as Line Producer. Among her other UPM credits are Garry Marshall's *Raising Helen*; Sydney Pollack's *The Interpreter*; *Before the Devil Knows You're Dead* directed by Sidney Lumet; Jonathan Demme's *Rachel Getting Married*; and most recently, *Men in Black III* for director Barry Sonnenfeld.

Joseph P. Reidy, First Assistant Director

Joseph Reidy is a long-time collaborator of Martin Scorsese, having served as First AD on many Scorsese films, ranging from *The Color of Money, The Last Temptation of Christ, Goodfellas* and *Cape Fear* to *Casino, Gangs of New York, The Aviator*, and *Shutter Island*. He has also worked with directors like George Cukor (*Rich and Famous*), Sydney Pollack (*Tootsie*), Francis Ford Coppola (*The Cotton Club*), and Steven Soderbergh (*Che: Parts 1 & 2*). Recent credits include Darren Aronofsky's *Black Swan* and *The Dictator* directed by Larry Charles.

Michael Ballhaus, Cinematographer

Michael Ballhaus made fifteen films with the iconic German filmmaker Rainer Werner Fassbender. He has also worked with directors like John Sayles (*Baby It's You*), James L. Brooks (*Broadcast News, I'll Do Anything*), Mike Nichols (*Working Girls, Postcards from the Edge, Primary Colors*), and Francis Ford Coppola (*Dracula*). In addition to

The Departed, Ballhaus has collaborated with Martin Scorsese on six films, including *The Color of Money, Goodfellas,* and *Gangs of New York*. He has been nominated for three Academy Awards for his cinematography on *Broadcast News, The Fabulous Baker Boys* and *Gangs of New York* and received The American Society of Cinematographers' 2007 International Award.

Kristi Zea, Production Designer

Kristi Zea started her career as Design Coordinator for Woody Allen's *Interiors*. She went on to become Production Designer for films like *Silverado* directed by Lawrence Kasdan; *Married to the Mob, The Silence of the Lambs,* and *Philadelphia* directed by Jonathan Demme; *Sleepers* directed by Barry Levinson; and *The Brave One* directed by Neil Jordan. Zea has been twice nominated for an Academy Award, the first for Art Direction in Sam Mendes' *Revolutionary Road* and the second for Best Picture on *As Good as It Gets*, sharing producing credit with Bridget Johnson and director James L. Brooks. Most recently she worked with directors Oliver Stone on *Wall Street: Money Never Sleeps* and Brett Ratner on *Tower Heist*.

Sandy Powell, Costume Designer

In addition to *The Departed*, Sandy Powell has worked with Martin Scorsese on *The Aviator, Gangs of New York, Hugo* and *Shutter Island*. She has also worked with Neil Jordan (*The Crying Game, Interview with the Vampire, Michael Collins*), Mike Figgis (*Stormy Monday, Miss Julie*), John Madden (*Shakespeare in Love*), and Julie Taymor (*The Tempest*). Powell is the recipient of ten Oscar nominations, winning three Academy Awards for her work on *The Aviator, Shakespeare in Love* and *The Young Victoria*, which also earned her a Costume Designers Guild Award for Excellence in Costume Design.

Thelma Schoonmaker, Editor

Thelma Schoonmaker began her collaboration with Martin Scorsese in 1967 on the film *Who's That Knocking at My Door*. She has been nominated for seven Academy Awards, six of which have been for her work on films directed by Martin Scorsese and the seventh for editing the documentary *Woodstock* directed by Michael Wadleigh. She won Oscars for editing the Scorsese films *Raging Bull, The Aviator,* and *The Departed*, as well as American Cinema Editors Awards for all three films, and an ACE Award for editing *The Gangs of New York*.

Howard Shore, Composer

Howard Shore is the recipient of seventeen ASCAP Film and Television Music Awards and three Oscars for his scores on films such as Peter Jackson's *The Lord of the Rings* trilogy, *Philadelphia* and *The Silence of the Lambs* directed by Jonathan Demme, and David Fincher's *Se7en*. He also received an Academy Award nomination for his work on Martin Scorsese's *Hugo*. After spending his early career as Music Director for *Saturday Night Live*, Shore ventured into features, working on such films as *Scanners* and *The Fly* for David Cronenberg, *Big* for Penny Marshall, David Fincher's *The Game* and *Panic Room*, Stephen Frears' *High Fidelity*, *The Twilight Saga: Eclipse* directed by David Slade, and the Scorsese films *The Aviator*, *The Departed* and *Hugo*. Howard recently worked with David Cronenberg on *Cosmopolis*.

THE HURT LOCKER (2009 DGA AWARD)
KATHRYN BIGELOW, DIRECTOR

Tony Mark, Unit Production Manager

Tony Mark is a Unit Production Manager and Producer who has worked with directors like Kathryn Bigelow (*The Hurt Locker*) and Robert Rodriguez (*Desperado, Once Upon a Time in Mexico*), Keenen Ivory Wayans (*Scary Movie 2*), and Terry Gilliam (*The Fisher King*). He has been nominated for two Emmy Awards for the television films *And Starring Pancho Villa as Himself* directed by Bruce Beresford and *Georgia O'Keeffe* directed by Bob Balaban. Most recently, Tony Mark produced the action thriller *Code Name: Geronimo* directed by John Stockwell.

Lee Cleary, First Assistant Director

Lee Cleary began working in the film industry as a Runner on *Chariots of Fire* for director Hugh Hudson and Producer David Puttnam. He worked as Key Second Assistant Director on Sydney Pollack's *Out of Africa*. Moving up to Assistant Director, he worked for filmmakers like Terry Gilliam (*The Adventures of Baron Munchausen*), Sydney Pollack (*Havana*), Tim Story (*Fantastic Four*), Joe Carnahan (*The A-Team*) and Bryan Singer (The *X-Men* franchise, *Valkyrie*). Most recently, Cleary made his feature directorial debut on *Fairytale of New York*.

David Ticotin, First Assistant Director

David Ticotin began his career as a Production Assistant on Martin Scorsese's *Raging Bull*. He has since worked as a Location Coordinator on Milos Forman's *Ragtime*, as Location Manager on John Avildsen's *Lean on Me*, and as Second AD on such features as Robert Zemeckis' *Contact*, David Fincher's *Se7en*, and *Collateral Damage* directed by Andrew Davis. His First Assistant Director credits include *Alpha Dog* directed by Nick Cassavetes, Danny Boyles' *127 Hours,* and *Cowboys & Aliens* directed by Jon Favreau. Ticotin most recently worked with director Ang Lee on *Life of Pi*.

Barry Ackroyd, Cinematographer

Barry Ackroyd has been a frequent collaborator of director Ken Loach. On Loach's films like *The Wind that Shakes the Barley* and *Bread and Roses*, Ackroyd developed the distinctive naturalistic, neo-realistic cinematographic style that earned him an Oscar nomination and a BAFTA Award for Best Achievement in Cinematography for *The Hurt Locker*. His most recent feature credits include *Coriolanus* directed by Ralph Fiennes, and *Green Zone* and *United 93* directed by Paul Greengrass. Ackroyd's work also includes the HBO movies for television *The Miraculous Year* (directed by Kathryn Bigelow) and *The Special Relationship* (directed by Richard Loncraine), as well as the HBO dramatic series, *The Newsroom*, and documentaries such as *Aileen Wournos: The Selling of a Serial Killer* and *Tracking Down Maggie: The Unofficial Biography of Margaret Thatcher* (both directed by Nick Broomfield).

Karl Júlíusson, Production Designer

Karl Júlíusson is an award-winning Icelandic production and costume designer, who is best known for collaborating with Lars von Trier (*Antichrist, Dancer in the Dark*) and Kathryn Bigelow (*The Hurt Locker, K19: The Widowmaker, The Weight of Water*). His work on *The Hurt Locker* garnered him an Art Directors Guild Award for Excellence in Production Design. Karl recently worked on the film *Kon-Tiki* about Thor Hyerdahl's legendary crossing of the Pacific on a balsawood raft.

George Little, Costume Designer

George Little started out as a Costumer for Francis Ford Coppola's *Apocalypse Now*, Robert Aldrich's *The Frisco Kid*, and Sam Peckinpah's *The Osterman Weekend*. He worked as Assistant Costume Supervisor on films such as *Jarhead* directed by Sam Mendes, and *Lucky Numbers* directed by Nora Ephron. He was the Costume Supervisor on films like Barry Levinson's *Bugsy*, John Milius' *Red Dawn* and Alan J. Pakula's *The Pelican Brief*. His Costume Designer credits range from the Television Miniseries *Lincoln* (directed by Lamont Johnson) which earned him an Emmy nomination, and the feature films *Things You Can Tell by Just Looking at Her* directed by Rodrigo Garcia, and Kathryn Bigelow's *The Hurt Locker* and *Zero Dark Thirty*.

Chris Innis, Editor

Chris Innis shared the 2010 Oscar, BAFTA and American Cinema Editors Award for editing *The Hurt Locker* with co-editor Bob Murawski. Chris started out in the editorial department of Oliver Stone's *JFK*. She also worked on Ridley Scott's *G.I. Jane*, Sam Raimi's *The Quick and the Dead* and *Spider-Man 3*. She has also worked as an editor on the television series, *American Horror Story*.

Bob Murawski, Editor

Bob Murawski has mainly worked as a film editor for director/producer Sam Raimi, on films including *Army of Darkness, Drag Me to Hell, The Gift* and the *Spider-Man* series. He co-edited *The Hurt Locker* with Chris Innis, which won them an Oscar, as well as BAFTA and American Cinema Editors Awards. Other editorial credits include John Woo's *Hard Target*, and most recently, Sam Raimi's *Oz: The Great and Powerful.*

Marco Beltrami, Composer

Marco Beltrami is best known for scoring horror films such as Troy Nixey's *Don't Be Afraid of the Dark,* Guillermo del Toro's *Mimic, The Woman in Black* (directed by James Watkins) and Wes Craven's *Scream* franchise. Beltrami is a long-time collaborator of Wes Craven's and has scored seven of the director's films. Among his other credits are Guillermo del Toro's *Blade II* and *Hellboy,* Luis Mandoki's *Angel Eyes* and Roland Joffee's *Captivity.* Beltrami has received two Academy Award nominations for Original Score for *3:10 to Yuma* (directed by James Mangold) and Kathryn Bigelow's *The Hurt Locker.*

Buck Sanders, Composer

In 1997, Buck Sanders started out as Marco Beltrami's assistant, programming synthesizers for him and writing additional cues for his scores. His feature film credits include Guillermo del Toro's *Blade II* and *Hellboy,* as well as Kathryn Bigelow's *The Hurt Locker* which garnered him an Oscar nomination with Beltrami for Original Score. Sanders's most recent collaborations with Beltrami include *Scream 4, Soul Surfer* and *The Thing.*

THE KING'S SPEECH (2010 DGA AWARD)
TOM HOOPER, DIRECTOR

Erica Bensly, Unit Production Manager

Erica Bensly has worked as a Production Coordinator on films such as *Richard III* directed by Richard Loncraine, Renny Harlin's *Cutthroat Island* and Tim Burton's *Planet of the Apes.* Among her Production Manager credits are *Elizabeth* directed by Shekhar Kapur, *Atonement* directed by Joe Wright, *Lara Croft Tomb Raider: The Cradle of Life* directed by Jan de Bontand Tom Hooper's *The King's Speech.* Most recently, she worked as Production Supervisor on *47 Ronin* directed by Carl Rinsch.

Martin Harrison, First Assistant Director

Martin Harrison has worked on many features including *Billy Elliot* and *The Hours* directed by Stephen Daldry, Marc Forster's *Finding Neverland,* Tom Hooper's *The King's Speech, Nine* directed by Rob Marshall, and most recently, Joe Wright's *Anna Karenina,* and *Hummingbird* directed by Steven Knight. Harrison's credits for television include the HBO series *Game of Thrones* and the movies for television *Page Eight* directed by David Hare, and *Richard II* directed by Rupert Goold.

Danny Cohen, Cinematographer

Danny Cohen has collaborated with director Tom Hooper on projects including the movie for television *Longford*, the HBO miniseries *John Adams* (for which he received an Emmy nomination for Outstanding Cinematography) and the feature films *The King's Speech* and *Les Misérables*. His work on *The King's Speech* earned him Oscar and BAFTA nominations for Best Cinematography. Among his other feature film credits are *Pirate Radio* directed by Richard Curtis and *This is England* directed by Shane Meadows.

Eve Stewart, Production Designer

Eve Stewart earned a BAFTA nomination for her work on *Vera Drake* directed by Mike Leigh and Oscar nominations for Mike Leigh's *Topsy-Turvy* and Tom Hooper's *The King's Speech*. She has also worked on the films *De-Lovely* directed by Irwin Winkler, *The Damned United* directed by Tom Hooper and *Revolver* directed by Guy Ritchie. Most recently, Stewart worked on the British series *The Hour* and Tom Hooper's feature film *Les Misérables*.

Jenny Beavan, Costume Designer

Jenny Beavan is a nine-time Academy Award nominee, winning the Oscar in 1987 for James Ivory's *A Room with a View*. She was most recently Oscar nominated for her work on *The King's Speech*, and was also nominated for *Anna and the King* directed by Andy Tennant, Robert Altman's *Gosford Park* and *Sense and Sensibility* directed by Ang Lee. Beavan received a Tony Award nomination for Best Costume Design for the play *Private Lives* and has won Emmys for her work on the miniseries *Cranford* and the movie for television *Emma*. Most recently, she worked on Guy Ritchie's *Sherlock Holmes: Game of Shadows* and *Gambit* directed by Michael Hoffman.

Tariq Anwar, Editor

Tariq Anwar received an Oscar nomination for his work on *The King's Speech*. Other editorial credits include the Nicholas Hytner's *Madness of King George*, *The Crucible*, and *Center Stage*, *The Wings of the Dove* directed by Lain Softley, Franco Zeffirelli's *Tea with Mussolini*, the Sam Mendes films *American Beauty* (for which he was nominated for an Academy Award and won two BAFTA Awards) and *Revolutionary Road*, and *The Good Shepherd* directed by Robert De Niro. Most recently, he edited *Great Expectations* for director Mike Newell.

Alexandre Desplat, Composer

Alexandre Desplat has received four Academy Award nominations, five BAFTA nominations, five Golden Globe nominations, and two Grammy nominations, winning a BAFTA Award and a Grammy Award for *The King's Speech*, as well as an Oscar nomination and a Golden Globe nomination. He has also worked on such films as David Fincher's *The Curious Case of Benjamin Button*, Wes Anderson's *Fantastic Mr. Fox*, *Harry Potter and the Deathly Hallows—Part 1* and *Part 2* directed by David Yates, Stephen Frears' *The Queen*, Ang Lee's *Lust, Caution*, Roman Polanski's films *The Ghost Writer* and *Carnage*, and Terrance Malick's *The Tree of Life*. Desplat recently composed the score for Wes Anderson's *Moonrise Kingdom*, as well as *Argo* directed by Ben Affleck and *Rise of the Guardians* for Dreamworks Animation.

NO COUNTRY FOR OLD MEN (2007 DGA AWARD) JOEL AND ETHAN COEN, DIRECTORS

Robert Graf, Unit Production Manager

Robert Graf began working as a Location Manager with the Coen brothers on the films *Fargo* and *The Big Lebowski*. Continuing to work on their films, he has served as Executive Producer and Unit Production Manager on *Burn after Reading*, *No Country for Old Men*, *True Grit* and most recently, *Inside Llewyn Davis*. Other feature credits include *Friday Night Lights* directed by Peter Berg, *Paul* directed by Greg Mottola and *Smokin' Aces* directed by Joe Carnahan.

Betsy Magruder, First Assistant Director

Betsy Magruder's early credits include films like *Honey, I Shrunk the Kids* and *Jumanji* directed by Joe Johnston, as well as James Cameron's *The Terminator*. She has worked with the Coen brothers on several of their films including *No Country for Old Men*, *The Man Who Wasn't There*, *Burn After Reading*, *O Brother, Where Art Thou?*, *A Serious Man* and *True Grit*.

Roger Deakins, Cinematographer

Since *Barton Fink*, Roger Deakins has been the Coens' principal cinematographer. He has been nominated for nine Academy Awards and in 2011 the American Society of Cinematographers honored him with a Lifetime Achievement Award for his work on films such as *A Beautiful Mind* directed by Ron Howard, the Coen brothers' *No Country for Old Men*, Stephen Daldry's *The Reader*, Martin Scorsese's *Kundun*, and *The Shawshank Redemption* directed by Frank Darabont.

Jess Gonchor, Production Designer

Jess Gonchor won an Art Directors Guild Award for his work on *No Country for Old Men* and has also received an Oscar nomination and an ADG Award for *True Grit*. Gonchor has served as Production Designer on such features as Bennett Miller's *Capote* and *Moneyball*, as well as Art Director on Edward Zwick's *The Last Samurai*.

Recent credits include *Fair Game* directed by Doug Liman, the Coen brothers' *Inside Llewyn Davis* and Gore Verbinski's *The Lone Ranger*.

Mary Zophres, Costume Designer

Mary Zophres received an Academy Award nomination for her costume design on Joel and Ethan Coen's *True Grit*. In addition to her collaboration on many Coen brothers films, she has also worked with directors Jon Favreau (*Iron Man 2, Cowboys & Aliens*), Steven Spielberg (*The Terminal, Catch Me if You Can, Indiana Jones and the Kingdom of the Crystal Skull*), Nora Ephron (*Bewitched*), Robert Redford (*Lions for Lambs*), and most recently, Alex Kurtzman (*People Like Us*) and Ruben Fleischer (*Gangster Squad*).

Roderick Jaynes, Editor

Roderick Jaynes is the pseudonym used by Joel and Ethan Coen for editing many of their films.

Carter Burwell, Composer

Carter Burwell is the Emmy Award-winning composer of the HBO miniseries *Mildred Pierce* directed by Todd Haynes. Since 1984's *Blood Simple*, Burwell has worked on every film directed by the Coen brothers. Among his many other credits are the musical scores for *Where the Wild Things Are* and *Adaptation* directed by Spike Jonze, *Twilight* directed by Catherine Hardwicke, *Before Night Falls* by Julian Schnabel, Sidney Lumet's *Before the Devil Knows You're Dead*, Lasse Hallstrom's *The Hoax*, *The Blind Side* directed by John Lee Hancock, *The Kids are All Right* directed by Lisa Cholodenko, and most recently, *Gangster Squad* directed by Ruben Fleischer and *The Twilight Saga: Breaking Dawn—Part II* directed by Bill Condon.

SLUMDOG MILLIONAIRE (2008 DGA AWARD)
DANNY BOYLE, DIRECTOR

Sanjay Kumar, Unit Production Manager

Sanjay Kumar has served as Production Manager on the feature films *Eat Pray Love* directed by Ryan Murphy, Albert Brooks's *Looking for Comedy in the Muslim World* and *Slumdog Millionaire*. Most recently he worked on *The Best Exotic Marigold Hotel* directed by John Madden, *Mission: Impossible—Ghost Protocol* directed by Brad Bird and Ang Lee's *Life of Pi*.

Raj Acharya, First Assistant Director

Raj Acharya has worked as an Assistant Director on Hollywood features including *Eat Pray Love* directed by Ryan Murphy, the Jeff Tremaine and Spike Jonze film *Jackass Number Two*, Danny Boyle's *Slumdog Millionaire* and *The Way Back* directed by Peter Weir. He recently completed work on two Bollywood films, *Gandhi of the Month* and *Talaash*, as well as *Code Name: Geronimo* directed by John Stockwell.

Anthony Dod Mantle, Cinematographer

Anthony Dod Mantle is the Oscar-winning cinematographer of *Slumdog Millionaire*. He has collaborated on several Danny Boyle films including *28 Days Later, 127 Hours* and *Millions*. He also worked with Lars Von Trier (*Breaking the Waves, Dogville, Antichrist*), Thomas Vinterberg (*The Biggest Heroes, The Celebration*), and Harmony Korine (*Julien Donkey-Boy*). His most recent feature credits include *Dredd* directed by Pete Travis, *Trance* directed by Danny Boyle, and *Rush* directed by Ron Howard. Mantle also worked on the British television series *Wallander*, which was the first to use the RED One digital camera.

Mark Digby, Production Designer

Mark Digby was honored with the Excellence in Production Design Award from the Art Directors Guild for his work on *Slumdog Millionaire*, his third collaboration with director Danny Boyle after *28 Days Later* and *Millions*. He's also worked as Production Designer on such features as *The American* directed by Anton Corbijn and *A Mighty Heart* directed by Michael Winterbottom, as well as *Dredd* for director Pete Travis and *Rush* for director Ron Howard.

Suttirat Anne Larlarb, Costume Designer

Suttirat Anne Larlarb has worked with Danny Boyle on *127 Hours, Sunshine*, and *Trance*. The Costume Designers Guild honored her with its Excellence in Costume Design Award for her work on *Slumdog Millionaire*. She also received an Emmy nomination for Costume Design for the HBO movie for television *Cinema Verite* directed by Shari Springer Berman and Robert Pulcini, then later collaborated with them again on the feature *The Extra Man*. Other feature credits include *K-Pax* directed by Iain Softley, *The American* directed by Anton Corbijn, *Men in Black II* directed by Barry Sonnenfeld, and Mira Nair's *The Namesake*.

Chris Dickens, Editor

Chris Dickens received an Academy Award, BAFTA Award, and American Cinema Editors Award for his work on *Slumdog Millionaire*. He has worked on several projects for director Edgar Wright, including the television series *Spaced* and the features *Hot Fuzz, Scott Pilgrim vs. the World* and *Shaun of the Dead*. In addition, he has edited *Paul* for director Greg Mottola and *Les Misérables* for director Tom Hooper.

A. R. Rahman, Composer

A. R. Rahman is a composer, singer-songwriter, music producer and musician. He won two Academy Awards for his work on *Slumdog Millionaire*, including Original

Score and Original Song. Music from the film also earned him a Golden Globe Award, a BAFTA Award and a Grammy. Rahman also served as composer for Danny Boyle's *127 Hours* and has worked on many notable Bollywood films including *Fire, Earth, Water*, and *Bollywood/Hollywood* directed by Deepa Mehta, as well as *Lagaan: Once Upon a Time in India* directed by Ashutoth Gowariker. In addition, he has provided music for Spike Lee's *Inside Man*, Andrew Niccol's *Lord of War*, and Julian Schnabel's *Miral*. Most recently, Rahman composed the scores for *Chennai Express* directed by Rohit Shetty, *Kochadaiyaan* directed by Soundarya Rajinikanth, and *People Like Us* directed by Alex Kurtzman.

Appendix D: The Directors Guild of America Nominees and Winners

Each year since 1948, the members of the Directors Guild of America have bestowed an award on the film director whose theatrical feature has been judged as the most distinguished of that year. In the following listing, both winners and nominees are cited, with this exception: from 1948 to 1952, quarterly as well as annual winners were announced; for these years only, the nominees in each quarter are not included. Winners are indicated in bold.

1948–49	Quarter	Howard Hawks	*Red River*
1948–49	Quarter	Anatole Litvak	*The Snake Pit*
1948–49	Quarter	Fred Zinnemann	*The Search*
1948–49	**Winner**	**Joseph L. Mankiewicz**	***A Letter to Three Wives***
1949–50	Quarter	Carol Reed	*The Third Man*
1949–50	Quarter	Mark Robson	*Champion*
1949–50	Quarter	Alfred Werker	*Lost Boundaries*
1949–50	**Winner**	**Robert Rossen**	***All the King's Men***
1950–51	Quarter	John Huston	*The Asphalt Jungle*
1950–51	Quarter	Vincente Minnelli	*Father's Little Dividend*
1950–51	Quarter	Billy Wilder	*Sunset Boulevard*
1950–51	**Winner**	**Joseph L. Mankiewicz**	***All About Eve***
1951	Quarter	Alfred Hitchcock	*Strangers on a Train*
1951	Quarter	Vincente Minnelli	*An American in Paris*
1951	**Winner**	**George Stevens**	***A Place in the Sun***
1951		Laslo Benedek	*Death of a Salesman*
1951		Michael Gordon	*Cyrano De Bergerac*
1951		Elia Kazan	*A Streetcar Named Desire*
1951		Henry King	*David and Bathsheba*
1951		Mervyn Leroy	*Quo Vadis*
1951		Anatole Litvak	*Decision before Dawn*

1951		George Sidney	*Showboat*
1951		Richard Thorpe	*The Great Caruso*
1951		William Wyler	*Detective Story*
1952	Quarter	Charles Crichton	*The Lavender Hill Mob*
1952	Quarter	Joseph L. Mankiewicz	*Five Fingers*
1952	Quarter	Fred Zinnemann	*High Noon*
1952	**Winner**	**John Ford**	***The Quiet Man***
1952		George Cukor	*Pat and Mike*
1952		Michael Curtiz	*I'll See You in My Dreams*
1952		Cecil B. De Mille	*The Greatest Show on Earth*
1952		Stanley Donen	*Singin' in the Rain* (co-director)
1952		Gene Kelly	*Singin' in the Rain* (co-director)
1952		Hugo Fregonese	*My Six Convicts*
1952		Howard Hawks	*The Big Sky*
1952		Elia Kazan	*Viva Zapata!*
1952		Henry King	*The Snows of Kilimanjaro*
1952		Akira Kurosawa	*Rashomon*
1952		Albert Lewin	*Pandora and the Flying Dutchman*
1952		Vincente Minnelli	*The Bad and the Beautiful*
1952		George Sidney	*Scaramouche*
1952		Richard Thorpe	*Ivanhoe*
1952		Charles Vidor	*Hans Christian Andersen*
1953	Finalist	George Stevens	*Shane*
1953	Finalist	Charles Walters	*Lili*
1953	Finalist	Billy Wilder	*Stalag 17*
1953	Finalist	William Wyler	*Roman Holiday*
1953	**Winner**	**Fred Zinnemann**	***From Here to Eternity***
1953		Melvin Frank	*Above and Beyond* (co-director)
1953		Norman Panama	*Above and Beyond* (co-director)
1953		Henry Koster	*The Robe*
1953		Walter Lang	*Call Me Madam*
1953		Joseph L. Mankiewicz	*Julius Caesar*
1953		Daniel Mann	*Come Back, Little Sheba*
1953		Jean Negulesco	*Titanic*
1953		George Sidney	*Young Bess*
1954	Finalist	Alfred Hitchcock	*Rear Window*
1954	Finalist	George Seaton	*The Country Girl*
1954	Finalist	William Wellman	*The High and the Mighty*
1954	Finalist	Billy Wilder	*Sabrina*
1954	**Winner**	**Elia Kazan**	***On the Waterfront***
1954		George Cukor	*A Star Is Born*
1954		Edward Dmytryk	*The Caine Mutiny*
1954		Stanley Donen	*Seven Brides for Seven Brothers*
1954		Melvin Frank	*Knock on Wood* (co-director)
1954		Norman Panama	*Knock on Wood* (co-director)
1954		Samuel Fuller	*Hell and High Water*

1954		Alfred Hitchcock	*Dial M for Murder*
1954		Henry King	*King of the Khyber Rifles*
1954		Anthony Mann	*The Glenn Miller Story*
1954		Jean Negulesco	*Three Coins in the Fountain*
1954		Don Siegel	*Riot in Cell Block 11*
1954		Robert E. Wise	*Executive Suite*
1955	Finalist	John Ford	*Mister Roberts* (co-director)
1955	Finalist	Mervyn Leroy	*Mister Roberts* (co-director)
1955	Finalist	Elia Kazan	*East of Eden*
1955	Finalist	Joshua Logan	*Picnic*
1955	Finalist	John Sturges	*Bad Day at Black Rock*
1955	**Winner**	**Delbert Mann**	***Marty***
1955		Richard Brooks	*The Blackboard Jungle*
1955		John Ford	*The Long Gray Line*
1955		Henry Koster	*A Man Called Peter*
1955		Daniel Mann	*The Rose Tattoo*
1955		Mark Robson	*The Bridges at Toko-Ri*
1955		Charles Vidor	*Love Me or Leave Me*
1955		Billy Wilder	*The Seven Year Itch*
1956	Finalist	John Ford	*The Searchers*
1956	Finalist	Alfred Hitchcock	*The Man Who Knew Too Much*
1956	Finalist	Alfred Hitchcock	*The Trouble with Harry*
1956	Finalist	Nunnally Johnson	*The Man in the Gray Flannel Suit*
1956	Finalist	Henry King	*Carousel*
1956	Finalist	Walter Lang	*The King and I*
1956	Finalist	Carol Reed	*Trapeze*
1956	Finalist	Robert Rossen	*Alexander the Great*
1956	Finalist	Roy Rowland	*Meet Me in Las Vegas*
1956	Finalist	George Sidney	*The Eddy Duchin Story*
1956	**Winner**	**George Stevens**	***Giant***
1956		Michael Anderson	*Around the World in Eighty Days*
1956		John Huston	*Moby Dick*
1956		Joshua Logan	*Bus Stop*
1956		Daniel Mann	*Teahouse of the August Moon*
1956		King Vidor	*War and Peace*
1956		Robert E. Wise	*Somebody Up There Likes Me*
1956		William Wyler	*Friendly Persuasion*
1957	Finalist	Joshua Logan	*Sayonara*
1957	Finalist	Sidney Lumet	*Twelve Angry Men*
1957	Finalist	Mark Robson	*Peyton Place*
1957	Finalist	Billy Wilder	*Witness for the Prosecution*
1957	**Winner**	**David Lean**	***The Bridge on the River Kwai***
1957		George Cukor	*Les Girls*
1957		Stanley Donen	*Funny Face*
1957		Jose Ferrer	*The Great Man*
1957		John Huston	*Heaven Knows, Mr. Allison*
1957		Elia Kazan	*A Face in the Crowd*

1957		Stanley Kramer	*The Pride and the Passion*
1957		Anthony Mann	*Men in War*
1957		Leo McCarey	*An Affair to Remember*
1957		Robert Mulligan	*Fear Strikes Out*
1957		John Sturges	*Gunfight at the O.K. Corral*
1957		Billy Wilder	*Love in the Afternoon*
1957		Fred Zinnemann	*A Hatful of Rain*
1958	Finalist	Richard Brooks	*Cat on a Hot Tin Roof*
1958	Finalist	Stanley Kramer	*The Defiant Ones*
1958	Finalist	Mark Robson	*The Inn of the Sixth Happiness*
1958	Finalist	Robert E. Wise	*I Want To Live!*
1958	**Winner**	**Vincente Minnelli**	***Gigi***
1958		Stanley Donen	*Damn Yankees* (co-director)
1958		George Abbott	*Damn Yankees* (co-director)
1958		Richard Brooks	*The Brothers Karamazov*
1958		Delmer Daves	*Cowboy*
1958		Edward Dmytryk	*The Young Lions*
1958		Richard Fleischer	*The Vikings*
1958		Alfred Hitchcock	*Vertigo*
1958		Martin Ritt	*The Long Hot Summer*
1958		George Seaton	*Teacher's Pet*
1958		William Wyler	*The Big Country*
1959	Finalist	Otto Preminger	*Anatomy of a Murder*
1959	Finalist	George Stevens	*The Diary of Anne Frank*
1959	Finalist	Billy Wilder	*Some Like It Hot*
1959	Finalist	Fred Zinnemann	*The Nun's Story*
1959	**Winner**	**William Wyler**	***Ben Hur***
1959		Charles Barton	*The Shaggy Dog*
1959		Frank Capra	*A Hole in the Head*
1959		Richard Fleischer	*Compulsion*
1959		John Ford	*The Horse Soldiers*
1959		Howard Hawks	*Rio Bravo*
1959		Alfred Hitchcock	*North by Northwest*
1959		Leo McCarey	*Rally Round the Flag, Boys!*
1959		Douglas Sirk	*Imitation of Life*
1960	Finalist	Jack Cardiff	*Sons and Lovers*
1960	Finalist	Alfred Hitchcock	*Psycho*
1960	Finalist	Vincente Minnelli	*Bells Are Ringing*
1960	Finalist	Fred Zinnemann	*The Sundowners*
1960	**Winner**	**Billy Wilder**	***The Apartment***
1960		Richard Brooks	*Elmer Gantry*
1960		Vincent J. Donehue	*Sunrise at Campobello*
1960		Lewis Gilbert	*Sink the Bismarck!*
1960		Walter Lang	*Can-Can*
1960		Delbert Mann	*The Dark at the Top of the Stairs*
1960		Vincente Minnelli	*Home from the Hill*
1960		Carol Reed	*Our Man in Havana*

1960		Alain Resnais	*Hiroshima, Mon Amour*
1960		Charles Walters	*Please Don't Eat the Daisies*
1961	Finalist	Blake Edwards	*Breakfast at Tiffany's*
1961	Finalist	Stanley Kramer	*Judgement at Nuremberg*
1961	Finalist	Robert Rossen	*The Hustler*
1961	Finalist	J. Lee Thompson	*The Guns of Navarone*
1961	**Winner**	**Jerome Robbins**	***West Side Story* (co-director)**
1961	**Winner**	**Robert E. Wise**	***West Side Story* (co-director)**
1961		Marlon Brando	*One-Eyed Jacks*
1961		Frank Capra	*A Pocket Full of Miracles*
1961		Jack Clayton	*The Innocents*
1961		Peter Glenville	*Summer and Smoke*
1961		John Huston	*The Misfits*
1961		Elia Kazan	*Splendor in the Grass*
1961		Henry Koster	*Flower Drum Song*
1961		Mervyn Le Roy	*A Majority of One*
1961		Philip Leacock	*Hand in Hand*
1961		Joshua Logan	*Fanny*
1961		Anthony Mann	*El Cid*
1961		Robert Mulligan	*The Great Imposter*
1961		Daniel Petrie	*A Raisin in the Sun*
1961		Robert Stevenson	*The Absent Minded Professor*
1961		Peter Ustinov	*Romanoff and Juliet*
1961		William Wyler	*The Children's Hour*
1962	Finalist	Bernhard Wicki	*The Longest Day* (co-director)
1962	Finalist	Ken Annakin	*The Longest Day* (co-director)
1962	Finalist	Andrew Marton	*The Longest Day* (co-director)
1962	Finalist	John Frankenheimer	*The Manchurian Candidate*
1962	Finalist	Pietro Germi	*Divorce, Italian Style*
1962	Finalist	John Huston	*Freud*
1962	Finalist	Stanley Kubrick	*Lolita*
1962	Finalist	Sidney Lumet	*Long Day's Journey into Night*
1962	Finalist	Peter Ustinov	*Billy Budd*
1962	**Winner**	**David Lean**	***Lawrence of Arabia***
1962		Robert Aldrich	*Whatever Happened to Baby Jane?*
1962		Morton DaCosta	*The Music Man*
1962		John Frankenheimer	*Birdman of Alcatraz*
1962		Lewis Milestone	*Mutiny on the Bounty*
1962		Robert Mulligan	*To Kill a Mockingbird*
1962		Ralph Nelson	*Requiem for a Heavyweight*
1962		Arthur Penn	*The Miracle Worker*
1962		Tony Richardson	*A Taste of Honey*
1963	**Winner**	**Tony Richardson**	***Tom Jones***
1963		Federico Fellini	*Fellini's 8 1/2*
1963		Elia Kazan	*America, America*
1963		Ralph Nelson	*Lilies of the Field*

1963		Martin Ritt	*Hud!*
1964	**Winner**	**George Cukor**	***My Fair Lady***
1964		Peter Glenville	*Becket*
1964		John Huston	*The Night of the Iguana*
1964		Stanley Kubrick	*Dr. Strangelove*
1964		Robert Stevenson	*Mary Poppins*
1965	**Winner**	**Robert E. Wise**	***The Sound of Music***
1965		Sidney Furie	*The Ipcress File*
1965		Sidney Lumet	*The Pawnbroker*
1965		John Schlesinger	*Darling*
1965		Elliot Silverstein	*Cat Ballou*
1966	**Winner**	**Fred Zinnemann**	***A Man for All Seasons***
1966		Richard Brooks	*The Professionals*
1966		John Frankenheimer	*Grand Prix*
1966		Lewis Gilbert	*Alfie*
1966		James Hill	*Born Free*
1966		Norman Jewison	*The Russians Are Coming, the Russians Are Coming*
1966		Claude Lelouch	*A Man and a Woman*
1966		Silvio Narizzano	*Georgy Girl*
1966		Mike Nichols	*Who's Afraid of Virginia Woolf?*
1966		Robert E. Wise	*The Sand Pebbles*
1967	Finalist	Richard Brooks	*In Cold Blood*
1967	Finalist	Norman Jewison	*In the Heat of the Night*
1967	Finalist	Stanley Kramer	*Guess Who's Coming to Dinner*
1967	Finalist	Arthur Penn	*Bonnie and Clyde*
1967	**Winner**	**Mike Nichols**	***The Graduate***
1967		Robert Aldrich	*The Dirty Dozen*
1967		James Clavell	*To Sir, with Love*
1967		Stanley Donen	*Two for the Road*
1967		Stuart Rosenberg	*Cool Hand Luke*
1967		Joseph Strick	*Ulysses*
1968	Finalist	Stanley Kubrick	*2001: A Space Odyssey*
1968	Finalist	Paul Newman	*Rachel, Rachel*
1968	Finalist	William Wyler	*Funny Girl*
1968	Oscar	Carol Reed	*Oliver!*
1968	**Winner**	**Anthony Harvey**	***The Lion in Winter***
1968		Paul Almond	*Isabel*
1968		Jiri Menzel	*Closely Watched Trains*
1968		Roman Polanski	*Rosemary's Baby*
1968		Gene Saks	*The Odd Couple*
1968		Franco Zeffirelli	*Romeo and Juliet*
1969	Finalist	Costa Gravas	*Z*
1969	Finalist	George Roy Hill	*Butch Cassidy and the Sundance Kid*
1969	Finalist	Dennis Hopper	*Easy Rider*
1969	Finalist	Sydney Pollack	*They Shoot Horses, Don't They?*
1969	**Winner**	**John Schlesinger**	***Midnight Cowboy***

1969		Richard Attenborough	*Oh, What a Lovely War*
1969		Gene Kelly	*Hello, Dolly*
1969		Sam Peckinpah	*The Wild Bunch*
1969		Larry Peerce	*Goodbye, Columbus*
1969		Haskell Wexler	*Medium Cool*
1970	**Winner**	**Franklin Schaffner**	***Patton***
1970		Robert Altman	*M*A*S*H*
1970		Arthur Hiller	*Love Story*
1970		David Lean	*Ryan's Daughter*
1970		Bob Rafelson	*Five Easy Pieces*
1971	**Winner**	**William Friedkin**	***The French Connection***
1971		Peter Bogdanovich	*The Last Picture Show*
1971		Stanley Kubrick	*A Clockwork Orange*
1971		Robert Mulligan	*Summer of '42*
1971		John Schlesinger	*Sunday, Bloody Sunday*
1972	Oscar	Bob Fosse	*Cabaret*
1972	**Winner**	**Francis Ford Coppola**	***The Godfather***
1972		John Boorman	*Deliverance*
1972		George Roy Hill	*Slaughterhouse Five*
1972		Martin Ritt	*Sounder*
1973	**Winner**	**George Roy Hill**	***The Sting***
1973		Bernardo Bertolucci	*Last Tango in Paris*
1973		William Friedkin	*The Exorcist*
1973		George Lucas	*American Graffiti*
1973		Sidney Lumet	*Serpico*
1974	**Winner**	**Francis Ford Coppola**	***The Godfather: Part II***
1974		Francis Ford Coppola	*The Conversation*
1974		Bob Fosse	*Lenny*
1974		Sidney Lumet	*Murder on the Orient Express*
1974		Roman Polanski	*Chinatown*
1975	**Winner**	**Milos Forman**	***One Flew Over the Cuckoo's Nest***
1975		Robert Altman	*Nashville*
1975		Stanley Kubrick	*Barry Lyndon*
1975		Sidney Lumet	*Dog Day Afternoon*
1975		Steven Spielberg	*Jaws*
1976	**Winner**	**John Avildsen**	***Rocky***
1976		Sidney Lumet	*Network*
1976		Alan J. Pakula	*All the President's Men*
1976		Martin Scorsese	*Taxi Driver*
1976		Lina Wertmuller	*Seven Beauties*
1977	**Winner**	**Woody Allen**	***Annie Hall***
1977		George Lucas	*Star Wars*
1977		Herbert Ross	*The Turning Point*
1977		Steven Spielberg	*Close Encounters of the Third Kind*
1977		Fred Zinnemann	*Julia*

1978	Winner	**Michael Cimino**	*The Deer Hunter*
1978		Hal Ashby	*Coming Home*
1978		Warren Beatty	*Heaven Can Wait* (co-director)
1978		Buck Henry	*Heaven Can Wait* (co-director)
1978		Paul Mazursky	*An Unmarried Woman*
1978		Alan Parker	*Midnight Express*
1979	**Winner**	**Robert Benton**	***Kramer vs. Kramer***
1979		Woody Allen	*Manhattan*
1979		James Bridges	*The China Syndrome*
1979		Francis Ford Coppola	*Apocalypse Now*
1979		Peter Yates	*Breaking Away*
1980	**Winner**	**Robert Redford**	***Ordinary People***
1980		Michael Apted	*Coal Miner's Daughter*
1980		David Lynch	*The Elephant Man*
1980		Richard Rush	*The Stunt Man*
1980		Martin Scorsese	*Raging Bull*
1981	**Winner**	**Warren Beatty**	***Reds***
1981		Hugh Hudson	*Chariots Of Fire*
1981		Louis Malle	*Atlantic City*
1981		Mark Rydell	*On Golden Pond*
1981		Steven Spielberg	*Raiders of the Lost Ark*
1982	**Winner**	**Richard Attenborough**	***Gandhi***
1982		Taylor Hackford	*An Officer and a Gentleman*
1982		Wolfgang Petersen	*Das Boot*
1982		Sydney Pollack	*Tootsie*
1982		Steven Spielberg	*E.T.: The Extra-Terrestrial*
1983	**Winner**	**James L. Brooks**	***Terms of Endearment***
1983		Bruce Beresford	*Tender Mercies*
1983		Ingmar Bergman	*Fanny and Alexander*
1983		Lawrence Kasdan	*The Big Chill*
1983		Philip Kaufman	*The Right Stuff*
1984	**Winner**	**Milos Forman**	***Amadeus***
1984		Robert Benton	*Places in the Heart*
1984		Norman Jewison	*A Soldier's Story*
1984		Roland Joffé	*The Killing Fields*
1984		David Lean	*A Passage to India*
1985	Oscar	Sydney Pollack	*Out of Africa*
1985	**Winner**	**Steven Spielberg**	***The Color Purple***
1985		Ron Howard	*Cocoon*
1985		John Huston	*Prizzi's Honor*
1985		Peter Weir	*Witness*
1986	**Winner**	**Oliver Stone**	***Platoon***
1986		Woody Allen	*Hannah and Her Sisters*
1986		Randa Haines	*Children of a Lesser God*
1986		James Ivory	*A Room with a View*
1986		Rob Reiner	*Stand by Me*
1987	**Winner**	**Bernardo Bertolucci**	***The Last Emperor***

1987		James L. Brooks	*Broadcast News*
1987		Lasse Hallström	*My Life as a Dog*
1987		Adrian Lyne	*Fatal Attraction*
1987		Steven Spielberg	*Empire of the Sun*
1988	**Winner**	**Barry Levinson**	***Rain Man***
1988		Charles Crichton	*A Fish Called Wanda*
1988		Mike Nichols	*Working Girl*
1988		Alan Parker	*Mississippi Burning*
1988		Robert Zemeckis	*Who Framed Roger Rabbit*
1989	**Winner**	**Oliver Stone**	***Born on the Fourth of July***
1989		Woody Allen	*Crimes and Misdemeanors*
1989		Rob Reiner	*When Harry Met Sally . . .*
1989		Phil Alden Robinson	*Field of Dreams*
1989		Peter Weir	*Dead Poets Society*
1990	**Winner**	**Kevin Costner**	***Dances with Wolves***
1990		Francis Ford Coppola	*The Godfather: Part III*
1990		Barry Levinson	*Avalon*
1990		Martin Scorsese	*Goodfellas*
1990		Giuseppe Tornatore	*Cinema Paradiso*
1991	**Winner**	**Jonathan Demme**	***The Silence of the Lambs***
1991		Barry Levinson	*Bugsy*
1991		Ridley Scott	*Thelma and Louise*
1991		Oliver Stone	*JFK*
1991		Barbra Streisand	*The Prince of Tides*
1992	**Winner**	**Clint Eastwood**	***Unforgiven***
1992		Robert Altman	*The Player*
1992		James Ivory	*Howards End*
1992		Neil Jordan	*The Crying Game*
1992		Rob Reiner	*A Few Good Men*
1993	**Winner**	**Steven Spielberg**	***Schindler's List***
1993		Jane Campion	*The Piano*
1993		Andrew Davis	*The Fugitive*
1993		James Ivory	*The Remains of the Day*
1993		Martin Scorsese	*The Age of Innocence*
1994	**Winner**	**Robert Zemeckis**	***Forrest Gump***
1994		Frank Darabont	*The Shawshank Redemption*
1994		Mike Newell	*Four Weddings and a Funeral*
1994		Robert Redford	*Quiz Show*
1994		Quentin Tarantino	*Pulp Fiction*
1995	Oscar	Mel Gibson	*Braveheart*
1995	**Winner**	**Ron Howard**	***Apollo 13***
1995		Mike Figgis	*Leaving Las Vegas*
1995		Ang Lee	*Sense and Sensibility*
1995		Michael Radford	*Il Postino*
1996	**Winner**	**Anthony Minghella**	***The English Patient***
1996		Joel Coen	*Fargo*
1996		Cameron Crowe	*Jerry Maguire*

1996		Scott Hicks	*Shine*
1996		Mike Leigh	*Secrets and Lies*
1997	**Winner**	**James Cameron**	***Titanic***
1997		James L. Brooks	*As Good as it Gets*
1997		Curtis Hanson	*L.A. Confidential*
1997		Steven Spielberg	*Amistad*
1997		Gus Van Sant	*Good Will Hunting*
1998	**Winner**	**Steven Spielberg**	***Saving Private Ryan***
1998		John Madden	*Shakespeare in Love*
1998		Peter Weir	*The Truman Show*
1998		Roberto Benigni	*Life is Beautiful*
1998		Terrence Malick	*The Thin Red Line*
1999		Frank Darabont	*The Green Mile*
1999		Spike Jonze	*Being John Malkovich*
1999		Michael Mann	*The Insider*
1999	**Winner**	**Sam Mendes**	***American Beauty***
1999		M. Night Shyamalan	*The Sixth Sense*
2000		Cameron Crowe	*Almost Famous*
2000	**Winner**	**Ang Lee**	***Crouching Tiger,*** *** Hidden Dragon***
2000		Ridley Scott	*Gladiator*
2000		Steven Soderbergh	*Erin Brockovich*
2000		Steven Soderbergh	*Traffic*
2001	**Winner**	**Ron Howard**	***A Beautiful Mind***
2001		Peter Jackson	*The Lord of the Rings: The Fellowship of the Ring*
2001		Baz Luhrmann	*Moulin Rouge*
2001		Christopher Nolan	*Memento*
2001		Ridley Scott	*Black Hawk Down*
2002		Stephen Daldry	*The Hours*
2002		Peter Jackson	*The Lord of the Rings: The Two Towers*
2002	**Winner**	**Rob Marshall**	***Chicago***
2002		Roman Polanski	*The Pianist*
2002		Martin Scorsese	*Gangs of New York*
2003		Sofia Coppola	*Lost in Translation*
2003		Clint Eastwood	*Mystic River*
2003	**Winner**	**Peter Jackson**	***The Lord of the Rings: The Return of the King***
2003		Gary Ross	*Seabiscuit*
2003		Peter Weir	*Master and Commander: The Far Side of the World*
2004	**Winner**	**Clint Eastwood**	***Million Dollar Baby***
2004		Marc Forster	*Finding Neverland*
2004		Taylor Hackford	*Ray*
2004		Alexander Payne	*Sideways*

2004		Martin Scorsese	*The Aviator*
2005		George Clooney	*Good Night, and Good Luck.*
2005		Paul Haggis	*Crash*
2005	**Winner**	**Ang Lee**	***Brokeback Mountain***
2005		Bennett Miller	*Capote*
2005		Steven Spielberg	*Munich*
2006		William Condon	*Dreamgirls*
2006		Jonathan Dayton	*Little Miss Sunshine* (co-director)
2006		Valerie Faris	*Little Miss Sunshine* (co-director)
2006		Stephen Frears	*The Queen*
2006		Alejandro González Iñárritu	*Babel*
2006	**Winner**	**Martin Scorsese**	***The Departed***
2007		Paul Thomas Anderson	*There Will Be Blood*
2007	**Winner**	**Ethan Coen**	***No Country for Old Men*** **(co-director)**
2007	**Winner**	**Joel Coen**	***No Country for Old Men*** **(co-director)**
2007		Tony Gilroy	*Michael Clayton*
2007		Sean Penn	*Into the Wild*
2007		Julian Schnabel	*The Diving Bell and the Butterfly*
2008	**Winner**	**Daniel Boyle**	***Slumdog Millionaire***
2008		David Fincher	*The Curious Case of Benjamin Button*
2008		Ron Howard	*Frost/Nixon*
2008		Christopher Nolan	*The Dark Knight*
2008		Gus Van Sant	*Milk*
2009	**Winner**	**Kathryn Bigelow**	***The Hurt Locker***
2009		James Cameron	*Avatar*
2009		Lee Daniels	*Precious*
2009		Jason Reitman	*Up in the Air*
2009		Quentin Tarantino	*Inglourious Basterds*
2010		Darren Aronofsky	*Black Swan*
2010		David Fincher	*The Social Network*
2010	**Winner**	**Tom Hooper**	***The King's Speech***
2010		Christopher Nolan	*Inception*
2010		David Russell	*The Fighter*
2011		Woody Allen	*Midnight in Paris*
2011		David Fincher	*The Girl with the Dragon Tattoo*
2011	**Winner**	**Michel Hazanavicius**	***The Artist***
2011		Alexander Payne	*The Descendants*
2011		Martin Scorsese	*Hugo*

Director Index

Page numbers in italic refer to photographs and figures.

Subject Index

Page numbers in italic refer to photographs and figures.

About the Moderator and Editor

 **Jeremy Kagan** is an internationally recognized director/writer/producer of feature films and television and a well-known teacher. Some of his feature credits include the box-office hit, *Heroes*; the political thriller *The Big Fix*; the screen adaptation of Chaim Potok's classic novel *The Chosen* (two-time Grand Prize winner, Montreal World Film Festival and Christopher Award); and *The Journey of Natty Gann* (the first US film to win a Gold Prize at the Moscow Film Festival).

Among his many television films are *Katherine: The Making of an American Revolutionary* and HBO's *Conspiracy: The Trial of the Chicago 8* (ACE Award winner for Best Dramatic Special). His film *Roswell, the UFO Conspiracy* garnered a Golden Globe nomination and he directed the pilot for the hit series *Dr. Quinn, Medicine Woman*. His movie *Bobbie's Girl* about a lesbian couple was one of the highest-rated films on Showtime and *Crown Heights*, also for Showtime, won the Humanitas Award in 2004 for "affirming the dignity of every person." This film also received an NAACP Award and a Directors Guild Nomination for Outstanding Directorial Achievement in Family Programs.

Mr. Kagan has won an Emmy Award for Dramatic Series Directing for *Chicago Hope* and has also directed for *The West Wing* and the Steven Spielberg series *Taken*. He produced and directed the ten-part series *Freedom Files*, broadcast on Court TV and on Link TV about threats to civil liberties covering issues from the Supreme Court and the Patriot Act to dissent, LGBT rights, and racial profiling. He has also made films for the Doe Fund, the most successful program in America helping the homeless; for Bioneers, the national organization for leaders in ecology and social justice; and for the National Cancer Institute.

Mr. Kagan is a full tenured professor at the University of Southern California where he teaches graduate courses in directing and where he founded the Change Making Media Lab. He has served as the Artistic Director of Robert Redford's Sundance Institute and is a member of the National Board of the Directors Guild of America and chairperson of its Special Projects Committee. In 2004, he was honored with the DGA's Robert Aldrich Award for "Extraordinary Service to the Guild." He is a Graduate Fellow of the American Film Institute, received his MFA from NYU and a BA from Harvard University. He has taught master seminars on filmmaking in Hong Kong, Hamburg, Jerusalem, Hanoi, France, Lebanon, Ireland, and India.